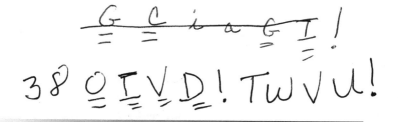

The Foundations
of Western Civilization

Thomas F. X. Noble, Ph.D.

THE
GREAT
COURSES

PUBLISHED BY:

THE GREAT COURSES
Corporate Headquarters
4840 Westfields Boulevard, Suite 500
Chantilly, Virginia 20151-2299
Phone: 1-800-832-2412
Fax: 703-378-3819
www.thegreatcourses.com

Thomas F. X. Noble, Ph.D.

Professor of History
University of Notre Dame

Professor Thomas Noble is the Robert M. Conway Director of the Medieval Institute and a professor of history at the University of Notre Dame. He assumed his current position in January of 2001 after teaching for 20 years at the University of Virginia and 4 years at Texas Tech University. Professor Noble earned his B.A. in history at Ohio University and his M.A. and Ph.D. in medieval history at Michigan State University, where he studied with the distinguished medievalist Richard E. Sullivan. During his years as a graduate student, Professor Noble held a Fulbright-Hays Fellowship, which took him to Belgium for a year and gave him the opportunity to study with François-Louis Ganshof and Léopold Génicot. Subsequently, he has been awarded two fellowships by the National Endowment for the Humanities, two research grants by the American Philosophical Society, a visiting fellowship in Clare Hall (University of Cambridge), a membership in the Institute for Advanced Study (Princeton), and a residential fellowship in the Netherlands Institute for Advanced Study.

Professor Noble's research interests are concentrated in the late antique and early medieval periods (A.D. 300–1000). He has worked on religious history, the history of Rome and the papacy, and the age of Charlemagne. His first book, *The Republic of St. Peter* (1984; Italian translation, 1997) explored the origins of papal temporal rule. He has edited two volumes, one a collection of essays on early medieval culture and the other a collection of saints' lives. He is now completing a study of controversies over religious art between 300 and 900. He has also published more than 30 articles and book chapters and around 150 book reviews. In 2002, Houghton-Mifflin published the third edition of his co-authored *Western Civilization: The Continuing Experiment*.

Professor Noble has taught courses in Western civilization for more than 25 years, along with surveys of medieval Europe and church history. He has taught advanced courses in late antiquity and Carolingian history. His

Ph.D. students now teach at colleges and universities across the country. In 1999, Professor Noble was presented with the Alumni Distinguished Professor award at the University of Virginia, that institution's highest award for teaching excellence, and a Harrison award for outstanding undergraduate advising. ■

Table of Contents

Table of Contents

Table of Contents

SUPPLEMENTAL MATERIAL

The Foundations of Western Civilization

Scope:

In this course of 48 lectures, we will explore the essential contours of the human experience in what has come to be called "Western civilization," from its humble beginnings in the ancient Near East to the dawn of the modern world; we will range from about 3000 B.C. to A.D. 1600. We will begin by asking just what "Western civilization" actually is, or what it has been thought to be. Throughout the course, we will pause to reflect on where Western civilization finds its primary locus at any given moment. That is, we'll begin in the ancient Near East and move to Greece, then to Rome; we will explore the shape and impact of large ancient empires, including the Persian, Alexander the Great's, and Rome's. When we take our leave of Rome, we'll move to Western Europe. We'll watch Europe gradually expand physically and culturally. Finally, we'll see the globalizations of Western civilization with the Portuguese and Spanish voyages of exploration and discovery.

But Western civilization is much more than human and political geography. We will explore the myriad forms of political and institutional structures by means of which Western peoples have organized themselves and their societies. These include monarchies of several distinct types, as well as participatory republics. Looking at institutions will draw us to inquire about the Western tradition of political discourse. Who should participate in any given society? Why? How have societies resolved the tension between individual self-interest and the common good?

Western civilization has always accorded a prominent place to religion and, by extension, to religious institutions and leaders. We will ask why this should be the case. Although we will pay some attention to the ancient religions of the Mediterranean world, we'll focus throughout on the three dominant monotheistic traditions: Judaism, Christianity, and Islam. Each of these religious traditions produced sacred books and vast commentaries on those books. Christianity also produced art, architecture, and music that have become living parts of the Western tradition.

If Western culture was at its source primarily religious, it was never exclusively so. This insight will invite us to probe the philosophical tradition of the West as it has asked how people should live, how they should conduct themselves, what they should regard as beautiful, and where they should find their pleasure. We will notice that the West has provided many answers to these fundamental questions. What has been common are the rational tools of debate used to seek answers and the ferocious critical tools elaborated to cross-examine every answer that has been offered.

Western civilization, finally, has bequeathed to us a library-full of literary monuments. We will discuss these from the standpoints of their technical artistry, their esthetic adornment, their political and social messages, their real and imagined audiences, and their long-term impact. We'll ask why we continue to read some works and forget others. With literature, indeed, as with other objects of our investigations, we'll continually ask what *is* more than what *was*; we will seek to understand why some things remain living elements of a civilization. ■

"Western," "Civilization," and "Foundations"
Lecture 1

The West has simultaneously had freedom and slavery. Does the West stand for freedom or oppression? Or, does the West stand for liberation from oppression?

For Sherlock Holmes, the first principle of detection was to begin with the obvious. Let's turn the old sleuth on his head and begin with what is not so obvious. What do we mean when we speak of "the West"? We can define this term culturally: free and participatory political institutions, capitalist economies, religious toleration, rational inquiry, an innovative spirit, and so on. We can define the term geographically: a cultural tradition that began around the Mediterranean Sea, spent centuries as a European preserve, then migrated to all the earth.

Any definition brings controversy: The West has had freedom and slavery; women have historically enjoyed fewer rights and opportunities than men; some have enjoyed vast wealth while others endured deep poverty. Definitions also bring paradox: Western civilization began in what is now Iraq, but it would be hard to make a case now for Iraq as Western. Today, Japan, in the "Far East," seems "Western"; in the Cold War years, Turkey was Western while Libya, far to the west of Turkey, was Eastern.

"Civilization" is no easier to define. The word itself is built from a Latin root *civ–*. We see this in such Latin words as *civis* (citizen), *civitas* (city), *civilis* (civil, polite, citizen-like). Thus, cities appear crucial to our sense of what civilization is. The Greek vocabulary is similarly revealing. *Polis* (city) gives us our words for politics and political. Cities emerged as a result of what is called the Neolithic Revolution, which occurred about 9,000 to 10,000 years ago in Mesopotamia and Egypt. Essentially, this process involved the rise of agriculture and the domestication of animals. The process was *revolutionary*, but it took a long time to produce cities and, then, civilization.

Extracting food from arid regions surrounding great rivers demanded social cohesion and cooperation. Irrigation was a key motor process. Concentrated populations grew as more people could be fed more predictably. This led to the specialization of labor, which in turn, resulted in social and political differentiation. Gradually, arts and crafts emerged and, finally, writing. With writing, we cross into the historical period.

These key elements seem to mark all civilizations, but one may also speak of Western civilization or African civilization, or somewhat more narrowly, of Maya or Aztec civilization. The West is unique, but it is not uniquely civilized. Civilization arose about 5,000 years ago. That is a long time. But the earth is about 4 billion years old. People like us—*homo sapiens sapiens*—have been around for some 40,000 years and their ancestors, for about 100,000 years. Human ancestors go back to Africa a million or so years ago. These time spans are humbling!

Finally, then, what do we mean by "foundations"? We mean origins, of course, but not just origins because all things grow and change. Durability is important but paradoxical: The oldest institution in the world today is the papacy, but Catholics are just under 20 percent of the world's population. The Athenian polis lasted in its highest manifestation less than a century, but its ideals have fired imaginations for 2,500 years. Few places today live by Roman law, yet Rome's law was the most influential ever conceived.

Foundations seem somehow related to revivals: Think of Greek or classical revival architecture. Think of one of the West's great movements: the Renaissance (allegedly a revival of classical antiquity). The Protestant Reformers thought they were reviving primitive Christianity, not creating something new. Foundations seem to be related to traditions, but these can be both invented and discarded. Those famous and "ancient" Scottish tartans were mostly invented in the 18th century; I passed a restaurant the other day with a sign that read, "A Tradition Since 1979."

In the following 47 lectures, we'll proceed through some 4,500 years. We'll begin in the ancient Near East and end with a Western European world beginning to globalize. What themes will we follow? Without being clumsy determinists, we'll talk of ecology, geography, and climate. Both the visible structures and invisible ideologies supporting them will draw continuous and comparative attention.

Although pagan religious beliefs and practices will engage us from time to time, we shall concentrate on the three "Abrahamic" faiths: Judaism, Christianity, and Islam. We'll ask how people lived, how they earned their livings, what their manners and customs were like, how their families were organized, and how they spent whatever leisure time they had. We will explore key philosophical ideas, always with a view to understanding them in specific historical contexts: Why did those people think those things in those times?

We will discuss great works of literature, the ideas they expressed, and the forms in which they were presented. We'll look into their backgrounds, their intended audiences, and their actual audiences right down to today. And we'll talk about art and architecture as the most public and visible manifestations of the Western tradition. But alongside these concrete issues, we'll repeatedly tease out perspectives on celebrity versus distinction; values versus virtues; changing understandings of the "good, the true, and the beautiful"; the respective roles of faith and reason; the competing claims of the individual and the community.

So "West" is a little messy. It's not absolutely easy to define; it's not so self-evident— "obvious," as [Sherlock] Holmes would've said— what the West is.

We will end around A.D. 1600, when many of the major features of modernity have come into view and the essential traditions of Western civilization have attained maturity. Two great backward-looking movements—the Renaissance and the Reformation—anchored tradition firmly into the Western worldview. "Christendom" was durably divided into Catholic and Protestant communities and cultures. Interlocking relationships of great-power diplomacy foreshadowed the modern state system. The Scientific Revolution altered the old balance of "science" and "wisdom." ∎

Suggested Reading

Braudel, *History of Civilizations*.

Diamond, *Guns, Germs, and Steel*.

Fagan, *Journey from Eden*.

Mellaart, *Neolithic of the Near East*.

Questions to Consider

1. If we were playing a free-association game, what would come most readily to your mind when you heard the words "Western" and "civilization"? (Keep this in mind. I will repeat the question at the end of the course!)

2. How do you think about such large-scale notions as change, continuity, revolution, evolution, and tradition?

Lecture 1: "Western," "Civilization," and "Foundations"

"Western," "Civilization," and "Foundations"
Lecture 1—Transcript

My name is Thomas Noble, I'm the Director of the Medieval Institute and Professor of History at the University of Notre Dame. It's going to be my pleasure to share with you over, the course of 48 lectures, some of my reflections on the foundations of Western civilization.

We have a lot of time to cover; we have a lot of space to cover. I often say this is going to be a bit like riding through the Louvre on a motorcycle. You will see a lot of things. I hope we can raise some interest, I hope we can put some things in perspective for you. I hope, in a way, that this exercise will be a bit like rummaging about in Granny's attic.

You're going to find a lot of familiar things as we go along. I hope that you'll frequently have what is sometimes called the "aha" experience: "Aha, that's where that comes from, that's why they say that, that's why they do that, that's why we talk that way, that's where that word came from." But in one way or another, we're going to go from the dawn of civilization to the dawn of the modern world, and that is a very long time.

Now you may know that, for Sherlock Holmes, the first principle of detection was to begin with the obvious. Let's start by standing the old sleuth on his head, and beginning with what's *not* so obvious. That is to say, what I'd like to do for the next little while is reflect on these words: "Western," "civilization" and "foundations." In other words, the title for this course. What do those words mean? What does this imply? What are we going to talk about in this course?

Let's begin with "the West." What does that mean? How would we proceed to define it? We might do so culturally. We might say the West is characterized by, for instance, free and participatory political institutions. We might say the West is characterized by capitalist economies, a form of economy that permits individuals a large measure of control over their own life, permits them to make rational choices. We might say the West is characterized by a tradition of religious toleration, the ability to accommodate simultaneously a variety of different, sometimes diametrically opposed, religious points of view.

We might say the West is characterized by a spirit of rational inquiry. I shall apply my mind to the world around me, and I will have only those answers as are achieved by my mind in reflecting on the world around me. We may say it means an innovative spirit, a willingness to do new things, to try new things, to make new departures. We could go on and on. We could talk of aesthetics and many other things, but I think you'll perhaps see the point. We could define the West as a cultural phenomenon.

But we could also define it geographically. We can say that we're going to deal with a cultural tradition that began in Mesopotamia, moved into the Mediterranean basin, crossed into Western Europe, and then—at the dawn of the modern world—globalized itself so that it wound up being everywhere.

Any definition we pose is going to bring some controversy. Let me mention a couple of examples to illustrate what I mean. The West has simultaneously had freedom and slavery. Does the West stand for freedom or oppression? Or, does the West stand for liberation from oppression? It must be said that throughout all of its history, women have enjoyed fewer opportunities, fewer possibilities than men have enjoyed. What implications does that have for how we think about the West? The West has generated enormous material wealth, but it has distributed that wealth unevenly. Some have enjoyed unimaginable richness, others unbearable poverty. We must acknowledge those realities as well.

Definitions, I dare say, bring paradox. For example, Western civilization began, as we'll see in our next lecture, in what we now call Iraq, Sumer in antiquity, but I think you'd have a pretty hard time making a case that Iraq is Western. Today, Japan, in the "Far East," seems more "Western" than parts of the West, at least on economic grounds—for example, technological grounds. Think, for a moment, about some of the curiosities of the Cold War era. Again, let's think of the Mediterranean world, where we'll spend a lot of our time and energy in this course of lectures. During the Cold War years, Turkey, which was East, was more Western than Libya, which was West but more Eastern.

So where is the West? Quite simply, physically, geographically, where is the West? We'll have to try to figure that out again and again and again.

We'll be very conscious of where are we. So "West" is a little messy. It's not absolutely easy to define; it's not so self-evident —"obvious," as Holmes would've said—what the West is.

How about "civilization?" Is that any easier to define? Alas, no. The word comes from a Latin root, *civ-*. We see this, for instance, in Latin words like *civis*, which means citizen, *civitas*, which means city, *civilis*, which means civil, yes - but it means polite, yes - but it means to behave like a person from a city, to behave like a citizen. A citizen is a person from a city. These very words sneak something into our consciousness about what civilization is or it must be. It must have cities. Our words tell us that.

Greek vocabulary is much the same. Greek for city is *polis*, and that gives us our words like "political" and "politics." The Greek word *politea* means a constitution. So we have again a sense that there is a whole vocabulary and a whole culture lurking behind it, rooted in the idea of cities. So to get civilization—to begin to form any kind of an understanding of civilization— we've got to make cities.

How do we do that? How do we make cities? How do we make cities happen historically? Cities emerged, it is now pretty generally thought, as a result of, as a consequence of, after a process which we call the Neolithic Revolution. This is a revolution which began probably something on the order of 9,000 or 10,000 years ago. At the end of its process, perhaps something like 5,000 years ago, the Neolithic Revolution had generated cities, and more than that, probably what we would call civilization, in both Mesopotamia—the land between the rivers Tigris and Euphrates—and in Egypt.

In our next lectures, we'll look in more detail at what actually happened in the historical period in Mesopotamia and Egypt. For the moment, what we want to say is what was this Neolithic Revolution, this rather leisurely revolution that took perhaps five millennia to work itself out? Its effects and consequences were revolutionary, there's no doubt about that, but it did move along at a rather genteel pace.

Fundamentally, we can put names on the things that happened during this revolution: agriculture and the domestication of animals. *Neolithic* is Greek;

9

it means "new stone." *Neos lithos*—it means "the new Stone Age." If we were to think in images, if we were to think in metaphors about the Neolithic period, it would mean the period when people began, for the first time, to fashion tools and weapons that permitted them to exert some control over the world around them rather than being controlled by it.

Let's not exaggerate it; anyone who has lived through a great natural disaster—a hurricane, and earthquake, a tornado—knows perfectly well that even now with all our vast technology we cannot control nature. But we're talking about a time, 10,000 or thereabout years ago, when people began for the first time to exercise some control over the world around them. But moving away from images and symbols and metaphors, we can say that in agriculture and the domestication of animals, we see some real changes in the kinds of things that groups of human beings did.

So this is a very long process, this Neolithic Revolution. We can think about it in concrete terms or in symbolic terms, but however we think of it and however long it took, it produced cities and then civilization. Extracting food from arid regions lies behind the story we must tell. Civilization arose in river valleys, as far as we know. It arose in the Tigris and Euphrates river valley, in Mesopotamia. It arose in the Nile river valley in Egypt. It arose in the Indus river valley in India. It arose in the Yangtze river valley in China. It arose in the Congo in Africa.

In some of these places, the climate was very different than that—for example, in Africa where you have an equatorial, humid, hot climate. It was not quite like the desert climate of Egypt or Mesopotamia. Egypt and Mesopotamia are more like, for example, the Indus than like the Congo, but there are differences here as well.

We're going to focus on Mesopotamia and then on Egypt. Hot, dry, arid climates, from which we wish to extract life, from which we wish to extract food. This is going to be a significant problem of human organization. It's going to require social cohesion. It's going to require cooperation. As near as we can tell, the great motor process is irrigation. I have a river. I have water in the river. I have land. The land is dry. I want that water out on that dry land. How am I going to do that?

Once I begin to develop an intricate system of dikes and channels and dams and pumps, I have something that is going to root me where I have built all that. This is not portable. You don't build something like this and then move on. You build something like this and then you settle where you built it, and more and more and more people settle. And this permits you, for example, as you water this land along the course of a river, to grow more food, to grow more kinds of food, to grow food more predictably, and to feed a population more stably than had ever been the case before.

But as you do this, as you begin to concentrate populations and to produce predictable, replicable food supplies, you begin to confront certain interesting problems of social, and then, beyond that, of political organization. In Biblical language, we think that there must be hewers of stone and drawers of water. There must be people who do different things.

Who decides? Is this done by social class? Is this done by some other mark of privilege? Is this done by aptitude? It's very hard to say, at the very earliest moment, how you make these distinctions—how you draw these differentiations—but the fact is that there will be people in society, for instance, who will tend the fields, perhaps other people who will tend the flocks, perhaps other people who will work on the irrigation systems. And then, eventually, there will be craftspeople, and there will also be persons charged with religious responsibilities, perhaps others charged with governing responsibilities. As the system goes, it will get more and more and more complicated.

But we are at the emergence of the specialization of labor. And the specialization of labor puts us at the front edge of political differentiation. At one level, we can say that this is all relatively simple. It is societies providing for themselves their most basic and fundamental needs. Food, in one way or another: if we control the fields and we grow our food, we are not responsible as foragers for finding whatever happens to be available. If we tend our flocks and raise our flocks—for instance, from a sheep— we can get a renewable source of material to make clothing. We can get, for example from cows, dairy products. Of course, if we want a steak I have to kill the cow. But we can get also reliable food supplies.

We may find that we can get beasts of burden; these animals can carry things for us. But in one way or another, we are managing these animals and managing the kinds of things that they can provide for us. But then we can take a step or two beyond that.

Arts and crafts will emerge. As a way for us to differentiate ourselves, we may wear slightly different jewelry from the person next door. We may adorn our homes with slightly different products, objects of beauty and of interest, from the people next door. We may adorn our towns, we may adorn our temples, we may adorn our palaces with products of human invention and human skill, and put them around us. And the arts and the crafts as we know them will begin to emerge.

Finally, we get writing, one of the great early achievements. We'll talk much about writing and forms of writing, and why we have writing at all, and why we have writing in the forms in which we have it, in later lectures. Right now, I simply want to signal that, with the emergence of writing, we see one of the remarkable achievements of this Neolithic Revolution, one of the remarkable achievements of the emergence of civilization, and we cross a threshold into the historical period.

For now, we begin to have durable forms of evidence that permit us, in the present, to eavesdrop on the doings and the thinkings of people long ago. We get to watch them telling us concretely what they did, and we get to watch them trying to manage how we will think about them. And thus history, as a dual process of discovering what happened and of reflecting on all of the different reflections on what happened, is born almost simultaneously.

These key elements seem to mark virtually all civilizations: this basic process, something like this Neolithic Revolution, something like the emergence of cities, agriculture, the domestication of animals, and so on. Our job here is going to be to talk about Western civilization. This is not to imply that there are no other civilizations. That would be absurd. We could speak, for example, of African civilization. We could talk of Chinese civilization. On somewhat smaller scales, we might talk of Maya civilization or Aztec civilization.

It will be my contention, in discussing with you some of these foundations of Western civilization over this course of lectures, that the West is unique, that the West is distinctive, that there are things about the West that make it different. But you won't hear me leading cheers. I am not here to praise; I am here to explain. Our task is to understand. That, it seems to me, is crucial.

Civilization arose perhaps 5,000 years ago. For just a moment, let's build a little perspective. The earth is perhaps 4 billion years old. *Homo sapiens*, people like us, perhaps 40,000 years old. Our basic human ancestors, perhaps 100,000 years old. Our remotest ancestors in East Africa, perhaps a million years old. That already puts that civilized period into some perspective.

Let's imagine 4 billion years as a calendar of a single year. So, everything begins on January 1st. If we want to study the civilized period, which is not surprising—we're humans, we're interested in ourselves—if we're interested in the civilized period, it's a few minutes before midnight on December 31st in our imaginary calendar. I think that perspective is humbling. Nevertheless, however humbled we may be, we're going to plunge forward and talk about that civilized period, at least in the West.

So "West" is a little messy. "Civilization" a little less messy, but still fairly complicated as a proposition. What about "foundations?" Surely, that word seems easy. Well, maybe not. For example, if we're going to talk about foundations, are we interested in the first place in origins? Of course we are, but only in origins? Are we only interested in how everything started, and we have no interest in its life, its vitality, its vigor, its span over time? Everything grows, everything changes, everything evolves over time. Nothing stays the same. So, origins will certainly figure in our story, but foundations cannot be equated with origins. Foundation's got to be bigger than that.

We might say durability is important. Sure it is, absolutely, durability is important. Some things really have staying power. They've been around a long time, we've studied them a long time, they have influenced us for a long time. But durability is tricky. If we poke at this, for example, from a couple of different angles, we could say the oldest continuously functioning institution in the world is the papacy, the head of the Roman Catholic Church. But about 20 percent of the world's population is Catholic.

The Athenian *polis* lasted, in its highest manifestation, less than a century—its golden age barely more than a generation—but it has fired imaginations for two-and-a-half thousand years. Rome's greatest legacy, perhaps, was her law, the most influential legal system that the world ever created. And yet, relatively few people today live, strictly speaking, under Roman law. So, what does durable mean? How exactly do we understand this phenomenon of durability?

Foundations may seem somehow to us to be connected to revivals. In other words, something was there at the start—was the foundation—and then we revive it periodically. Think of Greek or classical revival architecture. At the dawn of the United States, Greek and Roman revival architecture was very prominent. And why was it prominent? Perhaps those people liked it. But more importantly, it made a powerful ideological statement. It was an attempt to attach this new nation to an older history, to an ancient world, to a great tradition, to say we are not something brand new, we are the best manifestation now of what is richest in the old.

Think of postmodern architecture. Very often, we take modernist geometry run amuck, pure form and all that, and we put classical details on it, simply to echo an earlier time, an earlier way of thinking. The West has a couple of great movements, the Renaissance for example, that are fundamentally about reviving the past, taking us back to the past, going back to our roots. Exactly what the Renaissance is, we will have occasion to discuss in several lectures later in the course.

In the 16th century, the great religious reformers—the Protestant reformers—thought they were recapturing primitive Christianity, not creating something new. Martin Luther didn't say, "I have a new idea." He said, "Something has been tragically lost; let us recapture it."

Foundations may seem to us somehow related to traditions. But these can be invented, and they can be discarded. Tradition is a very complicated matter. I'll give you a couple of rather amusing examples. Think of those ancient Scottish tartans. How many people have been tempted to buy this or that or the other tartan because it belongs to the ancient Clan this, or Clan that, or Clan something else. Those things were almost all invented in the 18ᵗʰ century by people surrounding the culture of the great poet Robert Burns.

Robert Burns and his contemporaries were writing after the Act of Union attached Scotland to Great Britain, and people in Scotland were saying let us make a separate past for ourselves as a way of thinking about a different future. I passed a restaurant the other day with a sign hanging on it that said, "A tradition since 1979." I don't know about you, but that doesn't quite measure up to my sense of tradition. But I dare say, we know what the person who hung that sign was trying to do.

In the next 47 lectures, we're going to proceed through 4500 years. We'll begin in the ancient Near East, and we'll end with a Western world that is beginning to globalize. What themes will we follow? What questions will we ask? What subjects will engage our attention again and again, not necessarily in every single lecture, but often? Without being clumsy determinists, we're going to talk about ecology, geography and climate. Where people lived and what the natural world around them was like is important. Not, perhaps, determinative, but important.

We'll talk about both the visible structures and the invisible ideologies that supported them. What did governments look like, societies look like, economies look like, and how did people describe them? What did people think they were doing? And we'll compare one time to another, one phenomenon to another.

We'll discuss the pagan religious beliefs of people in Mesopotamia and Egypt to a degree, and of Greece and Rome as well. But essentially our focus will rest on the great "Abrahamic" faiths: Judaism, Christianity and Islam. These have been formative in the West.

We'll ask, from time to time, how did people live? How did they earn their livings? What were their manners? What were their customs like? What were their houses like? What were their families like? What did they do with whatever spare time they had? What did they imagine as leisure activity?

We'll explore certain key philosophical ideas. We'll try to say something about these philosophical ideas on their own terms and for their own right, so that, as we move along, we have a little bit of understanding of what Plato thought, or what a Stoic thought, or what St. Thomas Aquinas thought.

But also, and fundamentally, we'll be asking, "Why did those people think those kinds of things, in those places, and at that time?" Our approach will be that of history. So, too, for instance, we'll discuss a number of great works of literature, and the ideas which they express and the forms in which they were presented.

In other words, we will appropriately consider them as great works of art. But we're also going to look, and fundamentally, we're going to look at these works of literature as things that tell us two things above all else. When were they made? For whom were they made? Why were they made? Why were they made at a certain time and place, and what can we learn about that time and place from these works? And then, second, who have been the audiences for those works, from the time they were produced down to today? Why do they matter?

We'll talk about art and architecture, the most visible and public manifestations of the Western tradition. But alongside these concrete issues, we're also going to try to tease out perspectives on certain slightly more thematic, more fundamental issues. For instance, we'll try to tease out an understanding of the difference between celebrity and distinction. Think today of how we talk about the currently hot rock stars or athletes, and ask yourself how many of these people will, in a decade, still be interesting or important. How many of these people will be in your grandchildren's school books? How many of these people will, in 500 years, be distinguished, as opposed to merely famous?

We'll explore a little bit, for example, the distinction between values and virtues, between those things that seem somehow irredeemably and always and for everybody true, and the values which are, in a way, the social compacts made at any time, made in any place, and changeable. I can change my values as often as I change my hairdo. Well, perhaps I can't, I haven't got much hair anymore. But if I did, I could change my hairdo quite often. Can I change virtues so often? What have people thought about that problem?

We'll try to understand an issue, as the Greeks put it, the "good, the true, and the beautiful" aesthetics.

We'll try to understand the complementary and competing roles of faith and reason: what I believe because it has been revealed to me or told to me, and what I know because I have discovered it.

We'll try to explore the competing claims of the individual and the community. What rights have I against those with whom I live, and what rights have they against me?

These are some of the basic themes and issues that we'll pursue again and again. They won't all come up in every lecture, but every one of them will come up again and again.

We're going to end our course around 1600 A.D., when many of the major features of the modern world have come into view, and the essential traditions of the Western tradition have anchored themselves. They have attained a certain kind of maturity. In the first place, two great backward-looking movements, the Renaissance and the Reformation, anchored the past into the present, and made the past the way through the present into the future forever for the Western world. These kinds of revivals had happened before, but now it has made an operative dynamic of how we think.

Christendom—a uniform Christian society, never fully achieved but for a millennium an ideal—had, by 1600, been permanently driven into Protestant and Catholic communities and cultures, with their very different ways of thinking about the world. A set of interlocking power relationships between great nations was in place in 1600, and the diplomatic and, in many ways, the military history of the modern world from about 1600 until the collapse of the Soviet Union in 1989, left that great state system in place. By 1600, it's there.

And finally, the scientific revolution, emerging in the 16th century, triumphant and regnant in some ways in the 17th, had begun to alter the ancient balance between what people had long called "science" and what people had long called "wisdom." New modes of authority, new places to look for truth, had supplanted long-standing and traditional ways of finding authority and finding truth.

Those, then, are the themes, the issues and the problems that we'll explore in looking at the foundations of Western civilization. To begin building our foundations we turn next time to Mesopotamia.

History Begins at Sumer
Lecture 2

These kings were thought to have been put in place by the gods to rule with the special favor of the gods, to be accorded victory (for example, in battle) by the gods, to be accorded prosperity by the gods.

Although Mesopotamia is all the land between the rivers Tigris and Euphrates, the earliest traces of civilization appeared in Sumer, in what is now southern Iraq, and possibly, at Tell Hamoukar, in what is now northeastern Syria.

The Uruk period (3800–3200 B.C.) was tremendously creative, with the invention of the wheel and plow; the planting of the first orchards (of dates, figs, and olives); and the development of metal casting. Perhaps most significant was writing: cuneiform.

People built cities with walls—circuits up to five miles—and buildings of mud brick. The most impressive early buildings were temples: *ziggurats*. Temple priesthoods dominated society.

In the "Dynastic period" (2800–2350 B.C.), fierce competition between cities, and perhaps inside them, too, led to the emergence of local strongmen— *lugals*—who evolved into kings. Kings claimed to be the representatives of the gods and to rule by the favor of the gods. This process introduced *theocratic kingship*. As warfare became more important, large landowners formed a military aristocracy.

Mesopotamia is a broad, open plain surrounded by deserts and, beyond the deserts, by mountains. The region has no natural frontiers to ward off migrants or conquerors. Areas beyond Mesopotamia were inhabited by people of lower cultural development who coveted the comparative riches and security of Mesopotamia. After about 2350 B.C., Sumer was several times overrun by outsiders.

Babylonian bull relief sculpture from the Ishtar Gate.

Sargon (2371–2316) conquered Sumer from Akkad to the north, then expanded his holdings, as did his son after him, to the east and west. This first imperial state demanded little of its subjects and, ironically, was itself conquered by Sumerian culture. After Akkadian rule eventually weakened, there was a period of relative independence for Sumerian cities, followed by Babylonian conquest. Hammurabi (1792—1750) was the most famous and powerful of the Babylonians (or Amorites). His law code was influential for centuries. Like the Akkadians before them, the Babylonians adopted and spread Sumerian culture.

In religion, people were *polytheists* and *syncretistic*. Sky gods were generally thought of as male and related to power; earth gods were thought of as female and related to fertility. Individual forces of nature were also invested with divine power: *Animism* is a habit of mind that sees nothing as wholly lifeless. Gods and goddesses differed from humans in supernatural powers and immortality. They were capricious. Religion sought to propitiate them. Religion was pessimistic and fatalistic; it had no ethical dimension at all. This outlook was perhaps related to the geography and politics of the region.

Religion served as an impressive attempt to begin to systematize knowledge about the natural world.

Law was issued by councils of notables in conjunction with priests and kings. Law was not abstract and philosophical. Publishing laws in public places established the important principles that all are subject to the law; that the law belongs to all; that law rules, not men.

Religion was important and the priestly class was very important. That seems pretty clear. But there are those walls.

In literature, *The Epic of Gilgamesh* was a remarkable achievement. The *Epic* is a Sumerian work dating to around 2500 B.C. that survives in later versions dating to around 800 B.C. (A tribute to its dissemination!) An "epic" is a work on a grand scale dealing with gods and heroes; it is serious in tone, elevated in language, and universalizing in outlook. *Gilgamesh* is a tale of the adventures and friendship of King Gilgamesh and his friend Enkidu. It contains a mythical account of the civilizing process and a poignant reflection on mortality as the irreducible element in the human condition. There were other works, too, for example, short poems by Enkheduana, Sargon's daughter and the world's first known woman writer.

Sciences probably derived from watching the heavens, measuring fields, and regulating irrigation hydraulics. Sumerians developed the decimal and sexadecimal systems (hence, we still have 60 seconds in a minute, 60 minutes in an hour, and so on). Sumerians understood place value in numbers, that is, the difference between 35 and 53. They anticipated Greek developments in mathematics.

Sumerian culture gradually spread over much of western Asia and directly or indirectly influenced all the peoples who emerged within or who conquered those lands, including the later empire-building Persians, Greeks, Romans, Arabs, and Turks. Specific Sumerian practices and beliefs were adopted and adapted for millennia. ■

Suggested Reading

Bottéro, *Ancestor of the West*.

Crawford, *The Sumerians*.

The Epic of Gilgamesh.

Kramer, *History Begins at Sumer*.

Lerner, *Creation of Patriarchy*.

Snell, *Life in the Ancient Near East*.

Questions to Consider

1. What specific examples of the civilizing process that we learned about in the first lecture have we encountered in this one?

2. What are some of the ways in which Mesopotamia's geography influenced the historical development of the region?

History Begins at Sumer
Lecture 2—Transcript

This lecture's entitled "History Begins at Sumer." The lecture borrows its title from a quite well-known book by a scholar named Samuel Noah Kramer, who taught for many years at Johns Hopkins University. This was a little book in which he recorded a whole series of firsts in human recorded history, all of which he associated with the people of Sumer.

What is Sumer? Sumer is a small region in the south of what is today Iraq, and so that is where our story is going to start. And then slowly but surely as we move through this lecture, we're going to go through the Mesopotamian world, that is to say the land between the rivers, Tigris and Euphrates.

Civilization takes its rise in Mesopotamia shortly before 3000 B.C., perhaps as early as 3500 B.C., and we'll begin at about that point in Sumer. We'll talk about some small city-states in that region. Then we'll notice that Sumer is conquered, again and again, by persons from the outside, by people generally from the north or perhaps from the east.

One of the interesting things that we'll observe in that process is that as Sumer is conquered, Sumerian culture conquers the conquerors, and spreads with them and begins to form a somewhat more uniform civilization throughout this larger Mesopotamia region, and then westwards towards the Mediterranean Sea and eastwards towards the frontier of what we would think of today as Iran.

Mesopotamia is all the land between the two rivers, Tigris and Euphrates. We'll come to this but we're going to start with Sumer, a little region in the south of what is now Iraq. I mentioned in the first lecture on "Western," "civilization," and "foundations" that we could debate all day whether civilization began in Mesopotamia or began in Egypt. We'll turn to Egypt in our next lecture, and we'll see that civilization arises in these places more or less simultaneously.

It's also the case, as a result of recent archeological work, that some think that a place called Tel Hamoukar, in what is now northeastern Syria, may go back just as far as Sumer itself. But at least at the present time we know a lot less about Tel Hamoukar, so we're going to focus on Sumer today, and Mesopotamia a little more generally, and then Egypt in the next lecture.

Now, the Uruk period—in Sumer there were a number of cities: Ur, Uruk, Eridu, Lagash; there was a whole series of them. A number of these cities have been excavated by archaeologists. Uruk gives its name to the early period, from about 3800 B.C. to about 3200 B.C. This was, in many ways, a remarkably creative place and time. Again, the development of the Uruk period was a bit leisurely, just as we saw that the Neolithic Revolution was a bit leisurely and took about 5,000 years to work itself out.

At Uruk, we see, for example, the invention of the wheel and the plow, two very important ways of controlling nature, controlling the environment, developing agriculture, as we discussed in the last lecture. We see the first orchards planted: dates, figs and olives. For the first time, people are actually planting orchards, trying to control crops for themselves, as opposed to simply picking and plucking whatever happened to be available. We find the development of metal casting, making weapons in the first place, but then also making jewelry and other objects.

This is also a time when writing first emerges in Mesopotamia, writing of a very particular kind—cuneiform. That comes from the Latin *cuneus*, which means wedge. So cuneiform writing is wedge-shaped writing. A scribe would take a wedge-tipped stylus—it didn't have a point, it has a little wedge on the end—and make various marks in wet clay. The clay would then be left in the sun to dry, or the clay might be put in an oven and baked. Eventually, it formed a very permanent record.

Gradually, and we'll talk about this a little bit later in the lecture, literature begins to be produced. But early on, what we have, basically, are government records, bureaucratic records, and a certain number of legal documents and religious documents. But in any case, this formed a durable and memorable tribute to those people.

It's also interesting to say that this was not a particularly efficient information technology, as we might say today. You can only imagine carrying any reasonably large book around, with each page, as it were, ensized on stone tablets. This didn't make it very easy to keep information, to disseminate information, but it did, for the first time, make it possible to preserve information in a fairly durable way. And there are thousands upon thousands of these clay tablets still surviving today for scholars to look at and to work with.

I emphasized in the first lecture on the rise of civilization that we've got to have cities, and, indeed, this is the period when cities arise, and when they begin to take on some of the characteristics of cities from then until much later times. As I emphasized long ago, there's a number of them. They are small, independent city-states. There is no nation-state of Sumer. There is Ur and Uruk and Lagash, and these are basically small, independent towns.

They began to have circuits of walls, sometimes up to about five miles in circumference, that's a fairly large settlement for such an early time, and buildings made almost entirely of mud brick, or mud brick over wooden framing. Now, it's very important to say that the Mesopotamians were not dull-witted. It wasn't that they couldn't build in other materials. They didn't have stone. Stone was very far away. So, for example, we don't find in Mesopotamia the kind of monumental architecture that we find in Egypt, or that we find later on in Greece, or in other places. They simply didn't have stone available, and you can only build so large using wood and mud brick.

The creation of the walls around the towns—there's a good deal of evidence that these walls were built in the first place as sort of symbolic representations of the towns, and gradually, over time, rebuilt and rebuilt and rebuilt to serve as defensive tools. Why? We'll come to that in a few minutes. Quite simply, rivalry among these cities.

In these cities, the earliest impressive buildings are always temples. The temples usually took the form of a *Ziggurat*. A *Ziggurat* is a sort of a high-banked structure, built up in a series of steps from ground level up a certain distance. This is probably the sort of thing, for example, that in the Old Testament we read about as the Tower of Babylon, the Tower of Babel, the thing that was being built that was going to reach all the way up to heaven. If the largest buildings in these cities are *Ziggurats*, are temples, what does this tell us about the people and about that society? Religion was important and the priestly class was very important. That seems pretty clear. But there are those walls, after all, and they are going to become a factor a bit later.

When we move into what we call the "Dynastic period" of Mesopotamian history, the period from about 2800 B.C. to perhaps about 2350 B.C., we see a time of fierce competition among these little cities, and perhaps inside them, too. In other words, the struggles on the outside, the struggles between cities, may very well have begun to lead the social struggles inside the cities. We begin to see, for example, the building of palace complexes, and we begin to see the rise of local big shots, the texts of the time called them *lugals*, which basically means big shots, kings, important individuals, powerful individuals on the local scene. And as I mentioned a moment ago, city walls began to be larger, stronger, and more important.

With these kings, we meet, for the first time in the Western tradition, a particular kind of institution—monarchy—which will be with us right through these lectures all the way to the end, and we meet a particular kind of monarchy. These kings were thought to have been put in place by the gods to rule with the special favor of the gods, to be accorded victory (for example, in battle) by the gods, to be accorded prosperity by the gods. They were not—this is very important—they were not themselves thought to be gods, but they were thought to have been put in place by and to be made specially answerable to the gods.

We call that "theocratic kingship;" two nice Greek words, *theos* and *cratos,* ruled by a god, but ruled by a god through a particular agent on Earth, a king. So one of the earliest justifications for kings, then, is that they are people chosen out by the gods. Why would that have been the case? Was that people's idea in the very first place? Probably not. Probably what we see here is that, as individuals came to exercise leadership over a society, they had to find some way of describing, of justifying who why were, the position they had, the power that they had, and so they did this through particular connections with their gods.

As warfare became more important, particularly between these various cities, we notice something else: large landowners. It's very hard for us today to say exactly why this happened, how it happened, what the mechanism was, that produced some people who owned a great deal more land than others, and then some people who worked on the land of these more powerful people.

The fact that these large landowners began to form a kind of a warrior aristocracy, that's not so difficult to understand, because these were obviously the most prominent people in a local town who had to assume some responsibility, either for defending that town against the attack of others or perhaps for leading an attack by your town on the next town over. So these people as warrior aristocrats, and warrior aristocrats are going to be with us right through this entire course of lectures, their presence is not surprising. Their presence is not that easy to explain.

What, in the first place, led to the social differentiation, so that some people had more land than others and thus a greater stake in the society than others? That's trickier. It's also important to bear in mind that, with any of these towns—even with a circuit of walls, let's say of five miles or thereabout—the agricultural land was not in the town. There might have been some house gardens in the town. The land was outside. If the city is going to be subject to attack by outsiders, then those persons who own that land are going to have a very real interest in what's going on outside of those walls, as well as inside the walls.

So, what we see is a society where kings are increasingly advised by other warrior aristocrats. Clearly, in the social dynamics and the social mechanisms of the towns, these kings had to get along with these warrior aristocrats. That's clear. And it's clear that they had to listen to them, it's clear that they had to take their advice, and probably the tension at the other end of that is precisely these kings trying to say, "No, no, we're here because of the gods; we answer only to the gods." "We answer to the gods," in the sense of, "we don't answer to these guys," because of course, what they had to do was answer to those guys.

So, we can see a sense of social tensions. We can also see tensions between these important people and others in society. I'll come back to that question in a few minutes, when I talk about law.

Mesopotamia is a large open plain. You have two rivers, surrounded by desert, with mountains at the far edges of this region. The area has no natural frontiers. There is nothing there to ward off invasion, nothing there to ward off migration. We could think, for example—today, there is an example that would give us some sense of the way it must have been in antiquity. I'm referring to the Kurds. These are people who live in northern Iraq, eastern Syria, southeastern Turkey, and northwestern Iran. They are a stateless people, they simply move around. They've been doing this for millennia, and in antiquity, this must have been the way this Mesopotamian world was virtually all the time.

The areas beyond Mesopotamia, or the areas on its fringes, along its edges, were inhabited by people who basically could see the higher cultural development, the higher political development, the higher economic development, the greater prosperity of the Mesopotamian cities. And not surprisingly, they were attracted like moths to a bulb on a summer night to these Mesopotamian cities. They came again and again and again and again, and eventually great conquerors—the Persians, and then Alexander, and then the Romans, and then the Arabs, and then the Turks—have overrun this part of the world. But on a much smaller scale, that process of overrunning Mesopotamia was happening even in antiquity.

So we have the period before 3000 B.C. is sort of the Uruk period, and we can see civilization taking its rise, and the period after 3000 B.C., when the various Sumerian cities are working out in the Dynastic period their own local political, social, economic development. After about 2350 B.C., we see, for the first time, one of these great conquests of the region of Sumer, southern Iraq, by an outside force. In this case, the individuals involved were the Akkadians.

If you're going up the Tigris and Euphrates rivers, you can always try to remember that the Tigris is on top. So we have the two rivers, Tigris and Euphrates; the Tigris is on top. Mesopotamia, technically, would be the land between those two rivers, precisely what the word means—what is between the rivers. But actually, we think of Mesopotamia also as the land lying on both sides of those rivers. Akkad is in the area where the rivers bow out just a little bit, north and west of Sumer, a slightly fat region in the middle, where the rivers bow out before they come close together again and flow into the mountains in Anatolia in antiquity, Turkey today. So, Akkad is up there a few hundred miles to the north of Sumer.

In Akkad, there emerged a very powerful, ambitious, and militarily gifted king. His name was Sargon. Sargon ruled from 2371 to 2316 B.C. He turned the Akkadians into a very effective fighting force, and then he began to move to the south. Later on, his son and successor moved eastwards towards what we would think of Iran, and westwards almost towards the Mediterranean Sea.

Let me tell you a story about Sargon. Sargon is an interesting fellow. He was found floating in a reed basket in the river Tigris by serving maidens of the queen. He was brought into the palace and found to be a fine and healthy baby boy, and was raised among the children of the servants in the palace, and of course, eventually he was so intelligent, capable, gifted, brave, and resourceful that he was brought in to serve among the king's assistants. Eventually, he became the king himself.

Now that may remind you of someone else you've heard of, I have in mind Moses, of course. Now Moses never got to be pharaoh in Egypt, but he rose pretty high in the Egyptian service. It's not surprising that riverine civilizations will tell two kinds of stories about rivers: stories where the rivers bring you wonderful things, and stories where the rivers crush you in terrible floods. And so, we have Sargon as a good thing that is brought to the Akkadians by their river.

One of the most important things for us to say about Sargon is that when he conquered the Sumerians to the south, rather than destroying their culture, rather than putting the Sumerians to death, rather than overrunning them and bringing the forces of darkness and barbarism to them, he actually absorbed Sumerian culture in all sort of important respects.

Very much later, the Roman poet Horace would say that "captive Greece took her captor captive." The point is that that has happened many times, historically, that people at a lower cultural level conquer people at a higher cultural level; and instead of destroying their culture, they absorb it. That's a first point with respect to Sargon. A second is that this is the first moment of the dissemination of Sumerian culture over a much larger imperial state.

Some years after Sargon and the Akkadians began to weaken, as their power began to decline, Sumer was overrun, as indeed much of Mesopotamia was overrun again by people whom we call the Old Babylonians. We meet these people in the Old Testament as the Amorites. Their most famous king was Hammurabi, the one who issues the great law code, and we'll have something to say about that law code in just a few minutes.

But once again, when the Old Babylonians conquer the area of Mesopotamia, and indeed the area of Sumer, what they do is spread Sumerian culture. They don't destroy it, they don't make it vanish; they spread it. As these slightly larger imperial states continued to grow, what began to happen is there was what we might call a Sumerianization of the culture of much of the Middle East, and this provided a kind of a common foundation, a common basis for cultural life in that part of the world. We'll return to this part of the world in some later lectures from some other angles.

For the moment, let's turn and ask ourselves a little bit about the culture of Sumer, the culture of these earliest of people. What were they like? What is their culture like? We might turn in the first place to their religion. What do we know about their religion? We know, for example, that these people were polytheistic. Quite simply, they worshipped many gods and goddesses. Polytheistic.

We know also that they were syncretistic. What that means—that's a fancy word that actually means something very simple: they were quite happy and willing to borrow things from their neighbors. If, for example, your neighbor conquered you, this might lead you to believe that your neighbor's gods were more powerful than your own. Now, you don't jettison your own and take on the new ones in their place; you add the new ones, you hedge your bets.

If your neighbors have finer flocks than you do, if your neighbors have more abundant crops than you do, their fertility goddesses may be a little more efficient than yours. So, you would borrow them. Again, you don't throw yours out, you add some new ones. Syncretism there: a way of spreading certain kinds of religious practices, certain kinds of religious ideas, certain kinds of religious cults.

When we think about these gods, we can divide them up in certain fairly basic ways, according to the ways the Sumerians themselves did. There were sky gods, gods who were thought to live on mountaintops, way up in the heavens someplace. These are generally thought of as male, and they are generally associated with war, sometimes with government, and sometimes with the more powerful forces of nature: thunder, lightening, the more terrifying forces of nature.

There were also Earth gods. Not surprisingly, Earth was understood as feminine, and therefore those divine beings, specially charged with Earth and its fertility and its richness and its abundance, were conceived of as female amongst various peoples of Sumer, and other places as well.

In between these sky gods and female Earth gods, there was a whole host of other beings, imagined more or less clearly at different times, in different places, among different people. What we see here is a process that we can characterize as animism. Animism means, quite simply, that you really don't see anything in the world as lifeless, that everything somehow is alive. From wind and rain and storms to animals, even to abstract forces: love, hate, fear. All of these things can somehow be imagined as divine and as greater than and external to ourselves.

These gods and goddesses differed from humans in a couple of very basic respects. They were immortal, and they were superhuman. In other respects, when we meet them (we know a lot more, for example, about Greek and Roman gods, we'll have more to say about them in later lectures), they appear much the same. They seem like us, except that they are immortal and they have superhuman powers. The religious rites practiced by the Sumerians were fundamentally aimed at propitiating these gods, at trying to keep them in order.

The religion was fatalistic; the religion was pessimistic. These were people who could be conquered at any time; these were people who could be flooded and destroyed at almost any time. The Nile floods absolutely annually and predictably and benevolently in Egypt. That is not true of the Tigris and Euphrates. Consequently, it's not surprising that people felt a bit pessimistic and a bit fatalistic about their religion. All they could do was try to keep these gods in order, and I think that that may have been related, in certain ways, to the geography, to the climate, and sort of to the political life of the area.

It's interesting, too, that these gods and goddesses served no ethical functions in these societies. As near as we can tell, how you lived your life made absolutely no difference. Good people didn't get a reward; bad people didn't get punished. You didn't turn to religion for explanations of how to live, of how to live well, how to live honorably, how to live justly. These were ideas that we will see emerge slowly and very much later.

We can say also of these various religions that they represent something else for us, and something quite different from what you might think. If we try to understand the natural order today, we would turn to the various natural sciences for the various rules of how the world works. What we see with the Sumerians was a first attempt, and I think in many respects an impressive one, to begin understanding the forces of nature, to systematize them, to give them names, to differentiate among them. The answers that they gave may strike us as primitive, may strike us as utterly incredible, but what is interesting is the beginning of the process of bringing some order into how we think about that world out there. That, I think, is actually a fairly impressive achievement.

Law is another important achievement of the Mesopotamian peoples, and, in particular, in the first place of the Sumerians. The laws appear to have been issued, first of all, by councils of notables in conjunction with priests and kings—priests early, kings later. These laws are interesting in a number of ways, distinctive in a number of ways. They are not abstract. They are not philosophical. No Mesopotamian law code comes with a great preamble like the American Constitution. There's nothing like our Declaration of Independence. There's no statement of first principles, no "*liberté, egalité, fraternité.*" There's nothing like that.

They are long lists of rules, "Do this, do this, do this, don't do this, don't do this, don't do this, don't do this," with oftentimes specific fines attached to the rules. If you do this, it's going to cost you this, and very often, the laws are very cruel. You could be sentenced to death for an enormous number of offenses. It is in these laws that we think we can see a lot of the social struggles of these societies—that people were somehow making rules to keep the powerful from destroying the powerless, to keep the rich from overrunning the poor. It's in these law codes that we think we get some kind of feel for the social stresses of these societies. Unfortunately, we have too little evidence really to hang much flesh and sinew on that skeleton, but it appears to be what we're looking at.

Now, the law's interesting to us in a second way. Most of these law codes were carved in great stone tablets and displayed in public places. And this creates the notion that the law is not the arbitrary possession of the powerful but the possession, in fact, of all people— that it belongs to everyone, that it was public, that obliges everyone, that everyone is subject to it.

So, religion and law, two important areas. A third is literature. The greatest of the Mesopotamian works, indeed the greatest of the early works of human literary production, is *The Epic of Gilgamesh*. This is a Sumerian work; in its oldest form, it goes back probably to about 2500 B.C. The versions we have today survive from about 800 B.C., which is a testimony to its longevity, a testimony to its durability, to its dissemination. It's an epic.

We're going to talk about a lot of epics in these lectures, so let's pause just for a moment and describe what an epic is. An epic is a long poem, usually. It's conceivable to have a prose epic, but generally speaking, it is a poetic work. It is conceived on a grand scale. It deals with gods and heroes. It deals with important subjects. It deals with them in elevated language. And it is universalizing. It makes its points as if for all time and not for a given place and time, for all people and not just for the people mentioned in the story. These are some characteristics of epics, and we'll talk about other ones as we go along.

What about this one? It's a story, basically, of friendship, of a friendship between Gilgamesh and his great friend Enkidu. Enkidu is the natural man. The poem has a mythic account of the civilizing process. What that means: Enkidu runs with the animals; he's the natural man. The people in the city are worried about him. He comes down to a pool to drink all of the time, so the people in the city send a harlot out to seduce him. He has sex with the harlot, now the animals won't come near him anymore; he's been civilized. Once again, the woman becomes the bad guy in the story about the civilizing process, the fall of Enkidu. Enkidu then comes into the city.

Gilgamesh, who's a big, tough guy himself, has been looking for a buddy—two bubbas who can hang out together. Now one bubba's got another one. And they go and have all kinds of amazing adventures, and they kill the bull of heaven, and they fight with Humbaba, and they travel all over the place. And then Enkidu gets sick and dies. And the poem has a poignant refrain, "and the worm fastened on him." And it poses this quite wonderful existential problem. You're born, you live, you die, the worm gets you. So what? What did it all matter?

Now, Gilgamesh goes in search of immortality. He goes off chasing a guy named Ziusudra in some versions of the story, Utnapishtim in others. He gives him a branch, which presumably if he consumes it or something will grant him immortality. He fails to consume it right away, and a snake takes it away from him; the snake's back in the story now, and of course, the immortal snake and so on. And Gilgamesh is forced to realize that we will only have such immortality as exists in the memory of those who come after us. We cannot live forever.

Quite a remarkable work. Not the only work. There was, for example, a woman Enkheduana, daughter of Sargon, who was the first known woman poet. Quite a remarkable figure she was.

We can say, for example, in areas like mathematics and sciences, perhaps the Mesopotamians derive this from their hydraulics, perhaps they derive this watching the heavens above them, perhaps from measuring fields, hard to say. They developed pretty sophisticated mathematics: they developed the decimal, but also the sexadecimal system.

You ever wonder why we have 60 seconds in a minute and 60 minutes in an hour? Thank the Sumerians for that. They understood place value in numbers; for example, they understood why 35 is different from 53.

That's not obvious, that's not self-evident that you go left or right; they understood that.

They anticipated a number of Greek developments in mathematics and in science, and they left them a very considerable legacy. The legacy was of the Sumerian people conquered again and again and again—who provided in religion, in law, and in certain basic sciences a foundation from the eastern shore of the Mediterranean to the western border of Iran, or Persia in antiquity—on which one civilization after another would build, or which we may regard in a sense as kind of the foundation under the Western civilization that we'll continue to pursue in our later lectures. As indeed, in the very next one, when we turn to Egypt.

Egypt—The Gift of the Nile
Lecture 3

> Quite simply, the first thing you need to know about Egypt: no Nile, no Egypt. The Nile is a very long, very powerful, very important river.

The Greek writer Herodotus called Egypt "the Gift of the Nile," and so it was. The Nile is a long, powerful river running in a northerly direction some 750 miles from the last cataract to the Mediterranean. It floods—annually and predictably—an area five to 15 miles wide. About five percent of Egypt is habitable. Without the Nile, there would be only barren desert. From as early as 5000 B.C., small communities along the Nile began to drain marshes, irrigate, and plant regular crops (mainly cereal grains).

Slowly, these communities coalesced into *nomes* (the word is Greek; we do not know what word the Egyptians used) under *nomarchs*. Then the *nomes* of the south—"Upper Egypt" because it is nearer the source of the Nile—and the north—"Lower Egypt," nearer the mouth of the Nile—formed as larger entities. It seems that a need to control irrigation led to political organization on a larger scale. Much about this period is shrouded in legend, but about 3100 B.C., Menes united Upper and Lower Egypt. This unification ushered in the historical period.

Historians divide Egypt's historical period into 30-some dynasties, or families, of rulers. The dynasties are grouped into the Old, Middle,

The Nile River valley as seen from space.

and New Kingdoms, with intermediate periods in between. The Old Kingdom (2695–2160 B.C.) was an era of great vitality, security, and prosperity. Egypt was isolated and untroubled by invaders.

A distinctive Egyptian kingship evolved. The word *pharaoh* comes from *per aa*, meaning the "Great House." Pharaoh was one of the gods and guaranteed Egypt's prosperity and security. In turn, Egypt's prosperity and security

King Akhenaten of the 18th dynasty of ancient Egypt.

legitimized the pharaoh. The Great Pyramids at Gizeh symbolize the Old Kingdom.

The Middle Kingdom (2025–1786 B.C.) was a period of more widely dispersed rule. Pharaohs shared power with local notables. This period was important in the elaboration of Egyptian religion because the emphasis moved beyond the royal dynasty to nobles and even ordinary people.

Around 1700 B.C., the Hyksos, Semitic-speaking peoples from Palestine, conquered Egypt. Hatred for foreign rule eventually led a dynasty from Upper Egypt to drive out the Hyksos and inaugurate the New Kingdom (1550–1075 B.C.). Fired by ambition and a desire to ward off future conquest, the Egyptians now built an empire that extended into Mesopotamia and along the shore of the eastern Mediterranean. This was a brilliant and cosmopolitan period.

After about 1400 B.C., the Egyptians confronted the Hittites, a powerful and expanding people from Anatolia and the first Indo-European speakers in recorded history. In 1274, at Qadesh in northern Syria, the Egyptians and Hittites fought a battle that left them both crippled and declining.

Everything starts with the pharaoh in a two-class society (the pharaoh and everybody else). Egypt first displayed an abstract sense of rule—the separation of ruler and office and the complete removal of the ruler from the ordinary realm of humans.

Religion grew more complicated over time. The peace and prosperity of the Old Kingdom led to a happy, optimistic outlook. The concept of the afterlife—as a continuation of this life, not something better!—was reserved mainly to the pharaoh, his family, and perhaps a few key advisers. The Middle Kingdom saw a profusion of temples and new cults. Herodotus called the Egyptian the "most religious of all people." This might have been a reemergence of predynastic religion or a response to unsettled conditions. At this time, the afterlife seems to have been considered available to all.

The concept of *Ma'at* became crucial, that is, the idea of truth, justice, balance, and order. The myth of Osiris revealing the Middle Kingdom was popular. The New Kingdom saw the remarkable religious experiment of Akhenaton. He abandoned traditional worship to promote the cult of Aton (henotheism or monolatry), but this died with him.

As later people, Greeks and then Romans, admired the Egyptians; they were very interested in preserving these Egyptian preservations' memory.

Scientific and artisanal advances were striking. The use of papyrus facilitated writing and record-keeping. Hieroglyphic (= pictographic) writing gave way gradually to demotic, which was more efficient than cuneiform. The desire to preserve bodies intact (mummification) for the afterlife led to advances in medical science, including surgery and knowledge of anatomy.

Greeks and Romans were impressed, even dazzled, by the Egyptians, as have been most visitors to Egypt since antiquity. Seeing just what influence Egypt actually had, however, is not so easy. Political control lasted a short time. Divinized kingship recurred but not necessarily because of the Egyptians. No new literary forms were added. Monumental architecture as propaganda recurred, but this idea is not "Egyptian."

Early Egyptologists were eager to claim the ancient Egyptians for the West. After World War II, as colonial empires crumbled and black consciousness arose, some people claimed that Egypt was an African civilization, indeed, that Egypt was Africa and vice versa. In its most extreme forms, this view has held that Western civilization was stolen from the Egyptians by the Greeks. This view again puts a sharp focus on Egypt but without solid reasons for doing so. Perhaps these historical mysteries explain the mysterious smile of the Sphinx. ■

Suggested Reading

Bernal, *Black Athena*, vols. 1 and 2.

Murnane, *Penguin Guide to Egypt*.

Redford, *Akhenaten*.

Strouhal, *Life of the Ancient Egyptians*.

Questions to Consider

1. Explain the impact of geography on the course of Egyptian history.

2. How is Egyptian historical development both like and unlike that of Mesopotamia?

Egypt—The Gift of the Nile
Lecture 3—Transcript

This time we're going to talk about Egypt.

The Greek writer Herodotus, a historian whom we'll meet in a later lecture, once called Egypt "the Gift of the Nile," and so it was. Quite simply, the first thing you need to know about Egypt: no Nile, no Egypt. The Nile is a very long, very powerful, very important river. It runs in a northerly direction some 750 miles, from the last cataract, the last waterfall, up to the Mediterranean Sea. It floods annually. It floods predictably. And what it does is it deposits a layer of silt over a ribbon of territory extending from about 5 to about 15 miles wide, all along the course of this great river. About 5 percent, in other words, of the actual land of Egypt is habitable, is usable. So again, no Nile, no Egypt. If you don't remember anything else, you want to remember that. Without this great river, this would only be barren desert, as indeed much of the rest of the course of North Africa is.

In this lecture, we're, in a sense, going to refer again and again to the way that organizing life along this great river has dictated the way (and I think dictate is not too strong a term) that Egyptian history has unfolded. And it will tell us some things about how Egyptian culture has unfolded. And it will tell us something about the Egyptian outlook, their religious values, their political and social organization and so on. So, the Nile is always our great fact here.

From as early as about 5000 B.C., there were small communities up and down the Nile, and it began to drain marshes. The riverbed, of course, is exactly what you would expect, but alongside the river, on both sides, it's very marshy territory. This is also where this great silt is deposited, so one of the things you need to do is you need to get the water out of the marsh so that you can plant things in the silt. So early on, these small communities up and down the Nile began to try to manage their little areas of the river. They began to irrigate, they began to drain, and then they began to irrigate, which is to put the water back somewhat more systematically. They began to plant regular crops, mainly cereal grains: bread, the staff of life. In one way or another, you've got to have bread.

Very slowly, these communities coalesced into things we call nomes, that's a Greek word, actually comes from the Greek word *nomos*, which means the law, so a law district, a law territory. We actually don't know what the Egyptians called these little communities that began to evolve along the Nile, and then eventually, there were leaders in these nomes called *nomarchs*. Once again, that's a later Greek name, a ruler of a nome. Once more, we don't know precisely what the Egyptians called them. In any case, what we see is that the nomes began to form slightly larger districts, we might think of them today as counties or something like that in a state, up and down the Nile. And gradually, Upper and Lower Egypt were organized into two much larger areas, and then all of Egypt was unified.

A quick word about Egyptian geography. To understand what I'm going to say now, it would be very helpful if you could stand on your head, because the point is that Upper Egypt is on the bottom and Lower Egypt is on the top, and that's because the Nile flows in a northerly direction from where it rises in Africa to the Mediterranean Sea. So Upper Egypt is on the bottom, but it's nearer the beginning of the Nile, so it's actually the top, you see? In other words, it's perfectly backwards. So as I said, if you were standing on your head just now, that made perfect sense to you. If you weren't, then you just have to trust me.

Eventually, Lower and Upper Egypt coalesced, and then, slowly but surely, all of Egypt began to be pulled together into a single kingdom. It appears—we're working in a realm where our evidence is pretty thin—that the need to control irrigation really drove the creation of larger and larger and larger scale political organizations. This is something that we know from many places in the globe, over many moments in human history.

Rivers have been used, let us say for example, to take a quite easy case, to power a mill. If I'm parked at a certain point along the river and I have a mill, and somebody up the river dams the river up because they want to control the water—perhaps they want to have a mill up there—my mill stops. So we have to cooperate, you see, along a river. So, if too much irrigation is undertaken, if too much water is diverted at one point along the Nile's course, this would be dangerous for people downstream.

Probably the need to cooperate in the management of the Nile is what drove people to a more unified form of political organization. This, by the way, is a very good example of how geography can affect how history unfolds itself. I'm not going to tell you that, absent cooperation along the Nile, all of Egyptian cooperation wouldn't have happened, but I can say I think it would've been different.

In legend, in myth, and probably, too, in history, a ruler by the name of Menes (that again is a Greek word) unified Upper and Lower Egypt. Tradition says that this was done about 3100 B.C. But this unification of Upper and Lower Egypt really ushers in for us the historic period. This is really when we can start talking in some reasonably meaningful sense about Egyptian history.

Before this time, our evidence is legendary, our evidence is archaeological, and it has to be pieced together with lots of great gaps. One way to think about this is to imagine a great fishing net. It's been strung out and suspended, and what we know is the string and what we don't know is all of the holes. That's sort of a way to think about the earliest stages of human history. Yes, we know a lot, but boy, is there a lot we don't know.

The course of Egyptian history. The Egyptians were fanatical about remembering things and about recording things. As later people, Greeks and then Romans, admired the Egyptians; they were very interested in preserving these Egyptian preservations' memory. What that means is that historians in antiquity, and so also in modern times, divide Egyptian history into 30-some dynasties. That means families of rulers. Family after family after family, with the names of the rulers in each dynasty recorded one after another with their reignal years. And we think actually that these reignal years are quite accurate.

For purposes of discussion, then, historians have spoken of the Pre-dynastic period and then the Old, Middle, and New Kingdoms, with the First and Second Intermediate periods falling between Old and Middle, and Middle and New. That's a modern division that enables us to manage Egyptian history. But the dynasties, the kingdoms, are an old Egyptian way of thinking about their own history.

Egyptian history, then, begins in a very serious way with what we call the Old Kingdom, with the Pharaonic dynasties. What's a "pharaoh?" We'll come to "pharaoh" in just a moment, but the names of kings in Egypt are Pharaohs. The Old Kingdom, from about 2695 B.C. to about 2160 B.C.—500 years plus or minus a bit—was an era of great vitality, of great security, of great prosperity. This was the time, for example, when Egypt was largely isolated from outside influences. Egypt was not overrun, as Mesopotamia was. There was some trade, there was certainly some movement of peoples back and forth, but on the whole, Egypt was isolated in ways that Mesopotamia never was, with important consequences as we'll see as we move along through our discussion of Egypt here in the next little while.

Now a very distinctive Egyptian form of kingship emerged, called "pharaoh." This came from the Egyptian words *per aa*, which means the "Great House," the big house. The pharaoh was the guy who lived in the big house. There's something very interesting hiding in this. We might any given night hear on the television news, we might read in the newspaper, that the Oval Office reported yesterday, Downing Street says that the Quai d'Orsay issued a bulletin. We have learned somehow to differentiate a person and an office, and to think of abstract and symbolic ways of referring to an office. We differentiate, for example, between the president and the presidency. The one, an office and institution that is durable, the other, a person who momentarily holds that office.

In the very fact that the Egyptians called their rulers "the guy who lives in the big house," we see, for the first time, this interesting separation of office and holder of office, the idea that an office can be understood abstractly and symbolically. This is a development which will be with us through the rest of our lectures, but it is something that emerges here, for the first time, at least as far as we know, in Egypt.

The pharaoh was basically the person assigned responsibility for guaranteeing Egypt's prosperity and security. In an interesting way, it was pretty easy to be pharaoh in early times. The pharaoh had one job, one really important job; he had to make the sun rise every morning in the east and make the sun set every evening in the west. Well, as far as we can tell, pharaoh did a pretty good job. So this didn't generate a lot of distress, it didn't generate a lot of trouble.

Egypt, as I mentioned a moment ago, was largely isolated from foreign invasions, the Nile floods predictably and benevolently, the land was prosperous, the land was peaceful. Life went on. There was no reason to challenge the way things were. So, security legitimized the pharaoh and the pharaoh legitimized the security of Egypt.

In many respects, we can take the three great pyramids at Gizeh, the pyramids of Khufu, Khafre, and Menkare, as symbolic of this Old Kingdom period, this early period. From one point of view, these are astonishing feats of engineering, built by people who hadn't had an opportunity to come and take engineering degrees from modern universities.

The Great Pyramid, for example, is almost exactly 481 feet on a side. It's aligned only a few minutes off true north. It has stones, some of them weighing up to 20 tons, that have been moved very high up. You may be thinking, am I going to tell you how they built the pyramids? No, I'm not, because we don't actually know. There are lots of theories, and I could take up much of the rest of your life going through these theories with you, but I'll spare you that. The fact is they built them; let's just leave it at that for the moment.

What I want to do is draw a historical fact out of it, and that is that almost certainly these pyramids required teams of thousands of men, years and years to build. This is a remarkable commitment of human and material resources to a particular project. What is that project? To make a tomb for a king. That king has to be very popular, people have to be very loyal, that society must have the opportunity to commit such resources to a project like this. That's the interesting way in which we can think about what those pyramids represent about the stability, the harmony, the peace, and the security of Old Kingdom Egypt.

The Middle Kingdom is rather different in a number of ways. We generally date the Middle Kingdom 2025 to 1786 B.C. This is a period of more widely dispersed rule. In other words, it appears that up and down the Nile, pharaohs were now increasingly required to share power with local notables. Who would those local notables have been? Almost certainly, major landowners.

In other words, we're finding a certain amount of social and economic differentiation up and down the land of Egypt, something for which we don't have very good sources. We can't easily say precisely why some people began to be wealthier, more powerful, more influential, on a local basis than they had been formerly. What is clear is that these people were less and less willing to accord all power, all privileges, all rule in Egypt to the pharaohs. They began to try in various ways to share power.

This is also an important period in the elaboration of Egyptian religion. I'm going to turn to the subject of religion specifically, on its own terms, in a few minutes. But for right now, what we can say is that emphasis began to move beyond the royal dynasty. In many respects, in the Old Kingdom, Egyptian religion focused on the pharaoh, possibly on some of the members of the pharaoh's family, possibly on some of the pharaoh's closest associates. But fundamentally, religion focused on the pharaoh.

In the Middle Kingdom, we begin to see a profusion of gods and goddesses; we begin to see a larger number of sites of temples and temple cults, a large number of priesthoods that began to be more important. So, in an interesting kind of way, religion mirrors politics in Middle Kingdom Egypt. A little bit more diffused political control; a little bit more diffused religious experience.

When the Middle Kingdom was drawing to an end, the land of Egypt was overrun by Semitic-speaking peoples from the outside. These are people whom we call the "Hyksos." They came into Egypt from Palestine around perhaps 1700 B.C. They conquered Egypt by seizing control of the Nile delta—in other words Lower Egypt, the end of Lower Egypt—and then exercising a certain amount of control further south.

What we can say is they really collected tribute from some of the big shots who had been prominent in Egypt during the Middle Kingdom, or the descendants of those big shots. To put it a little bit differently, we can say they were sort of running protection rackets in terms of how they managed

Egypt. They did not physically take over every square inch of Egypt and reduce all Egyptians to servitude under themselves; they were sort of a conquering minority who ruled from the north.

Very gradually, hatred for this foreign rule led the Egyptians to begin to organize themselves, led them to begin to try to unify in some way, to drive out the Hyksos. And when they did this, when the Egyptians were able finally to drive out the Hyksos, they inaugurated what we call the New Kingdom. This runs on for about five centuries, from about 1550-1075 B.C.

The New Kingdom was driven by a couple of very basic dynamics. First of all, there was a desire to ward off future conquest. Remember, under the New Kingdom [sic Old] and under the Middle Kingdom, Egypt had been very largely isolated, and been very free from any kind of foreign invasion, and then sort of the unthinkable happened and Egypt was conquered. So one of the things, then, that drove the New Kingdom was to ward off any possibility that someone would conquer Egypt.

The way, in a sense, to ward off this outside influence, to ward off outside conquest, was sort of preemptive. Strike your neighbors before they can strike you. And so we find the Egyptians, for the first time, building an empire, an empire that extended all the way into Mesopotamia, that extended to the west along the southern shore of the Mediterranean Sea, in the direction of what we would call Libya.

This New Kingdom was in lots of ways quite a remarkable period for the Egyptians. It was brilliant, and it was cosmopolitan. Egyptian culture spread very widely. We're going to bump into some examples in later lectures of the spread of Egyptian culture in precisely this period of time. But Egypt was also, for the first time, open to cultural influences coming in from the outside, open in a very decisive kind of way. Specialists can see this in Egyptian art, particularly. Some have found it, for example, in Egyptian literature, particularly in poetry, that Egyptians are now open to influences coming from outside the land of Egypt. So the New Kingdom, or as it's sometimes called, the New Empire, is a decisive period for the Egyptians.

During this period, the Egyptians began to encounter also, as they spread to the east in particular, peoples called the "Hittites." The Hittites were the first Indo-European speaking peoples of whom we have secure historical information in this period. Indo-European basically means that they're speaking a language like the one I'm speaking now. English is an Indo-European language, as is French, as is German, as is Swedish, as opposed to the Semitic languages that were oftentimes spoken in the whole land of Mesopotamia.

The Hittites were basically expanding from their bases in Anatolia. Anatolia is, in antiquity, what we call Turkey today, but couldn't be called Turkey yet because the Turks hadn't come. We'll get Turks into Anatolia later in the course. So, don't worry about that for now. For now, Anatolia, think Turkey. So, the Hittites are spreading south from Anatolia and spreading along the eastern shore of the Mediterranean Sea, just as the Egyptians are spreading to the north in the same area. They warred and warred and warred and warred, over several centuries. Finally, in 1274 B.C., at Qadesh in what is today northern Syria—so think where that is, Syria is about halfway between Egypt and Anatolia—a great battle is fought between the Egyptians and the Hittites. And it was essentially a draw.

It's very interesting because we also have the treaty documents that were issued in both lands, in Anatolia and in Egypt, after this battle. And interestingly enough, domestic consumption being what it is, both claimed a great victory. In fact, it wasn't a great victory for anybody, it was a draw. Probably what had happened, or perhaps we might put Qadesh into the context of a longer unfolding process, was these two states just wore themselves in this long unfolding battle. Really, after the battle of Qadesh, both more or less go into a state of decline. They carry on for quite a while, but they are never really in the kind of powerful, preeminent, influential, dominating position that they had been for at least a brief period of time, say from 1500 B.C. or thereabout down to the battle of Qadesh in 1274 B.C.

So Egyptian history is not so terribly interesting to us from the standpoint of their great conquests, of their great empire building. Is it perhaps the case, then, that what interests us about Egypt is the culture of Egypt? Let's talk a little bit about Egyptian culture, then. What are some of its distinguishing characteristics? What are some of the things that are most interesting and important about it? If we talk about Egyptian culture, everything starts with the pharaoh. This is really where our story begins.

We put tongue in cheek and say that, in a way Egypt, was a two-class society. There was Pharaoh, and there was everybody else. But it's also important to emphasize, in connection with the pharaoh, and we talked about this a little bit earlier on, that this represents the first appearance of an abstract sense of rule, of a separation of ruler and office. That point is sufficiently important that it bears repeating. It's also important that this was a time when the pharaoh is really separated from the ordinary run of human beings, from the ordinary realm of human beings.

For instance, an ordinary person was only permitted to speak in the pharaoh's presence. You could not speak to the pharaoh. So, for instance, if the pharaoh were sitting on his throne, and a person would approach at right angles and speak, as it were, past the pharaoh, that person could not look the pharaoh in the face and speak directly to him. So, whereas in Mesopotamia, for example, we talked about theocratic kingship—the king rules as the agent of the gods, chosen by the gods, on behalf of the gods, at the gods' pleasure—in Egypt, Pharaoh was a god, and in the Old Kingdom the most prominent and most important of the gods.

Over the course of Egyptian history, Egyptian religion grew considerably more complicated over time. For example, peace, the prosperity, the security of the Old Kingdom basically led to a very happy, optimistic outlook. This was not a time of great challenge. The Egyptians weren't being conquered by anybody, the country was prosperous: there were not famines, there were not violent, unpredictable floods. People didn't have reason to ask tough questions about life, the way, for example, that the people who wrote *Gilgamesh* asked tough questions.

If we think about the afterlife of the Egyptians at this period, it's a continuation of this life—many religious traditions, a new or better life. In Egypt, people wanted this life to continue. So, for example, when archaeologists have found tombs that weren't robbed in antiquity, they are typically full of all of the ordinary products of life. You needed in the next life all the things you had in this life. In the Old Kingdom, this wonderful afterlife was clearly meant for the pharaoh, for members of the pharaoh's family, perhaps for the most important advisors of the pharaoh, but perhaps not for everyone.

Then, during the Middle Kingdom, we begin to see a profusion of temples, a profusion of cults, many more gods and goddesses whose names we know about. This is the period about which the Greek historian Herodotus was speaking, when he said the Egyptians are the "most religious of all people." I don't think that they were the most religious of all people, but even for the Greeks, who were polytheistic, the Egyptians seemed sort of unbelievably polytheistic. This might have been the reemergence of pre-dynastic religion that had been repressed after the unification of Egypt. It may, perhaps, have been new developments. The afterlife, for example, seems now to have been considered much more available, available perhaps to everyone, certainly to larger numbers of people in the society.

We meet the concept of *Ma'at*. *Ma'at* means truth, justice, balance, order, harmony—that there is some sense that things will level out, out there. You may, for example, have seen depictions of Egyptian art where you have seen a scale. Perhaps you've been to the Supreme Court building in Washington, D.C. and you've seen the scales of justice depicted there on the building. During the Middle Kingdom, the myth of Osiris began to be very, very popular. Osiris had been killed, and then Isis went to find his killers, to avenge his death, and also to find his body. It had been carved up and divided; she had to find the parts and bring them back together.

One part of this myth is that Isis would measure a *kah*, the soul, against a feather. If the *kah* was light, that is to say not burdened with evil, it would be lighter than the feather, and then this *kah* could go and find its body again and live this happy afterlife. If, on the other hand, the *kah* were weighted down with evil, it would be heavier than the feather and it would be doomed to wander forever throughout all eternity. Now, what is interesting here is the first faint hints of an ethical dimension. There is something here suggesting that how you live your life is going to matter in how you live your afterlife, how you live your next life. You'll recall, perhaps, that we saw in Mesopotamia that we didn't have that.

The New Kingdom in Egypt saw many quite remarkable religious experiments. The Pharaoh Akhenaton, servant of Aton, the sun disc, abandoned the traditional worship of the Egyptian gods and tried to promote the worship of the cult of Aton. In doing this, Akhenaton became, for the first time, a person whom we might call a "henotheist," or a "monolatrist."

Henotheism and monolatry are synonymous words; they mean the worship of one god without denying the existence of others. So it is not monotheism—only one god, period—but it means, "We'll worship one, but not the others." Akhenaton's experiment died with him; his successors returned to the worship of the traditional gods, and that was the end of that. But this was, nevertheless, a quite bold and interesting religious experiment.

Scientific and artisanal advances are also striking in Egypt—for example, the use of papyrus. When we talked about Mesopotamia, we saw that clay tablets with cuneiform writing were not particularly efficient writing technology, information technology. The Egyptians developed papyrus, which gives us our word "paper."

Papyrus is a paper-like product made from soaking and then weaving together and then hammering, soaking, hammering, soaking, and then finally drying papyrus, the reeds of papyrus plants. It makes a paper-like product on which it is possible to write, and which makes it much easier to carry that writing around. And Egypt, being a very dry, drought-like climate, this material can survive for very long periods of time, thousands upon thousands of these papyrus documents have been found.

But it would be not very efficient to try to write hieroglyphics on paper, on papyrus. You may have seen pictures of Egyptian tomb art, where these beautiful pictures that depict writing, pictographic writing. Hieroglyphic writing means priestly writing, writing over which priests had control, but technically it's pictograph, picture writing. So you have someone, you depict them running, you depict someone rowing a boat, and there are little tricks that can be introduced to indicate whether it's happening right now, whether it will happen tomorrow, or whether it happened yesterday. But in any case, hieroglyphics would be very inefficient to use. What began to happen was the emergence of a demotic—that is to say, a popular—script that could be used, more widely read, more widely made, more widely produced, but on papyrus sheets, and then preserved.

We could turn to other aspects of Egyptian culture. For example, the desire to keep bodies intact. You've got to have some place for the *kah* to go back to. So, if you keep bodies for the afterlife, if you're going to preserve them, then obviously, in the process of preserving them, you're going to learn a very great deal about the human body. The Egyptians then discovered that not only could you do things to cadavers, to dead bodies, you could do things to live bodies. So, they became precocious, for example, in surgery. They developed a knowledge of anatomy that was second to none in all of antiquity.

What, then, are we to make of the legacy of Egypt? It's a bit puzzling in a way. The Greeks and the Romans were impressed, they were dazzled by the Egyptians, they remembered them, they wrote about them, they were extremely curious about them. Egypt attracted a great many visitors in antiquity. But it's not so easy to see exactly just what influence Egypt actually had. For example, Egypt's political control in the New Kingdom lasted for a very brief time.

Divinized kingship, as the Egyptians practiced, did recur historically, but I don't think it recurred, strictly speaking, because of the Egyptians. The Egyptians didn't really give us any new literary forms. There's nothing in Egypt as good as *Gilgamesh*; there's a lot of wonderful poetry, there's nothing new. The Egyptians, having much stone available, built magnificent temples, built the pyramids, as we've seen. Building huge architecturous propaganda is, again, something that has recurred, but this isn't, strictly speaking, Egyptian—we didn't need the Egyptians to invent it.

The earliest Egyptologists, from the middle of the 19th century on, were very anxious to claim ancient Egypt for the West. It's always been, in some ways, a dubious proposition, whether Egypt is part of the West. And then the whole issue was given a new spur of influence in the years after World War II. With the crumbling of colonial empires, and particularly in North America the emergence of black consciousness, some people claimed that Egypt was particularly, specifically, an African civilization. This, of course, spawned a claim of, "No, no, no, it's not; it's Western. Africa is something different." But can one actually equate Egypt and Africa? That is a very controversial view. In its most extreme form, people would have said, some people argued, that Western civilization was stolen from the Egyptians by the Greeks, and that, in fact, therefore, it was Egyptian in the first place and African behind that.

Now that view puts a very sharp focus on Egypt, but perhaps without solid reasons for doing so, and perhaps by way of indicating that modern interests in Egypt had been rather more prominent than ancient interests in Egypt, it is, therefore, a mystery—just what it is we have learned from, gotten from, borrowed from the Egyptians. That just might explain the mysterious smile of the Sphinx.

The Hebrews—Small States and Big Ideas
Lecture 4

What the Phoenicians did, in particular, was this: they planted trading colonies all over the Mediterranean. They began doing this probably about 900 B.C., and they created, in the process, one of the first great commercial empires that the world had ever seen.

After the Egyptians and Hittites exhausted themselves, and before other large, powerful states emerged, there was a brief period of importance for some small states and peoples. Sea peoples, most famously the Philistines, attacked along the eastern shore of the Mediterranean after about 1200 B.C.

The Phoenicians managed to avoid conquest. They were Canaanites who spoke a Semitic language and who had been present in the region of what is today coastal Syria and Lebanon for centuries. After about 900, they created one of the first great commercial empires the world had seen, anticipating the Athenians, Venetians, and Dutch. Creating colonies all over the Mediterranean, including at Carthage and Massilia, the Phoenicians played a role in spreading Mesopotamian culture and in beginning the creation of a Mediterranean cultural network. By 600 B.C., they had almost certainly circumnavigated Africa and, by about 450, they had reached Britain.

The other significant people who emerged in this big-power pause were the Hebrews. Again, much of the Hebrews' history is shrouded in legend. A pastoralist, Abraham, who has been dated between 2000 and 1550 B.C., was the leader of a people who were on the outs with the settled city-dwellers and grain farmers of Sumer. Abraham and his God made a pact, and Abraham was told to leave Ur for the land of Canaan/Palestine. For some centuries, Abraham's descendants farmed the land, quarreled among themselves, and tried to ward off enemies.

Eventually, they were swept up in the struggles between the Egyptians and Hittites. The familiar story says that the Hebrews were carried off in bondage to Egypt. Some probably were prisoners of war, but others doubtless migrated there voluntarily because the area was more peaceful and prosperous. Moses arose as a leader who forged a people during the Exodus, a long process of departing from Egypt and reentering the "promised land."

For a time, the Hebrews lived under numerous independent judges, but the threat of the sea peoples, chiefly the Philistines, induced them to choose kings, first Saul, then David, and Solomon. Under Solomon, the kingdom reached its high point, and considerable commercial wealth flowed in. But a distaste for strong central authority led to a division of the kingdom into Israel in the north, with its capital at Samaria, and Judah in the south, with its capital at Jerusalem. Eventually, these small kingdoms were conquered by more powerful neighbors: Israel fell to the Assyrians in 722 and Judah, to the Neo-Babylonians in 586. The Assyrians in particular physically dispersed the Hebrews all over the Near East: the "Exile."

Over time, this notion of a covenant and this notion of a chosen people led to a series of more mature reflections on the very nature of that deity.

Never has a people been so politically insignificant, yet culturally so critical in the history of Western civilization. It is the religion of the Hebrews that has left so deep an imprint. Our knowledge of the beliefs of the Hebrews comes from a collection of writings that in some ways cover the period from about 2000 to 200 B.C., but that were mostly written down after 1000 B.C. These writings are properly called the Hebrew Bible, or the Hebrew Scriptures. To Christians, these materials are the Old Testament. The Hebrew Bible consists of three major kinds of materials:

> The Torah: The first five books, sometimes called the "Books of Moses." The name means "the teaching," and these books contain the prescriptions that governed the life of the Hebrews.

> The Prophets: This group of books contains both historical books, such as Kings, Samuel, and Chronicles, that reveal God's unfolding relationship with His people, and the more obviously prophetic

books of the "Greater Prophets," such as Isaiah and Jeremiah, and the "Lesser Prophets," such as Amos and Micah.

The Writings: This is a catchall designation for the poetic material, such as the Psalms and Canticles, and for the beautiful and moving advice literature, such as Proverbs and Wisdom.

Three central religious ideas contained in the Hebrew Bible, taken together, constitute the key foundations of Western civilization.

The idea of the *covenant* was created between Yahweh and Abraham—between God and a tribe—and renewed between Yahweh and Moses—between God and a people. It was redefined by the Prophet Ezra during the Exile—between God and a people adhering to the Torah. The unique notion of reciprocity appears here for the first time. The covenant also embodies the unique notion of a *chosen people*: One God for one people, not a god for a place or a state.

The idea of *exclusive monotheism* has a long evolution, from henotheism, still present in the time of Moses, to monotheism in the time of Isaiah. This occasioned a profound tension between the idea that Yahweh was the only God and the God of the Hebrews, and the possibility of universalism. The idea is seen most vividly in the Book of Jonah.

The idea of *ethical monotheism* is the profound sense of social justice that runs through the prophetic books is unprecedented in the previous religious experience of known peoples. God demanded a particular kind of behavior as a guarantee of his continuing benevolence. This idea is seen in the *Decalogue* and *Shema*, in Micah.

Philosophers and theologians have long acknowledged the importance of monotheism for everything from natural philosophy to political ideology. Numerous peoples in the West have called themselves a "New Israel" as a way of claiming a unique, chosen relationship with providence. Historically, social justice has sometimes been a secular concern, but much more often, one with religious roots. Western literature is unimaginable without its fundamental, formative text: the Bible. ■

Drane, *Introducing the Old Testament.*

The Hebrew Scriptures (Old Testament). From a historical and cultural point of view, read Genesis, Exodus, Kings, Jeremiah, Isaiah, Psalms.

Moscati, *World of the Phoenicians.*

Shanks, ed., *Ancient Israel.*

Questions to Consider

1. How do the religious and ethical ideas of the Hebrews differ from those of the Mesopotamians and Egyptians?

2. Does it seem odd to you that a people who were not politically, militarily, or economically powerful exercised such a potent influence on Western civilization? Can you think of any comparable examples?

The Hebrews—Small States and Big Ideas
Lecture 4—Transcript

You may remember that last time we talked about Egypt, and in the concluding remarks to that lecture I observed that the Egyptians have been, perhaps, more important for how they have been remembered than for what they did. In some very real ways, we're going to turn to two little peoples today, the Phoenicians and the Hebrews, who likewise are important for how they are remembered, but also for certain things that they did—yet not because they built great empires, not because they were great conquerors, not because they were particularly gifted in the arts, but because, particularly with the Hebrews, of a profound religious tradition.

These small peoples—Egyptians and Hittites having worn themselves out, as we saw, in this long series of wars that they fought with one another—these small peoples were able to emerge. There was a kind of a gap, an interstice, that runs from about 1200 to 700 B.C., and in that period of time, a number of small states emerged. Some of these really don't need to attract much of our attention.

We might say, for example, that this is the time of the Philistines. Contemporary records speak of sea peoples, a group of peoples who raided and invaded all along the eastern coast of the Mediterranean and the southern shore of the Mediterranean as well, particularly around Egypt. But these were not people who left any durable impact, who made any long-term contributions.

The Phoenicians, on the other hand, are rather different. So let's spend just a few minutes thinking about them, reminding yourselves again that these were a very small people who had an opportunity to emerge, because, for a moment, their great and powerful neighbors had been much weakened. The Phoenicians, actually they're Canaanites—they're a people who live roughly in what is today Lebanon, the area north of what we think of as Israel, south of what we think of as Syria. They're called "Phoenicians" because they were very famous, among other things, for exporting purple dye, and the Romans therefore called them the *poeny*, the purple people. But actually, they were Canaanites.

The Phoenicians emerged along what we would think of as the Lebanese coast. They built a series of very important trading cities, like Tyre, Sidon, Byblos and Beirut. These are Phoenician cities, and very important ones. What the Phoenicians did, in particular, was this: they planted trading colonies all over the Mediterranean. They began doing this probably about 900 B.C., and they created, in the process, one of the first great commercial empires that the world had ever seen. In this, they really anticipated the Athenians, they anticipated the Venetians, they anticipated the Dutch. That is, they were not people who conquered enormous amounts of territory, but they were people who built a commercial empire that was, in some ways, more valuable and less expensive.

Where were these colonies? For instance, Carthage. We will be much occupied with Carthage later on, when we talk about the Romans, for example. But Carthage was a Phoenician colony. We might think of Massilia, we know that better as Marseilles, in the south of France. That was another Phoenician colony. There were Phoenician colonies along the coast of Iberia, what we call Spain. There were Phoenician colonies in southern Italy and in Sicily. The Phoenicians built trading colonies all over the Mediterranean world, and they began, slowly but surely, by dint of these communities, stitching that world together, making one kind of cultural basin in the Mediterranean area.

This was their great contribution, spreading ideas that had arisen in Mesopotamia, and spreading through much of the Middle East, now to much of the Mediterranean world as a whole. It's worth saying, too, with respect to these Phoenicians, that they were really intrepid sailors. It's a shame we don't know more about them. It's a shame, for example, that we don't know more about their naval technology. For example, by about 600 B.C., they had almost certainly circumnavigated Africa. That wouldn't happen again for more than 2,000 years, at least not by someone coming from the Mediterranean basin.

By perhaps 450 B.C., they had reached the British Isles—the Tin Isles as they were called in antiquity—probably sailed up to the coast to what we would think of today as Cornwall, southwestern Britain. So, the Phoenicians, then, are one of the small peoples who emerged in this sort of gap left after the Egyptians and Hittites had worn themselves out, and before other imperial powers (to whom we'll turn really in our next lecture in more detail) had arisen.

By far, however, the most important people who emerged in this brief gap, in this brief moment of opportunity, were the Hebrews. To raise the subject of the history of the Hebrews is to raise one of the most fundamental and foundational issues in all of Western civilization; though, we'll see, there's a certain irony in it. We're not going to stress them because of their politics, because of their government, because of their war, because of their diplomacy, because of their economics, but rather because of their religious ideals.

We know a lot, and there's a great deal that we don't know. For example, much is shrouded in legend. We're told that a pastoralist by the name of Abraham was told by his god to move his people from Euratha Caldese, from Sumer, which we talked about in an earlier lecture, up to a land that God would show him. That land wound up being roughly what we think of today as Israel, or, from another point of view, Palestine.

The story tells us, of course, that God bid his people move, and that's perhaps true. But it's also important to say that Abraham was a pastoralist, and in Sumer, you have a land basically of settled agriculturalists, of farmers. There are no places on earth where pastoralists and farmers get along well together.

One has only to think, for instance, of the American frontier in the 19th century—the great struggles between the cattlemen and the farmers. So there's probably a sense that pastoral peoples were less numerous and less powerful and, therefore, were invited to leave; but, perhaps, maybe were induced to leave. And they migrated off to someplace else. They settled in a barren, godforsaken part of the world, even though God had given it to them. In a very real way, it was like Joseph Smith settling the Mormons in Utah. This was a land, surely, that no one else wanted, so they settled in this new land.

What about this Abraham? When did he do this? Scholars have confidently dated Abraham everywhere between about 2000 and about 1550 B.C. We can build very convincing cases for a whole series of dates. Suffice it to say that this begins during what we would have called the Dynastic Period at Ur, the Dynastic Period in Sumer, and then extends a little bit beyond that period.

Once the Hebrews had settled in the land that had been pointed out to them, the land that would become Israel, they were very much divided up. They didn't come as a single people who were firmly unified, who had a firm government, who had a firm structure of authority, a firm structure of organization around themselves. They settled in small groups and small bands.

If one reads, for example, the early books of the Hebrew Scriptures, about which we'll have a lot more to say in just a minute, one notices the names of large numbers of families, and struggles, and contentions, and rivalries, and jealousies, and envies among those families. And one also notices that they weren't the only people about the place. They were also struggling with other small groups of people—none so powerful that they could conquer the Hebrews, the Hebrews not so powerful that they could conquer all of their neighbors.

After a long period of time, during which this local society—this local community divided up into many small groups—had been settled in this region, we encounter a series of stories about the Hebrews having been carried off into bondage in Egypt. Now, it's quite likely, indeed, that a certain number of these people were taken away as prisoners of war in these great struggles between the Egyptians and the Hittites.

The Egyptians and the Hittites, after all, were marching back and forth, back and forth, through much of this territory. It's also very likely that certain numbers of people, finding life difficult in the barren and harsh plains of the land of Israel—a land that has really been brought to much fruition by the technologies of modern agriculture, by chemical fertilizers and by modern farm machinery and so on—very hard to get a living out of that land in antiquity. It may very well have been, then, that some of these Hebrews elected to migrate into Egypt, a land which we have seen was legendary for its prosperity.

Now what probably happened was that during the New Kingdom in Egypt—you'll perhaps recall from our lecture on Egypt that during the New Kingdom, the pharaohs first of all rose up to throw off the Hyksos, these external invaders who had come in at the end of the Middle Kingdom, and that they then began building an empire of their own, partly to ward off foreign conquest, and partly to ward off foreign influences. It may very well have been at that time that the Hebrews living in Egypt were really reduced to bondage. They may have been sort of resident aliens; I wouldn't want to say that they had a privileged status before this, although the story of Joseph certainly suggests to us that some of them had a reasonably privileged existence in Egypt. But in any case, probably during the New Kingdom, many of the Hebrews were reduced to subjection.

Gradually, a leader rose among them, Moses. In the years after the Egyptians and Hittites had really begun to weaken, and that's fairly important, Moses was able to forge his people into one, and then to lead them out of Egypt. A century or two centuries before, such an activity would have been unthinkable. Egypt would simply have been too powerful. So it's important that Egypt had actually weakened a good deal when the exodus, the journey out, the departure, took place.

We have a series of accounts of that departure. The Hebrews left Egypt; they wandered for a period of 40 years in the desert of Sinai before they settled again in the land presumably from which they had come, while obviously some of their fellows were still there. Not all of them had left. And they came back in. We have two very different accounts. One account suggests that they reentered this land slowly and in small groups, and settled all over the territory. Another account is the one where Joshua fought the battle of Jericho. They came in, there was one great battle, and they won and they took over. Probably there were great battles, and that's remembered. And probably there was a very slow, patient entry into this new land.

For a long time, the Hebrews lived under rulers called judges, a group of local notables, who were responsible for the leadership of relatively small groups of people. There was considerable contention among these small groups of people. It was only in the face of external threats, of the Philistines, of the sea peoples to whom I alluded a few minutes ago, that the Hebrews really induced to unify. And they created for themselves kings: Saul, and then David, and then Solomon.

Under these kings, the Hebrews were unified as they had not been before. Under Solomon, a very considerable commercial state was created, a state of considerable prosperity, of considerable influence. But the unification had only really come in the face of an external threat, in the face of an external challenge. A certain disinclination to accept strong, centralized authority then led to a situation where the small, unified kingdom broke down into two even smaller kingdoms: one in the north called Israel, with its capital at Samaria, one in the south called Judah, with its capital at Jerusalem.

These two kingdoms existed, then, for a period of about two or three centuries. They struggled often with one another; they struggled often with external foes—no great foes yet, no great powers yet. All of the evidence that we have, the evidence of the Hebrew Bible, suggests that these were contentious folk, that there were a great many struggles inside the kingdoms of Israel and Judah. Gradually, however, powerful neighbors arose.

In 722 B.C., the kingdom of Israel, the northernmost of the kingdoms, was conquered by the Assyrians. We'll talk in our next lecture about the Assyrians. About a century-and-a-half later, in 586 B.C., the kingdom of Judah, the southern kingdom, fell to the Neo-Babylonians. When the Assyrians conquered Israel, they deported a very large portion of the population. They spread them throughout the far-flung Assyrian empire. This is remembered, then, in tradition, as the "Ten Lost Tribes." It's also remembered as the "Exile," the time when the Hebrews have been exiled from their land, the first such exile that they experienced.

We're faced, then, with an interesting puzzle. We have a people, not very numerous, not very powerful, not very well united, momentarily economically significant but never anything like the Phoenicians were. And yet, they have left us a religious heritage second to none in the Western tradition. This is a reminder that you don't have to be powerful, you don't have to be top dog, to be important. Indeed, I think it would be fair to say that there is no other people so politically insignificant and so culturally significant in the history of Western civilization.

What, then, is the nature of this imprint that the Hebrews have left? To put that question a little differently, how do we know about it? Our knowledge of Hebrew beliefs comes from a very large, a very rich, a very complex set of writings. We know those writings as the Bible. We know them in particular as the Hebrew Bible, or the Hebrew Scriptures. It's that collection of materials that Christians call the Old Testament. But of course, it's not the Old Testament at all for the Jews, for the people who made these books.

The books themselves provide us with a series of revealing insights into these people from about 2000 B.C., if one dates Abraham that early, down to about 200 B.C., down really to the beginnings of the Roman conquest of the Mediterranean world. Most of the writings, however, that we have, in the form in which we have them, are written between about 1000 and 500 B.C. There are some that are written after 500 B.C., and there are certainly, in the materials that take shape as we know them after 1000 B.C., older materials embedded. Essentially, this great body of material witnesses most precisely to the period from about 1000 to 500 B.C. In other words, from the creation of the unified kingdom down into the full period of exile. That's the period chronologically where the material comes from, and the period that it reveals to us.

The Hebrew Bible consists of three basic kinds of materials. There's three bodies of material here. The first five books of the Hebrew Bible— Genesis, Exodus, Leviticus, Numbers and Deuteronomy—are called the Torah. Sometimes we call these the Books of Moses. The name means "the teaching." Now, what, precisely, is it that these books teach? Two things. It tells the Hebrews about the initiation and the unfolding of their early relationship with their God, and of their settlement in the kingdom, the land that had been assigned to them. I shouldn't have said "kingdom," the land before it was a kingdom that had been assigned to them.

In the second place, and in particular in Leviticus, Numbers and Deuteronomy, is an enormous array of prescriptive material: "Do this, and don't do that." In that regard, this early legal material is very much like the law codes that we saw in Mesopotamia, in other places, and in earlier times. That is to say, no great scientific jurisprudence, not yet informed clearly and directly and systematically by ethical principles, but rather a whole series of requirements and prohibitions, relatively simple at this particular stage. The Torah, the first part of the Hebrew Bible.

Second, there's an enormous collection of material called "the Prophets." The prophetic books—immediately you'll think of Isaiah, Jeremiah, Ezekiel, the great prophets. But, in fact, there's a series of historical books that are reckoned among the prophets before—as the Scriptures are laid out—we typically come to the prophets themselves. These are, for example, the books of Kings, and Samuel, and Chronicles.

These are books that are prophetic in the sense that they show the unfolding of God's relationship with His people. When they observe his law, when they keep his rule, when they keep his commandments, they prosper. When they fall away from his law, from his rule, from his commandments, they suffer. So, it is in that sense that these books are imagined later as prophetic, and, therefore, charting a future. We've talked about that in earlier lectures, the way people create histories as a way of imagining pasts that point them to a future. So these books were supposed to be, and were designed to be, ways of understanding how to live tomorrow according to what had happened yesterday.

But then, there are also the collections of the prophets themselves, the major prophets—Isaiah, Jeremiah, Ezekiel, for example—and the lesser prophets— Amos and Micah and Habakkuk and the rest. The prophets are, in a sense, the great theoreticians of the religious message contained otherwise in these historical books. The historical books contained information, presumably immediately accessibly relevant, easy to understand for anybody. They did well, and things worked fine for them. They did badly, and things worked poorly for them. But along come the prophets to provide a kind of a theological explanation, to provide a kind of a philosophical explanation, to provide a message, to explain what it all means. A very large body of material, and in many respects quite beautiful and quite moving literature.

In the third place, there's a collection of material that bear the not terribly helpful name "the Writings." What we have here is a kind of a catchall designation for wisdom literature, for poetic material like the Psalms (sometimes these were thought of as prophetic, sometimes they were simply reckoned among the Writings, these instructive and uplifting documents), the Canticles, books like Proverbs, books like Wisdom—full of pithy sayings, full of guides to life, full of ways to organize how you do things. Not so powerful, not so clear, not so direct as the Prophets, but certainly nothing like the historical books in that they don't tell a story, they don't narrate anything. Or if they narrate tiny stories; each story is simply meant to have a moral and doesn't necessarily connect to the story after it or to the one before it.

So, a large body of material designed in fundamental ways to tell people how to live well. How to live well meant not how to be happy, how to enjoy yourself; it meant how to keep God's law. The central religious ideas contained in the Hebrew Bible are, in the time that we have available to us, a little difficult to capture briefly. Let's try to do that anyway.

Here we have, unquestionably, one of the real foundation stones of Western civilization. What I want to do is look at some very basic ideas which can inform one's reading, one's appreciation, one's understanding of this body of material, but which also has the advantage for us as historians of saying what is important then, what was happening then, what did it mean then? And this reiterates a point that I've made any number of times in previous lectures already. History is always a kind of a dialogic process. There is, on the one hand, finding out what happened then, and why, and what it meant to those people. And then there is the process of the way that has been remembered subsequently all the way down to our own time.

So, in some very real ways, and talking about some of the basic ideas in the Hebrew Scriptures, what we're trying to do is understand "then," and many "thens" following on the first one. The first of these great ideas is the idea of a covenant, a pact, a bargain, a contract. It's created, in the first instance, between Yahweh and Abraham, between a god and a tribal leader, between a god and the followers—in fiction, the family of Abraham. They weren't necessarily all related to him, but this was the way it was remembered, that this was his great family, his extended family, a tribe. This was, then, a covenant renewed on Mt. Sinai between God and Moses, for the people who had been forged in the exodus from Egypt, in the wandering in the desert. A new people in a way, and so a new covenant with them.

The covenant was then renewed a third time, and we find this, in particular, in the writings of the prophet Ezra. This was a time when these people had been dispersed, when these people had been exiled from their land. And so, now the covenant—Yahweh doesn't fall out of it, nor does Abraham, nor does Moses, nor does the tradition, nor do all of these books that we talked about a moment ago. But now, the covenant is understood, particularly, to be all those people who observe the Torah—wherever they may be, under what political system they may live—there is always the hope, perhaps, that they might be unified again. But for the time being, insofar as they're enduring exile, their covenant is now with the Torah.

The very idea of covenant itself is unique and distinctive, and quite remarkable. It is the idea of a reciprocal relationship between a god and his people. One finds this again and again and again; and in the prophetic books, one finds it in the Psalms, for example. There are expressions there unlike those found anywhere else in the religious literature of any other people before this time in the world.

When the psalmist cries out, "My God, why have you forsaken me?" this is utterly remarkable. Looking into the face of God and saying, "We made a deal, pay off," when the prophets again and again and again call upon God to honor his promises—this is so very and fundamentally different from the sort of thing we see in Mesopotamia, where all those people want is "Please don't let somebody conquer us. Please don't let the Tigris and Euphrates flood so violently again this year."

The propitiatory religion of Mesopotamia is utterly unlike what we find among the Hebrews. The idea of a pact, of a covenant, of a contract, of a mutual and reciprocal deal. It's not to trivialize to call it a deal; it was really understood that way. Each party had rights and obligations.

Next, the idea of a uniquely chosen people. One god for one people. You'll perhaps recall again that, in an earlier lecture, we said that there very much a tendency in Mesopotamia—and we saw this in Egypt as well but it worked a little differently in Egypt—a tendency towards syncretism. In other words, you add deities all the time. Physicists speak of the law of the conservation of energy, or the law of the conservation of matter. We might say that in antiquity, there was a law of the conservation of divinity. You didn't want to lose any; you just added. Not so for the Hebrews. One god for one people. A remarkable notion.

Over time, this notion of a covenant and this notion of a chosen people led to a series of more mature reflections on the very nature of that deity. There emerged the idea of exclusive monotheism. We have some hints of this in the various earliest sections of Genesis, the first book of the Hebrew Scriptures. There we find plural words used for God. Now this could be polite; it could be a royal "we." One has to acknowledge that possibility. But when, for example, Moses goes upon Sinai and is there given the law, the covenant is renewed; he is given what we think of as the Ten Commandments. The first of those commandments, "I am the Lord, your God. You shall not have false gods before you." Translated more strictly, the gods of strangers, the gods of other people. It doesn't say they're not out there; it says don't mess with them. What we seem to see at that point is what we learned to call, in connection with the Egyptians, "henotheism" or "monolatry." You worship one god, but you don't deny that there are other ones out there.

By the time we come to the prophet Isaiah, this sense of monotheism has evolved in an interesting kind of way. Now we meet the notion that there is one God, period. There are no others. That generated a very interesting tension. The covenant had been, in the first place, between God and Abraham. It had been, in the second place, between God and the people who Moses had forged into one. And it meant, in the third place, between those people and the Torah.

What now? If there is one God only, are all other people consigned to godlessness, or is this God eventually to be for all of them as well? This was a question to which Jewish thinkers in antiquity gave many answers, as indeed they have given many answers in modern time. It remains a very controversial subject. But we can feel this tension most vividly in the book of Jonah.

The book of Jonah has often attracted attention for all the wrong reasons. Jonah, you may recall, had been told to go and preach in Nineveh, to go and preach to the Assyrians. As we'll see in more detail in the next lecture, these were really bad guys. These were awful people, and they were Gentiles to boot. They were not Hebrews. Jonah tries to flee; he doesn't want to accept this responsibility. He tries to flee; he takes a ship, probably in one of the Phoenician ports, and sails out into the Mediterranean. A great storm comes up, Jonah's pitched into the ocean, a whale or big fish or something swallows him up and spits him out on the coast, and God says, "Listen, I told you you're going to Nineveh, now get on about it." The point is that, in the way the story is told in the Hebrew Bible, and the way the Hebrews would've understood that story, it had nothing to do with whether Jonah was really in the belly of a fish or not, and why didn't he get digested and so on. The story was told in this wonderful and richly exaggerated way to say if God tells you to do something, you're going to do it. You can't escape it. That moral was pretty clear, but what is fascinating is that God had told Jonah to go to Nineveh. Does this suggest universalism? Does this suggest now that this faith is for all people, and not merely for the Hebrews? As I said, that was a controversial point in antiquity, it has been controversial since, but we can feel the tension.

The next important point to make is the emergence, very clearly, of the idea of ethical monotheism. A profound sense of social justice runs through the prophetic books. This again, as we saw, is something that does not appear in Mesopotamia. It is something that, as we saw, is hinted at in Middle Kingdom Egypt. But in the ways that it works itself out in the Hebrew Bible, it is unprecedented. There is the fundamental idea that God demands a particular kind of behavior as a guarantee of his continuing benevolence.

We can see this in several quite vivid places. For instance, the Decalogue, the Ten Commandments. The first commandments tell the Hebrews how to behave with respect to their God, and the rest of the commandments tell the Hebrews how to behave with respect to one another. Honor God and honor him alone, make no graven images and keep his Sabbath holy. And then, honor your family—always it starts there—and then don't lie, don't cheat, don't steal, don't covet. Behave yourselves. We find the same kind of thing worked out in Deuteronomy 6, the *Shema*: "Hear, O Israel, the Lord your God is One, and Him alone shall you serve." We find it in the great statement of the prophet Micah: "This alone the Lord your God asks of you, that you do justice and walk humbly with your God"—the last commandments and the first commandments.

The Hebrew legacy, then, is an enormously powerful one. Philosophers and theologians, for example, have long acknowledged the importance of monotheism in the Western tradition. It makes a great difference if you imagine the world as one, or if you imagine the world as many. Numerous peoples historically—in the West in particular—have called themselves, by reference to the Hebrews, a "New Israel," of claiming for themselves a unique relationship with God like the one that the Hebrews enjoy. Historically, social justice has much more often been a religious than a secular phenomenon. Think, for example, of abolition in the United States, something that rose in the Protestant churches of New England. And finally, and very richly, Western literature is inconceivable without its fundamental formative text, the Bible. You hear a quote, make a wager. If you bet Shakespeare or the Bible, you'll rarely lose your bet. Next time we turn to the peoples who conquered the Hebrews.

A Succession of Empires
Lecture 5

> The main achievement of the Neo-Babylonians, whose high point lasted only about a century ... was the massive rebuilding of the city of Babylon, creating there the famous Hanging Gardens, one of the Seven Wonders of the Ancient World, an elaborate palace complex with beautiful pleasure gardens surrounding it.

The period of Phoenician and Hebrew independence ended with the rise of the Assyrian Empire. The Assyrians were a Semitic-speaking people who had been important in northern Mesopotamia in the second millennium B.C., then declined, and reemerged around Nineveh in about 900. They began a series of campaigns that carried them to Persia in the East and Egypt in the West. Their success was facilitated by a huge army, iron weapons, and cavalry. In 722, the Assyrians conquered Israel and deported its inhabitants, the Ten Lost Tribes. Their policies were cruel; state terrorism was their normal practice. Even their art glorified fear and destruction.

The Assyrians eventually evoked a challenge from a coalition of peoples who were seen as liberators by those whom the Assyrians had conquered. One key group was the Neo-Babylonians. The dynasty of whom Nebuchadnezzar (r. 605–562 B.C.) was the most famous built a large realm in Mesopotamia after the fall of the Assyrians. The main achievement of this dynasty was the massive

Assyrian wall carvings.

© Hemera/Thinkstock.

rebuilding of Babylon. The Hanging Gardens were one of the Seven Wonders of the Ancient World.

Minor players were the central Anatolian Lydians. The Lydians' main historical achievement was the invention of coinage around 700 B.C. Their most famous king was Croesus, whose wealth—probably because he heaped up coins—was legendary. The greatest members of the anti-Assyrian coalition were the Medes and Persians.

The Medes were from the Zagros Mountains, and the Persians were from the Iranian plain. They were ethnically related and spoke similar languages. Until Persian Cyrus (r. 559–530) assumed leadership, the Medes had generally been the dominant partner. Cyrus began a series of lightning campaigns that were continued by his successors, Cambyses (r. 530–525 B.C.) and Darius (r. 521–486 B.C.). They built the largest empire the world had yet seen.

> **[The Persians] left a profound religious heritage that interacted reciprocally and fruitfully with Judaism, with Christianity, and later with Islam.**

There were several reasons for Persian success. The Persians had a huge army—up to 300,000 men—with an elite core of 10,000 "Immortals." They practiced brilliant cavalry tactics and were the first to understand the significance of the cavalry. They were tolerant of the customs of local peoples and often left their own people in charge. They were highly skilled at administration. The Persians set up an elaborate administrative network under satraps. They developed common systems of weights, measures, and coinage; the Persian imperial post; and great roads, including the "Royal Road." They also used the widely known Aramaic language instead of Persian.

The chief manifestation of Persian culture was the religion Zoroastrianism. Scholars dispute the dates for Zarathustra. He may have lived circa 1000, 750, or 550 B.C. His teachings are revealed by *gathas* (songs) preserved in the Avesta, the holy scriptures of Zoroastrianism. Zarathustra taught of a single, benevolent god, Ahura Mazda, who was the creator of all. But he also was much intrigued by the problem of evil.

Zarathustra taught that Ahura Mazda had twin children, one benevolent and one evil. These two played out a great cosmic challenge between good and bad, truth and falsehood, and so on. Human beings are endowed with free will to choose one path or the other. Zarathustra stressed superiority of the spiritual over the material. This dualism would recur time and time again in the West, such as among the Manicheans, Bogomils, and Cathars. The Assyrians and Babylonians left some impressive ruins but not much else. The Persians left a legacy of civilized rule, ideas about kingship and government, and a profound religious heritage that interacted reciprocally with Judaism and Christianity. ■

Suggested Reading

The Avesta.

Cook, *The Persian Empire.*

Saggs, *The Might That Was Assyria.*

Questions to Consider

1. Given the example of Assyrian failure, why do you think regimes have continued to believe that they can rule by terror?

2. Can you think of inheritances from Zoroastrianist dualism, for example, in the realms of art or literature?

A Succession of Empires
Lecture 5—Transcript

Last time, we talked in particular about the Hebrews. Today we're going to turn to a succession of great empires. In particular, and in the first place, the Assyrians, who conquered the Hebrew kingdom of Israel, then to the Neo-Babylonians who conquered the kingdom of Judah. And then we'll move on through a number of smaller imperial states to a consideration of the Persian Empire. In a certain sense, the theme of this lecture, the central point that we'll be tracking, is the building of larger and larger and larger states on the land of Mesopotamia, on the land of the Middle East—the land with which we began in Sumer in our second lecture.

The period of Phoenician and Hebrew independence, and you'll recall, perhaps, my saying that this independence emerged because there was a kind of a gap between great imperial states. The Egyptians and Hittites had worn themselves out; the Assyrians had not quite come on the scene yet. But this period of independence for people like the Phoenicians and the Hebrews was brought to an abrupt end by the Assyrians, who built a very large empire, the largest that had been built up until that time.

The Assyrians were a Semitic-speaking people, who had been important in northern Mesopotamia in the second millennium B.C. They then declined for a period of years, and then after about 900 B.C., from their capital at Nineveh, they began a lightning series of military campaigns that created an empire stretching from the boundaries of Persia—Iran, to us—over to and including the north of Egypt.

I've several times mentioned Semitic-speaking peoples. For example, I mentioned the Hyksos, and now I've mentioned this in connection with the Assyrians. And, of course, also the Hebrews spoke a Semitic language. It's important, perhaps, just to say here, so that in later lectures we can refer to it, that scholars now divide people, historically, around the globe, by language groups. No longer do we try to divide them by races, no longer do we try to divide them by ethnicity. These are modern and constructed categories. They're not biological; they're not in the blood. You can't take somebody's blood and say, "Oh, that person speaks a Semitic language," or "that person is Irish," or "that person is something else." So, we divide people up, more or less neutrally, by languages.

We're dealing now with another of the Semitic peoples. You'll recall, perhaps, my mentioning the Hittites were the first Indo-European speakers whom we encountered. We'll encounter many more of those as we go along.

Now, back to our friends, the Assyrians. They built this enormous imperial state, largely on the basis of a very large army, the use of iron weapons, and the use of cavalry. A large army is not so remarkable in and of itself; the use of iron weapons is important. Previously, we have been working through what we might call the Bronze Age, and the weapons were Bronze. The Assyrians, with their iron weapons, simply had a higher grade of military technology than the peoples whom they encountered.

Cavalry, for the Assyrians, was basically a tool of getting to the battlefield quickly. They didn't really understand the use of cavalry on the battlefield. The Persians, as we'll see in a few minutes, were the ones who discovered how to use cavalry on the battlefield. But the Assyrians were able to get there fast. That was really what they learned from the use of horses.

In 722 B.C., as we saw in our last lecture, they conquered the kingdom of Israel, and they deported its inhabitants, the Ten Lost Tribes, beginning the period of the Exile. The Assyrians were, as I hinted in the lecture on the Hebrews, bad guys. Their basic policies were cruel; their basic policy was state terrorism. They routinely rounded up and killed large numbers of people just by way of sending a message to everybody else that they could do that to them, too, at any time and for no reason. Even their art glorified fear and destruction. If you've ever seen, for example, any of the great Assyrian stone carvings, there are some in this country in the Metropolitan in New York, but there are particularly large and fierce ones in the British Museum in London, if you've ever been in the room there of antiquities. To walk by one of these panels is actually to feel eerie, to feel scared. That's exactly what they meant to evoke in you: fear, terror.

Not surprisingly, the Assyrians didn't evoke much loyalty; they didn't evoke much affection. And what they did evoke was a challenge. This challenge arose from a coalition of peoples who, very often, were seen as liberators from the Assyrians. They didn't necessarily want to be conquered by these new guys, but they really wanted out from under the thumb of the Assyrians.

In this great coalition of people, one key group was the Neo-Babylonians. You'll remember we talked of the old Babylonians, that's the people of Hammurabi, he of the great law code. The Neo-Babylonians are the people whose most famous king was Nebuchadnezzar, who turns up in some of the later books of the Hebrew Bible. He reigned from about 605 to 562 B.C.

He built a very large realm based in Mesopotamia, based in the same areas where the Assyrians had been. Their capital now is at Babylon and not at Nineveh, but the point is that the center of this realm is basically in the same place that the center of the Assyrian realm had been based. The main achievement of the Neo-Babylonians, whose high point lasted only about a century—they were not really on the scene very long—was the massive rebuilding of the city of Babylon, creating there the famous Hanging Gardens, one of the Seven Wonders of the Ancient World, an elaborate palace complex with beautiful pleasure gardens surrounding it. So, then, the Neo-Babylonians were one of the peoples in the great coalition that brought down the Assyrians.

There were also a number of minor players at this time. For example, up in central Anatolia, people called the Lydians. The Lydians might very well have disappeared from history—they weren't particularly remarkable—were it not for two things. One, they invented coinage, as far as we can tell. And eventually, of course, virtually everyone who came after them used coined money. Did they always borrow it from the Lydians? It may very well be, as we'll see in a minute, that they borrowed it from the Persians, who borrowed it from the Lydians, who disseminated it a great deal further. But the point is, the Lydians invented coinage.

The second thing is their legendary King Croesus. His wealth was legendary, probably because he heaped up coins, because he collected a large number of these coins as taxes and tribute. His very name meant wealth in the ancient world. We still say somebody's as rich as Croesus, or maybe some of us say things like that. So, Croesus is famous and the Lydians made money, but they also walked their weary hour on the stage and departed, not really much to be heard from afterwards.

Not so for the other great party to the anti-Assyrian coalition. These were the Medes and the Persians. These were peoples who had been living, the Medes, in the Zagros Mountains, the mountain range basically that divides Iran from Iraq. They'd been living in those mountains for a very long time, and we haven't heard much about them. And indeed, people in antiquity hadn't heard much about them. The Persians, on the other hand, lived down on the Iranian plain. They had been there for a very long time, but again had not been particularly interested in the lands to their west in Mesopotamia.

We can say of the Medes and the Persians that they're ethnically related—they speak a similar language, they're roughly the same kinds of people—but there are some differences among them. In any case, they began to forge a great unity under the great King Cyrus. Cyrus was the Shah; he was the Shah-in-Shah, the King of Kings, founded a monarchy which ceased in 1979 when the Shah of Iran was put off his throne—the oldest reigning imperial regime in the world.

In any case, Cyrus forged this great unity between the Medes and the Persians, and formed a temporary alliance with the Neo-Babylonians that had, as its first goal, as its first aim, putting an end to the Assyrian menace. In a certain sense here, this was probably, from the standpoint of the Medes and the Persians, a preemptive strike. The Assyrians had not conquered Persia, but there was always the great fear that they might do so. So, in a sense, the Medes and the Persians finally say it's in our interest to get rid of these guys. And that's basically what happened then to the Assyrians.

Very quickly, the Persians, who were at a much higher level culturally, who were at a much higher level economically, who had much more sophisticated political organization, became the dominant partner in the Mede-Persian fusion. The Medes and Persians, or as we'll call them from now on, the Persians, then began themselves a series of lightning military campaigns. These campaigns went east, virtually to the frontiers of China. These campaigns went southeast, virtually to the frontiers of India. And these campaigns went west; they went to the Mediterranean Sea, overrunning the eastern shore of the Mediterranean. They went to the west into Egypt, and overran Egypt and small portions of the coast of North Africa, even to the west of Egypt.

They conquered virtually all of Anatolia, all of what we would think of as Turkey, including its Mediterranean coastland where large numbers of Greeks lived. In a later lecture, we're going to bump into these Persians as the Persians and the Greeks were bumping into each other. But the point, for now, is simply to say that the Persians built, in a series of remarkably fast campaigns, the biggest empire that had ever been built anywhere up until that time, and indeed one of the largest that has ever been built.

How did they do it? There's a number of reasons for the Persians' success. Again, like the Assyrians, they had a very large army. The Persian army, we think from later reports, may have numbered on a regular basis as many as 300,000 men. The Greek historian Herodotus tells us when the Persians invaded Greece, they had an army of a million men. First of all, that number is suspiciously round. I mean, it might have been 997,326. But probably the number is way too big.

But even an army of 300,000 men—stop and think now, in a modern society, of the cost and all of the administrative problems that would be associated with maintaining 300,000 men. War may strike us as something unpleasant, as something unthinkable even. But war is one of the most sophisticated things any society can do, and maintaining a military establishment is one of the most complicated things that any society can do. In some very real ways, to peer into a society and figure out how it works, ask questions about its military establishment, and you'll learn a very great deal about that society.

So, the Persians had a very large army, which, at least in antiquity, was imagined to be as large as 300,000 men. There was also, inside that army, a quite interesting group, the 10,000 "Immortals." They weren't immortal in the sense that they didn't die. They were immortal in the sense that if one of them fell in battle, another immediately came up to take his place, so that central core of the army always stayed at, in tradition, 10,000 men. They also had the responsibility of guarding the shah, guarding the emperor, guarding the king—of protecting him. And indeed, Persian rulers did not fall on the battlefield, but they did appear on the battlefield. They didn't sort of sit way far away and watch what was going on. So a very large army, one thing.

The second place, brilliant cavalry tactics. The Persians—as I mentioned a moment ago in connection with the Assyrians, who understood how to use cavalry to get someplace fast—it was the Persians who figured out what to do with men on horses once you got there. On any given battlefield, the challenge for those fighting is either to outflank the enemy or to avoid being outflanked by the enemy. Two long, relatively stable lines slugging it out with each other will create a lot of mayhem and destruction, and at the end of the day— think of the trench warfare in World War I: you may have moved forward a few yards or fallen back a few yards, but not much will have changed.

What the Persians discovered is that once the main bodies of infantry had engaged, if you used cavalry at just the right moment in just the right numbers, you could turn your enemy's flank. This, then, would produce the rout. This, then, produces an enemy that is not surrounded but who's being attacked on two sides simultaneously. So, in that sense, some aspects of military strategy from antiquity persist right down to modern times.

There were other reasons for Persian success, too. I don't want to put all of the stress on the Persian military establishment. The Persians were very tolerant of the customs of local peoples. They often left local people in charge. The basic local officer of the Persian administration was called a "satrap." The Persians built a very sophisticated and complicated administrative structure. It all culminated in the shah, it culminated in the emperor. And then there were these officials at the local level, called "satraps."

Under the satraps, there were various minor, and subordinate officials; then, interestingly enough, above the satraps, there were officials called "the eyes and ears of the king." They were, in effect, state spies. And they were sent out to observe, but you didn't know who they were, you didn't know when they were coming, you didn't know when they would leave, you didn't even know quite what message they'd been given, what they were supposed to go discover about the peoples on whom they were spying. But, in any case, this was a very effective way of making sure that people at the local level were behaving themselves.

Mentioning these satraps and mentioning the fact that the Persians sometimes, not always, but sometimes, left local people in charge raises another interesting point, something that will recur again and again and again in future lectures, and it may be worth pausing just for a minute to put a little bit of focus on it right now. If you're going to create a large administrative structure, if you want to build an empire, if you want to build a kingdom, if you want to build a state, you're going to have to have help at the local level.

In building a state, and in securing help at the local level, you have basically two choices. You can use your own people and send them out. At this stage, they have no connection to the local societies where they're working, they're not married into those societies, they didn't grow up there, they don't own property there, they have no local loyalties, they have no local interests, they're not going to be sympathetic necessarily to the locals. They will be entirely loyal to the central administration, which has appointed them and sent them out. That's one theory. Generally speaking, it's reasonably effective, at least in some cases.

The other theory is that what it is best to do, what it is wisest to do, most prudent to do, is raise up prominent local people precisely because they're anchored in the local society. They are married in that society. They own property in that society. They know the customs of that society. They know everybody's secrets, they know what's going on, and all of that local knowledge can be turned to your benefit.

How? If you're very clever—and the Persians were very clever at this, and we'll see in later lectures that the Romans were absolute masters at this—if you pick out people of some local prominence, of some local authority, of some local respect, and you elevate them very far beyond what they could ever have hoped to achieve at the local level on their own, they don't now all of a sudden change their stripes. They're not any longer local people who know the local scene. But they're completely loyal to you because you can take away all that you gave them, and if you take away all that you gave them and reduce them to mere locals again after they've had power over the locals, things may not go so very well for them. So there is simultaneously a kind of loyalty at the local level and to the central level.

The Persians, clever folk that they were, used both of these systems. Later on, we'll see the Romans blending both of these systems. We'll see rulers in medieval Europe using both of these systems. But always these are the two basic choices: I send my guys out there, or I find and promote people who are already out there. The Persians didn't go one way or another; they blended the two systems.

Persian success is attributable also to a number of other important developments. For instance, they created a very common system of weights and measures throughout this enormous empire. Any of us who travel, we go off on holiday to Europe and all of a sudden everything's in kilos and things, and we go, "Oops, how much is that?" Now we have the new euro coinage in Europe so we don't have to try to figure out how many lire make a dollar and all of those wonderfully complicated things that we used to have to figure out.

But let's suppose, for example, that you were traveling around the United States, and one state used the system of ounces and pounds and another state used grams and kilograms. It would be rather confusing, wouldn't it? It would be hard to trade. How would you buy products? If your breakfast cereal was made in a factory someplace, do they have to make two different boxes, one in kilos and one in pounds?

The point is that the example is not absurd. It would be very complicated if, for example, we had different money in our 50 states. Every time you crossed the state line, you have to change your money and reorganize yourself, rethink how to do things at the local level. What the Persians did is create a not absolutely 100 percent unified, but a very substantially unified system of weights and measures throughout this vast empire, which facilitated trade in crucial ways.

They created a single coinage throughout this vast empire, which, again, facilitated trade, facilitated travel, facilitated the building and the maintaining of an effective state. They built roads. The great Royal Road ran from the Persian capital city of Persepolis right up to the Mediterranean coast of Anatolia, right up to where those Greeks lived, with whom the Persians got themselves mixed up, as we'll see in a later lecture. Building roads facilitated travel.

Now it's perfectly true that the Persians didn't build their roads because they were just benevolent and thought that this was a good idea. They built these great roads because you could move armies long distances fast, precisely why the Romans built their great road system. The Romans didn't build those roads so that later on people would admire them. They built those roads in order to move troops in a big hurry. But in any case, other benefits flowed from the creation of the Persian road system. There's no question about that.

The Persians undertook some other, smaller gestures, but nevertheless important ones. The language of administration throughout the Persian Empire was Aramaic, not Persian. Aramaic is another Semitic language; Persian is not. Aramaic is another Semitic language, and it had become, over a very wide area of the Near East, over a long period of time, a kind of *lingua franca*, a language that many people spoke. There's an interesting point hiding there. One of the things that we would have to encounter in all of these imperial states we've been talking about, in these successions of empire after empire, how is communication to be affected? What language is everybody going to speak?

Communications will have been, over long periods of time, a very complicated matter indeed. The Persians took the step of adopting Aramaic, which was a language that large numbers of people would have known at least a little bit. Therefore, communication would have been possible, just as, later on, Greek, *koine* Greek—the common Greek, not the highfaluting Greek of the Attic orators and of Plato and Aristotle, but a common Greek—became the language widely used in the Mediterranean world, more widely, actually, than Latin ever was. In the 18th century, French became the language of international communication. Today, obviously, English has become the language of international communication. But in a very real way, and a very long time ago, the Persians had an insight into that process, and so they used the Aramaic language.

The Persians built a number of beautiful buildings at their capital at Persepolis, for example. But we think of the Persians particularly when we think of their culture in connection with their religious ideas. The chief manifestation of Persian culture, of Persian religion, was what we call "Zoroastrianism." This is a rather complicated matter. Once again, as with Abraham, as with some of the other religious figures that we'll talk about this term, scholars dispute the date for Zarathustra, the great teacher of what we call Zoroastrianism. Sometimes you'll hear him referred to as Zoroaster, sometimes Zarathustra— same person. Some would say he goes back, perhaps, as far as 1000 B.C. Others would say more like 750 B.C. Others would say it's closer to the time of the King Cyrus and the spread of the Persian empire.

In my own view, we probably have something which is actually very old at its origins, and then grew and developed and took on new shapes at slightly different points in time. And as new manifestations of Zoroastrianism appeared, people would tend to attach novelty to them, would attempt to say this is where the origins are, this is where it all began. And as a result, we get this confused tradition of multiple dates of origin. What we have, as is often the case, is something that is evolving for a long period of time. It's developing over a long period of time. It's really a fool's errand to go and say that is the moment when it all got started.

Zarathustra's teachings are revealed to us in a collection of songs called *gathas*. Now the *gathas* are poems, basically, but the word apparently does mean song more than poem, so it may very well be the case that they were meant to be sung or perhaps intoned or chanted in some way. The *gathas* are preserved in a larger work called the Avesta. These are, in a way, the spiritual scriptures of the Zoroastrians and therefore of the Persian peoples. If we think about this body of materials as a whole, the *gathas* are a part of the Avesta. The *gathas*, most scholars think, is the section of the Avesta that is particularly to be attributed to Zarathustra himself, and the other parts here are parts of the tradition that have emerged over a longer period of time.

What did Zarathustra teach? He taught the idea of a single benevolent god, called Ahura Mazda. Zarathustra imagined Ahura Mazda to be the single creator of all. In this, of course, Zarathustra is not wholly unlike the Hebrews. But he is most certainly a henotheist or a monolatrist, more than a monotheist. So there is increasingly the idea of focusing on a single deity.

Zarathustra was also much intrigued by the problem of evil. How many people, over long periods of time, have been intrigued by the problem of evil? If there was a single god who has made all things, and who is somehow benevolent, why is there evil in the world? Why do bad things happen? Can one Supreme Being at once have created all that is good and all that opposes it?

Zarathustra's answer to this question is a rather interesting one. Zarathustra taught that Ahura Mazda had twin children; and after Ahura Mazda's own time, these two children struggled with one another, and that world history, in a certain sense, is a playing out of this struggle. The one child is wholly benevolent; the other child is wholly evil. If this begins to sound a little like, for example, the tradition of Satan as a figure who is wholly evil and opposed to another figure, God, who is wholly good, there are certain similarities. I think it would be an exaggeration to say borrowings. I think what we see here are people reflecting in comparable ways to similar phenomena. We have a very interesting problem of imagining a benevolent god and then looking at the world around us.

This perpetual struggle between the forces of good and the forces of evil produces a rather interesting way of thinking about the world. We call this "dualism." We meet this dualism, for the first time, here with the Zoroastrians. We'll meet it later again and again and again. It basically involves us in a series of polarities—good and evil. Sometimes it puts us in a realm of poetic images, light and dark. Sometimes it puts us in a series of emotional images, hope and fear. Sometimes it puts us into a series of spiritual and psychological images, flesh and spirit.

St. Paul says the spirit is willing but the flesh is weak. St. Paul was not a Zoroastrian, but there were certain common ways of talking, certain common ways of thinking, imagining these polarities as a way that each of us lives our lives, as we face the struggles that we go through, imagining the processes that we see around us all the time—this sense of duality.

It may be worth pointing out that if we reflect back to what I was saying in the previous lecture on the emergence of exclusive monotheism among the Hebrews, and the fact that this produces, for Western civilization, one powerful but challenging tradition, the notion of thinking in ones, in monads. It's very hard to think in ones. It's much easier to think in twos, perhaps easier, still, to think in "manys," polys, polytheists, many gods. But at the very least, two seems a superior way of imagining the world, at least for some, than to think in terms of strict unities.

Zarathustra was very much more interested in the spiritual realm than in the earthly, in the temporal, in what we see around us. This, again, will be a very powerful part of later philosophical and religious traditions. We'll see this, for example, particularly in connection with Plato. But there is this insight, and we find it in Zarathustra—and I don't want to suggest later that Plato was somehow a closet Zoroastrian, that's not the point—but people are arriving at fairly common understandings of problems. The world as I see it, as I look out at it, is messy and confusing and troubling and complicated. Surely there is a world beyond this one that is better, that is clearer, that is more easy to understand. And perhaps this world is somehow but a false impression of that other realm. You see? Very interesting to think about the superiority of the spiritual realm to the temporal realm in which we live.

But these dualisms, I must emphasize once more, are going to come back again and again. We're going to meet them with people called "Manicheans," at the time of the Roman Empire. We're going to meet them as people called "Bogomils," 20 or so lectures on. We're going to meet them as "Cathars." We're going to meet them in people in the south of France called "Albigensians." So, these dualists who trace a direct legacy to Zoroaster are an impressive and important part of the Western tradition.

What's the legacy of this imperial age? The Assyrians and the Babylonians built some impressive buildings, but didn't otherwise leave much else behind. They were not the kind of people to leave much behind. As I said before, these were bad guys. The Persians, on the other hand, left a legacy of civilized rule. They left a particular way of thinking about government and about kingship. And they left a profound religious heritage that interacted reciprocally and fruitfully with Judaism, with Christianity, and later with Islam.

I mentioned several times that the Persians bumped into the Greeks. In our very next lecture, we, ourselves, will bump into the Greeks.

Wide-Ruling Agamemnon
Lecture 6

What we do know comes overwhelmingly from archaeology. These Minoans left us some pretty impressive hints about themselves, about what they were like.

C ivilization in the Greek world began on the Mediterranean island of Crete about 2000 B.C. The civilization there has been long called the Minoan, from the mythical King Minos. We do not yet know exactly who these people were. Examples of their writing have been discovered, but the language is unknown. It is not Greek.

The massive palace complex at Knossos, which covers 5 acres and has a central courtyard that is 55 meters by 25 meters, provides clues about the Minoans. The size, beauty, and decorations of the complex suggest wealth, leisure, and a developed aesthetic sense. Storehouses and Linear A documents suggest bureaucracy. Artistic motifs and, perhaps, architectural forms suggest contacts with the Near East and Egypt. The complete lack of fortifications suggests that the people were peaceful and nonaggressive.

This is the period of the great cities of Mycenae and Corinth and Pylos, the very cities that are mentioned in Homer's *Iliad*.

Minoan civilization flourished from 1800 to 1550 B.C. In 1626 B.C., a volcanic eruption on Thera, 70 miles away, caused heavy damage and may have initiated the decline of the Minoans. Much of the island was devastated by conquest circa 1550 B.C. The conquerors almost certainly came from mainland Greece. Civilization took hold slowly in Greece. The land is rocky; the soil, poor; and the climate, especially in the north, harsh. By 6500 B.C., villages showed signs of the Neolithic Revolution. Around 3000 and again around 2300 (or, to some, c. 1700), the Balkans saw impressive migrations. By 2600–2200, we see the first signs of urban development and the "Mediterranean triad" of crops: cereal grains, grapes, and olives. From about 2000 B.C., we can discern

The Temple of Apollo, at Delphi, Greece.

Mycenean civilization—named for the great citadel at Mycenae. Almost certainly, the Myceneans conquered the Minoans. Apparently, they had been learning from, and grew jealous of, the Minoans. The highpoint of Mycenean civilization was from 1400 to 1200 B.C.

The sources of our knowledge of the Myceneans are three.

> Linear B documents: Linear B documents were found in profusion. These were deciphered by Michael Ventris and others in the early 1950s. They revealed a world of bureaucratic regulation.

> Archaeology: Impressive remains have been found at several major sites, such as Mycenae, Sparta, Pylos, Corinth, and so on. Large fortified sites with strong defensive works and imposing royal residences suggest strong kingship and military rule. Tomb complexes suggest historical memory and dynastic continuity.

Homeric poems: Homeric poems, especially the *Iliad*, are the most important sources, but also difficult and controversial. The Homeric poems were put into something like their current shape after 800 and probably around 725 B.C., then written down about 550. How can they tell us much about the period from 1400 to 1200 B.C.?

After World War II, Milman Parry and Albert Lord studied poetic bards in Yugoslavia and discovered that they could recite up to 500,000 lines of material. Think of Alex Haley and *Roots*. Or of performers today with scripts and lyrics! Therefore, it is legitimate to think that much authentic material was transmitted over a long time to "Homer."

The Mycenean elements in the story are the basic and concrete details: names of key places and, perhaps, people; some aspects of warfare in the "old" days; a vague sense of the diplomatic structure of the time. The Trojan War (traditional date 1194 B.C.) was probably a trade dispute and may have been a Mycenean inheritance from the Minoans. The ethical teachings of the *Iliad* relate more precisely to the period when the poems were put into coherent form, our next subject. ∎

Suggested Reading

Allen, *Finding the Walls of Troy*.

Dickinson, *The Aegean Bronze Age*.

Edwards, *Homer*.

Finley, *The World of Odysseus*.

Homer, *The Iliad* and *The Odyssey*.

1. Assess the impact of geography on the historical development of the Minoans and Myceneans.

2. What similarities do you detect between the Myceaneans and the peoples of the Near East whom we have encountered?

Wide-Ruling Agamemnon
Lecture 6—Transcript

Hello again, and welcome to the sixth lecture in our series on *The Foundations of Western Civilization*. You may recall, at the end of the last lecture, I said we're now going to bump into the Greeks.

If I said, "You were born in Greece," you'd probably say, "No, I wasn't; I was born in Punxsutawney," or someplace. But for a very long time, intellectuals were in the habit of saying, "You were born in Greece," the fundamental notion being that, somehow, the Western tradition was born there, and that there's a straight line from then until now.

We have spent some time looking at people who lived before the Greeks, or as we'll see in this lecture, contemporaneously with the Greeks, because the Greeks learned things from these people. That's one reason to study them. And because some of them made, as for example with Zoroastrianism, as for example with Venetian commerce and colonies, as for example with Hebrew religions ideas, some of these people made durable contributions of their own. But now we come to the Greeks, and we'll occupy ourselves with the Greeks over the next several lectures, from a number of different points of view.

But to get the story started, we must say that civilization in the Greek world began on the Mediterranean island of Crete, lying off of the Greek mainland, about 2000 B.C. Again, nothing terribly sacred about that date, but that's approximately when we really see civilization taking its rise there. So a bit later than, for example, in the Near East.

This civilization that arose on the island of Crete, we've always called—not always but for the last couple of centuries—Minoan, from the legendary King Minos, whose palace—it may or may not have been his palace, actually—but whose great palace was found on the island of Crete. So Minoan civilization attaches to the name of Minos, the legendary king. Legend not only attaches just to Minos, and mystery, it attaches to much else about Minoan civilization. For example, we don't know exactly who these people were. They wrote, they wrote a great deal, they wrote what we call Linear A documents. We don't know the language. It's not Greek, we know that, but it isn't any other known language.

I mentioned in the last lecture, you may recall, that today's scholars tend to classify people, to organize people, by language groupings. So we've got a real problem with the Minoans. We don't know what group to put them in, so we can't give them a history. We can't even give them much of a past. We just don't know a lot about them.

What we do know comes overwhelmingly from archaeology. These Minoans left us some pretty impressive hints about themselves, about what they were like. For example, in the enormous palace complex, this legendary palace of Minos at Knossos—this is an enormous complex. The building itself, the complex of buildings, occupies some five acres. It has, in its center, a great central courtyard, a ceremonial space. It was about 55 meters by 25 meters. That's a very large interior space inside a house, though, of course, this is a royal house, so it's very big. The size, the beauty, the decorations of this palace suggest wealth, suggest leisure, suggest a rather comfortable life, suggest very elaborate aesthetic standards. I'll come back to a couple of issues in just a moment. But the point is that this palace permits us to make certain inferences, but we don't have the kind of written documentation or later tradition that permits us to confirm our inferences.

One of the things that is true about this palace is that all the way along its exterior flanks are great storehouses, so obviously the kings who lived there stored up various products: cereal, grains, and olive oil, what have you. And we think that these Linear A documents, much like, for example, the cuneiform documents that we find from Sumer, are bureaucratic records. They're probably attached to the administration of the palace, to the administration of the island of Crete, and perhaps, indeed, also to the administration of the Minoans' fairly far-flung commercial ventures. So we have a sense of bureaucratic rule; we can infer certain things about a fairly sophisticated administration, even though we cannot strictly speaking write its history.

The architectural forms in the palace, and some of the artistic forms in the frescoes, the wall paintings inside of the palace. "Fresco" is painting on wet plaster; it is not painting on a dry plaster wall, but it is putting paint actually into the wet plaster so that, as the plaster dries, the painted surface, in effect, becomes part of the surface of the wall. Alas, if the wall falls down, you lose everything, but the point is that a fresco is a fairly durable art form, and fragments of many frescoes have been found from the palace of Minos at Knossos.

The artistic motifs that we see, and architectural motifs that we see, suggest contacts with the Near East and with Egypt. We know the Minoans were great trading people, we know they were substantial seafarers, so that's not surprising. And here we can see the transfer of ideas, a point that I've raised several times in earlier lectures. But, again, we work at the level of inference. We can't work at the level of confirmation.

There are some other interesting things about Minoan Crete that permit us inferences: an utter lack of fortifications. None. Not a few, none. These people apparently had no fear of being attacked by anybody. This suggests that they were, themselves, not aggressive, that they weren't interested in attacking anyone; no fortified harbor complexes, even though they were great traders; no fortified palace complexes, even though they were wealthy and powerful.

Inside these palaces, we find evidence of a very elegant life—for example, depictions of women wearing cosmetics with beautiful hairdos, with beautiful jewelry and beautiful clothing. No one would paint so lovingly and so accurately, and in such great detail, were these things not appreciated. And it's probably fair to say that, at least for queens, for princesses, for important women of the court, that these depictions may come close to reality. I don't want to suggest that they're something like photographs; they may come very close to reality, so it may provide us an insight into what gave these people pleasure, what they liked to look at, what seemed pleasing to them. But again, that's an inference.

We might say, for example, we have some very interesting depictions of bull leaping. This appears to have been their favorite sport. Perhaps you've watched the vault in the Olympics, where an athlete runs down a long runway, leaps into the air, turns over in the air, touches hands on a vault, and springs over the other side of it, perhaps sometimes doing various somersaults and spins and flips in the air. Well, the Minoans did that, except, instead of a stationary vault, they went at a running bull. One suggests that the penalty for slipping up was more than getting the judges to give you a bad score. But in any case, it suggests peaceful sporting activities. Unlike other arts that we see, where military affairs and military men and weapons may be featured, I mention the Assyrians in this connection in the last lecture, we don't see that sort of thing. We see peaceful sporting activities. That is what the Minoans presented us.

Minoan civilization flourished from about 1800-1550 B.C. This is really the high point of Minoan culture. In 1626 B.C., there was a volcanic eruption on the island of Thera, about 70 miles away. This caused, apparently, a massive tidal wave, which itself produced heavy damage and may very well have begun, have initiated, a process of decline on Minoan Crete. Coincidentally, this eruption of this volcano on the island of Thera and the disappearance of about half that island into the Mediterranean may be what lies behind the story of the lost city of Atlantis. But we can't actually confirm that, and once again that's an inference; there's no concrete history there.

Seventy-five years, or thereabout, after the eruption of the volcano on Thera and the destruction of much of Crete by a tidal wave, Crete was conquered. It was conquered from the outside by persons who certainly came from the Greek mainland. It was conquered by people whose early arts and crafts again suggest long contact with the Minoans. These people who conquered the Minoans we call the Myceneans. We'll turn to them in just a moment, but we have now moved to the mainland of Greece.

Let's pause for just a second and take mental stock of the land of Greece. We may think of the Greeks for their stunning cultural achievements. But the land of Greece is hard and tough and rocky and craggy. The further north you go, the worse the weather is. The further south you go, the hotter the weather is. This is not an easy land; its soil is not good. This has never been an easy place to eke out a living. We have to remember, then, that the life of the Greeks is not played out against a wonderful, charming, pleasant geographical background. It's played out in a very tough spot.

The earliest hints that we have of the emergence of settled life in Greece go back to perhaps 6500 B.C. or thereabouts. So, 8500 years ago, we begin to see signs of the Neolithic Revolution in Greece. So we can say that the Neolithic Revolution comes to Europe, comes to the Greek mainland, a little after we see signs of the Neolithic in Mesopotamia or in Egypt. Now, this is neither here nor there; it doesn't suggest that priority is somehow precedence. But we do see that the Greek world is, perhaps, a little bit behind.

In about 3000 B.C., according to some scholars perhaps around 2300 B.C., according to other scholars perhaps around 1700 B.C., the Balkan Peninsula was subjected to invasions, or perhaps migrations from the north—two fairly substantial movements of people toward the south. They appear to have come from Central Europe, and some may even have come over from Anatolia; they may have come round the Black Sea region and down into the Balkans. These people are the historic ancestors of the Greeks. These people really bring the Greeks into the Balkan Peninsula.

From as early as 2600-2200 B.C., we see the first signs of urban development in the Greek world, and we also find clear evidence of the growth of the Mediterranean triad of crops. This triad of crops, cereal grains, olives, and grapes, has sustained life in the Mediterranean for 10,000 years. If you travel in the Mediterranean world today, you're in an oil culture, not a butter culture. If you travel in the Mediterranean world today, you're much more likely to drink wine than to drink beer. And you will find all of those wonderful products made, in one way or another, with cereal grains. This has been true for a very, very long time.

From about 2000 B.C., we can begin to discern a civilization which we give the name "Mycenean." Mycenean is not a made up name; Mycenae is the greatest of the Mycenean sites. The great citadel at Mycenae, this was the city of Agamemnon, the great hero, the great leader of the Greeks in the Trojan War. We'll come back to Agamemnon and his folk in just a few minutes. Mycenae, then, gives its name to a period in early Greek history. It is almost certainly these Myceneans who conquered Minoan Crete, to be sure conquered Minoan Crete at a very late stage in its development. They'd probably been learning from them for a long time. They probably grew jealous of them, and saw that they were ripe for the plucking, and they plucked them.

The high point of Mycenean civilization falls between about 1400-1200 B.C. —in other words, the couple of centuries following the conquest of Minoan Crete. This is the period of the great cities of Mycenae and Corinth and Pylos, the very cities that are mentioned in Homer's *Iliad*. We're going to talk about the *Iliad* more in a few minutes, but this is basically the world that Homer begins to bring into focus for us. This is a period of massive building projects. For example, at sites like Mycenae: a huge citadel built on the top of the hill, a massive road flanked on each side with stone walls leading up to that great citadel at Mycenae.

So these were people who could build quite impressive structures, who could build quite impressive buildings. It was a time, we think, of very considerable wealth. The Myceneans seem to have sustained themselves mainly by agricultural pursuits in the Greek mainland, but also by engaging in overseas trade and overseas contacts and overseas commerce, and in having contacts with people overseas as well.

We know about the Myceneans from three different kinds of evidence. In the first place, we have a great collection of what are called Linear B documents. There are thousands of these. Again, it turns out these are overwhelmingly bureaucratic records; we didn't find the first edition of the *Iliad*, or something like that, in these documents. It would have been lovely to have done so, but we didn't.

The Linear B documents differ from the Linear A documents in a couple of very important respects. The first and fundamental one is we can read them. We can read these documents. For a very long time, nobody could read them. We still can't read the Linear A documents; we don't know what the language is. For a long time, prevailing archaeological theory held that the Greeks came into Greece after about 1200 B.C., and therefore, theory held, those people before 1200, whatever they might have been, weren't Greek. So people went and looked in one place after another for the language in these Linear B documents.

Right after World War II, a group of individuals led by an Oxford classicist by the name of Michael Ventris, they had all worked at Bletchley during World War II, these were the Enigma code breakers. Very interesting people to put to work on the task of puzzling out a language. So they assembled all this brain power, and they were going to crack this code. Ventris gets the bright idea that maybe it's Greek, but written in a different script. Hello, it's Greek. So actually, they didn't need all that brain power in the long run. It took one simple flash of brilliant insight. And now it was possible to read these documents, and to adjust earlier archaeological theory. These people were speaking Greek, writing Greek; they're probably Greek in some way or another.

One other interesting thing to say about the Linear B documents, before we leave them, is you may be puzzled by what does this "Linear" mean. It means, simply, writing that is arrayed in lines. That doesn't sound terribly interesting. Cuneiform can be arrayed in lines; hieroglyphics would be arrayed in lines. It is writing that is arrayed in lines, running from left to right across the page, but it is a particular kind of writing. That's the point that I want to put a little bit of emphasis on at the moment. It is syllabic writing.

We can have, basically, three kinds of writing. We have talked already about pictographs—hieroglyphics, for example. Picture writing, where pictures stand for nouns and verbs, and then colored in certain ways can give us the other array of words, adjectives, adverbs, that modify things, and various connective words. Picture writing, as we saw, not terribly efficient. Syllabic writing is more efficient. The demotic, for example, that began to be used on papyrus in Egypt is syllabic. Cuneiform is syllabic writing; the languages which the cuneiform symbols represent are laid out syllabically. So in all certainty, the Linear A documents are like that, too, we just don't know what the language is. And the Linear B documents are laid out this way, as well.

Now, what on earth does this mean, syllabic writing? It's vastly more efficient than pictographs, but a lot less efficient than alphabetic writing, to which I'll come in just a second. Syllabic writing, let's suppose we're going to make up a "syllabary" for English. We would have to have a symbol for every possible sound combination. So I would have to have one for ba, ca, da, fa, ga, then I'd have to have one for bo, co, do, fo, go, and so on. But I'd have one symbol for each of those sound possibilities, and I could array them, and that's not so bad. But it makes a lot of symbols.

What I can do beyond that is alphabetic writing. I can have a certain number of letters—from *aleph* and *beth* in Hebrew, *alpha beta* in Greek—I can have a certain number of letters, and I can assign each one of them a sound value. And then, of course, what I can do is create all sorts of irregularities to terrorize schoolchildren down through the centuries, but that's another story entirely. I can assign sound values to letters, so that each letter holds a place of its own, and makes its own sound and forms new sound in combination with other letters.

The Greeks are going to learn an alphabet in our next lecture. They're actually going to borrow an alphabet from the Phoenicians. But at the moment they're writing in linear, syllabic writing. So, three kinds of writing: pictographs, syllabic writing, alphabetic writing. We've had two; we'll get the alphabetic in our next lecture.

What do the Linear B documents tell us? As I said a moment ago, a world of bureaucracy. I'm going to come back to that point in a little bit in connection with Homer in a minute, because if you've ever read the *Iliad*, there's not a lot of bureaucracy in the *Iliad*. So, are things slightly out of step? We'll come back to that.

In the second place, archaeology. The second way we know about the Myceneans is archaeology. Massive and impressive remains found at the sites of these great cities, found at Mycenae, found at Pylos, found at Tiryns, at Corinth, and so on. These people built big palaces. Not big temples, big palaces. Remember when we talked about Mesopotamia, we saw that temples might need the predominance of temple priesthoods, palaces might need the predominance of kings. Walls and palaces might mean kings and warrior aristocracies. Now, if you've read the *Iliad*, you have certainly met powerful warrior kings and powerful warrior aristocracies. That begins to sound a little bit more like—that is to say the archaeology begins to sound a little bit more like the world that we actually encounter in Homer's *Iliad*. We have a sense, then, of powerful rule, of local strongmen, of strongly exercised leadership.

The next type of source, the next thing that permits us to draw inferences about this Mycenean world, are the Homeric poems: the *Iliad* and the *Odyssey*. As you probably know, there are all sorts of theories about the *Iliad* and the *Odyssey*: that they weren't written by Homer, they were written by another guy whose name was Homer; that they were written by two different guys; and they have been confidently dated to a lot of different moments and a lot of different places; and so on. We don't have time here to pursue all of these issues. We'll skate through them rather safely, I think.

The Homeric poems, but particularly the *Iliad*, the poem about Ilion, Ilion is Troy. The *Iliad* is the great poem about the Trojan War. It's the Mycenean heroes, Agamemnon and company, going over to fight on the coast of Anatolia, to fight at Ilion, or what we call Troy. They're very controversial poems; they're very controversial sources. Why?

First of all, it is clearly a large body of all the material that is circulating in all sorts of different forms over a long period of time. Let me give you one example of this. If you've ever read the *Iliad*, for example, and you kind of remember the various gods and goddesses and the jobs they have, then you might have read one or another of the Greek plays. And you've encountered those very same gods and goddesses, and they've got different jobs. Obviously, the stories of the old days were remembered differently in different places.

Around 800 B.C., it appears that the Homeric *Iliad*, and perhaps the *Odyssey* as well, began to be put into something like the shape in which we now have them. They began to be assembled as a corpus of material. Probably by around 725 B.C., they had begun to achieve almost a canonical status in the growing Greek cities. There was no other way that you had to tell this story; people had certain expectations about how the story would be told.

By about 550 B.C., the poems were written down for the first time. That's a good thing and a bad thing. It's a good thing because they stabilized; it's a bad thing because it killed the living tradition, froze it, never to grow anymore. But our problem as historians is to say, "How on earth do we use a poetic corpus, built, as it were, between 800-ish and 500-ish B.C., to tell us about a world that played itself out between 1400 and 1200 B.C.?" That's the puzzle;

how do we use the Homeric poems? Now, the poems purport to tell us about the old days, to tell us about those people. So the problem is, what do they tell us, what can they tell us? For a long time, there was a great deal of skepticism on these subjects, and there was a battle that went back and forth in the scholarly world. To put this battle in its very simplest terms, there are some who said the Homeric poems are works of art. They spring, full-blown, from the mind of a great bard, a great teller of tales, Homer, whoever he was. And what we have is his artistic vision.

Others said, "No, that's not how we should understand the making of the *Iliad* and the *Odyssey*; we should understand them as all formulaic poetry." All formulaic poetry—again if you read the *Iliad* and you know about rosy-fingered dawn and the wine-dark sea and wide-ruling Agamemnon and Diomedes, of the loud war cry—all of these formulas that recur again and again and again because they fit a certain metrical pattern. It's not unlike sitting around of an evening with a great group of friends, and you're making up verses to a song as you go along. You have to stick with the theme of the song, and you have to stay with the beat of the music. So people can build poems that way.

If that's the case, then is this thing simply a free for all? In other words, if it's a composed epic by Homer, whoever Homer was, then we really aren't authorized to say that this Homer guy knew very much about Mycenae. And therefore we can't really read the poem for that, though we can appreciate it as great poetry. But if it's oral formulaic poetry, we say there's no rules here. People are kind of making it up as they go along. After World War II, two Harvard scholars, Milman Parry and Albert Lord, who had worked in Yugoslavia during World War II with the Office of Strategic Services, the predecessor of the CIA, working with various groups in the Balkans, attempting to hold that territory against Nazis in the first place, against possible Soviet incursion in the second place. One of the things they discovered up there was a local bardic tradition.

There were singers of songs, tellers of tales up there, and they discovered some of these guys who could keep in mind up to half a million lines of material. We've encountered this most recently in something like Alex Haley's famous book, *Roots*, and the television series *Roots*, where Haley went back to the Gambia and found the storytellers and had them start reciting the tale until he began to hear things that resonated. And then he tried to start stitching this tale together. We might think also, for instance, of performers today. Think of a really good popular singer. How many lyrics must that person know? It's an enormous number of things. Think of a great actor, Lawrence Olivier. How many scripts must he have had in mind? He did every Shakespearean play in his life. I don't suppose, necessarily, at every minute, he could remember every line from all of them, but he must have had an awful lot of it in mind. We don't exercise our memories today the way we did in earlier times, the way people did generally in earlier times. So the capacity to remember large amounts of things, and to hand it on quite faithfully, makes it legitimate to think that this all-formulaic poetry was not playing in a game with no rules, and, did in fact, transmit down over the centuries a great deal of quite substantial and accurate and authentic information.

Having said that, and probably at that stage today almost no one would disagree, we get to the hard part. How much of it is authentic? What of this material is really accurate? The Mycenean elements in the story are likely to be among the most basic and concrete. Names of characters, there's no reason for those to change. Names of places, there's no reason for those to change. There are certainly hints of warfare in the old days; there are some problems with that. Iron weapons crop up a couple of times in the *Iliad*, while there were no iron weapons at Mycenae. That was still the Bronze Age. There are some references, for example, to military armaments, to armor that didn't really appear at the time of Mycenae and almost certainly did appear later on.

So, there's a certain amount of basic information in the *Iliad* that is almost certainly authentic and that has come down from earlier times. What kinds of things? Let's remind ourselves, it's a story about the Trojan War. The Greek tradition remembers the Trojan War took place 1194-1184 B.C. It took place for ten years; the *Iliad* shows us the battlefield in the very last stages of that war. Quite remarkably, scholars today actually peg the Trojan War at between 1225-1200 B.C. So there's one place the tradition is remarkably close, in remembering when this war took place. It almost certainly was a Mycenean war against the Trojans, against the people on the other side of the Aegean

Sea. Alas, it was not a war launched by the beauty of Helen, whose face could send all these men off to fight and to die. It was probably a grotty little trade war, fought in the Aegean Basin. Probably it came at the end of a long series of contentions in this part of the world, and later on was remembered in much grander, in much more heroic terms. All of this seems quite certain.

There's lots of basic nuts and bolts of information, nuggets of information if you will, hiding in the *Iliad* that are useful to us, along with the Linear B documents and the archaeology, in reconstructing the Mycenean world. But surely, people say, it's the ethical teachings of the *Iliad*, it's the wrath of Achilles that we really want to think about; it is all of those remarkable people and the things that they did and said, or failed to do. All of that is almost certainly from the world of Homer himself and not from the world of Mycenae. It's to that ethical world of Homer, of the Greek Dark Ages and the Greek Archaic period, it's to that that we'll turn in our next lecture.

Dark Age and Archaic Greece
Lecture 7

It's very important to say, in other words, that Greek glory did not rise in a straight line from the Myceneans to the world of Pericles and Plato. There were a few bumps in the road along the way.

Greek civilization did not grow to glory in a straight line from the Myceneans. Between 1200 and 1100 B.C., there is evidence for widespread destruction of the major Mycenean sites, some of which—not least Mycenae itself!—were never reinhabited. These invasions were traditionally associated with the Dorians, a people from northern Greece who pushed south and settled primarily in the Peloponnesus with Sparta as their key city. But the Dorians were not alone in disrupting Mycenean Greece; they were alone in being remembered.

Introducing the Dorians provides an opportunity to clarify some terms. We speak of Greeks, oddly, because the Romans called them Graeci. The "Greeks" called themselves Hellenes and their land, Hellas. There were four major groupings of Greeks with modest ethnic and linguistic differences: Attic, Ionic, Aeolic, and Doric. The Dorian invasions ushered in a period traditionally called the Dark Ages. This was a time of small, illiterate communities. The Greeks forgot how to write! This period also saw depopulation, de-urbanization, and scant construction.

Between 800 and 700 B.C., the Greek world began to show signs of life and energy. Historians speak of the transition to the Archaic period (c. 750–550). The great achievement of this period was the *polis*, the city-state that was the key Greek political institution. We will take a detailed look at Athens and Sparta in the next lectures. For now, we will look at origins. Dark Age Greece was relatively peaceful, and after about 900, the population began to grow. This gradually produced fierce competition for resources in a poor land.

Also around 900 or 800 B.C., the commercial exploits of the Phoenicians were a spur to at least some Greeks. Wealth generated by trade also upset the delicate balance in modest agricultural communities. Beginning in around 750 B.C., various Greek cities displayed one or more of three responses to the tensions of the age.

> Conquest: Sparta conquered and enslaved their neighbors to the west, the Messenians.

> Trade: Athens, but also Corinth and other cities, entered into widespread commercial ventures. The Athenians and others may have been emulating the Phoenician example.

> Colonization: Corinth above all, along with many other Greek cities, exported surplus population to colonies that maintained emotional, political, and economic relations with their "mother-cities" (literally, *metropoleis*).

Of these processes, the commercial and, especially, the colonial, were of immense historical significance. Greek cities, language, culture, art, architecture, literature, and political institutions were scattered all over the Mediterranean world. But the Greeks learned, too. For example, they got their alphabet from the Phoenicians.

The later Dark Ages and the Archaic period give evidence for the emergence of some of the most familiar aspects of Greek culture. Decorations on pottery are revealing. Geometric designs show rationalism but also a sense of order, balance, and harmony. Figured pottery shows a tendency to abstraction, an attempt to discern behind what is visible to what is really "more" true. Aesthetic tastes and technical virtuosity are also on display.

The *Calf Bearer* statue is typical of the Archaic period.

Sculpture shows a steady progression that may have owed much to Egyptian styles but that also advanced the Greek quest to explore the particularities of the human condition. A return to Homer's poems also opens up a vista on the values and ideologies of the age and hints at some of that age's changes.

So the Greek world, Homer's world, provides us a vista on Greek politics, on Greek religion.

Intense competition, both verbal and physical, is portrayed in the poems. Compare the athletic contests. The poems evidence reflections on brains (Nestor) versus brawn (Achilles). The poems address respective obligations of the individual and the community. They examine the nature of authority: kings and great advisers versus the ordinary man. We also see changes in warfare in Homer's poems, from the single combat of the heroes to the *hoplite phalanx* featuring the ordinary soldier. This formative period, then, brought into view, albeit in embryonic form, many of the features of Greece's "classical" period. ∎

Suggested Reading

Boardman, *The Greeks Overseas*.

Burkert, *Greek Religion*.

Desborough, *The Greek Dark Ages*.

Murray, *Early Greece*.

Questions to Consider

1. You have learned how the Greeks responded to population pressure and competition. Can you think of examples of how other peoples have handled these challenges?

2. Did anything surprise you in the list of Greek values that you encountered in this lecture? Does anything seem to be missing?

Dark Age and Archaic Greece
Lecture 7—Transcript

Welcome to the seventh of our lectures on *The Foundations of Western Civilization.* In the last lecture, we introduced the Greek world, particularly the earliest stages of the Greek world, the world of the Myceneans and before them, the world of the Minoans. In this lecture, we're going to turn to the period that followed the Myceneans. Roughly speaking, we'll be talking about the period from 1200 B.C. on down to something like 550 B.C.

We're going to go through two periods that scholars call the Greek Dark Ages and the Greek Archaic period. It's very important to say, in other words, that Greek glory did not rise in a straight line from the Myceneans to the world of Pericles and Plato. There were a few bumps in the road along the way. Today we're going to drive over, carefully, some of those bumps.

Between about 1200 and about 1100 B.C., there's considerable evidence in the Greek world for widespread destruction of a number of the major Mycenean sites. One of the things that happens, when buildings burn, even if later on they are rebuilt or even if earth covers them over, archaeologists can dig down and find burn levels in the stone. So this is one of the ways that we discover when there has been widespread destruction. We could, on occasion, get fooled by just a fire that was incidental or coincidental, but generally it shows us destruction. And we find a lot of evidence for this in the Greek world after about 1200 B.C.—in other words, after the Trojan War.

This implies something interesting, or permits us again an inference. We talked much about inferences in the last couple of lectures. It may very well be that whatever we think of the Trojan Wars as having been—remember I said it was kind of a grotty little trade war probably, but it may have come at the end of a long period of contention. And it may very well be that the Myceneans spent themselves in this long period of contention. So, a bit like, for example, the Egyptians and the Hittites simply wearing each other out over a period of time and then entering on a kind of a long decline, there may have been some decline in the Greek world, occasioned by these struggles that come to represent themselves for us so vividly in the *Iliad.*

We find, then, in any case, this period of considerable evidence of destruction in these major Mycenean sites. It's interesting, too, that a number of them were never again re-inhabited. That's not true for all of them; Corinth was, Pylos was. But Mycenae, the greatest of the Mycenean sites, was never again inhabited. You can go to it today. It rests in a kind of a sovereign repose. It's really haunting, in a certain way, to go to that place and to think of Agamemnon and the other Greeks.

Later, Greek memory and the archaeological record both suggest that we can make some sense of these invasions in connection with some people called the Dorians. The Greeks basically later remembered the Dorian invasions as if it were somehow one process, one great invasion, with one people primarily involved, primarily making all of the trouble. It's certainly true that the Dorians were one of the groups who pushed southward into the Balkans at about this time. Probably there were people who had trailed behind those much earlier migrations of people into the Balkans. They may very well have settled up in what we call Thessaly, for example, considerably further to the north, and now, after the Mycenean period, had begun moving yet further south and entering the Peloponnesus—that is to say, the southernmost portion of the Balkan Peninsula, the great peninsula on the bottom of the peninsula, if you like, the land on the other side of the Gulf of Corinth, if you have a picture of the Greek world in your mind. What is clear is that the Dorians were not alone in disrupting Greece, even if Greek tradition later remembered the story that way, and remembered the Dorians as the great invaders.

Introducing the Dorians provides us with an opportunity to clear up a couple of pieces of terminology. If the Dorians, themselves, are a puzzle, so, too, are one or two other things. For example, why do they call the Greeks "Greeks?" Why do we call their land Greece? We do that because the Romans did. The Romans called them *Graeci*; they called the land *Graecia*, and we basically borrowed our terminology from Latin, which isn't playing fair with the Greeks. They called themselves *Hellenes*, and they called their land *Hellas*. And the word that we have as Greek, they would have as Hellatic. But anyway, we're probably not going to get away from Greek and Greece, so we'll stick with that.

It's also true to say that there are several kinds of Greeks. There isn't just one kind of Greek; there are several. We talked, in the last lecture, briefly, about how difficult it is to characterize people ethnically, biologically, over long periods of time. It's probably fair to say that there were some modest differences among the various kinds of Greeks, but the fundamental differences among them were linguistic. They spoke Greek in slightly different ways.

The basic groups are the Dorians, about whom we have spoken just a moment ago, and then the Ionic Greeks. Those are the Greeks who lived over on the Aegean coast of Anatolia, what the Romans would later call Asia Minor, what we would think of as western Turkey. The Aeolic Greeks are the ones who live in the northernmost portion of the Greek world, north of the Gulf of Corinth, or northwest of Athens. And there are finally the Attic Greeks. Those are the Greeks of Athens.

How did these Greeks differ from one another, how would you recognize one? If you take a word like *demos*, the Greek word for people, in Doric Greek that same word is *damos*. So, instead of saying *demos*, you said *damos*. It's not so unlike, for example, the differences in the way a person from Boston and a person from Savannah might speak our American English. It's basically the same language, slightly different vocabulary, slightly different expressions, slightly different pronunciation. But that's the kind of differences, that's the scale of differences we're dealing with. And they aren't so great. We do have different peoples, then, around the Greek world in different places.

The Dorian invasions ushered in a period that we refer to as the "Greek Dark Ages." We don't call this the Dark Ages because we're trying to be insulting to it, because we're trying to say that it was an awful time. It is a time of small, illiterate communities. I'm sure you're thinking along with me, and you're thinking, "He explained all of that business about language and linear scripts, and syllabic scripts, and Linear B documents and they were actually written in Greek, and all that. What do you mean illiterate?" The Greeks forgot how to write. They're the only people we know of, historically, who achieved writing and lost it. Now, they're going to get it back pretty soon, but the point is they forgot how to write.

So now we have no Linear B documents; we have no documents at all. And the later tradition, actually, doesn't seem to have known very much about this period, which we can say runs from maybe 1100 down to 900 or 800 B.C., roughly. The Greek Dark Ages. So it's dark, fundamentally, because it's a period about which we know little. We can shed very little light on it. That's the sense in which it's dark. But it doesn't appear to have been an entirely felicitous time either. It was a time of depopulation, it was a time of de-urbanization, and it appears to have been a time of scant construction. We just don't see the kinds of grand structures that marked the Mycenean period.

This is a good opportunity to pause and say just a quick word about archaeology, and the elaboration of the discipline of archaeology. Archaeologists found, without trouble, those spectacular Mycenean sites, many of them are sort of poking through the ground today and are visible to the naked eye, although excavators have had to take them down a great deal to really get to the root of things, to get to the bottom of things.

When archaeology first arose a few centuries ago, in a clear way in the middle of the 19th century but in a certain sense it actually arose before that, archaeology was essentially the servant of museum science and then of art history. Archaeologists went out and looked for beautiful things, to put them on display. That's fundamentally what they did. One might sort of put tongue in cheek and say that the great goal of early archaeology was to find the Venus de Milo's arms; this would have made you famous. You found these wonderful things, put them in museums, and arrayed them room by room, and so on.

There's no archaeologist in the world today who wouldn't love to find a beautiful thing. But archaeology today is based on, and is dedicated to, something very different. Modern survey archaeology is designed, basically, to take large sites and, slowly but surely, to strip the soil away, layer by layer by layer, to uncover life as it was lived: to find humble things—ordinary dwellings, ordinary crockery, ordinary ceramics; to go digging through garbage pits to find what percentages of chicken bones, and what percentages of pig bones, and what percentages of beef bones you find in order to make guesses about diets, about what people ate, their protein intake, and this kind of thing. Today, archaeology is really much more interested in figuring out how people lived than in finding the beautiful things that they left lying about.

What that means is that, day by day by day, the Greek Dark Ages are actually less dark to us than they were once before, even though we don't have these great, spectacular palaces, and, as near as we can tell, beautiful things to find and to look at and to admire.

Between about 800 and 700 B.C., the Greek world began to show the first clear signs of life and energy. Kind of a revival begins to appear all over much of the Greek world. Historians refer to this as the "transitional period" between the Dark Ages—less dark all the time, as I've said—and the Archaic period. The great classical period, to which we'll turn in a series of lectures beginning with the next one, follows this Archaic period.

The great achievements of this transitional period of the early part of the Archaic period, the great achievements of this period, the fundamental achievement, is the creation of the *polis*, the Greek city-state, the fundamental Greek political institution. A political institution that gave vocabulary, that gave ideals to the Western world ever since. In our next couple of lectures, we're going to look in some detail at Athens and at Sparta, two of the greatest of the Greek *poleis*. For now, I just want to emphasize that we can begin to see the first faint stirrings, like a small sprout coming through the ground in early spring, of what will later be a full-flowered *polis*.

Dark Age Greece appears, on the whole, to have been a pretty peaceful place, a fairly easy place. I said earlier, in the last lecture, that Greece was never an easy land to eke an living out of, and that's certainly true. But it's also true that, in a world that was depopulated, in a world with much less contention than had marked the Mycenean period, people were able to live their lives largely undisturbed by external forces. As a result, the population began to grow.

One of the great problems in the Greek world is that the mountain crags, the mountain ridges, tend to work in such a way as to leave kind of a patchwork quilt of small areas of arable land. And as a result of this, the population can pretty easily and pretty quickly outstrip the capacity of that arable land to support it. Now you've got a problem. You've got more people than you can feed. What are you going to do? This began to generate a whole series of important and complex social tensions in the Greek world. And it's probably this gradual pressure of population on resources that leads to some of the steps that begin to generate the *polis*, as I suggested a few minutes ago.

By around 900 or 800 B.C., the commercial exploits of the Phoenicians may very well have been, in the first place, a spur to the Greeks. Wealth generated by trade might either supplement or upset the very delicate balance of life in essentially agricultural communities. The Greeks know that the Phoenicians were trading, there were some Greeks who were already beginning to engage in trade. There's no place in the Greek world that's more than about 150 miles from the sea. It's much easier to get to the sea and travel around by sea than it is to travel overland in Greece. If any of you have ever driven in Greece, if any of you have ever tried to take a train in Greece, you know this to be the case. It's not an easy land to move about in.

Around 750 B.C., or thereabouts, various Greek cities began to display one or another of three responses to these tensions generated in this period, occasioned by rising population and limited resources. The first response, particularly associated with Sparta, you conquer your neighbors. You don't have enough soil? You don't have enough land? You conquer your neighbors. The Spartans conquered the Messenians, the people who lived to the west of them in the Peloponnesus, and reduced them to slavery. Turned them into helots, state slaves. We'll talk more about them in the next lecture when we turn to Sparta.

Another way to do it is to Phoenicianize. Athens was the Greek city that decided that what they would do, essentially, is live by trade. Rather than making everything they needed, they would trade and generate the wealth to permit them to buy whatever they needed. So the Athenians turned, in particular, to commercial ventures. This made them, as I said, a bit like the Phoenicians, makes them a bit like the later Venetians and Dutch—a point that I've emphasized already in connection with the Phoenicians when we talked about them.

A third possibility—Corinth is, perhaps, the best example of this, but there were others in the Greek world—you colonize. You export your surplus population. You don't just sort of throw them out the door, that's not the point, because you do have pressures in the city. These are your fellow citizens; you want to maintain some connection with them. So you're sending these people to places where they will create cities of their own and maintain very close, very cordial, very effective relations with the mother city. Quite literally, that's what the Greek word *metropoleis* means, it means a mother-city. We, in English, tend to use the word metropolis for a big city. We think of New York as a metropolis. Actually, strictly speaking, it's a mother city. You have to have sent out colonies, and then it's a metropolis.

These colonies were planted all around the Black Sea region. They were planted along the North African coast, in the area that we would think of as Libya. They were planted in southern Italy, and in Sicily. Indeed, southern Italy and Sicily became so full of Greek colonies that the area came to be called *magna Graecia*, greater Greece. Did it ever strike you that the cities in Sicily bear Greek names? Syracuse, that's not a Latin name, that's a Greek name. And Naples—Napoli. What could be more Italian than Napoli? *Neapolis*, new city, a Corinthian colony. So the Corinthians planted colonies, but other Greek cities planted colonies as well.

This process of colonization is interesting and important to us because it reveals the inventiveness, the cleverness, the adaptability, the flexibility of the Greeks in responding to a problem. They all faced more or less the same problem, and they dealt with it in quite different ways. That's one important thing. Another important thing is to say that spreading these colonies all around the Mediterranean world was of enormous historical significance. If you've traveled in the Mediterranean world, you have seen beautiful Greek temples in Sicily, and you have seen beautiful Greek temples in southern Italy, and you've seen beautiful Greek temples along the North African coast. Greek art, Greek architecture, the Greek language, Greek values, Greek literature, Greek political institutions, Greek ways of life were spread all over the Mediterranean basin.

I suggested, when we talked about the Phoenicians, that they represented the first such evidence of a spreading of a common culture around the

Mediterranean. But the Phoenicians were never as numerous, and they were never as self-conscious as the Greeks were about spreading themselves and all that they represented. And remember, these colonies were meant to maintain close relationships with their mother-city. They weren't meant to be something wholly new, something wholly different. They were meant to be little extensions of Greece, wherever they went. And so they were. This was crucial in continuing this process, but accelerating this process, of making the Mediterranean basin a common cultural realm.

It's important to say, too, the Greeks did not merely spread out and take themselves all about the place. They learned; they borrowed. We have occasion, when we talk about Greek philosophy, perhaps we talk about Greek history, to see some concrete ideas which the Greeks learned from others and borrowed from others. But for the moment, let me just instance one crucial thing: they borrowed an alphabet from the Phoenicians. So that when the Greeks finally started writing again, probably in the eighth century B.C., they write in the familiar Greek script that we know, basically the Greek script that has been used since about the eighth century B.C. right down to now. Not like the script of those Linear B documents. And then, of course, as I mentioned, they stopped writing altogether for a period of some two or three hundred years.

So the Greeks were never unwilling to borrow. We mustn't suppose that Greek influence is always a one-way street. The Greeks are giving things to people, but they also knew how to take things from others.

The latter stages of the Dark Ages and the first phase of the Archaic period—this transitional period, perhaps the eighth century B.C. more or less—also begins to show us evidence for some of the most familiar aspects of Greek ways of thinking, Greek attitude, Greek values, issues that will be with us for the next several lectures. So let's suggest a little about what some of these emerging ideas were, say a few things about them, and see if we can't see how we may take them with us in some of our following lectures.

Decorations on pottery. You may think this a humble place to start, but designs on ceramics. The Greeks were able to make beautiful pots, but the Greeks were not the first people historically to make beautiful pots. But they were among the first people to put beautiful geometric designs on their pots. Geometry, the science of measuring the earth. But what does this suggest to you? If I asked you to close your eyes, if you're listening to this in a car, you probably don't want to do that, but if you could close your eyes and think geometry, you think shapes, you think forms. You think, don't you, of a certain sense of order, of balance, of harmony, of measure, of proportion. And don't a lot of those things sound awfully Greek?

There's a tendency on some of these pots to reduce the shape of living things to geometric forms. A very common motif, for example, often around the neck of a Greek pot, is to have a series of deer all following one another, or stags, actually. And in each instance, the bodies of each deer are described in almost exactly the same way. It's a highly stylized kind of image. It's a very abstract kind of image. It is an image that abstracts something from the world around us, something from the familiar world that we see. It is to turn the familiar into what is even more familiar but less visible. That is to say, geometry. It is to suggest in another way that behind all that we see there may be another realm, another kind of truth, another kind of beauty, another kind of perfection, of which all things in this world are but imperfect examples, or suggestions, or hints, or possibilities.

We saw that, did we not, in connection with Zoroastrianism. I'm not trying to turn the Greeks into Zoroastrians, I'm not trying to turn the Zoroastrians into Greeks. I'm saying again it is a common phenomenon, a common way of thinking about certain issues. But the next time you're in a museum, and you see a Greek pot with these geometric designs, or these highly stylized animal designs, think. Stop and think, what do they suggest to you? What do they invite you to think about? And I think you'll see this sense that not everything is quite as we see it, and that there is a quest for order, balance, harmony, and proportion.

It's also very important to say that, at a very early stage, the Greeks achieve a spectacular level of technical virtuosity: in their sculpture, in their ceramics, in vase painting eventually when they put pictures on ceramics, and so on. So this is important, too. And we'll come back to that point, because with that Greeks there is always *tekhnē*. *Tekhnē* is Greek for skill. There's always skill, accomplishment, but then there is the vision that informs the use of that skill. The Greeks are not alone in that. What is alone, what the Greeks are unique in, is the ways in which they put these two things together.

Early Greek sculpture across this Archaic period begins, sometimes in stone, sometimes in bronze—bronze figures, obviously, are cast not carved. But early Greek sculpture begins to give us some interesting and important hints about little differences between the way the Greeks think of the world, and the way some of their neighbors did. If you looked, for example, at Egyptian sculpture, at a good deal of Mesopotamian sculpture, Hittite sculpture, one of the things you would see is figures that are rigid and frontal and unblinking, unfeeling, unchanging. What they communicate is all that does not change. There's again a sense of abstraction there, that's true. But with the Greeks, we begin to get (in a later lecture we'll bring this more fully into view) a hint, a suggestion that an image represents an actual person who walked upon the earth, who is distinctive, who is different from everybody else, who looks like that and not like a rigid, lifeless, eternal kind of figure.

So the Greeks had the capacity to be technically proficient. They had the capacity to look for abstraction behind the world we live in. And they had the capacity to observe very, very closely the world we live in. This blend, we will see later, is enormously positive, creative, and generative.

Let's go back to Homer's poems. We left off poor Homer as we were trying to extract from his poems certain things that we might be able to learn about the Mycenean world. Now, let's put Homer back in his own time and place, 800-700 B.C. So what do we see in these poems that may begin providing us with hints about this *polis* that is just beginning to emerge, like late winter's first crocus? What we open up, I think, now, and I suggested this at the end of the last lecture, is a vista on ideologies, on values. But also, I think, some hints of that world's changes. Remember we've talked about this period, 800-700, as transitional between the Dark Ages and the Archaic period. I think in the very Homeric poem, we can feel some of these changes.

For instance, one of the things that we find in the *Iliad*, you find these things in the *Odyssey*, too, but I'm essentially focusing on the *Iliad*, one of the things that we find is intense competition. These Greeks are very competitive people. Now, we may think, they after all invented the Olympic Games, and the Olympic Games happened every four years, but in the other three years there were other games, the Isthmian, the Nemean, and the Pan-Hellenic games. So there were games going on in the Greek world all the time. Athletic means "about prizes." You didn't play for the fun of it. The game was not the thing, winning the game was the thing. These Greeks were competitive.

Now, think of the soldiers in the *Iliad*. We have a picture of two great armies arrayed on a battlefield. But they're basically nameless and faceless to us, aren't they? What we have is two warriors, our vision is always on two warriors. They come out on a battlefield and they make speeches to each other. They fight verbally before they ever strike a blow in earnest. And then they fight and they speechify, and they fight and they speechify, and they fight and they speechify. So there's physical competition and there's verbal competition. What would the Greeks have loved more than verbal competition? Somebody will be struck a mortal blow. He doesn't just die and kind of just get himself off. He dies for a hundred lines, making speeches, telling us—he's fighting with us sometimes, the audience—"Here's what you're supposed to think about this. Remember this; do that." This powerful sense of competition is very Greek.

Reflections on brains and brawn. Kind of poor, big, dumb, lummox Achilles. He never quite gets it. Various other figures in the story are like that. Wise, old master, the wise old man. He's the one, when the going gets tough, they always turn to. What do we do now? The question of whether the kings are as smart as they ought to be, as wise as they ought to be. A great play, what is important in this great battle playing out before the walls of Ilion: brains or brawn?

Respecting obligations of the individual and the community. The *Iliad* begins, "Sing, muse." Aida, hence the name of a great opera, "Sing muse, the wrath of Achilles, Peleus' son." The whole story is about whether Achilles' wrath is justified or not. He has been affronted, so he thinks; he takes himself off from the battle. The Greeks suffer and suffer and suffer and they go to him: "Won't you fight, won't you fight, won't you fight?" "No." And we are not presented with a story as if Achilles is simply a bad guy. He has a case, he has been affronted; his honor has been damaged. How can his honor be repaired and remedied, so that he might rejoin the battle? Only when his great friend, Petrocus, is killed does he go back, and then not because he owes anything to the Greeks, but because he owes something to the memory of his dead friend.

So we're beginning to see the struggles of a political community. What do I owe you? What do you owe me? What demands can I make on you? What demands can you make on me? What's the nature of authority? Who participates? The great, the powerful, the important, or ordinary people?

There's the one powerful scene in the *Iliad*, when Tosedes, an ordinary soldier, dares to speak in the presence of his betters and gets flogged for it. But, in fact, in the new *polis*, it's going to be a world where citizens do the talking, and where they come increasingly to see that they have no betters; they have equals, and they will speak to them as equals. We also see in this period powerful changes in warfare, as these towns must attack their neighbors or defend their neighbors, they must mobilize the ordinary citizens. They must mobilize the *hoplite*, who now fights in a full-length serried row, one after another of *hoplite* soldiers. You cannot ask people to fight, bleed, die for their city, and deny them participation.

So the Greek world, Homer's world, provides us a vista on Greek politics, on Greek religion, and we'll turn to Greek religion in somewhat more detail in a couple of later lectures. And it opens up the dawning classical world. The world of the *polis*. And it is to the two greatest of the Greek *poleis*, Sparta and Athens, that we will turn in the next two lectures.

The Greek Polis—Sparta
Lecture 8

We'll speak, in particular, about the *polis* of Sparta and then Athens as political and then social entities, and we'll then turn in a series of lectures to the *polis* as a cultural phenomenon.

The classical polis (plural: *poleis*) was a political, social, and cultural entity. Over the next several lectures, we will look at it from each of these points of view. First, we address some preliminary considerations. The physical characteristics of a polis may be expressed by a formula: *asty* + *chora* = polis. *Asty* is the Greek word for the city proper, the core of the polis. *Chora* means region or district; in our formula, it refers to the agricultural hinterland around a polis. A polis, therefore, is always an urban core and a rural zone: Athens + Attica = Athenian polis; Sparta + Laconia = Spartan polis.

Supposedly, a mythical law-giver by the name of Lycurgus, on the command of the gods, gave Sparta a constitution, all at once, in about the year 750 B.C.

The urban area usually had an *agora* (market area), temples, a building or area where public decisions were reached, and entertainment facilities, such as theaters and stadiums. Some poleis had natural fortifications: *acropolis*. Aristotle believed that people "naturally" lived in poleis. He and his pupils studied more than 100 Greek poleis. The amount of variation from one to another could be considerable. We shall look in detail at only two.

Sparta's early development is shrouded in legend. Supposedly, Lycurgus, a mythical law-giver, on the command of the gods, gave Sparta a constitution all at once circa 750 B.C. In fact, the Spartan system emerged piecemeal after the conquest of the Messenians circa 725 B.C.

One outstanding feature of the Spartan system was the social classes. The *homoioi* (equals) were adult male Spartan citizens over the age of 18. They had substantial rights of political participation, which was unusual at so early a date. The *periokoi* (dwellers about) were what we would call "resident aliens." These people were not citizens but enjoyed basic protection. There are many theories about just who they were. The *helots* (state slaves) were, essentially, the conquered Messenians; the helots belonged to Sparta and not to individual Spartans.

There were two kings, drawn from the same two families, who had veto power over each other. One was usually at home, and one away with the army. And there were two deliberative councils. All equals belonged to the assembly. This body could propose laws, wars, or treaties but could not legislate by itself. Real power was vested in a council consisting of the kings, the *ephors* (whom we will discuss in a moment), and equals over the age of 60. This body could ignore or act on suggestions from the assembly of equals.

There were five *ephors* (overseers) whose job it was to ensure that any law passed by the council or any verdict passed by a court was in accordance with Spartan tradition. They were always old and wealthy equals. *Krypteia* (secret police) were young men between 18 and 20 who primarily spied on the helots but also snooped on ordinary equals.

Spartan statue of a sphinx.

The Spartan constitution depended on the social system, the *agoge* (the training, or upbringing). Babies were inspected at birth, and the healthy ones were returned to their parents until age seven. At age seven, boys were enrolled in military brotherhoods to which they belonged the rest of their lives. From seven to 18, they underwent rigorous physical and military training. From 18 to 20, many served in secret service, then entered a regular army unit until age 60.

Marriage was not companionate; its sole function was the production of more equals. The system aimed to create military excellence, discipline, and loyalty. Spartan life was austere and simple. Spartans believed that book-learning made men effeminate. Spartans used iron money to make hoarding unattractive.

The Spartan system aimed to hold the helots in check (their labor made the life of the equals possible) and to ward off any threat of attack. By about 550, Sparta had formed the Peloponnesian League, which gave it the opportunity to control the constitutions of member states. Sparta tried to prevent democracies and social turmoil. The Spartan system was still in place when Rome conquered Greece in the 2nd century B.C., but there were only a few equals left by then. Contemporaries admired Sparta's strength, simplicity, and stability. ∎

Suggested Reading

Cartledge, *Sparta and Lakonia*.

Questions to Consider

1. Would the Spartan constitutional system have functioned without the *agoge*?

2. Why do you think that authoritarian regimes, like Sparta's, have been so attractive throughout history?

The Greek Polis—Sparta
Lecture 8—Transcript

Last time, we talked about the Greek Dark Ages and the Greek Archaic period. Perhaps you'll recall my saying that during the Archaic period, during the period from about 800 to 700 B.C., the first faint stirrings of the Greek *polis*, the classic Greek political institution, are visible.

In today's lecture, we're going to talk about Sparta. In the next lecture, we will talk in some detail about Athens. So what we're going to try to do is understand the classical Greek *polis*. The plural of that word, by the way, is *poleis*, not polises. We're going to try to understand the *polis* as a political, as a social, and as a cultural entity. In this lecture and in the next one, we'll speak, in particular, about the *polis* of Sparta and then Athens as political and then social entities, and we'll then turn in a series of lectures to the *polis* as a cultural phenomenon.

A few preliminary considerations may help us to enter on this discussion of a *polis*, and what a *polis* is, and what it represents. First of all, for example, physical characteristics. What exactly was a *polis*? We may think it's a city. That goes without saying, that's self-evident. But it's not quite so simple.

We can express what a *polis* was by means of a formula. We can say *asty* + *chora* = *polis*. What that means is this. *Asty* is the Greek word for city proper, and it refers to the urban core, the urban center of the *polis*. *Chora* is a Greek word that means region or district. What this refers to is the agricultural hinterlands that surrounded a *polis*. So a *polis* is always an urban core, *asty*, and a rural hinterland, *chora*. For instance, in Athens, you have Athens plus Attica, which makes the Athenian *polis*. In Sparta, you have Sparta and Laconia, which makes the Spartan *polis*. We always have to bear in mind that there are at least two elements, and that they have a very important symbiotic relationship.

Inside the urban area itself, the *poleis* of the Greek world had certain features in common. There would be great variation, but there were certain features in common. An *agora*. Think of "agoraphobia," the fear of public places. An *agora*, in a Greek city, in a Greek *polis*, was the marketplace. An open market that was where products were exchanged, people bought things, people sold things, but also where people encountered one another, where they talked to one another, where they shared gossip with one another. In a sense, the life of the *polis* was really played out informally, in many ways, in the *agora*.

There would almost always be temples. Temples dedicated, in the first place, to the god or goddess to whom that city was most particularly dedicated, and then for other cults that were important to the people in that place.

There would also be either a building or a public area—it could be either one—where the public life of the *polis* was played out in more formal senses. This is where assemblies met, where legislative institutions met, perhaps where courts of law met. In other words, different from the *agora*, where informally the public life of the city was played out. The institutional center was where formally the life of the *polis* was played out.

There were also entertainment facilities. Generally, these were of two kinds: theaters—many of the surviving Greek *poleis* will show us the remains, sometimes, as for example, in Athens or in one or two other places, very impressive remains of the ancient theater—and sometimes also stadiums. You may recall I was saying last time that the Greeks were very much enamored of competition, and that started with athletic competition that began with the Olympic Games, and then eventually extended itself to games played in many Greek cities. So not surprisingly, many of the Greek *poleis* had stadiums.

Some *poleis* also had natural fortifications. These could involve walls around the city, but often there was a high point. Cities started off and were built around, or even on, a high point. In Athens, for example, we have the Acropolis. This is a stone butte that sticks up right in the middle of the city, several hundred feet above the level of most of the urban core down below it. This was a place where temples and important buildings could be built, so that people would go there in ritual procession. But it was also a place to which people could retreat if the city were ever attacked by any of its neighbors.

Not every city had an acropolis; Athens doesn't have the only acropolis. We always think of the famous Athenian Acropolis, but there were acropoleis in a number of Greek cities. Corinth had one, for instance. Usually, there was also some provision provided for defending the *polis*.

Aristotle, who wrote a great deal about Greek government—we'll have occasion in some later lectures to talk in much more detail about Aristotle—Aristotle believed that people naturally lived in *poleis*. By nature, we associate with one another. You may have heard the old statement: Aristotle said man is a political animal. Point of fact, that's not quite what Aristotle said. What Aristotle said is man is by nature a creature who lives in a *polis*. Now of course, what you do in a *polis* is *politike*, is in a sense politics. But that really means city-ics, and we don't quite have that word. I mean, I need it right now, but I don't have it. So politics is what you do in a city. And that's what Aristotle said is natural for us; we come together in community, and we regulate our affairs.

Aristotle was very much interested in, as a philosopher might well be, the fact that over the Greek world there were a large number of these *poleis*. We know something, historically, about nearly 200 of them. Aristotle and a number of his pupils, he was sort of running like a research institution, studied the constitutions of more than 100 of these *poleis*.

Aristotle reserved it to himself to study the constitution of Athens. In some later lectures, we'll have occasion, once in a while, to draw on some of Aristotle's observations about Athens. So he studied Athens; he had his pupils sort of write theses, we might almost say, about a large number of the other Greek *poleis*, because Aristotle was very interested in discerning what was different. Were there any underlying, any fundamental principles? Alas, all of these other works vanished. We have, thankfully, Aristotle's treatment of the Athenian constitution, but all of these other studies of the other Greek *poleis* have vanished.

So we know a little from other sources, from histories and chance references in plays, and all sorts of things. We know a little something about these other cities, and we know that the variation could be considerable from one city to another. They were by no means alike. If we were really interested in the *polis*, and we really wanted to explore that subject in great detail, we'd have to assemble everything we've been able to learn about all of these *poleis*, and compare them and contrast them in all sorts of ways. We don't have time to do that here.

What we're going to do instead is focus on the two most famous, and in many ways the two most distinctive, of the Greek *poleis*: Sparta, in the first place, and we'll turn to that in more detail in just a second, and Athens, to which we'll turn in our next lecture. But I don't want to leave the impression that all Greek cities were either like Sparta or like Athens. That's not true.

Sparta's earliest development is shrouded in legend. By now, that's not going to surprise us. The origins of everything, it seems, are shrouded in legend. The Spartans told a story. Supposedly, a mythical law-giver by the name of Lycurgus, on the command of the gods, gave Sparta a constitution, all at once, in about the year 750 B.C. There are several things wrong with that. First of all, we do think Lycurgus is a real historical person. We do think there was such a person at Sparta, and that he may very well have been an important reformer; he may very well have played a significant role in the elaboration of the Spartan system. But it's also clear, it seems, that the Spartan system emerged over a long period of time, and slowly. And probably, in fact, reached its culmination at about the time when the Spartans conquered the Messenians.

Perhaps you'll recall, in the last lecture, we had said that the pressures of the early Archaic period, or of this transitional period, could be met in the Greek world in various ways. You could colonize and export your population, you could engage in trade, or you could conquer additional land. The Spartans, in particular, chose that option. They conquered their neighbors to the west, the Messenians. So it seems that some aspects of the Spartan system, however old they might have been, however many embryonic features they may have contained, were really sharpened, were hardened, after the conquest of the Messenians.

That takes place in the eighth century B.C., so the tradition remembering that somewhere in the eighth century B.C. the constitution was made is not bad. Remember we talked about how close Greek tradition on the date of the

Trojan Wars is. We talked about handing things down orally over long periods of time. Traditions are not false because they're traditions, and legends often have much in them that is true. It's sorting out what is true and what is false, in terms of facts, that is tricky. But when we discuss myth, when we discuss legend, if we are seeking only those few kernels of truth we're going to miss the whole point. Because myth and legend are meant to tell stories that tell much larger truths than the tiny and humble facts which they contain.

What the Spartans thought, then, about their past was that a great law-giver had given them their system at once. Now that's worth pausing to think about for just a minute because, in that regard, the Spartans are not unlike a lot of other peoples. The Athenians, for example, also thought their laws were given to them by a person called Theseus. Now they never quite—the Athenians didn't associate their whole system with Theseus the way the Spartans did with Lycurgus, but we might think about Moses, to whom "the law" is attributed. And yet clearly, "the law" evolved over a long period of time. Much later, the Romans remembered a figure called Numa Pompilius as having given them their law.

There is a tendency, always, to imagine a founding father, not a founding mother, and that is interesting as well, to imagine a founding father or perhaps founding fathers. Think of how frequently we Americans speak of the Founding Fathers, and how much legend and myth has attached to what they did. Sometimes we're interested in the facts, and sometimes we're interested in the larger story, the big picture.

The Spartan system, then, is revealed to us by a number of ancient writings. We actually have quite a lot of source materials. We don't have Aristotle's constitution of Sparta, but we have a lot of writings about Sparta, and we know a lot about the system. It was, in many ways, quite a peculiar system. We might very well think in the modern world that a particularly successful political system is one that is designed to accommodate change. In other words, one that can incorporate contention, institutionalize contention, diffuse contention, and move forward. The Spartan system, on the other hand, was designed not to accommodate, but to prevent change. This was one of the most conservative political systems created in human history, and created as such by design and not at all by accident.

The first feature of the Spartan system, what we want to think about as we proceed along to try to understand it as a political system and as a social system, because these two systems complement one another in important ways. The first feature, then, that we want to talk about is the social classes in Sparta. Who were these Spartans?

The first and the most important class of people at Sparta were called the *homoioi*. That means the "equals"—all adult Spartans who were male. Adult meant above the age of 18. If you were 18, and a Spartan, and male, you were an equal. These people had very wide opportunities for participation in the Spartan system. They had substantial rights of political involvement, of political speech, of voting on key issues. This is interesting and important to us. However conservative, however traditional, however stodgy the Spartan system was, it accorded earlier a wider degree of political organization, at least within the equals, than virtually any other political system had done before this time.

One could actually ask, was Sparta in some sense democratic? One could say that Sparta was a quasi-democracy, at least among the equals. Whether or not Sparta was democratic is something that may come into a little bit sharper focus for us in our next lecture, when we're talking about Athens, and we can perhaps develop one or two comparative insights on the two cities. So the equals, first.

Second, a group of people called the *periokoi*. A *urokos* is a house in Greek. *Peri* means "round." These were the people around the house. Well, not actually around your house, or anybody else's house. It meant the "dwellers about." We would say "resident aliens." There's a good deal of scholarly controversy over who, exactly, we are to understand by these resident aliens. I won't go into great detail on this. Some suggested that they may have been the indigenous population of Laconia, who were there when the Dorians came. Remember the Dorian invasions, around about the 12th century B.C.?

Some have suggested they may have been people who migrated into Laconia from surrounding regions. Some have suggested that they may have been people who fell out in political contention in Sparta in earlier times. It's very hard to say. They were people who lived in Sparta, who were protected by the Spartan system, who had certain rights and certain opportunities; but they could never be Spartan citizens, and, therefore, they could never participate politically in the Spartan state.

Finally, a very interesting class of people, the *helots*. The *helots* were state slaves. Essentially, these were the conquered Messenians, those neighbors to the west of Sparta, whom the Spartans conquered as a way of relieving the demographic pressures in their own area. What is very distinctive about the *helots* is that they did not belong to individual Spartans; they belonged to Sparta. Slavery is an old institution, but in most places, slaves belonged to individuals, as individuals. In Sparta, the *helots*, in a sense, as a corporate body, belonged to Sparta, as a corporate body. And it is clear, it seems, that some aspects of the Spartan system were really designed to keep those *helots* in place.

If we turn from the main social classes at Sparta to the institutions of the Spartan system, how was the place set up, how did it operate? There were, in the first place, two kings. Not one, two Very interesting. The idea being that one was a check on the other. Over a very long period of time, these kings always came from two families, son succeeding to father generally speaking, occasionally again brothers and others entered into the line of succession. But kings drawn from two families. One was usually at home, functioning as, in some sense, the Chief Executive Officer of the Spartan state, and one was generally in the field with the Spartan armies. They didn't send out both kings with armies, and usually there weren't both at home. These kings had an absolute veto over each other. If one of them decided to make a decision, the other king could veto it.

There were two deliberative councils at Sparta. Was this the origins, in a sense, of bicameral legislatures? In a way, but it's very important to understand what these two deliberative bodies at Sparta were like, and how they worked in conjunction with each other. The assembly at Sparta was an assembly of direct participation, we might have said direct democracy, by all the equals. If you were an equal, you were a member of the assembly. You weren't elected, you didn't represent anybody, you didn't represent a territory. As an equal, you belonged.

The assembly could propose laws. It could propose going to war. It could propose concluding a war. It could propose striking a treaty with someone. But it could not finally legislate by itself. What it could do, in a sense, was set an agenda. That agenda was then forwarded on to the council. The council is really the body that guarded the Spartan system, that really made it work. The council consisted of the two kings, five *ephors* (I'll come back to these *ephors* in just a second, judicial officers, basically) and then all equals above the age of 60. That's very important, and I want to explain that, but a question may have come up in your mind right now. This is the ancient world. This was a long time ago. Who in the world was 60? Good question.

Figuring life expectancy as an average of the ages at death of all those people who belonged to a society will give you one number, which starts in antiquity as a fairly low number, probably in the high 20s. And as we come forward in time, gradually moves, for example in the United States, it moves to a fairly high number, in some parts of the undeveloped world today it remains a depressingly low number.

If you reckon life expectancy at certain moments in the lifespan, the numbers change pretty dramatically. If you lived to be 20, and you were male, your expectation of life was very long. It was easy to live—well, "easy" is an exaggeration—it was likely, it was possible to live well into your 60s. If a woman lived to be 30 or into her early 30s, she was very likely to live a long time. Childbirth was the great killer of women in the pre-modern world. The point is that enormous numbers of babies and adolescents died.

These were societies which could not solve all of the problems that occur at the moment of birth, and all of the problems associated with the diseases of youth and adolescence. That's where large numbers of people died. So if you had a large number of people who died at one, one, one, one, one, one, one, 50, and you average it up, you get a small number. If you put all of the ones in one category, and think about the people in the other category, you get a very different number. So it's not so shocking that there were lots of men at Sparta above the age of 60 to operate in the council.

Back to Spartan politics. All the equals could propose things to a body made up of the kings, the *ephors*, and the equals over 60. They finally said "yes" or "no." They didn't really have the initiative in the legislative process. That did come from the assembly of all the Spartans. But they could stop things they didn't want. That was their great power. Once you had been a member of the Spartan system, to the age of 60, you were not likely to go off on tangents. You were not likely to have a lot of new ideas. You were not likely to entertain, happily, new ideas.

I mentioned *ephors* a moment ago; who were these *ephors*? There were five of them. The word basically means "overseers," inspectors in a sense. Their job was to ensure that any law passed by the council, or any verdict passed by an Athenian law court, was in conformity with the laws of Sparta. So here was yet another brake on the system; here was another check on innovation.

There was also the *krypteia*. Think of the word crypt, you see, secret. A crypt is a secret place; cryptography is secret writing. The *krypteia* was the Spartan secret police. These were generally young men, usually between the ages of about 18 and 20, whose job it was to go around and, in the first place, keep an eye on the *helots*. But in the second place, to snoop on ordinary Spartans, just to make sure that they were behaving themselves.

That, then, was the basic Spartan constitution. It depended on a very curious, very interesting, very rigid social system, which we call the *agoge*. The *agoge* means the upbringing, the training, the leading along. So this is the social system, the *agoge*, that generated the political system of which we've just been speaking.

Babies were inspected at birth, and healthy ones were returned to their parents to about the age of seven. This occasions a pause. The idea of exposing babies at birth, the idea of infanticide. There are lots of famous instances in antiquity. You may think, just for a moment, of the play *Oedipus Rex*. Remember, Oedipus is displayed at crossroads, and left there. He's found, and the story goes on.

In antiquity, exposing a baby was not actually infanticide. Just think of the familiar images from literature. They were exposed in market squares, they were put in the steps of temples, they were put at crossroads. They were expected to be found. Oedipus was found. He was raised. He lived to a ripe old age, until various other things intervened in his life. Exposing babies is certainly not a practice I would want to recommend, and certainly not one that we would wish to praise, but it was not the same thing as killing unwanted children.

Babies were inspected, and if they seemed healthy, they were returned to their parents until the age of seven. At the age of seven, boys were enrolled in military brotherhoods, to which they belonged for the rest of their lives. In a sense, you were sort of put in a military unit, and you now were a member of that unit for the rest of your life. From seven to 18, they underwent rigorous physical and military training. As I mentioned a moment ago, from 18 to 20, many of them, not all, but many of them served at least a brief period of time in the secret service. They then entered a regular army unit, and remained a member of that unit to the age of 60. There were exceptions made if a person were wounded or physically impaired as life went along. But you could, in principle, have to serve actively in the field to the age of 60.

Marriage at Sparta was not companionate. It was not co-residential. That is to say, husbands and wives, generally speaking, didn't live together. Men lived with their military units. Marriage at Sparta had one fundamental purpose: to make more equals. That was the purpose of marriage at Sparta. And that means, of course, that the institution didn't generate family ties, family loyalties, bonds of family affection, and so on, as we might expect to see in other societies. The system was designed to create military excellence. It was designed to create discipline. It was designed to create loyalty. It was designed to create a group of equals with very powerful bonds to one another, and very powerful bonds to Sparta.

Spartan life was austere and very simple. Archaeology, for example, does not show us great elaborate housing complexes. Spartans lived very simply; men lived in barracks, basically. They ate very simple food. They prided themselves on their simplicity. They prided themselves on not being gabby and talking too much. Their land is called Laconia, and what does "laconic" mean? It means you don't have much to say. And in much Greek literature, there are wonderful stories about Spartans who didn't have much to say.

The Spartans didn't like book learning. There's a very interesting point here; that notion that recurs quite a number of times in Western civilization, amongst other peoples and in other places—there was a notion that book learning made men effeminate. It weakened them; it softened them. There is a wonderful irony there because, if it was thought to be the case that book learning made men effeminate, that sort of implies, doesn't it, that lots of women read a lot of books, and somehow that this was a characteristic of females. And yet, in most of these societies, women were actually denied opportunities to acquire a lot of book learning. Prejudices get built in very, very funny ways, and then operate in very funny ways.

But there is the notion—remember we talked about the struggle between brains and brawn—that if you got too much brains you don't have enough brawn. And in Sparta, you want brawn. So enough with the brains stuff.

Spartans used iron money, in big bars of small denomination. The whole point of this was to avoid hoarding, to avoid accumulating. What do you want money for?

The Spartan system, as I've suggested a couple of times, was designed fundamentally to hold the *helots* in check. Without the labor of the *helots*, the Spartan system simply would not have worked. How would all of these men have been in military service, in effect, from the age of seven to the age of 60, if they had to work in the fields or carry out other pursuits? So, the *helots* made Spartan life possible. Of course, the Spartans' idea was that this gave them the freedom to ward off attack, to ward off invasion, to keep foes at bay.

By about 550 B.C., the Spartans had pulled most of the cities of the Peloponnesus, southernmost Greece, together into the Peloponnesian League. This was not kind of a Spartan version of the United Nations. The members of the Peloponnesian League were under absolutely no circumstances Sparta's equals.

Sparta basically dictated to the Peloponnesian League what its plans would be, what its policies would be. Essentially, Sparta exercised some control over the constitutions of member states. Spartans did not want democratic regimes—they thought they were too unstable, too tumultuous. And they wanted to control the foreign policy of the states of the Peloponnesian League. They didn't want any military adventurism amongst their neighbors that might have implications for themselves.

The Spartan system was still fundamentally in place when the Romans conquered Greece in the second century B.C. By then, alas, there was a relative handful of equals left.

Contemporaries, interestingly enough, had a tendency to admire Sparta. They admired its strength, they admired its simplicity, they admired its stability. There is, for us, an interesting puzzle and an interesting challenge in that admiration that was accorded to Sparta, and it's just this. Most people, I think, would like to live in stable political systems. And then many people had been tempted toward authoritarian kinds of regimes that seemed to them to promise stability, even if such regimes reduced dramatically the rights of individuals. There is a tug, there is a pull, there is something that demands from us a kind of a grudging admiration for systems like the Spartans. And in antiquity, the Spartan system was much admired.

No one, I think, would say that the Athenian system was stable. Curiously, it was also not as much admired in antiquity as it would be subsequently. So, having gotten some understanding of Sparta, we'll turn in our next lecture to the most famous, and in many ways the most interesting, of the Greek *poleis*, Athens.

The Greek Polis—Athens
Lecture 9

It is probably safe to say that at no moment during Athens' long political evolution did any leader wake up one morning and say, "I have an idea: let's invent democracy. Let's have a democracy," though the system became more and more democratic.

The great story in Athens is the gradual shift of political power from the *eupatrids* (the well-fathered ones) to the *demos* (the people). With the luxury of hindsight, we can see an orderly process that has, almost, an air of inevitability. That process also seems natural to us because we suppose that others would share our admiration for democracy, that is, for rule (*crateia*) by the people. But ancient writers disliked democracy in general and the democracy of Athens in particular. Athens created democracy accidentally as the city's leaders responded to one crisis after another.

In the 7th century B.C., most of the Greek world, except Athens and Sparta, experienced tyranny. This was rule by a strong man who set himself up as the leader of the people. Popular discontent, as we have seen, arose from economic and demographic stresses as the beginning of the Archaic period. We have seen how Sparta escaped tyranny. Now we turn to Athens. Circa 621 B.C., Draco codified the laws of Athens and posted them in the Athenian agora. This code was harsh—"Draconian"—but it represented a concession to those who opposed the arbitrary rule of the eupatrids. Athens was, in principle, now ruled by laws, not by men.

Ordinary Athenian farmers still suffered cycles of boom and bust, and the city was home to more and more rich merchants who had no place in a society dominated by wealthy land-owning eupatrids. In 594, Solon, a eupatrid who had made a fortune in trade, was appointed lawgiver, with wide authority to introduce reforms. Solon was a moderate without personal ambition. He abolished many debts and debt slavery. He changed the basic qualifications for office holding from birth to wealth and distributed offices and the right to vote quite widely according to a sliding scale of wealth. He created a Council of 400 that set the agenda for the assembly of all citizens. (This is just the opposite of Sparta's system.)

The next generation saw squabbling among many who felt that Solon had not gone far enough and some who felt that he had gone too far. The lowest classes elevated Peisistratus to a mild tyranny in 560. He and his sons dominated Athens for about 40 years. He respected most of Solon's system but did redistribute land. Peisistratus also inaugurated festivals and initiated public building projects, partly to make people loyal to, and proud of, Athens and partly to put them to work. Eventually, the Athenian eupatrids allied themselves with some eupatrids and drove out the Peisistratids. A blueblood named Cleisthenes was given powers to make reforms.

As Athens's leaders responded to problem after problem, crisis, indeed, after crisis, they accidentally stumbled upon a democratic system.

From Cleisthenes to Pericles, Athenian democracy came into full force. Because Cleisthenes was disappointed with the eupatrids, he turned to the demos. He created a new Council of 500 based on residence, not birth or tradition. He bound together people of different social and occupational backgrounds. He opened almost all offices to almost all men. He introduced *ostracism*.

Themistocles was a popular leader during the Persian Wars. Because many of Athens's sailors were still denied some political rights, he worked to remedy this situation.

Between 461 and 450, Ephialtes and Pericles ended all aristocratic privilege by stripping the eupatrid *Areopagus* of the right of judicial review and by instituting pay for public service.

We will reflect on the Athenian system. How did it work? The Athenian system encompassed a weak executive; powerful role for the assembly, that is, for participation of ordinary people; and vigorous debate. There was a danger of *demagogues*. There was no necessary continuity in policy.

For whom did it work? For Athenian citizens, that is, adult males with two Athenian parents, perhaps 10 percent of 400,000 people. Not for women; *metics*—resident aliens; or slaves, which were increasingly numerous.

How was it financed? By tribute from the Athenian Empire. By slave labor. Who defended it? Pericles, in his "Funeral Oration."

Who criticized it? Almost all ancient writers. Plato and Aristotle believed that it did not advance the "best" men. The "Old Oligarch" believed it lacked deference and was too unstable, changeable, and subject to demagoguery. Historian Thucydides gave examples of folly, cruelty, and perversity.

What was the verdict? The Athenians demonstrated *what* a democracy might be. It remained for others later to show *for whom* a democracy might work. ∎

Suggested Reading

Andrewes, *The Greek Tyrants*.

Forrest, *The Emergence of Greek Democracy*.

Ober, *Mass and Elite in Democratic Athens*.

Sealey, *Greek City-States*.

Questions to Consider

1. Can you think of examples in U.S. history where the "law of unintended consequences" extracted very different political or institutional results from policies designed with different ends in mind?

2. Think of some of the democratic regimes in the world today and ask yourself how they differ from one another and how well they measure up to an ideal standard of democracy.

The Greek Polis—Athens
Lecture 9—Transcript

In our last lecture, we talked about Sparta, one of the most famous and important of the Greek *poleis*, and in this lecture we turn to Athens, surely the most famous, the most important, and in lots of ways, the most interesting of the Greek *poleis*. We saw, in talking about Sparta, that a very orderly, and therefore very stable system was created. When we turn to Athens, we can forget about that. Order and stability are not words that we would use if we talk about Athens. We can actually say that what the Athenians did is proceed in orderly fashion from crisis to crisis. That probably captures the Athenian system and the Athenian situation as well as anything.

The great story in Athens is basically this. It is a shift in power from a relatively small number of *eupatrids*. Eupatrids are well-fathered people; that's literally what the word means. *Pater* in Greek means father, as *pater* means father in Latin, as *vater* is father in German, as "father" is father in English, as *per* is father in French, as *padre* is father in Spanish. That, by the way, is a little lesson on the Indo-European family of languages, how we can see one word that is so similar across a range of languages. But that doesn't help us understand Athens very well; back to the story.

Athens had been run by well-fathered men. And over the period of about two centuries, political power was shifted to the *demos*, to the people as a whole. What people? That'll be part of our job to explain, what people indeed. But we move from *eupatrids* to the *demos*. With the luxury of hindsight, we can see in Athens what seems like a very orderly process that has almost an air of inevitability about it. The Athenians marched forward to create a democracy. The process, perhaps, seems natural to us because we admire democracy and we suppose that others would share our admiration for democracy. And therefore, we assume that the Greeks would have shared our admiration for democracy, and that that's what they'd have done. They'd have said, "Well, we have a job to do; let's create democracy." Rule by the people is what democracy means.

But ancient writers, as a matter of fact, were not positively disposed towards democracy, for the most part. A little bit later in this lecture we'll have occasion to see why that would have been the case. Democracy was messy, it was turbulent, it was unstable. Ancient writers didn't think that democracy was necessarily a good thing, or the thing towards which political evolution ought naturally to tend.

It is probably safe to say that at no moment during Athens' long political evolution did any leader wake up one morning and say, "I have an idea: let's invent democracy. Let's have a democracy," though the system became more and more democratic. There is something ironically accidental about the creation of Athenian democracy. As Athens's leaders responded to problem after problem, crisis, indeed, after crisis, they accidentally stumbled upon a democratic system. Let's observe that evolution over a period of time and see how exactly it worked itself out in the great *polis* of Athens.

In the seventh century B.C., much of the Greek world experienced a brief period of what the Greeks themselves called "tyranny." Tyranny didn't mean bad guys; it meant something like a strong man who was a popular leader. In other words, the word didn't necessarily carry negative connotations; it was a sort of a strong man who was a popular leader. The two cities that, in the seventh century, quite interestingly, escaped tyranny were Athens and Sparta.

What was generally happening, again if we think back to those tensions, in that generative period as the Greek Dark Age was giving way to the Greek Archaic period, we talked, you may recall, a couple of lectures back about the emergence of the *hoplite*, the ordinary soldier as opposed to the aristocratic man on horseback. And if as city is going to ask ordinary people to serve it, and perhaps to die for it, it may very well have to give them some share in the political process.

There was a great deal of social strife, a great deal of social contention in Greek towns. And in some towns, the popular classes, the popular groups who felt that they had been insufficiently rewarded for their contributions or had not been permitted to participate in the system, would wing forward one of their own as a great leader. Or they might rally behind an aristocrat, who sort of turned into a popular leader in the town. So tyranny spread across much of the Greek world, and this popular contention might have had economic roots, might have had political roots, it may have been rooted in the demographic pressures that we have talked about already.

What is interesting, then, is, how did Athens respond to this period of political contention, as compared, for example, to Sparta? So everywhere else in the Greek world, or almost everywhere, tyranny. Sparta creates the Lycurgan system, which we talked about in our last lecture. In Athens, the process works a little differently.

In 621 B.C., a man by the name of Draco was empowered in Athens to codify the laws of the city. He did this, and he posted them, on tablets, in the *agora*—the Athenian marketplace, this big open square that I referred to in the previous lecture. The law code was extremely harsh. "Draconian" is still a word we use for very harsh laws.

But it represented a very interesting and important concession to those who opposed the arbitrary rule of *eupatrids*. Aristocrats could basically rule at their pleasure, at their whim. In some ways, they really only had to answer to one another and not to anyone else. Making Athens' laws public was to establish, in principle—not yet, truth be told, in fact, but in principle—the idea that Athenians would henceforth be governed by laws and not by men.

It may occur to you to ask, "Well, didn't men make those laws? And didn't some men have more power than others? So didn't the law still provide the opportunity for the powerful to rule?" And the answer, of course, is yes. But the principle was established, that with the law as the public business of the people. You may recall, we had mentioned that very same point several lectures ago, or a couple of millennia ago, depending on how you look at it, in Mesopotamia.

Publishing the laws didn't relieve all of the problems. Ordinary Athenian farmers still suffered cycles of boom and bust, boom and bust. Remember, Athens has become a trading state. Farmers are always subject to the vagaries of the weather; they are subject to the vagaries of prices for crops. If there are tremendous amounts of cereal grains, for example, produced in the Black Sea region at one time, the price of Athenian grain goes down. If there are failures of crops elsewhere in the Mediterranean world, let's say on the coast of North Africa, the price of Athenian grain goes up. So farmers were suffering cycles of boom and bust. This generated problems.

Then there's another interesting group of people in Athens who have problems, and that's precisely the merchants. If Athens is going to be, as indeed it was, a great merchant city, it's going to attract large numbers of people who are fundamentally living by commerce. But these are not local landowners. They are not necessarily people with long traditions in the city, long-rootedness in the city, family connections in the city. They are not, simply, the old, wealthy, landowning *eupatrids*. What will be their place in this new Athens? They are responsible for generating a great deal of its wealth, but they really don't have any place in the system.

In 594 B.C., the Athenians appointed a man by the name of Solon. To this day, we still think of law-givers as "solons." They appointed a man by the name of Solon, a *eupatrid*, a man from a very old, important family. As law-giver, he was given an opportunity to make a whole series of legal provisions to try to introduce some reform into the Athenian system. Solon was an interesting person in lots of ways. He was a moderate. He was a person without personal ambition himself, as far as we can tell. He didn't seek to make himself famous. He didn't seek to aggrandize himself. He didn't seek to line his own pockets. He was able to do this because he was wealthy enough to sustain it. After he passed his reforms, he left Athens for 10 years because he wanted the system to work without him there, to pull the strings and push the buttons. He wanted the system to work for the Athenian people.

So what kinds of things did he do? He's got wealthy landowners who really don't want to share power. He's got merchants who haven't quite found a place in the system. And he's got farmer who are suffering from economic cycles of boom and bust. So, what's he going to do to help these people out?

One of the first things he did was he abolished many debts and debt slavery. One of the things that happened to large numbers of farmers, and of course, many farmers face this situation today, you borrow this year to get your crop in the ground, and you hope that you can get that crop back out of the ground and harvested in the fall, and have enough money to: (a) pay your debt back, and (b) to put something in your pocket for yourself until next spring, when you put your crop in the ground again.

If the crop fails or if the price falls dramatically, you fall into debt. And in Athens, when farmers fell into debt several years in a row, they could actually be enslaved by those to whom they were in debt. Some of these Athenians had even been sold overseas as slaves. Solon puts an end to debt slavery and actually bought back a certain number of the people who had been sold away.

He changed the basic qualifications for office holding and for voting in Athens, from birth to wealth. At first, you may say that doesn't seem like such a big change, changing from birth to wealth, distributing the right to hold office, the right to vote for office holders. But what Solon did was actually very clever: he created a system that we could call "timocracy"— that is to say, division of political power according to wealth.

"Plutocracy" is a system where the wealthy rule. You know, the golden rule: whoever has the gold, rules. That's plutocracy. Timocracy is to say, "According to a scale of wealth, you have power; you have places in this society." One of the things he did was immediately equate the wealthiest of the merchants at the very top of the system, because of their wealth, with the greatest of the landowners. He built a place in the system for them. And so, then right on down a scale.

Basically he created four classes by wealth. But he divided up political participation according to wealth, and he found a way to build the merchants in. And he found a way, even, to mitigate some of the old, powerful families who were a bit less wealthy than some of the other old, powerful families. You might end up with less power under Solon's system than you had had previously.

He created a Council of 400 that set the agenda for the assembly of all Athenian male citizens. That's interesting. That's exactly the opposite of the system at Sparta. Here, in Athens, a relatively small group, chosen amongst the population as a whole—not men over 60 or something of the sort—a relatively small group set the agenda. But the large group, the assembly of all citizens, got to say "yea" or "nay." Now, it's true that the assembly was not accorded early on much initiative. Nevertheless, they had the opportunity to vote on issues put to them by a Council of 400. Solon institutes this system, fairly moderate, actually.

Solon was also a bit of a poet. He wrote a poem talking about how he was like a great bird, and he put one wing over one party and another wing over the other party. Both parties were, in the generation after Solon, angry about what he had done. Some felt he had gone way too far; some felt he hadn't gone nearly far enough. It's an interesting thought. If you were a politician and you had people on both sides of you who disliked you equally, might that be a hint that you'd done about the right thing? I don't know; I'll leave it to you to decide that. But there did remain problems. Not all of the difficulties, not all of the stresses in the Athenian system, had been addressed by Solon's reforms.

As a result, around 560 B.C., the lower classes elevated a man by the name of Peisistratus to a very mild form of tyranny in Athens. He really left most of the existing institutions in place and ruled alongside them, even ruled through them. He didn't really supplant the institutions, so he wasn't quite a tyrant in the 7th century Greek sense. And he certainly didn't have the kind of domineering power that some of those tyrants had. He, and then his sons after him, dominated the Athenian political scene for about 40 years.

What did Peisistratus do? In the first place, he respected most of Solon's system. He didn't really change Solon's system dramatically, but he did redistribute some land. One of the interesting problems with Solon's system was Solon put an end to debt slavery, and Solon bought back certain numbers of people who had been sold into slavery. But if you bring back a former farmer, and you don't give him any land, what's he to do? He becomes part of an urban poor. He becomes part of a permanent underclass. So one of the things that Peisistratus did was, mildly, to redistribute land. How many times, historically, has land redistribution been a fundamental issue of people who are or who see themselves as reformers?

Peisistratus did some other interesting things, too. He inaugurated a whole series of festivals at Athens. The great Pan-Athenaic Festival, about which we'll have more to say in later lectures, for instance. He initiated massive public building projects in Athens; the first great set of public buildings in Athens were built mainly in the time of Peisistratus. He did this for a number of reasons. At one level, it was boosterism. He was really trying to make people proud of Athens. He wanted Athens really to be something, and to stand for something. And that was important. He was trying, in a certain way, to get people to focus their loyalty on the city and not on their particular class, their particular economic group, their particular geographical area, their own partisan interests.

But there's another side to this. It has led some historians to speak of an Athenian "New Deal." Somebody had to do the work of building all these buildings; and, as you had this increasing underclass, and you couldn't redistribute enough land to take care of all of them, you could put large numbers of them to work, basically at state pay, to build these buildings. So these, then, in the time of Peisistratus and of his sons who came after him, were some additional measures that the Athenians envisioned as ways of sort of siphoning off some of the political tension in the Athenian system.

Eventually, the Spartans allied themselves with a number of *eupatrid* families in Athens and threw out the Peisistratus regime. The Spartans had had enough of this regime; it looked a little bit too democratic to them. It looked a little bit too unstable to them. It just might give other people, like members of the Peloponnesian League, for instance, funny ideas about politics. What the Spartans wanted was a nice, stable Athens in the hands of a bunch of rich old men who wouldn't disturb the situation very much.

There's a wonderful law of unintended consequences in politics. What happened is a *eupatrid*, a real blueblood, a man by the name of Cleisthenes, was elevated to power and given the opportunity to make some new reforms. Well, Cleisthenes was on the outs with a lot of the other *eupatrids*. He really wanted to introduce some fairly moderate reforms; they were going to block him at every step of the way and say, "We've had enough of all of this reform business; we don't need any more." So Cleisthenes was sort of drawn to do a great deal more than he would have ever dreamed, probably, at the beginning, and certainly a whole lot more than the Spartans ever envisioned when they thought they had thrown out exactly people like this.

From Cleisthenes to Pericles, let us say then from about 510 B.C. down to about 450 B.C., over a period of about 60 years, two generations, let's say, full democracy emerged in Athens. Or, we can say the Athenian democracy became as fully democratic as it would ever become. How did that happen?

Cleisthenes, as I've indicated, was very much disappointed with the *eupatrids*, so he turned to the *demos*—he turned to the Athenian people. He began to build the people into the Athenian system, in a much more decisive way than Solon had ever done. And even where Peisistratus had done this emotionally, psychologically, and, to a degree, economically, Cleisthenes began to do it institutionally. He began to build the *demos* into the system.

He created, for example, a new Council of 500. It was divided up into groups of 50, which formed a kind of rotating executive committee that sat for a month at a time. The way he developed this council—it's actually very, very complicated, but there's a very simple idea underlying it. It's quite interesting. People then in Athens spoke of the plain, the coast, and the hill. These were shorthands. The plain was the plain of Attica, the great farmland. The coast meant the port, meant the merchants. The hill meant the uplands, the bad farmlands.

What Cleisthenes did, in a way, was gerrymander the political structure of Athens so that he took a group of people from the plain, a group from the coast, a group from the hill, and made them one group. Then another group from the plain, a group from the coast, and a group from the hill, and made them one group. He made 10 such groups. And then each of these groups could choose 50 members annually for the Council.

What he was trying to do was break down local interests, break down family interest, break down occupational interest, and make people cooperate—make them think about Athens. Peisistratus, remember, had the idea of doing this by making Athens beautiful. Make something you're really proud of. Cleisthenes said, "No, I've got a different idea; I'm going to build an institution that makes people cooperate." He opened virtually all offices to almost all men. Remember Solon's timocracy, Solon's system of arraying political participation by wealth. Cleisthenes opened up virtually the whole system to almost all men. There remained a few political disabilities, we'll see one or two of them go away here in 10 or 20 years, or in just a couple of minutes, depending on how you want to look at it. But essentially, men could now vote, and men could now hold office.

Cleisthenes introduced something else very interesting, too, one of the most distinctive features of Athenian system, "ostracism." Now, we know what "ostracism" is; we ostracize somebody we don't like, and we won't talk to them, and so on. Ostracism worked a little differently in Athens. *Ostraca* is the Greek word for a potshard. Once a year, the Athenians were bidden to come to the *agora*, and they could vote. They voted by writing a name on potshard. If a sufficient number—several thousand—if a sufficient number of votes were cast, then whoever got the most votes had to leave Athens for 10 years.

Cleisthenes's idea here was that anybody who really angered the *demos*, either by doing things that were foolish and stupid on the one hand, or by doing things that were damaging to the interests of the people on the other hand, would get their comeuppance by being thrown out. Obviously, you didn't campaign for ostracism, but people might and people did get ostracized—so ostracism. Potshardism is actually what the word means, from the *ostraca*.

After Cleisthenes, there were some additional reforms that came into the Athenian system. For instance, from 490 to 478 B.C., the Greek world fought a massive war with the Persians, a war in two great phases. We'll have something to say about those Persian Wars in a couple of later lectures. For now, I simply want to say that it was the Athenian navy—finally and above all else—it was the Athenian navy that won the war.

The lowest class citizens in the state, the ones who had been left at the bottom by Solon, the ones who had really not been quite fully incorporated by Cleisthenes, were the rowers in those ships. They found a great leader in the Athenian general—we would actually say admiral—Themistocles. Themistocles, then, managed to get laws passed through the Athenian assembly essentially to make the lowest class, represented by those sailors, fully able to participate publicly and politically in Athens—to vote, to hold office, and so on. In crucial respects, then, the last pieces of the Solonic and Cleisthenic limitations were knocked down.

In the 460s and 450s B.C., Athens experienced a period of leadership, by Ephialtes and then by Pericles. Ephialtes and Pericles, together, removed, in many respects, the last vestiges of aristocratic privilege in the Athenian system. They did basically two things. A number of things, but two that I think are particularly important. First, they stripped the old *Areopagus* of all its rights of judicial review. This is not unlike the *ephors* in Sparta. It was a body of *eupatrids* who could pass judgment on the constitutionality of measures passed by the assembly. It remained as a kind of an institutional brake on the full operations of the Athenian assembly. So the last review powers of the *Areopogus* were struck down.

The second thing they did is they introduced pay for public service. This is often, for us in contemporary America, a controversial issue. Should we do it all, do we pay our legislators too much money, should we pay them less money, do they have the right to vote themselves raises?

We get very heated up about this issue, and we should. That's fine. But there's something very fundamental about paying people for public service. If you did not do it, and if you were an Athenian or you were an American living right now, only the idle rich could serve. Only the idle rich, not even the working rich. Because if you're a person who has to get up every morning and go to your job, you can't—for months at a time, weeks at a time, or maybe even more or less permanently over a period of years—simply give up everything you do. So pay for public service is also, in critical respects, a democratizing force.

So, we get to about 450 B.C., and as a result of one crisis after another, virtually all men can participate, virtually all men can vote, and there are no checks on the system such as wealth: "If I'm not wealthy I can't afford to serve," or an old aristocratic body serving as a brake on the laws.

How did the system actually work in practice? The Athenian system had a very weak executive. The executive officers, they were called *arcons*—*arcon* in Greek means a "ruler"—there were three of them elected every year. They were relatively weak; they weren't powerful. They weren't as powerful, for example, as the kings at Sparta. The critical institution at Athens became the assembly. It was here that the ordinary Athenians could participate.

And from all indications we have—indications in the Greek historians, indications in dramas, indications in surviving speeches from some of the great Athenian orators—debate was vigorous in the assembly. People really did speak; they really did argue. That's important, if we want to think about a democratic system.

It's also true to say that there was a danger of demagoguery in Athens. A demagogue is a leader of the people, and the word does carry a slightly unsavory connotation. The assembly was, certainly its critics said, too easily swayed. It was too changeable. That produced a situation that also means that there was really no continuity in Athenian policy, or at least constitutionally there was no necessity of continuity. Remember the Spartan system was designed, in a sense, to ward off change, to make change almost impossible? The Athenian system could accommodate change, but what it couldn't do very easily was put the brakes on change.

We'll have occasion in a couple of later lectures to see some of the consequences, some of the implications of that fact. For now, I just want to remark it. Athens was freewheeling and wide open, and that's a good thing. But Athens was freewheeling and wide open, and that's not such a good thing. There's two stories here, good news and bad news.

For whom did the system work? For Athenian citizens. Who's that? Adult males with two Athenian parents, perhaps 10 percent of a population of 400,000 people. So, for whom did it not work? Well, it wasn't for women. It wasn't for *metics*. *Metics* were residents aliens at Athens—people who had come there to work, people who had come there as merchants. It didn't work for slaves, who became increasingly numerous in the Athenian scheme of things. So for something like 10 percent of the population, it was a remarkably democratic system. For almost everybody else, it was not.

How was it financed? After the Persian Wars, some of the Greeks, led by Sparta, simply wanted to go home. The war's over, that's that. Some of the Greeks said, "No, there remain Greeks on islands in the Aegean Sea and on the Ionian coast on the western shore of Anatolia, who are still under Persian domination. Let us go and free them," Athens led that party.

For a period of years, there was much cooperation among the groups of people who went to liberate the Ionian Greeks. And then in 454 B.C., Athens turned this sort of voluntary association into an Athenian empire. And the Athenians collected, with a vengeance, tribute from that empire. Allegedly, that tribute was to pay for the military costs, the naval costs of fighting the Persians. In point of fact, it went into the pockets of Athenians. It paid their politicians, for example. And it built those glorious buildings, like the Parthenon.

The Athenian system was also paid for by slave labor. Slavery was less prominent, less visibly prominent, less structurally prominent in Athens than in Sparta. But it was, nevertheless, an important component of the system.

Who defended Athens? Pericles did, the great leader, in his "Funeral Oration" in Thucydides's great *History of the Peloponnesian War*—the wars between Athens and Sparta. And we'll turn to Thucydides's history and that oration in a later lecture.

So we're going to pause for the moment and say that almost everybody criticized Athens, attacked Athens. Plato and Aristotle said, for example, that what was wrong with Athens is it did not bring the best men forward. They said government should be by *hoi aristoi*, the best. Aristocracy is not a bunch of people born privileged, but in the Greek sense, aristocracy is ruled by the best. Plato and Aristotle said it would never happen. Democracy's not going to bring the best forward.

An enormous treatise written by someone known as the "Old Oligarch" said that what was wrong with the Athenian system was that it lacked deference; it lacked deference for the great and the good and the important citizens. It was changeable; it was subject to demagoguery. You never knew what they were going to do next. Here was this call for stability.

Thucydides gives us many examples of folly, cruelty, perversity. He was giving the concrete examples of the kinds of changeableness that the Old Oligarch, that Plato and Aristotle and others had commented on. Thucydides simply parades the follies of the Athenians and invites us to reflect on them. And he does this despite being actually favorably disposed to Athens.

What must our verdict be? Athenian democracy has, after all—as I've suggested in earlier lectures—fired people's imagination for two and a half millennia. The Athenians demonstrated what a democracy might be. It remained for others to show how it might work, and for whom it might work.

I said that a *polis* is a political and a social institution, and we've talked a little about Sparta and Athens as political and social institutions. I also said the *polis* is a cultural institution. And in the next several lectures, we'll reflect a little bit on the kind of culture that a *polis* makes.

Civic Culture—Architecture and Drama
Lecture 10

Let's begin with the most public of cultural manifestations, the most public of art forms. In Athens, this means architecture and drama.

No art form is so public and communal as architecture. We know that at least some temples already existed by about 725 B.C. because Homer mentions them. In the Dark Ages and Archaic period, Greeks no longer built palaces as in the Mycenean period. Architecture was increasingly civic. Colonies usually built buildings that mirrored the ones of the metropolis. Peisistratus, as noted, initiated a building program in Athens. In the Persian Wars (490–478 B.C.), Athens was sacked and burned, and her public buildings were left in ruins. The restoration of peace and the revenues from the Imperial Tribute permitted rebuilding on a grand scale.

We may take the Parthenon in Athens as the finest example of a Greek building and as an example that teaches us a great deal about the people who built it. The Parthenon was built between 447/446 and 438 B.C., with its sculptures finished in 432. The chief architects were Ictinus and Callicrates; the main sculptor was Pheidias.

To appreciate the Parthenon, let's consider the basic elements of a Greek building. The key elements of a floor plan were: stylobate with colonnade or peristyle; interior chambers; passageways. The key vertical elements were:

The Parthenon.

© Anthony Haigh/Alamy

stereobate and stylobate; column (shaft and capital); entablature (architrave and metope). Note, too, the Doric and Ionic orders. These were the most common in ancient Greece. The Greeks knew the Corinthian, with its Acanthus-leaf capitals, but it was the Romans who popularized this order.

The building was in almost perfect condition until 1687 when a Venetian shell hit it. Fortunately, there were 1674 drawings of the sculptures *in situ*. Many of the best sculptures—the "Elgin Marbles"—are in the British Museum and a bone of contention. The building is more than 100 feet long with eight columns across

A portion of the Panathenaic frieze from the Acropolis.

the front, instead of the usual six, and 17 columns on each side, instead of the usual 12 to 15. The floors all curve outward to the corners; the columns lean in slightly. The building is huge but elegant and graceful.

The Parthenon has three great sculptural programs. Pediments (triangular ends) show the birth of Athena and the battle between Athena and Poseidon for control of Athens. Metopes have scenes of battle, both historical (Greek and Trojan) and mythical (Lapiths and Centaurs, Greeks and Amazons). The continuous frieze around the cella depicts—probably—aspects of the Panathenaic Festival.

The building was meant to make several points to and about Athenians. Its immense size was meant to be impressive. The cost of the building was to make Athenians proud and to make them accept the empire. The "Historical" (including the mythical) sculptures put Athens's long and proud history on display for all to see, embrace, and cherish. The unusual secular scene of the Panathenaia held up a mirror to the Athenians themselves.

In Athens, the other great public art was drama, performed in impressive open-air theaters. Citizens got free tickets. The origins of the word *tragedy*, which means "goat song," are remote and go back to wild celebrations in honor of Dionysus (called Bacchus by the Romans; think of a "bacchanal").

In tradition, Thespis (hence, "thespian") performed the first dramatic tragedy in Athens in around 530 B.C. The oldest surviving play dates from about

Corel Stock Photo Library.

470. We know the titles of more than 100 plays, but fewer than two dozen survive intact and all are by three playwrights: Aeschylus (525–456 B.C.), Sophocles (c. 496–406 B.C.), and Euripides (485–406 B.C.).

For Aristotle, whose *Poetics* is the world's first work of literary criticism, tragedy was a kind of poetry that was serious; written in beautiful language; dramatic, not narrative, in form; arousing fear and pity that purify the emotions. In sum, a tragedy is an elegant story of an admirable person struggling nobly against insuperable odds.

When we think of the Parthenon as a building, when we think of the poetic arts of the Greek plays, we see an interest in craftsmanship almost unrivaled.

Aeschylus wrote trilogies, one of which, the *Oresteia*, survives. It is an account of the fall of the house of Agamemnon and becomes a parable for the origins of justice. The trilogy was performed in 458, just when the Areopagus was stripped of its last powers in Athens. Aeschylus also wrote *The Persians*, the only play about a contemporary theme.

Sophocles abandoned the trilogy. His plays explored justice and principle and the consequences of right action (*Antigone*) and of just punishments for unintentional acts (*Oedipus Rex*). He reflected and participated in the deep philosophical debates of his day.

Euripides was unconventional in all ways. He adapted dramatic forms (for example, choruses were less important) and looked at the power of emotions—love, jealousy, and revenge. His plays show the disillusionment of Athens as the Peloponnesian War dragged to a sorry end.

Not all drama was tragic. There was also comedy. Tragedy was set in the remote past amongst mythical characters, even though it often commented in pointed ways on current affairs. Comedy was set in the present and satirized, sometimes even ridiculed, prominent contemporaries. Comedy could be vulgar, but it still had a certain elegance and grace.

The most famous ancient comedian, and the only one whose plays survive, is Aristophanes (455–385 B.C.). *Lysistrata* is a famous anti-war play. In it, the women of Athens stage a sex-strike to end the war. In fact, there are serious themes and social commentary running through the play. *Clouds* pokes fun at currently popular philosophers and scoops up Socrates, unfairly, into the criticism.

Public arts, then, provide us with three insights: the pride of Athens; the technical mastery of Athenian craftsmen; and the remarkably open way in which ideas were aired. ■

Suggested Reading

Beye, *Ancient Greek Literature*.

Biers, *The Archaeology of Greece*.

Boardman, *Greek Art*.

Plays by Aeschylus, Sophocles, Euripides, or Aristophanes.

Questions to Consider

1. What are the most prominent public arts today and how do they work in our society?

2. Is your view of, or appreciation for, art affected by knowing that it was often the result of intense contemporary preoccupations of a nonartistic type?

Civic Culture—Architecture and Drama
Lecture 10—Transcript

In the last couple of lectures, we talked about Sparta and then about Athens, two of the most famous and most important of the Greek *poleis*, the Greek city-states. We talked about them as social and political institutions. What I want to turn to now, in a series of several lectures, is the culture of the *poelis*. What kind of culture did these cities make?

If we think about it for just a moment, there are certain common features to the culture of cities, and then every city has distinctive features all its own. Boston is not quite like New York, New York is not like Los Angeles, Los Angeles is different from Chicago. Perfectly natural to us. And yet they do have some things in common.

Most of what we know about the culture of the Greek *poleis*, we know about the Athenian *polis*. So in certain respects, we can't really generalize to the culture of the *poleis* overall. What we know is really about Athens. And so let us visit that great city, and let's take several vantage points on its finest period, the Golden Age, the fifth century B.C., the classical period. Let's begin with the most public of cultural manifestations, the most public of art forms. In Athens, this means architecture and drama.

No cultural form is more public or communal than architecture. Great civic buildings are just there. We see them every day. We like them or we don't like them. We argue about them, we praise them, we criticize them. But there they are. And so, buildings can tell us some interesting and important things about the places where they are and the people who built them.

In Athens, drama is very important, too, and we'll turn to that in a few minutes. Homer mentions temples. As we saw in an earlier lecture, the Homeric poems probably took something like their contemporary shape in about 725 B.C., plus or minus a bit. So we can't necessarily argue from Homer, again we talked about this, as proving that there were temples in the Mycenean world. But certainly the fact that Homer mentions temples means that they existed in his time.

In the Dark Ages, and in the Archaic period in Greece, as near as we can tell from the surviving archaeological record, people no longer built palaces, and no longer built urban fortifications on the scale of the Mycenean period. Architecture was, perhaps, we might say, increasingly civic, but it served the civic purposes of these emerging *poleis*—public buildings where, for example, legislative deliberations could take place; temples, for example, where the people of the cities might worship their gods.

Greek colonies. We've talked about the Greek colonies around the Mediterranean world and how important that was. The Greek colonies tended to build architecture that mirrored the architecture of the metropolis that has sent them out in the first place. So, not surprisingly, we find not great palace complexes in Mycenean fashion, but rather temples and public buildings in the fashion of the dawning *poleis*.

Peisistratus, as we saw, built a considerable number of buildings in Athens, or was responsible for having them built. And partly this was to generate pride, to sustain pride in the city of Athens. Partly it was to put large numbers of people to work, but it does point to this civic context for architecture. And building buildings in a city, that we're going to enter into some kind of a dialogue with the people who lived in that city.

During the Persian Wars—I keep referring to the Persian Wars and keep promising that eventually we'll talk about them, but once more we're going to pass right by except to say that during the Persian Wars, the Persian army entered, sacked and burned much of Athens. So much of the great civic structure, the great civic fabric that Peisistratus had created, was gone. This, of course, then, left a remarkable opportunity for people of the generation of Pericles. The restoration of peace, then, and the revenues that flowed into Athens from the Athenian empire, provided the wherewithal to build these buildings. So there was will, there was opportunity, and there were material resources.

There were a large number of buildings built between the 450s and about 420 B.C. in Athens, a number of very beautiful ones. But the greatest, the most important, I think in many ways the most interesting of these, is the Parthenon. So let's talk about the Parthenon a little bit as a way of talking about a Greek temple, a Greek building, and we can learn a little something about the form by discussing the Parthenon, and then move on a little bit to ask ourselves what does the Parthenon tell us about Athens, and about the Athenians? How can we read this building as a contemporary document?

The Parthenon is the temple to Athena Parthenos, Athena the Maiden. Athena, not surprisingly, is the patron deity of Athens. The building is built between about 447 or 446 B.C. and 438 B.C. So, the basic temple itself is built over a period of about eight or nine years. Its sculptural programs, more about them in just a couple of minutes, were completed by about 432 B.C. This great building is put up in less than two decades.

In case you're interested, we do actually know the names of the architects who were most responsible for designing the building, Ictinus and Callicrates. It's a bit puzzling here because we can't confidently identify other buildings that they built, and yet they were so good they must have done other work. Their signature must be someplace else. The principal sculptor was Pheidias. It was he who did the great golden statue of Athena that was inside the temple itself; that statue disappeared already in antiquity, we have no idea what became of it. But Pheidias, the greatest of the sculptors in Athens at that time, was commissioned to make the great sculpture of Athena.

In order to understand the Parthenon, in particular, let us, in general, talk about the elements of a Greek building. Let's talk about the elements of a temple, the temple structure. Though the temple structure was a form of building that could actually be adapted to a large number of other uses. We're going to see this later when we talk about Romans. The basilica is basically a large rectangular hall, which can be adapted to lots of purposes. So, I'm going to be talking about a temple form here, but that doesn't mean that every building like this is, and only is, a temple.

The key elements of a floorplan—let us imagine a Greek temple's floorplan from two points of view. Imagine that you are standing on the ground, even with the temple and looking straight at it, but, like Superman, you have x-ray vision. So you can look right through it, you can kind of see how all of the elements work. Now let's hoist you up in the air in a helicopter above it, and you look straight down at it. What I want you to do is to imagine those two views, so that in a certain sense what we have are horizontal and vertical dimensions. And we're going to try to understand how these horizontal and vertical dimensions operate in tandem with one another.

We can refer to the main horizontal dimension as the "stereobate," and we can refer to the main vertical dimension as the "stylobate." Those are terms that may or may not be helpful as we go along.

Let's put it this way, a bit more simply. You build a floor. Now the floor may be built up several steps and several levels, and then you build a structure on that floor. The structure will generally consist, then, of this base, of this floor, possibly with steps leading up to it. There will then be a colonnade. We can call that a "peristyle." We have a colonnade that runs around the building, usually on four sides—not always on four sides, but usually it goes around on four sides. Inside that colonnade is one or more chambers. We call this the *cella*, the cell, the room on the inside of a temple. So that's the very basic structure. There will ordinarily be passageways around the inside of the colonnade, for example, and then perhaps inside the temple itself.

If we start to think about the vertical dimensions of such a building, the key vertical element, the thing we see most obviously, are the columns. A column consists always of two, and sometime of three, parts. A column has a shaft. The shafts may be smooth on the outside or they may be fluted, as we say. "Fluted" means grooved. The column may have a capital. Excuse me. The column will always have a capital. This is a more or less elaborate design on the top of the column. The column may have a base, a pedestal. This we do not always see. So you've always got a shaft, and you've always got a capital, and you sometimes have a base or a pedestal at the foot of the column.

The Greeks elaborated three basic ways of designing and thinking about their columns. In the classical period, the period that concerns us, the Doric and the Ionic orders were the commonest. Now, it will occur to you to ask, does that mean the Doric came from Sparta and the Ionic from Asia Minor? The answer to that question is a resounding maybe. They are named Doric and Ionic, and the Greeks certainly had a sense that this is where they came from. It is not clear that, for example, the Doric is born in Sparta.

A Doric column is a column that is very slightly fatter in the middle than at the top or at the bottom. It usually does not have a pedestal. It usually has a very flat, very simple, very unadorned capital. It is sturdy, it is vigorous, it is powerful, it conveys a sense of durability, of strength.

The Ionic order is rather different. Tall, graceful, slender, elegant columns. Always fluted, fluted very deeply with relatively narrow flutes. It always rests on a pedestal, more or less complex from one place to another. And it usually has a scrolled capital. It looks like a great booked scroll; perhaps you've seen pictures of a scroll. So you imagine laying a scroll over the top of the column, and that's what the capital of an Ionic column looks like.

A Corinthian column, more or less, in many respects, splits the difference, in terms of size, shape, and look, of a Doric and Ionic. It's not quite as heavy and massive as the Doric; it's not quite as slender and graceful as the Ionic. Its distinctive feature is an Acanthus-leaf capital. This became popular later in the Greek world, really after the classical period, and it was particularly favored by the Romans. The Romans built in Corinthian again and again and again and again. But we can say that the Corinthian was somewhat less in evidence in classical Athens.

At the very top of these columns, we have a system called the "entablature." The entablature is basically the horizontal dimension that sits on top of the vertical columns. Imagine this. The Greeks build in what we call post and lintel architecture. If you could hold your thumbs up about six inches apart and balance a pencil across them, you have two posts and a lintel. The pencil is the lintel. Lintels can, of course, run from column to column to column to column along the exterior, along the colonnade, or they can extend from column tops back to the interior walls of the *cella*. And in most temples, they did both things. On the top of those lintels springs the roof, framed in, sometimes in wood, sometimes in stone, often a combination of the two, framed on top of the horizontal elements that sit on top of the columns.

Those entablatures—as we call this horizontal business that sits on top of the vertical columns—the entablatures are important to us for a couple of reasons. They were very beautiful, they could be very intricate, they could be very complex. But they very often have flat, rectangular, sometimes square but usually rectangular plaques called *metopes*. And here, sculpture was put. Here, sculptures were put. Flat frieze sculptures were placed in these *metopes*. So the buildings have architectural dimensions, and the decorative dimensions of the buildings also give us certain artistic opportunities.

The Parthenon itself was in almost perfect condition in Athens until it was hit by a stray shell in 1687. The Turks controlled Athens at that time, and they were actually using the Parthenon as a powder magazine, and a stray shell from a Venetian ship struck the Parthenon, blew the roof off, and blew off a considerable part of the colonnade on one side, and left it in the ruined state in which we find it today. Fortunately, there were drawings made in 1674 of the building as a whole. But we had other reason to know what the building as whole would have looked like. These drawings were crucial to us because they show us all of the sculpture *in situ*.

Now, of course, that sculpture is scattered all over the place, and much of the finest of it, the so-called "Elgin Marbles," are in the British Museum in London. This has been a considerable bone of contention between the Greek and British governments for a very long time. So if you really want to see the Parthenon's sculpture, you don't go to Athens, you go to London.

The Parthenon is more than 100-feet-long on its two lateral sides. It's a very big building. It has eight columns across the front, instead of the usual six. It has 17 down each side instead of the usual 12 or 15. It is a very big building. It's meant to be big and impressive. The floors all curve slightly outward from a point in the very center of the floor. They bow slightly out towards the corners as a means of trying to defeat the ordinary foreshortening that we have when we look at a building. In other words, the builders of the Parthenon tried very hard to play an optical illusion on an optical illusion.

The point of foreshortening, of course, is if you stand, say, between two railroad tracks and look down the track, it looks as if, at a point in the distance, the two tracks come together and converge. We know perfectly well that they don't. Normally, if you look at a temple, it looks, as you're looking down the colonnade, as if the columns at the back are shorter than the ones at the front. By building the Parthenon with curving surfaces, an attempt was made to limit, somewhat, that sense of foreshortening. It's also true that the columns of the Parthenon, at a point about a mile-and-a-quarter above the building, would touch one another exactly over the center of the floor. This is a remarkable building, and none of that was designed in by accident.

It's large, but it is also graceful. It is elegant, beautiful. Curiously enough, as you may know, if you wish to see what the Parthenon actually looked like, don't go to Athens, go to Nashville, Tennessee, where there is a scale model of it built in stone—actually, it's built from concrete. But one can see it to this day, looking rather like it looked in antiquity.

The Parthenon has three great sculptural programs. These programs are meant to depict important things from the history of Athens. The pediments—the triangular ends of the building—depict on the one hand the birth of Athena, and on the other end the battle between Athena and Poseidon for control of Athens. Two great mythical historical events in the history of the city. The *metopes*, these panels going around the entablature, have a whole series of historical stories. Greeks and the Trojans, the mythical battle of the Lapiths and the Centaurs, battles between the Greeks and the Amazons. This was not uncommon in temple architecture, to have mythical scenes from the past. In Athens, not surprising, Athenian contributions are featured. And Athens is given a very long, very glorious history.

Around the *cella*, however, there was a continuous frieze, which is a little bit new. This was probably—there's some controversy among art historians about exactly what was depicted there. But I think the prevailing view is it is a depiction of the great Panathenaic Festival. In other words, here the Athenians are shown themselves now, not their glorious past. That's something interesting and important to think about with respect to the Athenians.

The building was meant to talk to the Athenians. It was meant to make points to them; it was meant to make points about them. Its immense size was meant to be impressive. The cost of the building was to make Athenians proud. To make them accept the empire. To make them accept the price of all the sacrifices which they had paid. The historical, including the mythical sculptures, put Athens' long and proud history on public display for all to see—for anyone who was a citizen of Athens, for anyone who visited the city.

The unusual secular scene of the Panathenaia held up a mirror to the Athenians, in which they could see themselves reflected. So, this was a building whose technical proficiency we must admire but which also was a building engaged in a constant and continuing conversation with the people who built it. That's one public element of the culture of a *polis*.

Another is drama. In many respects, the great public art at Athens was drama. It was performed in impressive open-air theaters. From the time of Ephialtes and Pericles, citizens of Athens got free tickets, another of the things the empire paid for. Drama, a course, a running.

Tragedy, the great dramatic form. What is "tragedy?" The word means "goat song." That's not very helpful. It suggests that the remote origins of tragedy go back to rather wild celebrations in honor of Dionysus, called by the Romans Bacchus, so if we were to think of a bacchanal, what kind of a party would a bacchanal be? One you hope your teenage kids don't have, that's what it is. So there was some kind of a primitive and rather wild, and perhaps rather wooly, celebration.

By the sixth century B.C., this began to be tamed a little bit. Tradition has it that a dramatist and actor named Thespis—now, actors are still thespians—performed the first dramatic tragedy in Athens around 530 B.C. So the classical dramatic form began to lose whatever its origins were in the goat song and become tragedy/drama as we would more familiarly recognize it.

The oldest surviving play dates from about 470 B.C. Here is a tragedy about tragedy. We know the names of more than a hundred plays. Fewer than two dozen survive intact. We know the names of dozens of dramatists. We have plays by three: Aeschylus, who lives from 525 to 465 B.C., Sophocles, who lives from 496 to 406 B.C., and Euripides, from 485 to 406 B.C. Our losses are enormous.

For Aristotle, whose book the *Poetics* is the world's first literary criticism, tragedy was a kind of poetry. It was a kind of poetry that was serious, that was written in beautiful language, beautiful, elegant, moving language. And it aroused fear and pity; it aroused fear and pity in a way that was to purify the emotions of the audience. This was the great catharsis, the purification.

Tragedy is, fundamentally, an elegant story of an admirable person struggling nobly against insuperable odds. It is not the ordinary and the accidental. It is not when a great promise dies in an automobile accident today. Aristotle would say that's not tragic; it's not even interesting. Everybody's going to die anyway. It is the struggle that ennobles tragedy. That's the key point.

Aeschylus, the first of the great dramatists whose works survive for us, wrote in trilogies, as we think other early dramatists did as well. Only one of his trilogies survived—indeed only one trilogy survives at all—and this is the *Oresteia*. The *Oresteia*, the play's about Orestes; Orestes is a son of Agamemnon. While Agamemnon was off fighting the Trojan War, his wife Clytemnestra took up with another man, partly because she felt that her husband had abandoned her, partly because her husband had sacrificed their daughter, Iphigenia, to get favorable winds in order for the Greek fleet to sail to Troy. When Agamemnon came back from the Trojan Wars, Clytemnestra and her paramour killed him. Orestes was now faced with the task of avenging his father's death. So, the three plays become a long meditation on the nature of justice, the nature of divine justice, the nature of human justice.

It is cast way in the past, and yet this play is performed in Athens in 458 B.C., four years before the *Areopagus* was stripped of its last powers in Athens. Orestes is finally tried in the third play before the Athenian *Areopagus*, except there it's a court made up of the gods. Bu the play is speaking profoundly to contemporary issues, to hot issues. This is one important reason why this is a public art. It's not only public because it happens in public; it's public because it engages the great issues of the day. Aeschylus also wrote a play called *The Persians*, the only play on a contemporary theme. He wrote a play about the Persians. The Persians had just attacked the Greeks, had burned Athens to the ground, and Aeschylus writes a play to show that the Persians are people, too—that they have the same homes and dreams and fears and aspirations as everyone else.

The second of the great tragedians, Sophocles, abandoned the trilogy. His plays explored justice. They explored principle. They explored the consequences of right action. For Sophocles, there is always a profound tension between "what I ought to do" and "what I want to do."

Let's just think of two examples. One of his most famous plays is *Antigone*. Two men, Antigone's brothers, Polynices and Eteocles, have fought in single combat before the walls of Thebes. They both died. Eteocles had actually been defending Thebes; Polynices attacked. So the king of Thebes at that time, a man named Creon, swore that Polynices' body was the be left there on the field to rot, was not the be buried. Now this violated Greek taboos of all kinds, but Polynices's sister Antigone said, "The gods command that I bury my brother." She goes to the king and pleads to be permitted to bury her brother. They king says, "No, I made a rule, you do not bury Polynices." She goes out and buries him anyway. The king is then outraged, puts spies to find out who did this, they track Antigone down, he sentences her to death; she is to die by being walled up in a cave.

What's going on in the play? What Sophocles is showing us is Antigone is answering to a higher law than the law of men. Creon is a man. He makes rules; they come, they go. She is obeying the gods; she answers to a higher calling. Now, part of what is tragic about the play is Creon's son Hyman is Antigone's paramour, and they are to be married. She kills herself, he kills himself, and Creon is disgraced, and the play goes on.

The more familiar play is *Oedipus Rex*, the story of Oedipus the King. This wonderful man, this good, kind, just man, who through terrible quirks of fate has killed his own father and married his own mother. And the blind seer, Tiresias, again and again says don't push it, don't ask questions, don't try to find out, there's more going on here than you know. Now this play is beautiful and brilliant for a lot of reasons. When you read it, one of the things to notice is all of the rope, tying, bonding imagery in the play. These people are tied; they can't escape.

Sight. Again and again and again, there is discussion of sight. It is only blind Tiresias, who at the beginning of the play can see. And at the end of the play, it is only Oedipus, but he's plucked out his own eyes, and he becomes blind who then can see. We're all blind as we operate, but the point is that Sophocles shows us this man and says he has committed great offenses and for these he must be punished. We would probably say there's not a jury in the world that would convict Oedipus. Sophocles convicted him, and that is the power of that play. And he's entering, as we'll see in a later lecture, into some of the great philosophical debates of his day.

Euripides was unconventional in all kinds of ways. He gets rid of the chorus, he writes trilogies, he adapts to dramatic forms, he adds more actors, he's very inventive. He also is responding to the great philosophical issues of the day. His plays show emotion: revenge, jealous, envy. For example, his play *Electra*. Electra is Orestes's sister. She also is outraged at the death of her father. But whereas for Aeschylus, the *Oresteia* is a great play about justice, for Euripides, the play *Electra* is about the sheer blind fury of Electra at the death of her beloved father. She reacts like an ordinary human being. No march of divine principle here, the rage of an individual person.

So Athenian tragedy, one of the great public arts of Athens. There was another, comedy. Not all drama was tragic. Comedies tended to be stories set in the present, not in the remote past. Not among mythical characters, but among people who live now. Pointing again, as tragedy could do, into contemporary issues. Satirizing them, ridiculing them, holding prominent citizens up to spectacular abuse.

The greatest of the comedic writers was Aristophanes. His plays could be vulgar, but also beautiful and elegant and written in extraordinary verse. Aristophanes lived from 455 to 385 B.C.; he lived through the Golden Age of Periclean Athens.

If most people are familiar with one of his plays, I suspect it's the play *Lysistrata*, which is the play where Lysistrata, a woman of Athens, in order to stop the Peloponnesian War, the war between the Spartans and the Athenians, persuades the women of Athens to go on a sex strike. The whole scene is absurd, but perhaps in the end you see the play is not meant to be absurd. Aristophanes is telling us something about a society at war. Contemporary themes run through the play. Another of his plays, the *Clouds*, pokes fun at contemporary philosophers, and actually quite unfairly scoops up Socrates into the criticism, and ridicules Socrates.

So these comic arts and these tragic arts tell us a few very basic things about this Athenian *polis*. This is a very open society. This is a society where you can debate, and say, and argue about almost anything. This is a society of spectacular technical precision. When we think of the Parthenon as a building, when we think of the poetic arts of the Greek plays, we see an interest in craftsmanship almost unrivaled. But there is also a sense of fun, and there is a sense of seriousness.

Now another of the arts, and we've hinted at this many times, so now it's time to confront it straight on, it was very public in Athens, was the art of history. And to that we'll turn in our next lecture.

The Birth of History
Lecture 11

What we can see in the best of these Greek historians is people engaged with the world of their day, engaged with the art forms of their day, engaged with the great intellectual issues of their day, speaking to their contemporaries, yes, and speaking to the future as well—to us.

What is history? Voltaire said that it was lies the living told about the dead. Henry Ford said it was "bunk." The Greeks invented it. What did they think it was? Greeks did not invent historical mindedness. This we see among Mesopotamians, Egyptians, and vividly, among the Hebrews. For the Hebrews, history was a way of revealing the unfolding relationship between God and his chosen people. In a richly paradoxical sense, history was also prophetic for the Hebrews: The past pointed to the future. That was true for the Greeks also but without the religious component.

The Greeks invented history as a specific literary art. But Aristotle, who knew a bit about literary art, said that poets would never lie, but historians usually did. He meant, basically, that poets capture real motivations, while historians haggle over mere details. The greatest Greek historians wrote down many details, but they also developed large themes about human life and conduct, themes that they believed to be universally valid. The Greek histories, thus, have an "epic" quality about them.

Herodotus (c. 485–425 B.C.) is the "father of history." He wrote a long, highly entertaining account of the Persian Wars, which he saw as the watershed moment in Greek history. Born in Ionia of a good family, Herodotus was widely read (he quotes Homer and Hesiod) and voraciously curious. He traveled all over the Greek world, to Egypt, through central Mesopotamia, and in the northern Balkans. He constantly interviewed people. He placed primary reliance on "what he had seen with his own eyes," but he also collated "what he had heard."

Why did he write? He was fascinated by how the Greeks were able to defeat the Persians. To get an answer, he decided that he needed to know all he could about the Persians, about the lands conquered by the Persians, and about how, exactly, the war had begun. For Herodotus, *historiai* meant "researches" or "investigations." He took something of a dramatist's view of his task. There were underlying causes for historical events but also immediate triggers.

When I say that the Greeks invented history, I am saying that the Greeks invented a particular literary form that we know as history, or that we have come to know as history.

In the case of the Persian Wars, Herodotus believed that the attack by Croesus of Lydia on the Persians was the proximate cause because it brought the Persians into Anatolia, then into Ionia. But the longer term or underlying cause was the arrogance of great states coupled with a certain inevitability in the clash between East and West, the struggle between slaves and free men, as he saw it.

Thucydides (460/555–c. 400 B.C.) knew and admired the work of Herodotus (he even borrowed from it), but he put the writing of history on a new path. He wrote of the Peloponnesian Wars. This was the great contest between Athens and Sparta, between the Peloponnesian League and the Athenian Empire, which lasted from 432 to 401 B.C. but had begun brewing in the 450s. His account stops abruptly in 411.

Although Thucydides's work is incomplete and unrevised, enough survives to reveal his working methods and his overall views and intentions. He viewed the causes as Sparta's inordinate fear of Athens, stirred up by some of Sparta's allies. He is cautious about Athens's rise to greatness but thinks the glory of the Periclean age was worth the cost of empire and the danger of war. Pericles's "Funeral Oration" is Thucydides's great statement about Athens. Yet war itself can cause a society such stress as to make its savage character emerge, to change the quality and character of its leaders. His account of the Mitylene affair reveals his thinking.

Thucydides was subject to many influences of his time. Like Herodotus, he was influenced by the dramatists, even down to his use of archaic poetic language. The medical writers taught him something about the etiology, progress, and diagnosis of political and social problems. Sophists (more about them in the next lecture) taught him about rhetoric, the power of language to influence people, and about the problems surrounding ideas of absolute truth and justice. The Melian Dialogue is his famous treatment of this theme. Xenophon (428/427–354 B.C.) carried on the *History* of Thucydides and wrote independent works.

Historical writing has been a key feature of Western culture since the Greeks. Partly to preserve accounts of great deeds. Partly to teach one's own generation "lessons." Partly to fashion and shape how later generations will see things. ∎

Suggested Reading

Anderson, *Xenophon.*

Connor, *Thucydides.*

Gould, *Herodotus.*

Questions to Consider

1. Do the essential criteria that the Greek historians set for themselves measure up to what you think a historian does or ought to do?

2. Are you tempted to read one of the Greek historians? Which one?

The Birth of History
Lecture 11—Transcript

In the last lecture, we talked about drama and about architecture as two of the great public arts of the *poleis*, and, in particular, of the Athenian *polis*. We're going to turn today to another of the public arts, to another of the public conversations that went on in these poleis. We're going to turn to history.

You may say that that seems a bit odd, a bit paradoxical. I mean, haven't we, after all, for the last 10 lectures, been doing history? Well, I suppose we have. What is history? Voltaire once said famously that history is a bunch of lies the living tell about the dead. Henry Ford said history's bunk. The Greeks invented it, so what did they think it was? What is the point of history?

Let's say right away, and I've made this point on two or three earlier occasions, as I hope you'll recall, that we can think of history as what happened in the past, and we can think of history as the way things are remembered, which, in a certain sense, means that the events of the past will take on new meanings, perhaps even change their meanings, as we reflect on them differently. That would be a useful thing to have in mind as we think about the Greeks, and about what they thought history was.

Let's be very clear. The Greeks did not invent historical mindedness. When I say that the Greeks invented history, I am saying that the Greeks invented a particular literary form that we know as history, or that we have come to know as history. When we talked about the Hebrews, for example, we saw that there was a powerful sense of historical mindedness among them. We also saw that its force was prophetic. You may recall my saying that, to some degree, the Hebrews imagined the past as a way of charting a future.

We also saw among the Egyptians a very powerful sense of historical mindedness. To take but one example, the recording of all of those dynasties of kings, one after another after another; you don't do that without a very powerful sense of historic mindedness. But for the Egyptians, this was a way of charting the authenticity and legitimacy of their Pharaonic rulers.

For the Hebrews, for example, unfolding history in this way was a way of revealing an unfolding relationship between a God and his chosen people. But insofar as one party to that relationship, God, himself, was rather beyond the realm of ordinary human experience; that made historical mindedness, or even history for the Hebrews, something rather different from what it would be for the Greeks. The Greeks were less interested, quite simply, in pointing toward the future.

For the Greeks, history was a way of understanding now; and then in the second place, it was a way of understanding certain fundamental elements that marked each of us and all societies. There's a universalizing dimension. We can say, then, that there are certain similarities between the Greek view of history and the Hebrew view of history. But that some ways, in the Greek view of history, the religious component is much diminished, perhaps even absent.

To repeat, to say that the Greeks invented history is to say that they invented a particular literary form. Was this a good idea or a bad idea? Aristotle, in his *Poetics*, you may recall in the last lecture we mentioned Aristotle's *Poetics* in terms of the definition of tragedy. Aristotle's great book of literary criticism, the first book of literary criticism, as far as we know, that was ever written, also addressed itself to history. Fundamentally, it's a book about poetry, although there, there is something interesting hiding in a word yet again. The Greek word *poiein,* means to make. A poet is a maker; the creative act is to make poetry. Aristotle says that poetry is a superior art to history because poets never lie and historians frequently do.

Now, I haven't been lying to you over the last 10 lectures, but Aristotle's point is that the poets seek for deeper, more fundamental, more lasting, and more beautiful truths. And they adorn them in more elegant language. Historians merely haggle over details. They try to get down what happened. I've often wondered if Aristotle had his tongue in his cheek when he said that. I don't begrudge him that he liked poetry better than history; sensible people have preferred poetry to history. But I'm not sure that historians only haggle over details, and I'm not sure that they don't, at least sometimes, tell the truth.

The greatest Greek historians wrote down lots of details. Of this, there can be no doubt. If you go to the library and you take one of these books off the shelf, or if you go to your local bookstore and you take one of these books off the shelf, Herodotus is at ease; they have big fat books. There's a lot of information in there. But the story is not, finally, about that information. The story is, finally, about certain large themes, about certain large truths about the way human beings conduct themselves, about why they do what they do. What they do is important, yes, but why people did things is vastly more important.

There is an element in Greek historical writing, at its best, that is epic. There is a sense of transposing the ordinary into the extraordinary, as it were, of painting a small picture but on a very large canvas. Of universalizing. Of saying I see these events in this place at this time, but I can derive from them this large principle about the way human beings act. That is the goal that is the aspiration of Greek historical writing, not merely to record. We could agree or disagree with the points that they make, and that may be something of what Aristotle was driving at. In other words, not telling the truth is not so much falsifying, but not hitting the unquestionably universal in the way he supposed poets did, and hitting the questionably universal, as he thought historians might do.

Enough of all this beating around the bush; let's talk about some Greek historians. Herodotus, born probably 485 B.C. or thereabouts, right in the middle of the Persian Wars, dies in 425. He's usually called the "father of history." He wrote one great book, a long—let me repeat that—a long, highly entertaining account of the Persian Wars. He saw the Persian Wars, Herodotus did, as a great watershed moment in Greek history. He saw this as kind of a defining moment in Greek history. In many ways, we could look back and say he was not wrong to do so.

Herodotus was born in Ionia; he was born, in other words, on the western coast of Anatolia, on the opposite side of the Aegean Sea from the Greek mainland. This reminds us that large numbers of important Greeks came from various parts of the Greek world. I've been stressing Athenian culture here, and that's legitimate, but not everything happened in Athens or was done by Athenians.

We don't know a lot about Herodotus. He was very well educated, apparently; he was very widely read. He quoted Homer. He also quotes the poet Hesiod, a little bit younger contemporary of Homer who wrote important poetic works. What is, I think, most interesting and engaging about Herodotus—and here what I would challenge you to do, or invite you perhaps, if you're wandering through a bookstore, wandering through a library, take Herodotus down off the shelf, open it randomly, and read five pages. You'll enjoy the five pages you just read. You won't have much of a sense of how the whole work works, but the point is that you'll enjoy those few pages. Herodotus is a wonderful storyteller, and is voraciously curious. He's interested in everything. There are times when we might wish that he had spared us some of what he learned. But in any case, there is this wonderful sense of wonder at the world around him.

In order for him to explain the Persian Wars, Herodotus felt that it was essential that he inform himself of the necessary background. So he traveled very widely. He traveled in Egypt; he traveled in Mesopotamia. He traveled throughout the Persian Empire. He thought that if the Greeks and the Persians are going to have this great war, he needs to know something about these people, and the world they lived in. He traveled throughout the Greek world. He constantly interviewed people. He tells us again and again and again and again that he interviewed people. And he actually, here, is very honest about these things. He will say, "When I was in a certain place, someone told me that," or he'll say, "Everyone there believes that."

This has sometimes been missed by people who read Herodotus. They think he's sort of credulous and believes everything. In fact, if you read him carefully, he's often saying, "Someone told me this," or "All the people in that town believe that," as if, in other words, to distance himself from what he's now telling you. He's saying this may not be true, but this is what they told me. But it may not be true. This is a very interesting, and I think actually, Aristotle to the contrary, a very honest component of his work. In the end, Herodotus said you can really rely most on what you've seen with your own eyes.

That raised a very interesting question, and it is one that we will actually come back to a number of times in later lectures in this course. Is it possible to write the history of the remote past? It would, for a very long time, have been said "no," because this Greek notion that "only what I have seen with my own eyes am I authorized to write about" was very powerful and very influential.

If he wants to write about the Persian Wars, then, you see, he has to travel through this world. He wasn't content merely to know about it at second or third hand, or to read about it. Why did he write? Lots of people have been interested in things, lots of people have been engaged by things, lots of people have been fascinated in things over the years. What prompted him to write about the Persian Wars?

Something struck him about those wars, and indeed, it is something striking about those wars. The Persian Empire, the mightiest empire the world had known, was defeated by the Greeks. Now, if you're a betting person, if it were about the year 490 B.C. and the Persian Wars were about to unfold and someone said get down your bet, you'd bet on the Persians. Every sensible person would bet on the Persians. You'd have lost your bet, but that would have been the only smart bet to make. But the Greeks won. So Herodotus was fascinated by this. How is it possible?

We could say: "Couldn't one ask the question of how a bunch of haggling, quarreling, arguing colonists in the East Coast of North America could, in the late 18th century, have defeated the British Empire?" I dare say we can, and we have asked that question. Roll yourself back to 1776; who would you bet on? You'd bet on the British. You'd lose, but that would be the smart bet.

Anyway, Herodotus was fascinated in this business of how it was that the Greeks were able to defeat the Persians. He figured this must have something to do with character. It must have something to do with fundamental underlying issues. Because on the face of it, the disparity in resources made it perfectly clear that the Greeks can't win. But they did. So, to understand character, he travels through the Persian Empire, he interviews people, he asks questions, he reads books, he visits sites, he goes all over the world.

He has in mind a number of things, but, in particular, he wants know why did this war come about? Why did it happen? What caused this war to take place? For Herodotus, the word *historiai* gives us our word history, and the word *historia* in the singular, *historiai* in the plural, in Greek can simply mean story. Any story we would tell a child, any story that we might read in the newspaper today, could simply mean story. But it can have some other registers of meaning. For Herodotus, it meant researches, investigations. So right away, that tells us something about history, that it's an investigation. It's not merely telling a story; it's investigating all of those things that would go into the story.

Herodotus took something of a dramatist's view of his task. The dramatists, you may recall from our earlier discussion, would take particular incidents, particular scenes, particular moments, particular characters, build a wonderful and introducing story around them, and then extract large realms of meaning from that event. In other words, dramatists did not actually tell stories; they didn't narrate a story from beginning to end. A narrative presentation of their account was not what they were striving for. There was something of that in Herodotus. He is a narrator, and a very good one, but he also fixes on moments, on scenes, on events, and he does it with a dramatist's flair.

So what does he want to know? Just as in every Greek play there is the climax, there is the moment when you've got up to the top and you're going to come back down, when everything turns, when everything changes; so, for Herodotus, he's got to find, as it were, the climax. Where's it going to be? In other words, why did this war happen?

He recognized that there could be any number of very long-term trends. But there also has to be some immediate trigger mechanism. He is putting ideas on parade, he is looking for character, and I'll come back in just a second to what those large character trends are as Herodotus saw them. But for the moment, the point I want to make, the point that Herodotus makes, is that, given these long-term character trends, such a war could have happened at any time. But it didn't happen at any time; it happened at a particular time. So why then?

After Herodotus thought about this for a long time, he said it was all because of the Lydians. Remember our Lydian friend, Croesus, he of the heaping up coins, he of the wealthy person? I've got to tell you a little bit about Greek oracles in order to explain this whole business with Croesus and Herodotus and so on.

Oracles were places in the Greek world—temples usually—where there was a seer, a person who could see into the future, a person who could tell you hidden truths. When people wanted to know something about the future, they would send to one or another of these oracles, and they would ask a question. They usually got an answer that came in the form of a riddle. One thinks that the oracles were in the business of hedging their bets, and wouldn't want to run off the customers by being wrong too often. But anyway, they would get an answer in the form of a riddle.

Croesus of Lydia was an ambitious fellow. He sends off to the oracle of Apollo, over on the Ionian coast, and he asks the question, "What were to happen if I were to attack the Persians?" The answer came back from the oracle, "You will destroy a great empire." Croesus said, "Oh, boy!" He attacked the Persians, and sure enough, he destroyed his empire. Not what he had in mind.

But in any case, from Herodotus's point of view, when Croesus somewhat rationally attacked the Persians, that brought the Persians into Anatolia. Once the Persians came into Anatolia, they marched right on to Ionia. They conquered western Anatolia; they conquered the Aegean coast. They conquered a world where lots of Greeks lived, and eventually large numbers of those Greeks were unwilling to live under foreign domination. They revolted against Persia; various cities on the mainland lent more or less success. Athens actually lent more success to the Ionian revolt than anyone else did.

The Persians, then, came to feel—once they had suppressed the Ionian revolt—that they had to square accounts with the Greeks on the mainland. And so, in two great campaigns, one in 490 B.C. and one in 480 B.C., the Persians sent their massed military might against the Greeks. And the Greeks finally struck them down, beat them off, won the war. So for Herodotus, the Persian Wars, the battle you see between the Greeks and the Persians, was actually occasioned by Croesus of Lydia's rashness in the first place. There was the trigger mechanism.

That's how he builds his story; that's how it has this dramatic moment in it. And it's plausible. Most historians today would probably say there's more to it than that. But Herodotus' account was plausible. It commands respect. What we can say is that it serves Herodotus to open his big themes. What are they? The arrogance of great states, states that do not bear their capacity to rule with grace and elegance and dignity, but want to throw their weight around. The Persians just thought they had to show the Greeks something. They had to prove the Greeks something. The Greeks were being no threat to the Persians, could have been left alone.

More interestingly, and I think somewhat richer food for thought, Herodotus saw an inevitable clash between East and West. All of his great travels led him to believe that world over there is not like our world over here. And these two worlds are not going to live in peace with one another. One suspects that for 2500 years, the unfolding course of history suggests that Herodotus may have been more right than wrong. And one suspects that only if that changes are we likely to have a very bright future.

Herodotus also saw a people in the Persian Empire as subjects, as virtual slaves to a great king, and not as free men, as he imagined the Greeks to be. So another of his great themes was the inevitable struggle of freedom and tyranny. His belief was that free men fight for things which they value, slaves fight for nothing, and therefore free men will defeat slaves on every occasion.

Herodotus collects enormous amounts of information, true. Herodotus has a sense that there are proximate and distant events driving historical forces, true. But in the end, he has this large sense of the great issues of history.

His younger contemporary, Thucydides, born 460 to 455 B.C., died in 400, knew and admired the work of Herodotus, even borrowed bits of it in the earliest section of his own work. But he put the writing of history onto a very new path. He wrote of the Peloponnesian Wars. This is the great war between the Peloponnesian League—Sparta and her allies—and the Athenian Empire—Athens and her subjects—that began in 431 B.C. and carried on intermittently, with sort of one end in 411 B.C., another in 401 B.C., and finally spent itself in the year 400 B.C.

Thucydides begins his account of this war, in good Herodotean fashion, back in the 450s B.C. He's really trying to narrate, how did this whole thing come about in the first place? How did we get ourselves into this fix? He thought, we've got to go back in time; we have to understand the antecedents of the war. His account, alas, stops abruptly in the year 411 B.C. He just didn't finish it. We wish very much that he did.

He himself was a highly educated, a widely read person. He was also briefly a general during the Peloponnesian Wars. So he had the experience as really a kind of hands-on participation in the life of Athens at this decisive time. Even though Thucydides's work is incomplete, and as far as we can tell is unrevised, he doesn't seem to have been able to go back and polish it up and tidy it up in the way that one would with a long work, his basic workings are clear. His overall views and intentions are clear. We can see, from what we have, what he was trying to do.

His view of the causes of this war—again, there are, in his view, certain inevitabilities almost to the struggle—he said that this war came about because Sparta and its allies were inordinately jealous of Athens, and that Sparta's allies stood Sparta up, finally, to start the war. We could go back and look through this period, and say that there might be plenty of evidence that we could adduce to say that the Athenians actually had generated about as much of this contention as the Spartans ever did.

Thucydides creates speeches and puts them in people's mouths. He tells us that he does not have to quote exactly what people said; he must tell what they would have said on such an occasion. And he creates remarkable speeches and puts them into people's mouths. This is his way, and this again is a bit like the theater, because the speeches in Thucydides are not wholly unlike the choruses in Greek dramas, the chorus that turns, as it were, to the audience and says, "You know what's going on up there, don't you? You know what they're really saying right now don't you?" There's a certain sense in which Thucydides uses his speeches to accomplish the same kind of thing. You see these public arts, and how there is even communication among the art forms. Thucydides is cautious about Athens. He's aware of the problems, he's aware of some of the stupid things that were done, of some of the less able leaders that Athens produced, particularly in the time after

Pericles. He had great admiration for Pericles, not much admiration at all for those who came after him. And he felt, basically, that the glories of Periclean Athens were worth plunging into war, and were worth all the other costs that Athens had paid to have this brief moment.

His "Funeral Oration" is his great statement about Athens. At the end of the first year of the Peloponnesian War, it was common for the leading public citizen in Athens—Pericles was the person at that time, the head of the Board of Ten Generals—to deliver a public eulogy over those who had died in the previous year's campaigning. Normally a person, on such an occasion, would give a speech full of pious platitudes about these nice boys who had lost their lives, sit down, and be quiet. Pericles got up, in Thucydides's telling, and praised Athens. He praised that for which the boys had died. He spoke of Athens as a school of Hellas. He said everyone admires us, everyone emulates us, the whole world comes to us, not to other places. Here, he says, there is a spirit of freedom and openness in inquiry.

It's an interesting and remarkable move, and insofar as Thucydides has already told us that he's inventing speeches, except insofar as what people would have said, he could have put any words he wanted to in Pericles's mouth. But what he puts into Pericles's mouth is this remarkable speech in favor of Athens, in favor of the cause for which these young men had died. Is Thucydides then somehow a kind of an unvarnished clack for Athens? Is he sort of Athens's great public relations agency? No, not at all.

If we call Herodotus the father of history, we call Thucydides the father of scientific history. There is something cool, cold almost, rational, calculating, detached about the way Thucydides can describe what happened in the course of this war. He recognized that war can generate, perhaps, the greatest stresses of any large scale process through which a society can go. It can make its citizens savage, it can render the quality of public life coarse, it can make leaders do unpredictable things.

His account, for example, of the Mitylene affair is one particularly vivid example of this. The island of Mitylene was over in the Aegean, over near the coast of Ionia. It had long been part of the Athenian empire. The Mitylenians wanted to withdraw their allegiance. The Athenian assembly met and had a vote, one of the popular demagogues got up and said, "Alright, that's it, let's kill all the men, and we will enslave the women and children." They sent the fleet to execute the charge. The next day, the assembly meets again, somebody comes in, cooler heads prevail, they say, "Oh, my heavens, we can't do that." They send a ship to catch the fleet. The ship actually catches the fleet just in the nick of time, and the Mitylenians are spared. But this is Thucydides's way of saying that there are wonderful things about Athens, but, well, there's this, too.

Thucydides was subject to many of the influences of his time. Like Herodotus, he was very much influenced by the dramatists. There is a very powerful dramatic element in Thucydides, in the way he structures his account. But there is also much in Thucydides that is dramatic, for instance, in his use of deliberately archaic language. How often do we see writers using archaic language to add sort of an element of, a hint of, authenticity to what they write?

The medical writers taught him a great deal. This was the time of Hippocrates, the first of the great medical writers. They taught him about analysis, about etiology, progress in diagnosis. There is something profoundly medical about the way Thucydides examines the Athenian body politic. The Sophists, and we'll hear much more about the Sophists in our very next lecture when we turn to Greek philosophy, they taught him about the power of rhetoric, the power of language to influence people, the power of language to prevail, the power of language to trump absolute truth, to trump justice. The Melian Dialogue is his famous example of this.

The island of Melos, which lays off the coast of the Peloponnesus, had always been independent, utterly neutral—the Switzerland of Greece. The Athenians went to the Melos and said, "You must join our empire." The Melians said, "Thank you very much, we've always been neutral, we're not going to join your empire." The Athenians said, "Well, actually you are, or else we'll kill you all, and enslave the ones we don't kill." The Melians said, "That's unjust." The Athenians said, "Justice has nothing to do with it. We have the power to make you do this, and since we have the power, we have the right to use it." The Melians said, "Where's the justice in that?" The Athenians say, "Might makes right." There's no good evidence that Thucydides believed that at all, but he knew that that was one of the great currents in the Athens of his day, and he laid it out that way for people to see it.

There were other historical writers later in the Greek world, Xenophon, for example. A prolific writer, he continued Thucydides's history of the Peloponnesian War. He wrote a history of Greece in the first part of the fourth century B.C. He wrote a book, sort of a how-to manual, for a Persian King. He wrote an account of a Greek mercenary army in Persia. Some have said Xenophon was more almost journalist than historian. He was not the literary artist that Herodotus or Thucydides were, and he didn't have the same elevated sense of fundamental principles and fundamental ideals. But he carried on and extended the Greek historical tradition. And so what we can see in the best of these Greek historians is people engaged with the world of their day, engaged with the art forms of their day, engaged with the great intellectual issues of their day, speaking to their contemporaries, yes, and speaking to the future as well—to us. One final context, then, that we must sketch, is that of Greek philosophy. And we'll turn to that in our next two lectures.

From Greek Religion to Socratic Philosophy
Lecture 12

The Greeks invented philosophy as a form of intellectual discipline, with its own rules, with its own system, with its own way of asking questions and of answering questions.

The Greeks invented philosophy as a particular, formal intellectual discipline. *Philosophy* is a Greek work, as is *philosopher* (it appeared about 400 B.C.). Conventionally, the history of Greek philosophy is divided at the person of Socrates (469–399 B.C.). In this lecture, we will consider the pre-Socratics. The Greeks were not the first to marvel at the world around them or to accumulate large amounts of practical information.

People asked why everything, or anything, exists. Early Greek poets had done this and had provided "cosmological" answers. On reflection, it was seen that all peoples attributed the coming-into-being of the world to various religious beings. Their answers were contradictory and conflicted with experience.

People also asked how things worked. This might lead to an inquiry into first principles or might remain at the level of "applied" knowledge. Greeks began to inquire into the nature of things that exist all around us and into the processes whereby they had come into being and by which they changed. Consider, for example, a seed that is planted, grows, bears fruit, dies, withers, and decays. What is going on here?

The Greeks also saw that explanations about how the world "out there" worked demanded some hard thinking about the process of knowing and the means of communicating knowledge. Three questions may be said to lie at the base of Greek, and subsequent, philosophy: What is the world made of? How can we know? And what should we do?

The quest for wisdom, according to Aristotle, and to most modern commentators, began in Ionia. This was a land open to Persia and, through the Persians, to Mesopotamian knowledge. The people there were familiar, too, with the Greek world and literature. Around 600 B.C., Thales of Miletus began to think about what exists and how it came into being. He decided on water as a primordial element. It is not clear if he thought that everything started as water and turned into other things or if everything we can see is somehow composed of water.

Some of Thales's successors posed other "materialist" answers to the question "What is the world made of?" Namely, earth, air, fire, and water.

Parmenides (fl. c. 450) said that being is one, motionless, uniform, and eternal. In this view, change was illusory, which was a response to Heraclitus's idea that change was itself, so to speak, the one immutable thing. But Anaxagoras responded that the mind was critical. Things existed to the degree, and only to the degree, that they were perceived. By the middle of the 5th century B.C., Greek thinking on being had been put on the path it would follow thereafter.

Nothing is finally right. Nothing is finally wrong. Nothing is absolute. This quest for truth is foolish.

As thinkers reflected on being, they began to turn to the problem of knowledge. We may capture this issue with four questions: What does it mean to know? Can we really know anything? What means are available to us for knowing? How is the world constituted, and how am I constituted so that I can know something about the world?

Initially, knowledge was equated with what I have seen, what I have experienced myself. (Think of Herodotus and his eyewitness reporting or of the diagnostics of the medical writers.) Soon, this extended to the other senses (hearing, smelling, tasting, touching). But sense perception as a basis for knowledge evoked severe criticism. Senses are unreliable to the extent that they are subjective. There is the problem of hearsay, or second-hand knowledge: I know something because you have told me.

With the critique of senses came a critique of language: Is language capable of capturing and communicating reality? One way out of the impasse was offered by Pythagoras (fl. late 6th century). Pythagoras formed a mystical brotherhood in southern Italy. His philosophy was based on the idea that wisdom came only from a life wholly dedicated to intense thought.

Pythagoras somehow came upon the mathematical relationships between the musical intervals (and, perhaps, the Pythagorean theorem, too, although one of his disciples may have discovered this). This suggested—like Anaxagoras's concept of mind—that material answers were insufficient and that human reason might discover and reliably communicate law-like propositions that pertained to reality, to the world as it actually is.

Bust of Socrates.

© Photos.com/Thinkstock.

After some Greeks had spent a century and a half of thinking about reality and knowledge, the Sophists turned to the practical matters of ethics: How should we behave? Sophists and sophistry have a bad name, not without some justification. Sophists were wandering teachers who for a fee—sometimes an exorbitant fee—would teach people the artful use of language. This was important in Athenian assemblies and law courts. This art was so much taken for granted that Thucydides larded his *History* with speeches. Aristophanes pilloried the Sophists in his comedies.

Sophistic ethics were based on a few fundamental propositions. A distinction was made between *nomos* (law, convention) and *physis* (nature, the natural order of things). The Sophists held that because society's rules were not eternal, not imprescriptibly right, not universal, they were matters of convention, and people could change them if they wished or flaunt them if they could. "Man is the measure of all things," said Protagoras. The aim is to prevail, not to be "right."

Gorgias posed the hermeneutic paradox: "Nothing exists; if anything existed, I could not know about it; even if I could know about it, I could not communicate my knowledge. At this juncture, Socrates appeared, desiring to vindicate reality, knowledge, and absolute truth. But the Sophists had left their mark indelibly, as in Thucydides, Sophocles, and Euripides (and Aristophanes, as noted). In 399, when Socrates was put to death, the future of the now 200-year-old Greek philosophical heritage was an open question. ∎

Suggested Reading

Brunschwig and Lloyd, *Greek Thought*, pp. 3–93.

Irwin, *Classical Thought*.

Lloyd, *Early Greek Science*.

Questions to Consider

1. If you hear the word *philosophy* what comes to mind?

2. Do any of the key aspects of pre-Socratic philosophy seem useful to you today?

From Greek Religion to Socratic Philosophy
Lecture 12—Transcript

We've been talking about the public cultures of the *polis*, and today we turn to one of the most durable of all the Greek inventions, of all the inventions of that remarkable institution, the *polis*. This is philosophy, the love of wisdom. The philosopher is one who loves wisdom.

The Greeks invented philosophy as a form of intellectual discipline, with its own rules, with its own system, with its own way of asking questions and of answering questions. This is a process that began to emerge, as we'll see, about 600 B.C., over in Ionia. It has persisted until this morning. It has not stopped.

We ought to clear up one or two possible misconceptions. If I say the Greeks invented philosophy, do I mean to imply by that that no one before the Greeks had thought that seriously about anything? Do I mean to say that people before the Greeks had not amassed large amounts of information? No, of course not. That would be absurd. There is a difference between what the Greeks themselves had done in early times and continued to do, and what other people did, and philosophy. That's the crucial point.

Generally speaking, before the Greeks, among other people, in other words, and even among the early Greeks, what we would think of later as philosophical explanations worked at the level of religion, and worked at the level of what we would call cosmological explanations. *Cosmos* means, in a sense, everything, the ordering and arranging of everything. Cosmology is the study of the origins and arrangement of everything.

A poet slightly younger than Homer, for example, whose name was Hesiod, wrote a book called the *Theogany*, in which he attempted to explain how everything got here. And this was attributed to wars and battles and contests among generations of the gods and goddesses, way back at the mists of time.

There's a very interesting comparison we can draw, for instance, with the first 11 chapters of the book of Genesis, where we also have a very detailed account of Creation, but not there because of quarrels among the gods, but because a god had a particular purpose in mind and arranged things for a reason. Arranged things, as it were, with meaning. So the Greeks had cosmological explanations, as Mesopotamians did, as Egyptians did. They attributed the origins of everything to something or other that the gods had done that was more or less understandable, and that happened a long time ago.

Slowly but surely, the Greeks began to recognize that all of these answers were contradictory, that all of these answers were different, and that many of these answers seemed to contradict plain common sense. Surely, the world is not as these poems describe it.

You may say, but what about the Olympian deities? What about the familiar deities of the Greek world? Do they play some role in this process? The Olympian deities, that is to say Zeus, and Hera, and so on, the great gods and goddesses who were thought to live on Mount Olympus. The Greeks, generally speaking, did not turn to their Olympian deities for understandings of how the world got here, of what their world was. They would turn to those deities—and they did this, for example, in Homer's *Iliad*, and they did this in Greek drama after Greek drama after Greek drama, and in other poetic works, too—as a way of explaining how societies work, how human emotions work, how human feelings work, how we are motivated to behave as we are.

But there's an interesting problem that we face in connection with the Greek deities. We can certainly read Greek literature and say that we know how the Greeks talked about their gods. And we can be pretty confident that we know that in talking about their gods, the Greeks were talking about themselves. The deities were, in a sense, a great screen on which the Greeks projected themselves, so they could watch themselves. But those deities were not asked to explain the origins of everything, what underlay everything. That is the turn that the Greeks made. That is a parting of the ways from religious explanations for things that is at the dawn of Greek philosophy.

Did Greeks, once they began inventing philosophy, cease being religious? I dare say those people in Athens, about whom we spoke in one of our earlier lectures, who built the Parthenon, who built the temple to Athena Parthenos, were not people who had abandoned religion. But religion played different roles for the Greeks than it would subsequently for them, and that it already and would continue to have for other people.

If philosophy means the development of a formal intellectual discipline, what do I have in mind by that? I have in mind, basically, the elaboration of three very basic questions. It was in posing these questions, and elaborating these questions, that the Greeks took this step of inventing what we call philosophy.

First question: What is the world made of? Slowly but surely, as the Greeks thought about that, and I think we'll see this as we go along, they were working in a realm much closer to what we would think of as natural science. We will ask something about why they would have started there, and how then, slowly but surely, natural science may eventually part ways from philosophy in the strict sense.

In the second place: How could we know? What is the nature of knowing? We can put a fancy name on that; that's epistemology, the science of knowing. What does it mean to know? If I say I know something, what does that mean? How do we know?

Finally, third question: What should we do? How should we behave? We can turn philosophy towards ourselves, and we can elaborate ethics and morals.

So, philosophy asked questions about that world out there, it asked questions about how we know, and it asked questions about how we know what we ought to do. It is in the elaboration of formal questioning and formal answering, like that, that Greek philosophy is born. And this is something that, at least in that form, does rise in Greece.

The quest for wisdom, the Greeks always drew a distinction between wisdom and knowledge. Knowledge is the accumulation of information. Knowledge is the accumulation of facts and details. Wisdom is a way of thinking that stands behind this, that informs this, that is basic to this. What we really want, in the end, is wisdom. This is a bit like saying, how many of us have friends who are enormously intelligent people and have no common sense? We might say very smart but not very wise. That's a rather crude way of putting the same point, but it's as if some people can be very, very well informed, and yet there's something lacking just a little bit in how they go about their business.

Aristotle talked about the rise of the quest for wisdom. He and most of those who followed him said we must start in Ionia. We must start among the Ionian Greeks, the Greeks who lived over on the Aegean coast of Anatolia. This was a world that was open to Persia. As we've seen in earlier lectures, it had been conquered by the Persians; it rebelled against the Persians.

Intellectual traditions passed back and forth very easily in that part of the world. It meant that this was an area which, through the Persians, was open to Mesopotamian learning earlier. There were great commercial cities in Ionia; people from Ionia traveled all over the Greek world, all over the Mediterranean world. So even if we can't trace specific ideas as having come from this person or this place at that moment, to another person or another place at another moment, it's a reasonable inference that Ionia was a very lively intellectual environment.

There, about the year 600 B.C., a man called Thales gets our story started for us. He began to ask questions about how things had come into existence. How had things come into existence? How did things come into being? Then he began to reflect, a little bit, on what's out there. If I look out through my eyes, what do I see? What is all of that? He decided that a way of explaining that was to say that water was behind everything. Did he mean that everything is made of water, or that everything had started as water and sort of became something else? That's not so clear. What is clear is that he was trying to find something that subsists, something that is behind everything, something that is permanent, something that is unchanging, something that is, in a way, the hook on which you can hang things.

To this day, if a scientist is to conduct an experiment, you've got to control something in order to measure other things against it. At the most sophisticated levels of science and mathematics, we're now learning how to control several things at once, and compare several things against them. But in a simpler time, you control one thing and you measure other things against it. In a certain sense, that's what Thales was intuiting. You've got to get something that stays put so that you can understand other things in relation to it.

Some of Thales's successors posed other materialist answers. We say materialist, not because we're speaking of Marxian materialism; that's not the point. They were looking for materials. Thales had posed water as this substance. Others, asking questions about what is the world made of, posed different answers. For example, one of them said earth, air, fire, and water.

Remember when we talked about Mesopotamian religion, we said that even if some of the answers that they gave, some of the conclusions they reached, strike us as primitive, strike us as naïve, there was something interesting about it in the way that they were trying to systematize the world out there, to put names on things, and to make sense of it. Let's think about that earth, air, fire, and water. Remember, this is at the level of sheer intuition. These thinkers are not working in great laboratories financed by companies or universities. They imagine fire as a catalyst, while earth, air, and water just about do cover everything, don't they? He almost intuited, actually, how things do work. Think of these things as a kind of a periodic chart of the elements in embryo. There's a remarkable piece of intuition here.

Another said fire, and others looked for the catalytic element, the element that forces things to move, forces things to change. They began to realize that one of the interesting problems they were going to contend with was change. How do you cope with the problem of change? What is change?

Parmenides, who really flourished as Pericles was coming on the scene in Athens, said that being—this substance that we're looking for—must be one, motionless, uniform and eternal. What that really represents is an attempt to add definition, to add substance, to add meaning to the very intuitive processes that had begun with Thales. We're really trying to give a little more precision to whatever this thing is that we're going to try to pin down in order to understand other things in relation to it.

So being must be one, motionless, uniform, and eternal. On this view, change was illusory; change didn't really take place. In a certain sense, and this is an issue we'll tease out in several different ways over the next few minutes, but right away what we can say is that Parmenides is actually answering one of his predecessors, a man by the name of Heraclitus.

Heraclitus's model, *mato*, was *ponterei*—that everything flows. He's the one who said you can't stick your foot in the same river twice, because if you stick your foot in the river, and you withdraw your foot, and you stick your foot in again, the river's flowed on and you stuck your foot in a new river. He didn't really believe that, but he was making a rather interesting point, that everything changes. For Heraclitis, change was that which was immutable. Paradoxically, the mutable was the immutable.

There are a couple of interesting points hiding there. We see that Parmenides responds—no, he's going to give him a material answer again—but we've got to have something that is one, and motionless, and eternal, and so on. The other thing is that we are beginning to see thinkers move a step or two past the idea that there will be material explanations for things. Because with Heraclitus, we've really got a different kind of answer. If change is the one unchanging thing, that's a very different thing than saying earth, or air, or fire, or water. It's a very different kind of answer. The question is the same, the aim is the same, what you're trying to figure out is the same, but it's a different kind of answer.

It was at that point that a figure called Anaxagoras comes along, and says actually the mind is crucial. What does that mean? What he meant by that was things exist to the degree, and only to the degree, that they are perceived. You've all heard, perhaps without thinking about it, examples of this: if a tree falls in the forest and there's no one there to hear it, does it make a sound? Anaxagoras would say no, because the sound must be perceived. For things to exist, they must be perceived. This is another interesting step from pure materialism, through the beginnings of conceptual attempts to grapple with the material; now to the grappling tool itself, the mind.

So now we are moving back and forth, in a sense, along a spectrum, from the world that is out there, and from the active intelligence that is in here. We're beginning to understand that the processes of thought, the nature of thought, how thought works, is going to be crucial.

In a number of important ways, Greek thinking on Being, the state of existence, what "Be" is out there, what is the nature of Being? The Greeks basically put that question, more or less, on the platform where it's resided ever since. We have qualified it in a variety of ways, and we've approached it in a variety of ways. Subsequent Greek thought will, in a sense, here begin to part paths.

The path that followed natural science will explore being in greater and greater and greater and greater detail, as an objective understanding of that world out there. Philosophy is going to travel on a different path. It's going to spend more time thinking about thinking. It's going to spend more time thinking about getting in touch with that world out there, and then slowly but surely, and under circumstances that we'll come to in just a few minutes, philosophy began to turn to what we would call ethics and morals.

That being the case, how do we know? Go back to that, our second question. How do we know? As thinkers reflected on being, they recognized that our senses, in the first instance, are the tools that we have. So, if we are going to ask how do we know, and if we are going to cope with the tools that are at our disposal for knowing, we're going to pose an agenda of questions, let's say, four. What does it mean to know? What does that mean? What is the nature of that process? Can we actually know anything? Is knowledge possible? What means are available to us for knowing? How is the world constituted? And how am I constituted, so that I can know something about that world out there? Am I composed in such a way that I actually have some capability of understanding that world out there?

Initially, knowledge was very much equated with what I have seen myself. You'll remember, perhaps, when we first were talking about Herodotus, the Greek historian, we said that, among other things, he said you can write about what you have seen. You can write about what you know yourself. He traveled enormously and interrogated large numbers of people. We saw, for example, among the Greek, medical writers who were so influential, for instance, on Thucydides, that close study and observation were crucial.

If we extend our thought just a bit, what I have seen, we're talking about one of our senses, aren't we, the sense of sight. Eventually, people began to recognize that we have four more senses: taste, touch, sound, hearing, and smell. So we have five tools, in a sense, at our disposal to get in touch with that world out there.

But is sense perception a valid or a sound basis for knowing things? Our senses began to provoke, among the Greeks, very severe criticisms. Is there an objective reality that can be attached to senses? Or are senses utterly subjective? If, for example, I listened to a piece of music and find it pleasing, that's an interesting problem right away. I was pleased. How do we understand that? Let's suppose for a moment that's not problematic, and you really basically know what I just said. But perhaps you will be pleased by a different piece of music. How has the sense of sound communicated valid and replicable information?

I like asparagus. I don't know if you do; lots of people don't. Does asparagus taste good or taste bad? If I said asparagus tastes wonderful, but you don't like asparagus, have I actually communicated anything to you? Have I told you anything? Do you now know something? You might say yes, I know that you like asparagus. So we've posed the problem, in a sense, of second-hand knowledge.

Suppose a blind person, and you tell the blind person the sky is blue. The blind person knows for sure that you have told him or her that the sky is blue. The blind person might think you're a reliable person, and they ought to believe you, and you're generally credible, and so on. But does that person actually know something, or do they know what you told? How much of what we know is second- or third- or fourth-hand, and is not personal observation, and is not in any meaningful sense objective and, in fact, subjective? So does all knowledge exist only in relation to me? Can only I know things? And you, and you, and you, and you, but that we don't know things? That's an interesting problem.

With the critique of the senses, there began to arise a critique of language. Let's suppose, for a moment, there are things to be known. Let's suppose, for a moment, that knowing them, getting in touch with them, is unproblematic. Clearly it is, but let's suppose for the sake of argument that these are not problems. Now I have the problem of communicating what I know. I have one tool to do this, language. You might say I can communicate in other ways. I can do it with painting; I can do it with music. This is entirely true, and it's entirely true that we can think of those things as language, as tools of communication. But the point here is that they are no less ambiguous, no less difficult, no less complicated than the language that is ordinary words.

Imagine a very simple sentence, "Dog bites man." That occasions no problem. Now use those exact same three words, "Man bites dog." It's only by a trick of syntax, of organization, that I've changed the meaning utterly. But the words are all the same. Do words convey meaning? Or is language a series of artifices, that may be designed as much to conceal as to reveal? Is language itself ambiguous, and communicates something, but how much? 25 percent? 50 percent? 100 percent? What is the nature of language, and how does it work to communicate what we think we know? Philosophy has begun posing a series of very interesting puzzles for itself.

In the midst of this musing over the answers to the three questions I posed—what's out there, how do we know, what should I do—in southern Italy, think for a moment about Greek colonization, think for a moment about *Magna Graecia*, the transition of a lot of those Greeks over to southern Italy into Sicily. And over in that part of a world, there was a thinker who had created a kind of a brotherhood around himself. This was Pythagoras, who flourished in the late 6th century B.C.

Pythagoras' idea, in a certain way he's going back to Anaxagoras, he's going back to the idea of mind. He's thinking that the only way we're going to get in touch with the world is to think very long and hard about it. And in thinking about the world, and using mind to comprehend reality, we're going to have to try to keep ourselves to the formulation of law-like principles that always work, that are replicable, that work again and again, that work without subjectivity. He feels that to gain true knowledge, one must live a life dedicated to intense thought.

A couple of examples serve very well to show what Pythagoras was up to, and the implications of his thinking. And some of these implications, we'll see, we'll encounter again in future lectures. He came upon, for example, the mathematical relationships among sounds. For example, the musical intervals, is what this means. If you pluck a string, and you pluck another string half as long, it will produce a sound twice as high. One can think of the finest piece of music that any of us enjoys, and it's actually pure physics in action. It could all be described mathematically. There is nothing subjective about this. Now you'll say wait a minute, the same bit of Chopin played by one pianist and played by another will not necessarily sound the same. That's entirely true, but what's happening inside the piano is all physics.

Are there some laws that are just woven into the fabric of the universe, and our task is to discover them? And the more of them we discover, the more we will know, and the more we can communicate? Because if I tell you that plucking strings or setting columns of air of mathematical relationships to one another into motion will produce a certain effect, you can go off and test it. You don't have to take it as second-hand knowledge. You don't have to take it on my say-so; you can go and check it out.

He does the same thing with his famous Pythagorean theorem, though that may have been one of his pupils. $C^2 = A^2 + B^2$, the rule for figuring out the sides and the hypotenuse of right triangles. If something like that, a fundamental human shape, a triangle, could be expressed mathematically, how many more things, perhaps, could be?

We come again to our friend Anaxagoras and mind. Material answers are insufficient. Pure ratiocination may help us out; we must somehow try to get above language. And if we can get above the ambiguities of language, and the ambiguities of sense perception, we may then be able to communicate reliably.

It's at that juncture, in Athens, with all of these problems in the air, that a group of thinkers called the "Sophists" come into place. The Sophists have had a bad reputation; sophistry has a bad reputation, and perhaps with some justification. One thing very clear that Sophists did was turn to practical matters. They turned to this world, the world we live in. The Sophists and sophistry, in a way, got their bad reputation because they'd actually started out studying language, one of these fundamental problems that we've just been dealing with. They start studying language, and there were people who ultimately worked out the rules of what we would call rhetoric. Now, we think of rhetoric today as somebody trying to bamboozle us. Rhetoric is actually a formal way of expressing persuasive speech.

Sophists were teachers, who, for a fee, would teach you how to speak elegantly, yes, but persuasively. That is the crucial thing. They would teach artful use of language for persuasion. This was important in the Athenian assemblies, where people made speeches. It was important in Athenian law courts. Think of Thucydides and all of the speeches that we talked about as being littered through Thucydides' *History.* We see that the playwrights, for example Sophocles, pillories the Sophists. We see that the comedian Aristophanes pillories the Sophists. These were the great issues of the day.

Why? What was so engaging about what these sophists were doing? To understand that, we must turn, just briefly, to sophistic ethics. The Sophists drew a distinction between *nomos*, which means law, and *physis*, which means nature. Law, they said, is sheer convention. You and I make a deal; we can change the deal. You and I make a deal; somebody else can tempt either of us to make a different deal with them. We do this according to our own convenience.

Physis, in the natural order of things, justice works this way. The race is to the swift; the battle is to the strong. Asking whether that is right, or whether that is good, is utterly meaningless, beside the point. That's the way the world works. Since the Sophists held, society's rules are not eternal, they are not immutable, they are not universal, they are mere conventions, they are subject to change at any time we wish.

Let's pause for just a moment and remember *Antigone*. When we talked about the play, and what Sophocles has held out, does she answer the eternal truth of the rules of the gods? And that's a literary convention, not a religious one, fundamentally. Or does she obey Creon, who has made these rules, who may make different ones? There's no question, of course, where Sophocles comes down on that, but this is one of the ways that these kinds of issues were played out for the Athenian public.

All right, so we can make rules, we can change them, we can flaunt them, we can chuck them around, we can tease them out. Nothing is finally right.

Nothing is finally wrong. Nothing is absolute. This quest for truth is foolish. This quest for ultimate reality is foolish. Man is the measure of all things—that means me. I am the measure of all things. I measure everything in relation to me. The aim is not to be right, but to prevail. I go into a court of law. I'm not interested in justice; I want to win. Justice is another issue entirely; that's for theologians and philosophers to worry about. Gorgias posed the hermeneutic paradox, "nothing exits." If anything existed, I couldn't know it, I couldn't communicate it. Everything is relative, everything is relative to me.

It's at that juncture that Socrates appears. Socrates wants to vindicate reality. There is something out there; it really exists. He wants to vindicate our capacity to know, and he wants to vindicate our capacity to communicate what we know. But the Sophists had left an indelible mark. They had, in a certain way, handed Socrates his agenda.

We'll see, at the beginning of our next lecture, that Socrates attempts to answer these questions, partly in the context of the Athens in which he lived, and partly through his pupil Plato, and Plato's pupil Aristotle, moved philosophy off the dangerous promontory on which the Sophists had left it. But the durable contribution of the Sophists was to have forced us to ask these nasty questions about the eternal and the momentary. The true and the seeming. Justice and prevailing. We've been forced, ever since, to formulate our questions in that way. How the Greeks answered those questions in the fourth century B.C. we'll see in our next lecture.

Plato and Aristotle
Lecture 13

First and foremost, how much of Plato is Socrates, and how much of Plato is Plato?

S ocrates was smug, pompous, cantankerous, and brilliant. An Athenian jury condemned him to death for corrupting the young. His death disillusioned many of his followers, but caused one of them, Plato, to dedicate himself to defending the master's teachings. Socrates wrote nothing and almost all we know, or think we know, comes from Plato's dialogues. Plato clearly defended much of his teacher's thought, but gradually, Plato's thought became his own. The starting point was that there is something "out there" that we can know; that we have the tools to apprehend that something; that, having apprehended that something, we can reliably communicate about it with others.

Plato (429–347 B.C.) was a consummate stylist, an influential teacher, and a wide-ranging thinker. He came from a wealthy and influential family and traveled widely. He devoted his adult life to philosophy, founding his school, the Academy, around 385. To begin with, let's review the problems: Change appears to be a constant, and stability, elusive; the senses are flawed tools of perception; language has severe limitations as a tool of communication; laws are human contrivances, not eternal regulations.

Plato addressed himself to two big questions: What is the nature of knowledge and what means do we have of obtaining and holding it? What is morality and what is the best form of human life? Plato was a prolific writer. His earliest works were in dialogue form, perhaps because this accorded with Socrates's teaching methods. Gradually, the works became straightforward treatises.

At least three things are controversial about Plato's thought. How much of Plato is attributable to Socrates? Did he use the Socratic *elenchus* and essentially demonstrate what was wrong with other views, or did he advance positive doctrines of his own? And did he have a coherent system of thought, or is Platonism attributable to his commentators?

In general terms, we can understand Plato's theories of knowledge and morality. In his *Republic*, Plato said, "We are accustomed to posit some one form concerning each set of things to which we apply the same name." The "form" is the very thing to which the name is applied. The form is invisible and is grasped by thought, not by the senses. Its relation to the named thing is as original to copy. Such knowledge as we have of the form is true knowledge and all else is mere "opinion." In the "Myth of the Cave" from the *Republic*, Plato came as close as he ever did to making clear what he meant. We can for purposes of discussion take two examples, a concrete one—a shoe—and an abstract one—love. Plato speaks of an immortal soul. This is eternal and has knowledge of the eternal, transcendent realm that it communicates to each sentient being.

They did understand, they had come to understand in a profound way, that world out there may not be as it seems, and therefore we've got some work to do to figure out how it actually works.

Also in his *Republic*, Plato reflected on the human soul before it is imprisoned in the body, on the embodied soul, and on the kind of state that properly arrayed souls could create. The soul has appetites, courage, and reason. Virtue, which equates to knowledge, is a proper arrangement of these three. An ideal polity, therefore, would have: farmers with all desirable possessions; soldiers without property or family (Sparta?); and philosophers who had such elevated understanding that they felt a duty, not a desire, to rule and whose desires did not attach to material things.

Aristotle (384–322 B.C.) came from the far north of the Greek world. His father was a doctor and had ties to the Macedonian court. At 17, Aristotle entered the Academy. He spent some time as tutor to Alexander the Great and lived in Ionia for a while after Plato's death. In 335, he founded his Lyceum in Athens. Aristotle learned much from his master, and the differences between them should not be exaggerated. Aristotle was a prolific writer but also a rigorously systematic one.

Marked by what one scholar called "inspired common sense," Aristotle based his ideas on observation and close study, not on pure thought. His earliest work was in zoology and his most durable, in biology. Perhaps we see here the influence of his doctor-father. But we can also see the long reach of the Ionians, beginning with Thales. Aristotle did not see change as illusory or as a proof of the contradictory nature of being. The fact that an acorn became an oak tree, for example, did not prove somehow that being became non-being or that being came from non-being. Change is a natural process that can be explained (alternatively, there is actually no such thing as change). Forms do not have existence separate from the things by which they are named. Reality is in the specific and observable.

Bust of Plato.

Aristotle had a profound love of order. He classified all sciences (that is, branches of knowledge) as theoretical (those that aim at knowledge), practical (those that aim to improve conduct), and productive (those that aim at making beautiful, useful things). He wrote on specific disciplines, such as logic, rhetoric, poetics, and politics. He believed that the communication of what is known (or knowable) depended on careful description. Hence, his "categories": substance, quantity, quality, relation, location, time, position, condition, action, and affection.

Aristotle also laid down rules for syllogisms as a way of testing propositions, which in turn, helped him to discuss both knowledge and communication. He classified 256 kinds of syllogisms, with only 24 of them valid. Thinkers had long understood that knowledge of being depended on causation—how things came to be.

Pierre Pellegrin describes Aristotelian causation theory this way: There are four ways in which something "is said to be" responsible for something else. In one sense, the responsible element in the statue is the bronze from which it is made; in another sense, a certain numerical relation is responsible for the octave; in still another sense, the one who has promulgated a decree is responsible for it; finally, the health I would like to recover is responsible for the fact that I waste my time at sports. ... There are four causes at work in nature: taken in the order of the above examples, these are the material, the formal, the efficient, and the final. The concepts of essence and accident, act and power, provide for his way of assessing being and (non-) change.

Ethics for Aristotle were habits that could be inculcated by careful training from earliest youth. The goal of life is happiness, which Aristotle equated with virtue. Man's goal is to be happy, not to know what happiness is. The virtue of the shoemaker is not to understand the concept "shoe," but to be able to make a shoe. True happiness is achieved by moderation and self-control. But every person is different, and some are "high-minded."

Raphael's famous painting *The School of Athens* has Plato and Aristotle walking side by side. Plato points upward. Truth, reality, and knowledge of them are not here. Now we have only vague hints or impressions. Aristotle points down (or perhaps right out in front of himself). Truth, reality, and knowledge of them are right here in this world, but we must study attentively and reason correctly. As Plato and Aristotle built on the foundations of Greek thought before them, so Western thought ever since has been built on these two pillars. ∎

Suggested Reading

Annas, "Plato," in Brunschwig, ed., *Greek Thought*, pp. 672–692.

Kraut, ed., *The Cambridge Companion to Plato*.

Pellegrin, "Aristotle," in Brunschwig, ed., *Greek Thought*, pp. 554–575.

Plato, *The Last Days of Socrates*.

The Pocket Aristotle.

Questions to Consider

1. In what ways can you see Plato and Aristotle responding to the challenges thrown up by pre-Socratic philosophy?

2. What do you see as the most significant similarities and differences between Plato and Aristotle?

Plato and Aristotle
Lecture 13—Transcript

This lecture is going to focus on Plato and Aristotle. You may recall that at the end of last lecture we had left off with Socrates. Let's pick up the story with Socrates and use him as a bridge figure to take us from the world of fifth century B.C. thought, particularly from the world left by the Sophists, and to move us on to the world of the great fourth century B.C. thinkers, Plato and Aristotle.

Socrates was an interesting person, in a lot of ways. He was smug, pompous, cantankerous and brilliant. An Athenian jury condemned him to death. Closely, but they condemned him to death for corrupting the young. His death disillusioned a great many of his followers, but it did cause one of them, at least, Plato, to dedicate his life to defending his master's teachings.

Socrates wrote nothing, as far as we know. Everything we know about him comes from Plato's dialogues that describe Socrates' teaching: his companions, his associates, his friends. This does—and I'll have a little bit more to say about this later on—pose the interesting question that we can never be quite sure how much we know about Socrates, and how much we know about what Plato wanted us to know about Socrates. Plato clearly defended his master's teachings; that seems reasonably clear. It's also clear that as time went along, Plato's thought gradually became his own.

What Socrates, above all else, I think, can be said to have defended—what was so important to him—was that there are things to know, or actual objects of knowledge, that we have the capacity to know them and to communicate that knowledge. That having been said, Socrates was not, himself, someone who felt that he knew everything, that he had all the answers, that he had all of this knowledge. Point of fact, to Socrates, he was wise only because he would admit that he didn't know very much.

This produced something interesting and important, at least in our literary picture of Socrates, and that is his method of demonstrating that other people didn't know very much, either. We call this the *elenchus*. It is Socrates' elaborate and cunning and trenchant way of questioning people until he had utterly befuddled them, and demonstrated that they didn't really know what they pretended to know.

It's not hard to see why a person like that was not especially popular with his contemporaries. Who among us would like to bump into somebody in the grocery store who came up and started asking us a lot of questions and left us a blithering mass of confusion? This would not make us happy. Indeed, Socrates did not make his contemporaries happy. But the point is, it raises the question: did he formulate a positive body of doctrine, or did he really poke holes in what was out there?

Most of what we know about Socrates, as I indicated, comes from his pupil Plato. Plato, born in 429 B.C., the second year of the Peloponnesian War, dying in 347 B.C., the middle of the tumultuous fourth century. Plato was a consummate stylist. He's a beautiful, beautiful writer, an engaging writer. There is something seductive about reading Plato. He was a wide-ranging thinker; he was interested in an enormous array of problems. He came from a wealthy and influential family, he had traveled widely, he devoted most of his adult life to philosophy. It's important to say that he had the means to do so. He was able to lead kind of a leisured life.

In about 385 B.C., he founded his Academy—his school—and hence, people who study are ever after "academics." Plato could probably have had a distinguished public career in Athens. He probably could have held high public office and won the esteem of his fellow citizens in that way. It appears that he went off to a private life of study because he was so disillusioned over the death—the execution, indeed—at the hands of the Athenian institutions of his master, Socrates. And so he tells us that he dedicated his life to defending his master's teachings. We'll see, as we go along here, what we ought to think about that proposition.

Let's quickly review where philosophy had got itself to, at the moment when the Sophists were on the scene, when Socrates was on the scene, when Plato was becoming disillusioned and withdrawing from public life. Change appears to be a constant; stability is elusive; everything around us seems to be changing all the time. The senses are flawed. They are very flawed tools of perception. Language has severe limitations as a tool of communication.

Laws are mere human contrivances and not eternal verities, eternal regulations. That's the past, that's where things stand, that's the problem that you've got to solve—or the series of problems.

All is not negative because we can also say that if all of that is the red ink in the ledger, we can put some black ink in that ledger, too. The Greeks had demonstrated, in a very sophisticated way, that appearances could be deceiving. This was not something that then caused them to fly off in anguish at their inability to know anything. Socrates wasn't anguished, Plato wasn't anguished, as we'll see. They did understand, they had come to understand in a profound way, that world out there may not be as it seems, and therefore we've got some work to do to figure out how it actually works.

Second, and even more important, through its elaboration of epistemology—through its elaboration of thinking about thinking—the Greeks built into the western tradition an internal critique. The western tradition is virtually unique in providing positive doctrine and a large technical methodology for qualifying, analyzing, questioning, exploring that doctrine. This is a remarkable achievement, to spawn doctrine and all the tools to test it, and possibly to prove it wrong. This is quite remarkable, and that was there already by the time Socrates had come on the scene.

Plato wants to defend his master's teachings. In a sense, in doing this, he poses two big kinds of questions: what is the nature of knowledge, and what means do we have of obtaining it? We can see how that question is rooted in the experience of fifth century Athens. Second, what is morality and the best form of human life? How should we live? There's a very powerful, practical dimension to Plato's thinking.

Plato was a prolific writer; that's one of the interesting and challenging things about him. You go stand before all of Plato's books, and they make a pretty long shelf. That's a lot of writing to get to grips with. His earliest works were in dialogue form, possibly because this accorded with Socratic teaching. It may have been that he used the dialogue because that's the way his master had taught, and if he wants to defend and to advance his master's teaching, he'll do it in the form that his master had used. It could have been sheer literary contrivance from the very beginning. It just may have been his particular style. Slowly but surely, though, over the long period of time when Plato wrote, his works become more and more straightforward treatises, with the dialogue element almost absent—and sometimes, indeed, absent completely.

There are some things that are a bit controversial about Plato's writings. We could go on at great length about these things. I want to just notice briefly some of the controversies that surround Plato's writings. First and foremost, how much of Plato is Socrates, and how much of Plato is Plato? The honest answer is that we'll never know. My inclination is to say the early Platonic dialogues, the *Apology* for example—the remarkable discussion of Socrates' trial before an Athenian jury—there's probably a lot of Socrates there. And slowly but surely, I think it's safe to say, the dialogues become Plato himself, and they are no longer really his teacher. But we're never really going to know.

\Second, did Plato use the Socratic *elenchus*, or did he formulate positive doctrine of his own? We never see Plato, as it were, wandering around the Athenian *agora,* questioning people. But the *elenchus* can be a public rhetorical art or a private one that's put on the page. The point here, quite simply, is, "Is Plato always playing defense?" Is he defending against positions of other thinkers, other philosophers, other writers and, in a sense, showing what's wrong with them without actually formulating a positive doctrine of his own? Or does he actually lay out his own ideas? My inclination there is to say he does both, but, finally, there is more of the latter than of the former.

Finally, and we can put this paradoxically; was Plato a Platonist? You all think I've taken leave of my senses. Of course, Plato was a Platonist, what else would he be? The question is important for this reason. Did Plato have a systematic approach to knowledge, a systematic approach to ideas? Is there kind of a red thread that runs through his thought? Is there a kind of a Platonism that underlies, that undergirds, the foundation on which all of what Plato said is built? Or, is Platonism something that is actually developed by those in later times who commented on Plato, the people who analyzed Plato? Did they reassemble and repackage his thought? Did they find order and system there which Plato had not built in in the first place? In other words, was Platonism invented after Plato, or was Platonism indeed invented by Plato himself? My inclination there is to say that, once again, that both things are true. There is a certain core of ideas that are unquestionably Plato's. There is also a systematizing of those ideas that is clearly attributable to those who came after him.

In germinal terms, what we can try to do is understand Plato's theories of knowledge and of morality. Remember, he's asking these two big areas of questions: what's going on our there in the world, and how can we know about it? And what's the moral life, what's the best life to live? I've said that Plato wrote a very great deal. We could talk about many more things. But I'm just going to pursue these two issues a little bit, partly to see what Plato said about them, and partly to get a feel for how Plato went about his business, how he actually worked his way through problems philosophically.

First of all, then, let's turn to the world out there, and how Plato understands how we're going to think about the world out there, how we're going to talk about knowledge, and how we're going to talk about communication. In his *Republic*, Plato said we are accustomed to posit some one form, concerning each set of things to which we apply the same name. The form is the very thing to which the name is applied.

If that sounds abstract and difficult to grasp, think of it this way. If you're in a position where you can do so, look at a chair. Now ask yourself if you have, in any other room of your house or your office—wherever you might be—another chair just like that. Is there a chair just like that in your neighbor's house? Is there a chair just like that in your colleague's office? Have you ever seen a chair like that before? Is there a chair like that in your grandmother's house? All these things are chairs, but they're all different. What is it that makes them chairs? You might say, "Because you can sit on them." Well, I can sit on a table; that's not a chair. I can sit on the ground; that's not a chair. A functional answer won't help us. I see all of these objects and somehow my mind says "chair." I don't have any problem with that. And yet these things are all, really, quite different.

What I have in mind is the form, is the idea that lurks behind all of these visible things in the tangible world that we speak of as, in this instance, chairs. That's really what is involved. The form is invisible; it's grasped by thought. It's grasped in the mind. Its relation to the named thing is as original to copy. The Greek word *karakter* is a very interesting word. You think of someone's character, this is the imprint of their soul; this is what they really are. But *karakter* in Greek is, for example, the very word you would use if suppose I had a die, and I put a flat piece of metal on it and I put the upper die over it and I struck it to make a coin. I then have on that coin a *karakter*, an image impressed by the die. That is what *karakter* means.

The idea of object in the real world in form is of original to copy. The form exists in our mind. Now think—I think this is very clever—he has gone back to those earlier Greek thinkers who have said ratiocination—thought, mind—is actually the active, energetic agent here. There are real things out there in the world, confusing and unalike and complex though they may be, that conform in some sense to this idea that is in our mind. Such knowledge as we have of the form is true knowledge. Everything else, Plato says, is mere opinion.

Plato spells this out for us as clearly as he ever does in the "Myth of the Cave," or the "Allegory of the Cave," from his *Republic*. Perhaps you've heard this story before, perhaps not, but it bears repeating. Imagine a cave. You have a group of people who are chained down in the cave, and they are in a place of relative darkness. Behind them and perhaps above them there is sort of a pathway, a passageway, a walkway. In front of them, there is a great wall. Up near that passageway, there is a fire, a light source. And up there, various people are moving back and forth and carrying various objects, and they are projecting onto this wall, in front of these people who are chained in the cave, images—of course, shadows. This is Plato's image for the way we function in the real world.

We see shadows, we see hints, we see suggestions, we see intimations. But those people are up there on the pathway. They are carrying real things around. Reality exists, but it is not in what we actually see around us. This is not for fault of our knowledge; it's not for fault of our sense. It's because the nature of reality in the world around us is as copy to original. Plato has moved truth, he has moved reality, to a transcendent realm. He imagines, for example, that if a person were to come up out of the cave and actually to see one of these things, one of these forms, for the first time, he wouldn't recognize it. He wouldn't know what it was; he'd never seen it that way before.

Platonisms are more familiar to us than we might think. When St. Paul says, "Now we see as but through the glass darkly, then face to face," that is pure Plato. He's talking to his contemporaries in language they understand. Here, nothing is finally real or true. There, all is real and true. Then we will understand; now we do not. This is exactly the way Plato made his point. He has salvaged reality, and he has salvaged our capacity to communicate something about reality. The price he paid for that was to move that reality to an abstract world, to a transcendent world.

For purposes of discussion, we could use a couple of examples; we could go back to the chairs that I was talking about before. You could take a shoe—or look at the shoe you're wearing now—and think of the other shoes that you have in your closet at home, and think of the shoes that your husband, your wife, your partner, your friend, your children have. Think of the shoes that your friends have. Lots of different things that we call shoes. Some of them are boots. They're things we put on our feet. I can put boots on my feet, I put slippers on my feet, I put shoes on my feet. What I have in mind, to be silly but helpful, is a notion of "shoeness." I have in mind a notion of "shoeness." I know what a shoe is, more or less.

We can take something different, if we want to come, for instance, to the question of language. Imagine love. Seemingly unproblematic—not that love itself is unproblematic, but the word. You might say, "I love my life." And I say, "I love a good meal," and "I love the novels of a certain author," and "I love a nice bottle of wine," and "I love the Notre Dame football team." I daresay none of those statements occasioned any confusion. You understood me. But I suspect that, for example, the love I feel for my wife and the love I feel for the Notre Dame football team are not the same thing—and may actually cause some trouble once in a while. But that's quite a different matter, indeed. Presumably, my love for novels and my love for wine are rather different. What is this thing "love?" I have a notion, as it were, of "loveness," of which I see in the world many imperfect manifestations. But there is, finally, this thing, love. It exists, and I can communicate something about it.

Plato speaks in various places of an immortal soul, which is eternal, which has knowledge of the eternal, which has knowledge of the transcendent world. Somehow, it communicates that hint, that spark of knowledge to each person, because otherwise you would certainly be asking yourself, "How do I know anything about this transcendent world? Where do I get this idea of 'shoeness' or 'chairness' or 'loveness?' Where does that come from?" It comes, in some vague sense—Plato is not very clear about this—through this world soul. In the *Republic*, Plato also reflects a bit on the human soul before it's imprisoned in a body, on the kind of state that properly arrayed souls might produce.

Now, turn to the question of what's the moral life. Plato thinks a bit about the soul, and he says that it has certain very basic characteristics. A soul has mind, intelligence, knowledge, *gnosi*. A soul has courage, the capacity to look out for one's interests, the capacity to defend oneself. And finally, the soul has appetites. It wants things. It wants food, shelter, companionship, things. So Plato says this would be more or less typical of any soul, if it has these three qualities.

Virtue, in Plato's scheme of things, equates to knowledge. To know this is to be virtuous. By extension, it is a proper arrangement, for instance, if we're talking about the soul of these three qualities: of reason, of courage, and of appetites. So an ideal polity would have farmers, persons marked fundamentally by appetites. The essential characteristic which they possess is appetites; and they would be permitted to own all of the property, to have all of the fine things. In the second place, soldiers, people endowed particularly with courage; and they would defend the community. Did he have Sparta in mind when he was thinking about a property-less class of soldiers, whose role is sort of corporately to defend the society? It's an interesting question, and it's hard to say. Finally, philosophers, who have such an elevated understanding that they felt a duty, not a desire, to serve those—by leading—who were committed to material things and to the exercise of physical skills.

The point is that no one of us, as we exist in the world, is arrayed in just this way. We are each imperfect manifestations of this transcendent soul, which would have three qualities—of reason, courage, and appetites—absolutely, properly arranged. He says an ideal state would be one that matched this ideal soul. Is there a state like that? No. Has there ever been one? No. Could there be? Yes, because we could study this, we could understand this and we could do it. But we're not likely to do so.

Plato's greatest pupil—he had many—his greatest pupil was Aristotle. Aristotle came from the far north of the Greek world. His father was a doctor and had important ties to the Macedonian Court. We'll talk more about the Macedonians in the next lecture. At 17, Aristotle entered Plato's Academy. He spent some time, also, as tutor to Alexander the Great. He lived in Ionia for a while, after Plato's death. In about 335 B.C., he founded his own school, the Lyceum in Athens. Today, still, in France, a school is a *lycee*.

Aristotle learned a great deal from his master, and the differences between them should not be exaggerated, as has sometimes been the case in the past. Aristotle, like his master Plato, was a prolific writer, and also a rigorously systematic one, and also not a particularly elegant one. It is easiest to describe Aristotle's prose as a drum solo, when the drummer has one stick. Thump, thump, thump, thump, and it goes on. Now, I've probably offended all of the Aristotelians among you, but reading Aristotle is not the same pleasurable experience as reading Plato.

Aristotle is marked by what one scholar called "inspired common sense." He based his ideas on close observation and study, not on pure thought. His earliest important work, for example, was in zoology. His most durable work, in the long run, was in biology, which has been the despair of every high school student for 200 years. Perhaps we see there the influence of his father, the doctor. Hard to say. We can also see the long reach of the Ionians, beginning with Thales. Aristotle returns, in a way, to that world out there, in a way, that Plato spent most of his time on the world in here—the world in our heads. Aristotle turns back to the world out there.

Aristotle did not see change as illusory. He didn't see change as proof of the contradictory nature of being—that, for example, if you plant an acorn, you get an oak tree. Aristotle says this is a perfectly natural process. This is not change. I don't have to explain that. Now, if I planted an acorn and grew a donkey, I would have a serious problem. I would now have a change, and

I'd have something to explain. Earlier Greek thinkers had reflected on, for instance, planting a seed. If I plant a seed, it grows, it bears fruit, it withers, it dies, it decays. There seemed to be a progression, there seemed to be a cycle here. Was this change? Was this natural? Was this something that required explanation or not?

The problem of change—or perhaps you'll recall my saying the problem of motion—was one that taxed the pre-Socratic philosophers in Greece, all of those before Socrates, considerably. Aristotle says it's a non-problem if you understand things correctly. Change is a natural process, and we can explain it. He would have said, alternatively, there's actually no such thing as change.

Forms, he would have said, Plato's forms, have no existence separate from the things by which they are named. A chair is a chair is a chair is a chair. There's no such thing as "chairness." We don't need that. What he's really saying is we don't need that concept. What we do is study closely things around us, and eventually we'll realize that we've got a whole lot of things that we can call chairs, and that they aren't tables, that they aren't other kinds of things. Reality exists in the specific and the observable, but this requires close observation. Here he's very much like Herodotus, isn't he? I know what I've seen myself. Here he's very much like the medical writers. Well, his father was a doctor. Again, close observation.

He had a profound love of order. For example, Aristotle classified all kinds of sciences, and he said that there are various branches of knowledge. There are the theoretical—those that aim at knowledge, purely. Practical—those that aim to improve conduct, productive. Those that aim at making beautiful and useful things. So he takes everything we know, and he begins carving it up. He wrote on specific disciplines: he wrote on logic, rhetoric, poetics, politics. He divides these things up, observes them closely, understands the rules by which each one operates, understands the vocabulary that attaches to each one of them. You see no "chairness," no "shoeness." Let's look at shoes; let's look at chairs. That's the difference here.

He believed that communication of what is known or knowable depends on careful description. Aristotelian description can be one of the most complicated elements of this philosophy—or, actually, one of the simplest. He developed ten categories, and what it basically says is that these categories are elements of the description of anything that exists. What do I have in mind? Substance, quantity, quality, relation, location, time, position, condition, action and affection. I won't repeat that long list—I don't expect you to remember it. But what I will invite you to think about is Aristotle's mania for describing things precisely.

He laid down the rules for syllogisms, the most elementary tools of logic. How do you actually demonstrate that something is true? How do you prove that something is not true? Indeed, in classifying syllogisms, all men are mortal: Socrates is a man; Socrates is mortal. That syllogism works. He thinks that syllogisms communicate knowledge, and what he does, basically, is study over 200 of these, and finds, in the end, that there's only about 24 that are actually valid.

Aristotle also has had to think about these large problems that have been plaguing his contemporaries for a long time. He's worried, for instance, about causation. What makes things enter on the processes, which look like change to others? The French scholar Pierre Pellegrin describes Aristotelian causation theory this way. Just let me just quote a very brief line:

> There are four ways in which something 'is said to be' responsible for something else. In one sense, the responsible element in the statue is the bronze from which it is made; in another sense, a certain numerical relation is responsible for the octave; in still another sense, the one who has promulgated a decree is responsible for it; finally, the health I would like to recover is responsible for the fact that I waste my time at sports. ... There are four causes at work in nature: taken in the order of the above examples, these are the material, the formal, the efficient, and the final.

What Aristotle is able to do is lay out a series of explanations for what looked to others like change, for what looked to others like motion.

In the process of all of this, Aristotle—and we may perhaps leave him with this notion—said that the virtue of a shoemaker is to make a good shoe, not to know what a shoe is. There are certain modern designers who would do well to go to school on that proposition. In Rafael's great painting, *The School of Athens*, in a sense a comment on all of Western thought, Plato points up. Reality is there, beyond us, someplace. Aristotle points straight out, perhaps down a bit. Reality is here, in our midst. And this has been not a parting of the ways, but the two paths along which the quest of knowledge has proceeded for 2500 years, thanks to a process that began on the Ionian coast.

The Failure of the Polis and the Rise of Alexander
Lecture 14

Suffice it to say ... that the 4th century B.C., the period after the Peloponnesian War, was an extremely difficult period for the Greek world. Eventually, the Greek world fell to the Macedonians to the north.

The 4th century was a terribly difficult time for the Greek world, but the difficulties were not unprecedented. During the Persian Wars, there were quarrels over strategy and some Greek cities *medized*, went over to the enemy. During the Peloponnesian Wars, most of the Greek world was dragged into the battle. Brutality became a way of life. Sparta won and threw out the Athenian democracy, but the Thirty Tyrants quickly discredited themselves, and a more moderate democracy was restored. To finish off the war against the sea-wise Athenians, the Spartan landlubbers turned to Persia, the ancient enemy.

For a generation, the Spartans, aided by Persia, which was really pulling the strings, dominated the Greek world. The Thebans then pulled together an alliance to put an end to Spartan rule and established a hegemony for about a decade. The Athenians now recreated a smaller version of their former empire and liberated Greece from Thebes. Meanwhile, to the north, the Macedonian storm cloud was gathering force.

The Macedonians were a tough people whom the Greeks called *barbarians* (essentially, "babblers," people who did not speak Greek). Macedon's kings were, however, accomplished rulers. By conquering important silver mines, they secured access to financial resources. Philip II (382–336 B.C.) was a particularly accomplished soldier, a reasonably cultivated man (he hired Aristotle to tutor his son!), and ambitious.

Meanwhile, in the Greek world, idealized states and "Panhellenism" were taking hold. Aristotle called man a "political animal": He meant a being who naturally lives in a polis. But he knew perfectly well that poleis had failed badly; he and his pupils studied 158 of them. He imagined an ideal state governed by an oligarchy of aristocrats, that is, "rule by a few" and "rule by the best." It is not so clear how this could come into being. Plato imagined his ideal republic where "Kings would be philosophers and philosophers would be kings." But by the end of his life, he gave up on this ideal and settled for a very small state where a carefully chosen few saw to the implementation of the laws.

Isocrates (436–338 B.C.) gave rise to Panhellenism (literally, "all-Greek-ism"). His dream was that all of Greece would unite under Athens and Sparta to undertake a crusade against Persia. He imagined that the Greeks had once been united. Then, realizing that the Greeks would not bow to one of their own, he tried to persuade people to unite under Philip of Macedon.

Meanwhile, Demosthenes (384–322 B.C.), Greece's, indeed antiquity's, greatest orator, raised his voice in defense of the autonomy of the polis. But he also would have wished for a war against Persia. He delivered four *Philippics* against Philip and saw Macedon as such a threat to Greek liberty that he actually entertained the idea of allying with the Persians against the Macedonians.

> **We must dismantle the *polis*. Actually, to be more accurate, we must watch the Greeks dismantling their own *poleis*. For, in the end, the *polis* failed.**

Amidst a welter of wars, alliances, and idealistic dreaming, Philip attacked. At Chaeronea in 338, Philip's army won a decisive victory over the Greeks. The attacking wing was led by Philip's 18-year-old son, Alexander. Philip created a league with himself at its head to govern Greece. He began making preparations to attack Persia. This might have been his own idea, or it might have been suggested to him by the Greeks. In 336, Philip was murdered in a palace intrigue, the outlines of which are still not clear. After some work to patch up relations with his father's supporters, Alexander became king.

Alexander (356–323 B.C.) is an enigmatic figure: large, handsome, athletic, intelligent, charismatic, but also ruthless and immeasurably ambitious. He was ideologically clever. He depicted his war against Persia as a crusade to even the account for the long-ago Persian attack on Greece. But he was using this as a cover for sheer imperialism. He also used his campaigns as a way to distract and reward the Macedonian nobles who might have turned against him at any moment.

Still, one should not minimize the extent of Alexander's military achievement. With a force not larger than 35,000 men, he conquered the Persian Empire and marched beyond it into central Asia and northern India. His tactics and personal courage were important, but so, too, was his attention to materiel and supply lines. Scholars have long thought that Alexander was cosmopolitan, that he fostered a kind of multicultural world. He incorporated foreigners into his command structure. He married an Asian princess. He promoted the study of the regions he conquered.

Alexander died, probably of malaria, shortly before his 33rd birthday. He left no institutions in place and no plans, as far as we know. The question of what he might have done had he lived longer remains open. Alexander unintentionally inaugurated what we call the Hellenistic world. This was a period when Greek values and culture would dominate the Mediterranean basin. On a grand scale, this is like the other colonizing and imperializing ventures that we have encountered. The spreading of a culture in this way played a decisive role in pouring the foundations for a Western civilization with deep Greek roots, instead of a Greek civilization that passed into oblivion. ∎

Suggested Reading

Connor, *Greek Orations*.

Green, *Alexander of Macedon*.

Questions to Consider

1. Why do you suppose that people are inclined to adhere so firmly to ideas that they must know to be flawed?

2. Was Alexander "Great"?

The Failure of the Polis and the Rise of Alexander
Lecture 14—Transcript

Over the last several lectures, we talked, in various ways and from various points of view, about the Greek *polis*. We talked about it as a political and social institution, in connection with Athens and Sparta. We talked about its public arts, drama and architecture, for example. We talked about history as a way in which the *polis* reflected on itself and carried on conversations with itself. Then we talked about the philosophical culture that emerged in these remarkable Greek cities.

Now we have a less happy task. We must dismantle the *polis*. Actually, to be more accurate, we must watch the Greeks dismantling their own *poleis*. For, in the end, the *polis* failed. As we move along, we'll have one or two reflections on why that would've been the case, and why, perhaps, it's important that that was the case. Suffice it to say, for the moment, by way of introduction, that the fourth century B.C., the period after the Peloponnesian War, was an extremely difficult period for the Greek world. Eventually, the Greek world fell to the Macedonians to the north.

Difficulties were not unprecedented; difficulties did not arise in the fourth century B.C. for the first time. We could go all the way back, for example, to the time of the Persian Wars. There were very, very sharp differences—depending on where you lived in Greece—as to what your views were on the proper strategies to be deployed in fighting the Persians. If you lived far the north, you wanted the defense lines there. If you lived far to the south, you wanted the defense lines there. And there were some people who took one look around and *medized*, went over to the Persians. They thought, "These guys are going to win; we'd better get on the winning side right away." They obviously were treated rather harshly when, in fact, the Greeks won.

During the Peloponnesian Wars, which followed a generation after the Persian Wars, most of the Greek world was dragged into the battle. Athens and her empire on the one hand, Sparta and her Peloponnesian League on the other hand, fought a long and brutal and ugly and nasty war—a war which made brutality a regular part of life, which coarsened public life and public debate. Sparta won, finally, if one can say that anybody really won this war.

Throughout the Athenian democracy, which the Spartans believed—perhaps they'd made hobgoblins in their mind, but they believed—that it had been the Athenian democracy that had been the problem for all that. You'll recall Thucydides had said actually it was Sparta's inordinate fear of Athens that had generated this war. The Spartans introduced a regime into Athens, the "Thirty Tyrants" as they came to be called—30 rather brutal right-wing folks who were supposed to keep control over the Athenian situation. These fellows discredited themselves pretty quickly, and a moderate democracy was restored. But it was really only a shadow of its former self.

In the very last stages of the Peloponnesian War, something, in the Greek context, almost unthinkable had happened. Spartans were landlubbers; the Athenians had a great navy. The Athenians had actually lost big chunks of their navy on several occasions during the Peloponnesian War, but it became pretty clear that to defeat Athens, Sparta needed resources beyond its own infantry forces. They turned to Persia, the unthinkable. They allied with the ancient enemy. That meant that for a generation after the conclusion of the Peloponnesian War, the Greek world was in a kind of uneasy balance. From one point of view, Sparta was dominant. From another point of view, it was really Persia that was dominant because Persia provided Sparta with the resources—manpower and military power—to maintain their authority.

Eventually, various Greek cities chafed under Spartan domination and under this Persian intrusion into the Greek world, something which, for at least some of them, was just unthinkable. The most prominent among those who felt this sense of distress at the control of the Greek world by the Spartans, by the Persians, were those in the city of Thebes. Thebes produced, in the 360s and 370s B.C., a series of very, very able, very capable kings, very capable rulers, who gradually achieved what we refer to as the "Theban hegemony." They, basically, now subjected most of Greece to Theban rule.

The Greeks chafed under Theban rule, and Athens once again forged an alliance of a large number of Greek cities, designed to overthrow the rule of Thebes. The Athenians were basically successful in doing this, and they then began to form a much smaller version of their old empire. We call this the "Second Athenian Empire." But for the most part, most Greek cities were simply not going to let Athens get too big for its britches again. They remembered the Athens of the fifth century; they wanted no part of that. The Athenian Empire of the fourth century had been strong enough to lead in defeating Thebes, but was not strong enough to dominate Greece. It was relatively weak.

Meanwhile, whilst the Greeks are squabbling amongst themselves, storm clouds were gathering in the north. The kingdom of Macedon was consolidating its position. The Macedonians, the northern neighbors of the Greeks, were people with whom the Greeks had had various kinds of contacts over the years. They knew vaguely who these people were; they had traded with them and so on. But the Greeks, honestly, had not thought very much about the Macedonians.

The Greeks called the Macedonians—but, indeed, the Greeks called everybody—barbarians. Don't you hate people who say there are only two kinds of people in the world, and then proceed to divide the world into two kinds of people? The Greeks, in fact, divided the world into two kinds of people. There were those who spoke Greek, and those who didn't. There was a very clear connotation here. We, who speak Greek, are clearly better than they, who do not. But essentially, it was descriptive. There are those who speak Greek and those who don't. Those who don't speak Greek, the Greeks thought, babbled. They were incomprehensible. The Greeks even made up a word. They took two nonsense syllables and put a Greek ending on it, *babarus*. A *babarus* is a babbler who goes "Babababababa," but then by extension becomes the barbarian—the foreigner, the alien, the one who does not speak our language. Gradually, then, barbarian comes to acquire a whole series of other cultural and ethical connotations. But initially, they don't speak Greek.

So, the Greeks called the Macedonians barbarians. And this meant that they're not like us, they don't speak our language. Macedon's kings, in point of fact, were not barbarians at all. They were very accomplished rulers, very capable rulers. By conquering a very large set of silver mines, they got access to very substantial financial resources that enabled them to undertake substantial building projects, that enabled them to win or to buy substantial human and material resources in the development of their kingdom. The Macedonian kingdom, then, was, slowly but surely, gathering force, gathering power.

Under King Philip II (382 to 336 B.C.), referring to a man who was a particularly accomplished soldier—in fact, a very gifted military leader—a reasonably cultivated man. We know, for example, from his palace, from his art, that this was a man of some heightened aesthetic sensibilities. After all, this was the man who hired Aristotle to tutor his son, little Alexander, about whom more in a few minutes. He was ambitious, too. This seems to have been something that ran in the blood of these Macedonian kings. One of the most ambitious people who ever lived was his son, Alexander.

The Greek world has been through 150 years of problems, of struggles, of quarrels, of controversies. These quarrels and controversies have been occasioned by instability inside individual Greek *poleis*, and by constant battles between and among the Greek *poleis*. Pause for just a moment, and think with me. Whatever else it may have been, the Greek *polis* as an independent city-state, as a fiercely independent city-state, was at the very heart of Greek thinking about government and social organization. And yet, from really the end of the Archaic period right to the middle of the fourth century B.C.—the point we have reached now—it is leagues, alliances, associations, and empires constantly fighting one another. In a very curious way, that's not supposed to happen. We're supposed to have all of these tiny and fiercely independent cities, and yet what we have are shifting coalitions—this group against that group, another group against yet another group. The *polis* had, quite simply, failed as an effective agent of political organization.

But as the *polis* is failing before the Greeks' eyes, and as Macedon is emerging—before their eyes as well, to the extent that they were paying attention—down in the Greek world, we begin to see some very interesting reflections on government. Some of these very much attuned to the issues of the day. Some of these, we might almost say, bewilderingly out of step with what people ought to have been able to see with their own two eyes. In a sense, we can say that certain people, Plato and Aristotle—so we're going to come back to them for a moment or two—were imagining ideal kinds of states. They may have been occasioned to think of ideal states because the ones they had sure didn't seem to work very well. And then other thinkers were elaborating a doctrine—an idea, a complex of ideas—that we call "Panhellenism," "all-Greek-ism," a way of trying to forge the Greeks together.

Ideal solutions first, then, in the midst of all this trouble, all this struggle, all this chaos. Aristotle, and I hope that you'll recall that we had mentioned this in an earlier lecture, had said that man is a political animal. That is to say, man is an animal who by nature lives in a *polis*. Aristotle was not willing to abandon the *polis* as the locus for his thinking about government, about politics, and so on. Indeed, he and his pupils, and I repeat a point again that I had made in an earlier lecture, studied 158 of them. You'll recall my mentioning that we don't have all of those studies, and it would be wonderful if we did. Aristotle himself studied the constitution of Athens.

In reflecting on all of these different kinds of political organizations, all of these *poleis* that had existed at one time or another, in one place or another—and I think, too, in reflecting on the inescapable reality of the history that these *poleis*—the rather sad history that these *poleis* had made over some 100-150 years since the Persian Wars, Aristotle began to think about how a state might actually be organized. He said tha,t in the first place, a state should be governed by a few, by an oligarchy. *Oligos* in Greek means few, *archy* means rule, so an oligarchy is a rule by a few. Which few? That seemed self-evident to Aristotle, and probably would to any of us if we thought about it for a minute. The best. We want the best citizens to rule. *Hoi aristoi*, we want aristocracy.

You'll recall, perhaps, that when we were talking about the critiques of democracy, of Periclean democracy, that there were a number of writers that said that one of the problems here is that it does not bring forward the best. In a sense, Aristotle was one of those critics, thinking back about that earlier time. But now, in a sense, we see that thinking in its own context and in its own time. Aristotle has watched what has happened over a long period, and he said that we must somehow bring forward the best. In a lot of ways, that's an unobjectionable proposition; it's pretty hard to disagree with that. We could disagree with the idea of the few, but it's hard to disagree with the idea that we ought to be governed by our best.

What Aristotle wasn't so clear on was how many should the few be? Probably not very many. Aristotle once said, for example, that a state should be no larger than all its citizens could be assembled by the cry of a herald. What the few who led them might be is hard to say. How would we get the best? Aristotle goes very fuzzy on us there. By what process would we identify, promote, bring forward and reconcile others to the rule of the best? Aristotle's quite content to say things haven't worked as well as they should have done over a long period of time. What we need is a small number of rulers who are the best, but how do we get them? He didn't help us very much on that particular point.

Plato, meanwhile, thinks also about ideal states. He thinks of a state where kings would be philosophers and philosophers would be kings. You may recall that in the last lecture—when we talked about Plato and his idea of a moral society—he imagined the soul of an individual as made up of reason, courage, and appetites. He said that each of us is probably not perfectly arrayed, and so as each of us is not arrayed, so our societies are not arrayed so as to reflect this transcendent reality. For the moment, though, I just want to draw your attention back to the highest of these qualities: reason, *gnosi*, mind.

From Plato's point of view, it stood to reason that, in an ideal state, those best in mind should be entrusted with rule. They would be most apt to this task. Plato reckons that this will not be a large group. He does say, for example, that this is not attributable to birth, wealth, social class; and he even said he thought it improbable, but it could apply to women, that women could be among the governing class. He thought it improbable—unlikely—but he said it's possible. That's a rather interesting notion.

Plato leaves us, also, with an interesting problem. If we're going to have a relatively small number of people marked particularly by their intellectual capacity—by reason—and these are the people who will make laws, who will implement laws? Who will oversee the system? How do we choose them? Who are they? Where do we get them? How do we find them? How do we bring them forward? How do we reconcile others to them? Just like his pupil Aristotle, Plato sort of fails us at that point; he doesn't actually tell us how we're going to do this. Though it is interesting, is it not, that Plato and Aristotle, finally, on reflecting on the nature of the *polis* as historical experience or as intellectual proposition, both arrive at oligarchy. Both arrive at rule by a few. They don't quite tell us how many, they don't tell us how we're going to get them, and so on, but they say rule by a few. I don't know about all of you, for those of us in the academic world, it's a nightmare to think of government by committee. But in any case, that's something like what was proposed here.

Some people in the Greek world are now thinking about ideal states. They're basically looking around and saying that what we've got is not so hot. What about an ideal state? There are others—perhaps a bit more realistic, perhaps a bit more pragmatic—who are looking at the world around them and saying we have to deal with what's here, what are we going to do?

One of the first of these is Isocrates—mind the "I," Isocrates—not Socrates. He was born in 436 B.C., dies in 338 B.C. He gave rise to a doctrine called "Panhellenism," "all-Greek-ism." What does this mean? Isocrates' great dream, his great hope, his great desire, was to unite all the Greeks—Athens and Sparta in the lead—in a great crusade against Persia. There's something very interesting going on here. There is a creative process going on here. Isocrates is imagining a past, a past at the time of the Persian Wars, when all the Greeks were united, when they stood as one, when they faced the common foe. As I told you a few minutes ago, the Greek world was not united at the time of the Persian Wars. They did not stand as one, they did not share ideas about how to fight the enemy, and as we've seen, they sure didn't share ideas about what should happen after the war.

But Isocrates is now inventing a history of the age of the Persian Wars, as a way of telling the Greeks, "Once we were united; let us unite again. Let us put aside our petty squabbling and bickering; let us unite and fight the great enemy Persia." In Isocrates' own lifetime, the Persians had been sort of hired guns by the Spartans—although it very well may be the case that, as often with the mercenary, the mercenary realizes the person hiring him isn't strong enough already, or they wouldn't need them. And so, the Persians were probably in control here.

Realizing that the Greeks would not bow to their own—they were not going to unify under Sparta, they had enough of that; they were not going to unify under Athens, they'd had enough of that—Isocrates hatches the scheme of having the Greeks unify under Philip of Macedon to go and fight the Persians.

Isocrates has a foe in Demosthenes (384-322 B.C.), the greatest of the Greek orators—indeed, perhaps, the greatest orator of antiquity. You may know the stories of Demosthenes as a small boy who had a speech impediment and he went down to the sea coast and put pebbles in his mouth and shouted over the sound of the waves—even over the sound of the waves, even with a mouth full of pebbles—until he had learned to speak, not only correctly, but powerfully and persuasively. We can say, certainly, that Demosthenes fits in the tradition of the Sophists—persons who had learned to use language in elegant ways, in artful ways, but also in ways that would be persuasive.

In any case, Demosthenes raises his voice in defense of the autonomy, the independence, the validity of the *polis*. We could say what was he thinking, couldn't he see what was going on in his world? But that was his great commitment. That was his great vision. He also would have wished for the war against Persia—that seems pretty clear. Unlike Isocrates, who would have invited the Greeks to unify under Philip of Macedon to fight the Persians, Demosthenes saw Philip as the great threat, as the greater threat to Greek liberty. He delivered a series of four *Philippic* orations, orations against Philip. The point of these orations was to warn the Greeks that the great danger to their liberty was from Macedon.

Exactly what Demosthenes imagined was possible is hard to say. Did he imagine that the Greeks would somehow be able to unify under one of the Greek cities, or in some kind of an alliance? He even seems to have entertained the possibility that the Greeks might ally with the Persians against the Macedonians, even though he had begun hoping for a Greek alliance against the Persians. Neither Demosthenes nor Isocrates quite had it his own way.

Amidst this welter of wars, alliances, scheming, ideal states, real states, practical ideas, impractical ideas, Philip attacked. Was he invited to buy what he could see over his border? These quarrelsome, meddlesome Greeks? Did Isocrates encourage him to come south? Did Demosthenes simply make him mad? It's hard to say. What we do know is that he attacked; and near the city of Thebes, at Chaeronea, in 338 B.C., he won a great victory over a combined Greek force. Philip destroyed much of the nearby city of Thebes, but he demonstrated his cultural proclivities by leaving standing the house of the poet Pindar. He flattened everything else.

The battle of Chaeronea is interesting to us for another reason, as well. The attacking wing, the wheeling wing, the cavalry wing, the wing that delivered the victory that day, was led by an 18-year-old boy named Alexander. We'll hear more about him.

Philip, having conquered the Greeks, really, in one great battle, now created a league; these leagues and alliances had been going on in the Greek world for a long time. He creates a league with himself at the head. In a sense, he creates a league where all of the Greeks have a vote, and he has a vote; and he has a veto, and they don't. Philip is basically in charge in the Greek world. His aim, I think, was to provide peace and order in the Greek world, but I think the kind of peace and order that meant he really didn't want to be bothered by these guys. He wanted to sort of impose peace rather more than elicit peace because eliciting it was unlikely to work.

And then he began making preparations to attack Persia. It's very interesting to ask here, would Philip, all on his own, have formed the idea of making war on the Persians? Was this something suggested to him, for example, by Isocrates, in particular, but maybe by other Greeks as well? It's just hard to say, but he clearly had begun making preparations for a war against Persia.

In 336 B.C., he was killed in a palace intrigue. The Macedonian court was often a tumultuous and difficult place, and unfortunately, we don't have quite rich enough and detailed enough sources to say exactly what was going on. Anyway, there was a palace intrigue; Philip was killed. It took a short period of time before his son, Alexander, was able to win out among several potential claimants for the Macedonian throne. Alexander was 20. He immediately had to patch up relations with a number of his father's most important associates and supporters, and with a number of the most important military commanders in the Macedonian army. But once he had managed to patch up these relations, he decided on what would become—as we know, with the luxury of hindsight—as his life's work: to go and make war on the Persians.

Alexander is a quite remarkable and quite mysterious figure. He was a very tall man, a very handsome man, apparently. He was athletic, he was intelligent, he was charismatic. But he was also ruthless, and immeasurably ambitious. Few people, I think, have ever been more ambitious than Alexander. He was ideologically clever. For a young man, he was pretty smart.

He depicted his war against Persia as a crusade to even the score for this long ago Persian attack on the Greeks. He makes himself the great defender of the Greeks, the great defender of Greek liberty, the great avenger of Greek humiliation. Well, the Greeks hadn't been humiliated; they won that war. And the Greeks had, in some way, brought that war on themselves by implicating themselves in the Ionian revolt. But, just as for his purposes, Isocrates had managed the history of the Persian War, so now Alexander, for his own purposes, manages the history of the Persian War. This is a wonderful object lesson in a point that I've made many times: there's a history that happens, and a history that's remembered. Here we're watching two people battling over the same history, and each using fictitious versions of it. Quite interesting, that.

He was using all of this as a cover for sheer imperialism. Alexander set out to conquer the world. Yes, we have that legendary account of how, at one point, he sat upon a stone and wept for lack of worlds to conquer. That's probably not true, but it's interesting that someone would tell that story about Alexander. He used the campaigns as a very clever way to distract and to reward the great Macedonian nobles who had been responsible for all these palace intrigues, who might at any point turn against him. Still, having said that, and having appreciated that Alexander was pretty savvy politically, and pretty savvy ideologically, for a young person who, after all, had not had a lot of experience of the world.

We shouldn't minimize the extent of his military achievement. Alexander was a great military leader, whatever else we may say about him. With an army of about 35,000 men at the height—that's as large as it ever got—he conquered the Persian Empire. He marched into the Persian Empire and, one after another, won a series of great battles, systematically dismantled the Persian military apparatus, and brought it into his own hands. And he then marched beyond the Persian Empire. He marched into central Asia; he marched into northern India.

His tactics were brilliant. Alexander is still studied today for his military tactics. How do you learn that as a young boy? He sets out to conquer the Persian Empire at the age of 18. His earliest great victories come in the next two or three years. He's 20, 21, 22 years old, and he's up against the greatest military establishment in the then world—and he beats them. He led his own troops; he sometimes acted recklessly, some might say. He had a remarkable capacity to elicit loyalty, to make men follow him, to make men do what seemed somehow impossible.

As if all of that weren't impressive enough, Alexander organized astonishing supply lines. One of the things he recognized was he was moving further and further and further and further away from the Greek world, from supplies, from everything he needed to accomplish his great military objectives. Yet he organized supply lines; he organized the provision of material and of food to his troops over an enormous network. Where did he learn all of that? Hard to say.

Some have thought that Alexander was a very cosmopolitan figure, that he fostered a kind of a multicultural world. We're going to talk about the world Alexander made in our next lecture. For now, we can say he incorporated foreigners into his command structure. That's true—that may indicate a certain lack of prejudice, or a certain willingness to incorporate. He married an Asian princess, that's true—that may indicate a certain sensitivity to local cultures, a certain willingness to accept them. He promoted the studies of the regions that he conquered. He brought all kinds of scientists and naturalists along with him, who collected all sorts of information about all these remarkable places that he went and visited. Maybe this is the influence of his tutor, Aristotle.

Aristotle may have taught him this curiosity for the world, probably didn't teach him his ambition, his dreams, his hopes. What might they have been? We'll never know. He died shortly before his 33rd birthday, died probably of malaria, which just goes to prove that mortality afflicts us all, as Gilgamesh and Enkidu learned, much to their great displeasure. He left behind no institutions. He left behind no plans. We have no idea, for example, what he might have done had he lived to be 40, 50. How would he have organized this world? What would he have done with it? Would he have gone back to the Greek world? We just don't know.

What Alexander leaves us with, crucially, in the Western tradition, is a period and a set of problems that we call Hellenistic. We'll turn to those in more detail in our next lecture. Suffice it to say that this is a world where Greek values, Greek ideas, Greek culture came to dominate the Mediterranean basin. Because of the Hellenistic world, because of the sheer scale of Alexander's empire building, we have a Hellenistic civilization. A civilization based upon Greek roots, which informs, which infuses Western civilization as a whole—and not merely a Greek civilization, which having had its period of brilliance, died and passed away. How to turn so much of that Mediterranean world even more Greek than it already was, is what we try to explain in our lecture on the Hellenistic world, next time.

The Hellenistic World
Lecture 15

This is a world that we generally date from the death of Alexander in 323 B.C. until the Battle of Action, when the Romans defeated the last of the great Hellenistic rulers in 31 B.C.

Hellenistic is the name given to the period from the death of Alexander to the Roman triumph in the Mediterranean: 323–31 B.C. The name is meant to distinguish between Hellenic proper and Hellenic-influenced. Greek became the *koiné*; Greek art dominant in influence; Greek philosophy regnant but revised. This was a world of empires and kingdoms, not of poleis.

On Alexander's death, his leading generals carved up his vast realm. Antigonos—his descendants are called the Antigonids—took Macedon and the Balkans. Gradually, the Greek lands broke away into a league of their own under nominal Antigonid supervision. In the western Balkans, the kingdom of Epirus emerged (we will meet the inhabitants again as enemies of Rome). Syria, Palestine, northern Mesopotamia, and southern Anatolia fell to the Seleucids.

Mostly named Seleucus and Antiochus, they turn up in the last books of the Hebrew Bible: Judas Maccabeus revolted against them. They shared rule in Anatolia with Pergamum. Egypt fell to the Ptolemies, whose last ruler was Cleopatra. These kingdoms warred against, and allied with, one another repeatedly, until the Romans conquered them one by one.

It is the cultural, not the political, history of the Hellenistic world that is interesting and important. The Hellenistic world was one of vast wealth, easy movement of peoples, rapid cultural dissemination, and genuine cosmopolitanism.

Developments in Alexandria are revealing. The city was founded by Alexander (he founded more than 20). It had 500,000 people by 250 B.C. and a million by 50. The scholars in its *Museum* (that is, "house of the muses," or academy of all the branches of knowledge) were learned and professional, not great civic figures as in the polis.

Culture was increasingly an object of study, not a part of daily life and debate. Learned, elitist scholars began to develop the idea of a literary canon, of normative texts, of critically defined tastes and standards. Here, we see for the first time, the "ivory-tower intellectual." This opened the gap characterized by C. P. Snow in *The Two Cultures* insofar as many Alexandrians were "scientists" while philosophers worked elsewhere: hence, the division between the arts and sciences instead of the integration that had been the ideal of the Academy and Lyceum.

The Hellenistic world was a time of important scientific breakthroughs. Euclid (c. 300) formulated the rules of geometry. Archimedes (287–212 B.C.) created all sorts of gadgets and advanced experimental science. Aristarchus (c. 275 B.C.) formulated the *heliocentric* theory: the sun is at the center of the "universe." Eratosthenes (c. 225 B.C.) calculated the circumference of the earth. Ptolemy (127–48 B.C.) systematized astronomical information, created a theory of the motion of the planets and the moon, and added a crucial mathematical element to astronomical theory.

The Hellenistic world spawned new literary forms. Apollonius (B.C. 295) wrote *Argonautica*, a work on an epic scale but not an epic; an adventure story and a love story. Jason and his argonauts go in search of the Golden Fleece, but it is the cunning of Medea, not the bumbling brutishness of Jason, that wins the prize. Jason is a hero but not like, say, Achilles. And no epic would have told a love story. This was entertainment.

Menander (342/341–293/289 B.C.) was the greatest writer of "new comedy." His *Curmudgeon* is the only surviving complete play. It is intricate, verbally adroit, and very funny. It treats ordinary domestic concerns, the stuff of daily life—sort of *I Love Lucy* Hellenistic style. New, and long influential, philosophies also arose. The greatest of these—Stoicism and Epicureanism— may be called "therapeutic" philosophies. Classical values seemed to have failed. The world of the citizen had vanished. Alienation was common. The focus shifted to ethics: How to live seemed more important than how to know or what to know.

227

Stoicism rose with Zeno (335–263 B.C.), who taught at the painted porch (*stoa poikilé*) in Athens. He believed that knowledge was possible, and he equated knowledge with virtue. He believed that there was a divine reason that permeated all creation. Virtue consisted in becoming acquainted with this divine reason, in learning its laws, and in putting oneself into harmony with reason (natural law philosophy would later derive from this way of thinking). One has, then, a moral duty to learn the laws of nature and to live in accord with them. To do so would bring happiness to individuals and justice to societies.

Things were built, very largely, because the Romans conquered this Hellenistic world and conquered its culture.

Pain or distress in life, and even death, are not absolute, final evils. They can be overcome by apathy, which does not mean, "I don't care" but instead means, "I am beyond all pain." Suicide is permitted as, curiously, a form of happiness should pain become too great. Stoicism taught that all visible differences in the world are accidental and of no fundamental significance. The king and the slave are essentially alike. Stoicism had a deep influence on Roman and Christian writers.

Epicureanism takes its name from Epicurus (341–270 B.C.), who also taught in Athens. The aim of philosophy, for the Epicureans, was happiness, or pleasure. But this did not mean the hedonism that is often nowadays, and quite wrongly, associated with Epicureanism. Happiness was defined by Epicurus as "an absence of pain from the body and trouble from the soul." This philosophy was austere in the extreme. Pleasure was equated with renunciation.

Epicurus urged withdrawal from the world, avoidance of stress, and avoidance of extremes. Pain is occasioned by unfulfilled desire. Therefore, it is sensible to desire only those things that are easily obtained. The events of life are accidental, and death is merely dissolution of the chance combination of atoms that made us in the first place. Conditions of life are not to be regretted, and death is not to be feared.

Rome conquered this Hellenistic world, but its culture conquered the Romans. For several centuries, Roman imperialism locked Hellenistic culture into place and stamped it deeply on all the cultures that would follow the Romans. ■

Suggested Reading

Apollonius of Rhodes, *The Voyage of Argo*.

Green, *Alexander to Actium*.

Lloyd, *Greek Science after Aristotle*.

Long, *Hellenistic Philosophy*.

Menander, *Plays and Fragments*.

Questions to Consider

1. Do any aspects of the Hellenistic world seem comparable to aspects of our world today?

2. Can you see the debts owed by Zeno and Epicurus to Plato and Aristotle?

The Hellenistic World
Lecture 15—Transcript

In the previous group of lectures, we talked about the Greek *polis*. We talked about it as a political and social institution, we talked about its culture. And in our last lecture, as you may recall, we talked about its demise, its internal failure, and then its failure in the face of Macedonian conquest—when Philip II of Macedon conquered the Greeks, and when his son Alexander took over his father's control of the Greeks, and then went off on these vast military campaigns into what had formerly been the Persian Empire. In doing this, Alexander inaugurated a period of history we call the Hellenistic world.

This is a world that we generally date from the death of Alexander in 323 B.C. until the Battle of Action, when the Romans defeated the last of the great Hellenistic rulers in 31 B.C. Basically there was three centuries in time, chronologically speaking, following on the Classical period of Greek history. In later lectures, we'll see that, in the western Mediterranean, during this Hellenistic period, the Romans are rising to prominence. But that's for later lectures. Right now, we want to focus on the world that Alexander made, or in any case, on the world that followed him.

I've used the word "Hellenistic." We call this world, from Alexander on, Hellenistic to differentiate it from the "Hellenic." We are inconsistent in doing this because I was telling you a few lectures back that we don't actually refer to the Greeks as Hellenes, or their land as Hellas—that we call them Greeks and we call their land Greece. We should call them Hellenes, so the period that we have been speaking of in our previous lectures should be the Hellenic period. Instead of saying that we're going to talk about the "Greek-istic" period, we talk about the Hellenistic period. You mustn't ever ask professors to be logical or consistent or coherent. We just confuse those who listen to us. Hellenistic: Greek-influenced, Greek-ish, as opposed to Greek proper.

It's a period when, in fact, Greek culture became fundamental in the Mediterranean world. The *koiné* Greek language—*koiné* in Greek means "common"—the common language of this Hellenistic world became Greek. Not the highfaluting Greek of the greatest of the Athenian writers, a commoner, more ordinary form, hence the name; but nevertheless, it spread very widely. The Greek influence became dominant in, for example, art, in architecture. Greek influences in literature spread very, very widely. Greek philosophy remained dominant. But we're going to see it was changed in some very interesting ways during this Hellenistic period.

Alexander's death—to come first of all to the political shape of this Hellenistic world—let's get a sense of just how it was organized. Who was out there? Who were the players? On Alexander's death, his generals, basically—at least three of the most important of them—carved up this vast world that he had conquered. You may recall my having said that Alexander died very young, and he had not made any formal provision, either, for how he was going to rule this world or for, indeed, what might one day succeed to him. We don't really know what his plans would have been. What we know is what happened, and that is that his generals carved this world up.

One of these, whose name was Antigonos—his descendants are called the Antigonids—took Macedon and the Balkans. Basically he went back and took the old Macedonian homelands and the Greek peninsula where Philip II and Alexander had made their first conquests. Gradually, slowly, over time, the Greek lands to the south of Macedon sort of broke away and formed a more or less league, an autonomous realm, under their own supervision and government, but with supervision from the Macedonians to the north.

In the Western Balkans, a small kingdom called Epirus emerged. This is something that was actually characteristic of the Hellenistic world; a fair number of small kingdoms arose amidst these great ones. Epirus I'll mention simply because we'll encounter them again, in a later lecture, as enemies of Rome. I'm not going to detail again and again and again all these little kingdoms that arose. Basically, there were, as we'll see in just a second, three big ones. The Antigonids formed the first of these big ones.

The lands lying at the eastern end of the Mediterranean—Syria, Palestine, northern Mesopotamia, southern Anatolia—those territories fell to a general by the name of Seleucus. The dynasty, then, which he establishes the Seleucid dynasty—most of the rulers of the Seleucid dynasty were named either Seleucus or Antiochus. If those names ring a bell, you may have encountered them in the very last books of the Hebrew Scriptures, the very last books of the Hebrew Bible. Judas Maccabeus revolted against these rulers. They had a kind of a purchase on our attention, quite independent of their position as successors of Alexander the Great.

It's worth mentioning one of the other smallish kingdoms that emerged, and this is Pergamum, which emerged in central Anatolia, an area which the Seleucids were unable effectively to dominate. The little kingdom of Pergamum arose in central Anatolia. I mentioned that one because, again, the Romans and the Pergamons will have dealings with each other late in the second century B.C. That is a story for a later day. I just want to forecast that we will come back to this.

In Egypt, finally, the last of Alexander's great generals, Ptolemy, marched off to Egypt, took over the land of Egypt, and established a dynasty of rulers there, which persisted until 31 B.C. The last of the Ptolemies, of course, was the famous Cleopatra, who, it is important to say, was not Egyptian at all, but Macedonian.

These various Hellenistic kingdoms—the large ones and the small ones—warred with one another often, were great rivals of one another most of the time, allied with one another occasionally in the face of common threats—for example, later on, in the face of the threat posed by the Romans. What we will see in later lectures is that the Romans marched into the eastern Mediterranean and conquered these Hellenistic kingdoms one by one by one, and it was really the final conquest of these Hellenistic kingdoms that marked the definitive rise of the Roman Empire in the eastern Mediterranean world. So that's basically the political shape of the Hellenistic world. Three great kingdoms—the Antoginids, the Seleucids, and the Ptolemies—arrayed between and among a series of smaller kingdoms, with this rising threat to them of Rome.

It's the cultural, and not the political, diplomatic, military history of the Hellenistic world that is really interesting and important to us. And this is what we want to spend the majority of our time talking about. It was a world of great wealth, in part because a sort of a very large – something like a free trading zone – was generated by these vast conquests of Alexander and his successors. It was a time of rapid and easy movement of peoples. One of the things very interesting in the sources for this period is how many people from one place wind up prominent—active, at any rate—in places very far away. There's an enormous amount of travel, an enormous amount of exchange in this world. It's a time of rapid cultural dissemination. This is a period when we can really see cultures spreading.

The great statues themselves are, in fact, some centuries later than the period that I'm talking about now. A very interesting example of this are those spectacular Buddhas that were destroyed in Bamiyan in the year 2001 A.D. by the Taliban. The largest of them was arrayed with facial features and with general sort of iconographic details of central Asia, but the folds of clothing and garments were Greek. The statue was arrayed as if it was a Greek. Somebody who made that statue had certain Greek in mind, and blended them with the ideas that were native to that region. There's an example that is poignant for us now because of recent events in world history, but it's a good example of this spread of cultures that was characteristic of the Hellenistic world.

It was a time, many think, of great cosmopolitanism—*cosmos polis*, of the world as a city, the city as a world; of the spread of cultures; of people taking on the cultures of other people, other places, other times. If we look, for a few minutes, at the city of Alexandria, we have some very good insights into what this Hellenistic world was like. Alexandria was, in many ways, a very dynamic, very creative place during the Hellenistic period. We could turn to other places, but let's use Alexandria as a kind of an example, as a way of thinking our way into this period.

The city was founded by Alexander. He founded more than 20 cities, and somewhat immodestly, named them after himself: Alexandria. One evidence to his overweening pride, perhaps. This was a city that by 250 B.C., or thereabouts, had probably a half a million people. By 31 B.C., when the Hellenistic world was finally conquered by the Romans, probably a million. That's a big city in antiquity. That's a big city in the modern world. It was a city known particularly for its scholarship; it was really thought of as sort of a city of great scholars.

Most these scholars worked in a place called the *Museum*. *Museum* is a Latin word; *museon* is a Greek word. The Museon is the home of the muses. The muses were the poetic names, the allegorical names, assigned by the Greeks to each of the branches of knowledge. You think of Calliope, the muse of music, for example. The Museon was the great house where the muses lived, but they lived there in the sense that they were studied there, that they were held dear there, that they were analyzed there. The Museum eventually became quite famous as a place where all branches of knowledge were studied, and this began to produce a new kind of person. This began to produce a very different kind of intellectual tradition in the West. I don't want to say we have a 180 degree turn; what I say is that we will now generate a tension, and a tension that I daresay is with us still.

The people who did this study were learned. They were professional. They were enormously scholarly. They were no longer actually great civic figures. One of the interesting things about the figures that we talked about in Athens, for example—whether we're thinking of a Socrates or a Plato, whether we're thinking of the playwrights or the historians—these were people who functioned in an urban environment, spoke to that urban environment, absorbed that urban environment into their work, spoke back to that urban environment in their work. They were very much anchored in that world.

Now, in the Museum, we have scholars, people who study without necessarily being fully engaged with their world. Culture was an object of study; it wasn't a part of daily life. Learned and elitist scholars began, for the first time, to define literary canons, to decide what criteria of excellence marked those works that should be remembered, should be studied, should be analyzed, and those which were forgettable. They began to study the various works that existed, to collect many manuscripts of them, for instance, to compare the texts in order to prepare what we would call standard editions, to make definitive additions to texts.

They began to try to define taste, to define standards, to sort of say, "This is what you ought to think; this is what you ought to know." Previously, these kinds of things, for instance, were, again, very much more a part of civic culture. We could say, for instance, to take but one example, Homer's *Iliad* and *Odyssey* were in very many ways part of the *paideia*, which means in Greek "the leading up," the training up, the drawing up of the youth. It wasn't as if the youths were sent home at night to memorize 20 lines of the *Iliad* per night, and over the course of a few years through their adolescence they had the whole thing memorized. But it was something that they heard recited, they heard talked about. The stories were told, the messages were told, the morals were registered, of these great books. They simply became a part of the patrimony of the Greeks.

In Alexandria, it would be much more common to study the language, diction, syntax, vocabulary—to look at the *Iliad* in a very different kind of way. We're seeing, in a way, the emergence of the ivory tower intellectual. The intellectual, in a very real way, is divorced from his society, or at least is perceived that way.

This is, in a way, a world also that exemplifies the first faint beginnings of what C.P. Snow described in his very famous book, *The Two Cultures*. Snow was an Oxford don, and a generation ago, a little older than that now, he wrote a book, *The Two Cultures*. And what he was really talking about is the culture of the arts, the humanities, and so on, on the one hand, and the culture of science on the other. And he's talking about how, in the modern world, these two things have become divorced from one another, and there's very often a sort of an inability to study them. You go to any college or university, and if you think about liberal arts, people think that that means you're going to read English and study art, and so on. It doesn't mean you're going to study calculus and chemistry. We're going to ask why that should have been the case in some later lectures. For the moment, it is worth pointing out that, in Alexandria, we basically see science. Philosophy, actually, remains very much in Athens. What we are beginning to see is this division between what we would think of as the sciences and what we would think of as the arts.

The ideal, for example in the Academy and in the Lyceum—Plato's school and Aristotle's school—had been to unify, to integrate these bodies of knowledge. Think of Aristotle, to go no further, and his interest in the world of natural science going back to Thales, and his ability to develop a whole philosophical approach to things based on his understanding of the natural world. Slowly but surely, however, that begins to change. These two trends, these two traditions, these two possibilities of knowing begin to divorce, one from the other. And I think there has been some considerable tension throughout the history of Western civilization since Hellenistic times addressed to the problem. Are they separate and distinct, or can they again be brought together?

I think we've probably made a concerted effort to bring them together, but we have not succeeded very well. You stop and think, for example, of the distribution requirements—or the general education requirements, however you want to describe them—in most colleges and universities. You take some English, you take some language, you take some history, you take some math, you take some science. There's still this idea that to be liberally educated, you have to know this range of things. Then there's also the idea that if I'm interested in this, I don't want to do that. This break that comes in the Hellenistic period has been a durable one.

The Hellenistic period was important for a number of scientific breakthroughs. If I'm going to say that Alexandria was a place where science was important, let's have a few examples of this kind of thing. Euclid, around 300 B.C., formulated the rules of geometry, the rules of plane geometry—the essential rules, the essential formulae, the essential theorems for explaining plane surfaces.

Archimedes, of the important Hellenistic era scientists, 287 to about 212 B.C. Archimedes was a sort of a "Mr. Fix-It." He's famous for making all kinds of gadgets. Actually, there's something else rather interesting about Archimedes. This is the emergence of experimental science. This is the first time we really begin, concretely, to see something like experimental science. The attempt by experimentation to arrive at a point, and then to be able to confirm a point—a theory, an argument, an idea, a mechanical contraption, whatever it might be—to be able to confirm it by repeated demonstration, by repeated testing. Before this time, Aristotle, of course, and the traditions behind him that said you must observe closely, but there had not really been the experimental dimension. This is added in the Hellenistic period.

Aristarchus, around 275 B.C., articulated for the first time the *heliocentric* theory. *Helios* is Greek for sun. He put the Sun at the center of the universe. That's a rather interesting thing for an earthly person to do, I suppose. We now know, of course, that the Sun isn't the center of the universe, but we do think of the Sun as the center of our Solar System, which is merely one part of a large galaxy, which is merely one part of a much larger universe. That astronomical lore was not yet available in Hellenistic times, and as we'll have occasion to see, very near the end of our course of lectures, as late as the 17th century, fellows like Galileo could get themselves in trouble over this heliocentric theory. It had not, in fact, triumphed. It was not regnant.

Eratosthenes, 225 B.C., by process of quite simple intuition, calculated the circumference of the Earth, and managed to do it to a remarkable accurate degree.

Ptolemy—the Ptolemies, of course, were the rulers of Egypt, but there were members of the family, of course, who never got to be the ruler, so they went off and pursued other interests. One of these, Ptolemy, who lived from 127 to 48 B.C., began to systematize astronomical information. He began to collect enormous amounts of material that had been observed of the heavens above us, and he began, for the first time, to try to create a theory that would explain planetary motion. This, quite simply, is that if you collect a lot of information about the way the world works, and the way the planets are going around out there, you notice that there's something slightly odd. They're not all moving at exactly the same speed, at exactly the same order, in exactly the same place. They seem to kind of move around. How can this be?

One of the things Ptolemy recognized was that we were going to need more sophisticated mathematical models to explain what was going on. And he, for the first time, introduces mathematics into astronomy. There were some very elementary errors, or misunderstandings, in Ptolemy's time. He thought orbits were circular. It was a very long time later they realized that orbits were elliptical. It's already in the 17th century that Johannes Kepler can do the mathematics of astronomy as we know it now. Ptolemy made some pretty remarkable steps for his time. That's the kind of thing that we see as characteristic, perhaps, of the culture of the Museum.

Elsewhere in the Hellenistic world, we also see the emergence of some new literary forms. Some of the older Greek forms persisted; history continued to be written, poetry continued to be written, and so on. But we find something new, for instance, in the *Argonautica*, the journey of Argo, a story written perhaps 285 B.C. or thereabouts, by Appolonius of Rhodes. This is a work that is on epic scale, but it's not an epic. It's an adventure story. Jason and his Argonauts go off in search of the Golden Fleece. It's a mythical story, it's an adventure story, it's quite an engaging tale. It's not very long, it's easy to read, it's great fun. It's a cunning story, it's a clever story.

We're presented with a number of anomalies. There is a great love interest in the story, Jason and Medea. It's also the case that Jason is a big, strong, brash, spontaneous kind of fellow, who forever is getting himself in trouble. And it's Medea who is always getting him out of trouble, and is always figuring out exactly how to prevail in his quest for the Golden Fleece. That's, in a way, the old brains and brawn issue that we've seen in the Greek world before, but now the woman has the brains and the man has merely the brawn. Perhaps it's always so.

It's a story on epic scale: there are monsters, and ships travel long distances, and amazing things happen. But in a classic epic, you'd have had verse, not prose. This was a prose work. You wouldn't have had a love story told. It wouldn't have been told in common and ordinary language. There's nothing universalizing about this story. This is entertainment; this was pleasant diversion. You're not supposed to put the *Argonautica* down and feel that you have grown morally or ethically. You've been entertained.

Menander, who lives from perhaps 342 to 293, maybe as late as 289 B.C., is the great writer of comedies in the Hellenistic world, or at least the one whose name we know best. We have a problem here. One of his plays survives completely—one alone. We know the names—again, remember, as with the Greek tragedians—we know the names of a number of other plays. We even have fragments of a few of them, but what we have is one play in total. It's called the *Curmudgeon*. It's the story about an angry old man, and it is very funny. It's full of improbably funny circumstances.

But again, it is full of ordinary domestic concerns; it's full of daily life. This is, in a way, *I Love Lucy*. This is the sitcom; this is the remote ancestor of the situation comedy. This is not high comedy like Aristophanes, where humor—perhaps even ridicule, certainly satire—is used to poke fun at, to make comments about great events of the day. Menander is just funny. You read him, you learn, maybe there is a kind of a point. Good heavens, every time we watch a sitcom, there is a point, I suppose, of some kind in them. But they're pretty simple, they're pretty homely, they're not the kind of thing that are ever going to be carved in stone and put on the front of a building.

We also begin to see entertainment as escape. Let them take us to the philosophies of the Hellenistic world. The two great ones, of course, were Stoicism and Epicureanism—philosophies that specialists in these areas have called "therapeutic." Therapeutic because they were philosophies designed to make you feel better. They were philosophies for people who lived in a world whose values and institutions seem somehow to have failed.

Things seemed to have gone desperately wrong. The *polis* was gone; the world of the citizen was gone. Vast empires had arisen; impersonal government had arisen. From all accounts, in the literature of the time, alienation was common. And the focus began, therefore, for philosophical writers to shift to ethics. How can I cope with this world? How can I live? That, somehow, now seemed a lot more important than what is the world made of. What are the grand principles that underlie everything? I don't want to imply that no one was thinking about those questions, but fundamentally, thought was moving in slightly different directions.

The most famous, then, of these philosophies: Stoicism and Epicureanism. Let's begin with a few words about Stoicism. Stoicism takes its rise with Zeno. Zeno lived in Athens, 335-263 B.C. He taught, more or less in the open, at the *stoa poikilé*, the painted porch, near the Athenian *agora* in Athens. We ought to be speaking of "Zeno-ism," or something like that, but we talk of Stoicism, which literally means "porch-ism."

He falls very much in the tradition of Plato and Aristotle. He believes that knowledge is possible. He absolutely believes that. He believes there are things we can know. He believes it's necessary to equate knowledge with virtue. You may recall that Plato and Aristotle had both said the same thing, that knowledge could be equated with virtue.

Zeno believed that there was a divine reason that permeated all creation, that lay behind everything, that there was a point, a purpose, a law. Think for just a moment of Pythagoras and his theorem, discovering, in a sense, one law that appears to operate in all of nature. By extension, that kind of thinking suggests that there are laws, finally, behind everything. Virtue consists, therefore, in becoming acquainted with this divine reason, putting oneself into harmony with its laws and with its rules, accepting these propositions as necessary and benevolent. Stoics very often used the image of the theater. We should know our roles and play our roles. We should accept the roles that are assigned to us, that we should learn them very well.

This was also a way of thinking that, over time, would give rise to what we think of as "Natural Law." When Thomas Jefferson speaks of the laws of nature, and of nature's God, he is speaking in a way that a Stoic would have spoken about these laws that exist in the nature. "We hold certain truths," he said, "to be self evident." They are writ into the universe. They don't exist because a legislature made them, or a king made them, or somebody wrote a book about them. What is, then, a moral duty to learn the laws of nature and to live in accord with them? To do so would bring happiness. If I understood how the universe worked, and I behaved as if I understood that, I would be happy. Were I happy, I would not be distressed. You see the therapeutic dimension? Pain or stress that exists in any individual—that exists in any society—are a result of misunderstanding, of not possessing knowledge.

But pain and distress, themselves, are not final and not destructive. Even death is natural, not to be feared, but to be embraced. If you think of the apathy of the Stoic sage. When you hear the word "apathy," that's not a very pleasant word; you wouldn't want to be called apathetic. Stoic apathy does not mean, "I don't care." Stoic apathy means, "I am beyond all pain. I am unperturbed; I understand the way the world works. I have accepted it." Suicide is even permitted, curiously, as a form of happiness. If the pain becomes too great, we can escape. Stoicism taught that all visible differences in the world are illusory and accidental. Everyone, finally, is like everyone else. We are all equal, essentially—not by the way we see ourselves out there in the world, but fundamentally—we are all alike.

Now let's turn, for a moment, to Epicureanism. Epicureanism takes its name from Epicurus, who lived from 341 to 270 B.C., and who also taught in Athens. Epicureanism was, perhaps, less influential in later years than Stoicism was, but it was very, very important in antiquity. We have to be very careful not to imagine, not to think, not to embrace the caricature of Epicureanism that is the common understanding of, the common reaction to the word itself.

The only philosophy, according to the Epicureans, was happiness or pleasure. That's old; that's exactly what Aristotle said. The point of living well is to be happy. But this did not mean the hedonism that we often now associate, wrongly, with Epicureanism. Eat, drink, and be merry, for tomorrow you die. That is not ancient Epicureanism.

Epicurus defined happiness as an absence of pain from the body and of trouble from the soul. His philosophy was austere in the extreme. Pleasure was equated with renunciation. Epicurus urged withdrawal from the world— avoidance of stress, avoidance of anguish, avoidance of all those things: too much food, too much love, whatever it might be that would bring you stress, that would bring you anguish. It's sensible, the Epicureans taught, to desire only those things in moderation that will bring happiness. Only those things that are attainable. Don't go after things you can't get; it will make you unhappy, it will make too much stress.

These hedonistic philosophies are going to be influential for the Romans, then are going to be influential for all of those who came after. Stoicism, perhaps, a bit more than Epicureanism.

The Hellenistic world, again, leaves us this fundamental foundational basis for the spread of Greek culture. On that foundation, things were built, very largely, because the Romans conquered this Hellenistic world and conquered its culture. You may remember, in an earlier lecture, I spoke of captive Greece taking her captor captive. This is the world that the Romans captured. "*Tutte le strade portano a Roma,*" say our Italian friends. "All roads lead to Rome," and our next lecture will take us to the Eternal City.

The Rise of Rome
Lecture 16

> The area where the Romans emerged, the plain of Latium (which gives its name to Latin, it is Lazio today) is in the center of the Italian peninsula, but it's not a very big area.

T he Romans have been central to the Western tradition. They created stable, efficient political institutions that have been admired and emulated for centuries. They created the most influential secular legal system in the history of the world. They were masters of what we might call civil engineering: Need water 50 miles away? No problem. Rome will build an aqueduct. Need to conquer an enemy ensconced on a 1,300-foot-high plateau? No problem. Rome will build a ramp.

In many ways, the Romans were unlikely players on the world stage. They emerged in the plain of Latium (which gave its name to Latin and is called Lazio today) in the center of the Italian peninsula. Italy as a whole is some 750 miles long from the Alps to the sea. But Roman Italy ran from the Rubicon River to the sea. The whole Italian area divides into several distinct regions.

The Po River valley lies in the north, called by the Romans Cisalpine Gaul (Gaul "on this side of the Alps"). The area has rich agricultural land and a mild continental climate. Liguria-Tuscany was the region north of Latium and Rome. People called the Etruscans lived here when the Romans came on the scene. Campania, literally "the countryside," was the area south of Latium. The Samnites lived here amidst high (more than 2,000 meters), rough mountain ridges. Magna Graecia was the area in the south, the "heel" and "toe," as well as Sicily, where Greeks were a major presence from the 8th century.

The Iron Age came to central Italy circa 1000 B.C. The first settlements around later Rome date from circa 800. Roman tradition says that their city was founded in the year we call 753 B.C. Rome was pretty well sited: 15 miles inland on a navigable river at a good ford; seven hills provided residential areas above the swampy lowlands and defense in case of attack. But Italy's best harbors faced west and all the "action" in the Mediterranean was in the east; north of Rome, the Etruscans and, south of Rome, the Greeks were major threats; Latium itself was a region of small villages not yet under Roman sway.

Tradition says that the Romans expelled the last Etruscan king, Tarquin the Proud, in 509 B.C. and created a republic. That tradition bears a little scrutiny. During these two centuries, Rome progressed from a few scattered settlements to a city. Romans created their first *forum*, built their first stone buildings, laid out streets, and erected the first walls. Probably the influence of the Greeks to the south was decisive.

This renders controversial the relationship between the Romans and the Etruscans to their north. The Etruscans are a somewhat mysterious people who lived in 12 small cities and who became rich from farming, mining, and trade. Roman legend says that the Etruscans conquered the Romans, who then liberated themselves, but probably, there was a long period of rivalry and mutual influence.

The kings were assisted in ruling Rome in these early times by a group of men called "fathers," *patres*. Hence, patricians.

Tradition says that Rome was ruled by seven kings: kings, yes; seven, maybe. Kings had broad powers in war, religion, and daily life and left a deep imprint on Rome's later institutions. Kings were assisted by "fathers" (*patres*, hence *patricians*, "well-fathered ones," like the Greek *eupatrids*) who formed a council called a *Senate* (from *senex* = old man: compare Sparta). Ordinary people were *plebeians*. There was an assembly of all citizens that could take legislative initiative, although its measures had to be approved by the Senate. Early Rome was very much open to foreigners, unlike most Greek cities.

Almost all the evidence for the creation of the Roman Republic is late and tends to collapse into a short time development that took decades, maybe centuries. Two basic changes were crucial: *liberty*, the freedom of the people to participate rather than be ruled by a king, and *republic*, from *res publica*, the "public thing"—government, the state itself, was an affair that belonged to everyone. It was not *res privata*, the "private (or personal) thing" of a single ruler. Because Romans did not embrace the idea of equality, the idea of who the "people" were who were allowed to participate was worked out in the early years of the republic.

Two basic mechanisms drove political and institutional change in the early republic. Poor plebeians wanted land, debt relief, and published laws, while rich plebeians wanted access to public offices that were restricted to patricians. Rome's patricians carried out a policy of "expanding defense." Towns and regions around Rome were seen as potential enemies; therefore, the Romans attacked and either neutralized or conquered them. This more-or-less continuous warfare demanded participation of the plebs.

Several times, the plebs "seceded" from the Roman state to wrangle concessions from the patricians. Plebs organized themselves into a plebeian council that could pass laws binding on all the plebs. This created solidarity. Eventually, the plebs got 10 tribunes as defenders of their interests. They could veto acts of magistrates or laws of patrician assemblies. In 449, Twelve Tables bearing laws were erected in the forum. By 367, the plebeians could be elected *consul*, the highest office in the Roman state. In 287, the Licinian-Sextian law granted the legislation of the plebeian assembly full binding power on all the Roman people.

By the early decades of the 3rd century B.C., Rome was, formally at least, a democracy and dominant in central Italy. It remains for us to see how that Roman political system worked. The middle years of the 3rd century also saw the initiation of the military activities that gained Rome an empire. Yet already we can see that Rome had been a relatively stable and efficient system, with mechanisms for reforming itself, for much longer than any of the Greek poleis had managed. ∎

Suggested Reading

Barker and Rasmussen, *The Etruscans.*

Cornell, *The Beginnings of Rome.*

Livy, *The Early History of Rome.*

Questions to Consider

1. Thinking about Rome's early political development, what comparisons with the Greek world suggest themselves to you?

2. Can you discern in early Roman history any durable terms or practices of the Western political tradition?

The Rise of Rome
Lecture 16—Transcript

At the end of the last lecture, I mentioned that all roads lead to Rome, and our road has now brought us to Rome, to Italy, and to history in the western Mediterranean region.

The Romans have been central to the Western tradition in a variety of ways. They have been remembered in a number of ways—that's important, as we've been seeing. They did a number of very interesting things. The Romans created stable, efficient political institutions that were admired and emulated for centuries. There was stability that we saw in Sparta; Rome created greater stability and perhaps a somewhat more admirable kind of stability. The Romans created the most influential secular legal system in the history of the world. Roman law has been of enormous significance.

The Romans were masters of what we might call "civil engineering." You need water in a city, and the nearest water is 50 miles away? No problem, you build an aqueduct. You have an enemy ensconced on a plateau 1300 feet above sea level? No problem, the Roman military engineers simply build a ramp to get you up there. These were people with a remarkable sense of the real, of the practical, of the normal, of the objective in the world around them. They saw problems; they thought about them a bit; they solved them.

For all that, the Romans were, in some ways, unlikely players on the world stage. After all, they come from the western Mediterranean. All of the action has been in the eastern Mediterranean. They are on the west side of Italy, facing west. Again, the action is in the eastern Mediterranean. It is a curious phenomenon that, with one or two exceptions, Rome's great ports are on its western coast, facing, as it were, in the wrong direction.

The area where the Romans emerged, the plain of Latium (which gives its name to Latin, it is Lazio today) is in the center of the Italian peninsula, but it's not a very big area. It didn't really provide the kind of foundation, the kind of basis we might think, for people who would eventually build a world empire. If you ever have the opportunity to fly into Fiumicino Airport, and it's a clear day and you're sitting near a window and you look out, you can see the whole plain of Latium with the ring of hills surrounding it. You say, "That is where Roman history began. That is where the Romans were nurtured."

Latium's a part of Italy. Let's just, for a minute, fix the shape of Italy in our minds. It's a long peninsula, as you know. It runs about 750 miles from the Alps in the north all the way to the Mediterranean Sea in the south. To the Romans, however, parts of this peninsula were more important than others. If you were going up along the eastern coast of Italy, at just about the point when the coast begins to loop around and turn directly to the east, there's a small river. It's called the Rubicon. Very much later in history, and a few lectures later in this course, we'll see Caesar crossing the Rubicon, but that's not our point today. The point today that I wanted to make is the Rubicon separated Italy proper, Roman Italy proper, from *Gallia Cisalpina*—that means Gaul on this side of the Alps.

To the Romans, Italy is the area from the Rubicon River south. We can take this whole Italian area, however, and divide it into several regions. Let's go back up to this top region, Gallia Cisalpina. Of course, the Romans then later on would refer to Gallia Transalpina. Gaul, what we think of as France, that's Gaul on the other side of the Alps. We'll get Romans there a little bit later on. Here we're in the north of Italy proper, or at least of the Italian region. Gallia Cisalpina is, essentially, the Po River basin. It is an area of extraordinarily rich farmland. It was in antiquity; it is today. It's an area with a mild continental climate. It doesn't quite have the Mediterranean climate of peninsular Italy, but it doesn't quite have the harsh winters of the continent to the north. So, very valuable agricultural land, but, in certain respects, outside the immediate ambit of Roman interests.

Liguria-Tuscany is the region north of Latium, north of Rome, particularly along the western coast of Italy and extending over to the Apennine Mountains, which is the spine of mountains that runs up and down the Italian peninsula. Those Apennines, it's worth pausing to say, are not so terribly high, but they're high enough that they've always been a bit of a nuisance for travel and communications in Italy. If any of you have ever visited Italy, you know that it's very easy to take trains north and south, and very difficult take trains east and west, because if you go east and west, you've got to hop the Apennines at some point or another. Liguria-Tuscany was, as Roman history opens, the place where people called the Etruscans lived, and we'll see in just a few minutes that the Romans had some important encounters with the Etruscans in their early history.

On the other side of Latium, to the south, is Campania—literally, the countryside. The main people here were called the Samnites. In our next lecture, we'll encounter the Romans dealing with the Samnites as they begin to spread their authority inside Italy. The main thing we want to remember here is this is an area of tough, craggy mountain ridges, many of them rising to about 2000 meters in height. This is tough country. If you ever have an opportunity to ask a veteran of World War II who had to fight his way up through that country, you'll understand something of the task the Romans faced as they fought their way down through that country. Campania—the region to the south of Latium.

Finally, on the other side of Campagnia was Magna Graecia. You'll perhaps recall that we talked about this before. This is the heel and toe of the Italian peninsula, and coming all the way up to the Bay of Naples, and then the island of Sicily lying beyond. This is the area where, during the transition from the Dark Ages to the Archaic period in Greek history, we saw large numbers of Greek colonists come and settle. We even bumped into philosophers there, people like Pythagoras, for example. So, this had been a very important region, and had helped, in some ways, to begin linking Italy in the west to the world of the eastern Mediterranean, to the Greek world.

The Iron Age came to Italy in perhaps 1000 B.C., the transition from the Bronze Age to the Iron Age. The Italian peninsula seems to have experienced the same kinds of migrations from the north to the south that, for example, the Balkan Peninsula did, and probably on roughly the same chronology. But we can pick up the story, not in the prehistoric, not in the Neolithic, but rather with the advent of the Iron Age, the emergence of iron weapons and tools.

Archaeologists today, on the basis of their discoveries, would say that there seems to begin to be a history around Rome about 800 B.C. That's interesting for any number of reasons, but for one reason in particular. The Romans remembered the date of the founding of their city as the year that we call

753 B.C. Here again, we have one of these things a bit like, for example, the Trojan Wars in Greek memory. Roman tradition was pretty good in terms of remembering about when things got started. That said, what got started was pretty small and pretty humble.

Rome is well sited; the place where Rome sits is well sited. It's about 15 miles inland, up the River Tiber. It's not right on the coast and vulnerable, but the Tiber is navigable down to the coast. That meant that it was always possible to provision the city. Rome was at the point where there was a good ford of the River Tiber in the coastal road that ran right up through Liguria-Tuscany up into the Etruscan region, and then down to the south, all the way to Naples and beyond, into Magna Graecia. It was an area for commerce: good for exchange, good for the movements of peoples and ideas.

The point where the Tiber makes its great loop through the city of Rome is low and swampy and damp and fairly nasty. But Rome, as you probably know—like Cincinnati for example—is built on seven hills. The people at Rome were always able, early on, to move up and live on those hilltops, where they could catch afternoon breezes and also where they didn't have to live down in the malarial swamps. Then, slowly over time, the Romans began to drain those swamps, and to open up a flat area between and among the seven hills. Broadly speaking, you have a situation where, over the long course of Roman history, those with fewer financial resources live down in the flat and those with greater financial resources live up on the hills—up the edges of the hills or perhaps even on top of them. So Rome was reasonably well situated from a variety of points of view.

As I mentioned a moment ago, Italy's best harbors are actually on the west; they faced west. And, it bears repeating, the "action"—everything we've talked about until now in this course of lectures—has been happening in the eastern Mediterranean. What was going on in Rome, what was going on in Italy, what was going on in the West were all of these other issues that we have been talking about, were unfolding. That's perhaps the first issue, or one of the central issues, that we will talk about a little bit in this lecture. What's happening way over here in the West?

You may notice, and I have attempted from time to time with cross-references to stitch things together a little bit, that Mesopotamia and Egypt are unfolding roughly contemporaneously. We then move along and we begin to see the emergence of life at an early time in Minoan Crete, and then in Mycenaean Greece, and that the Greeks are moving along, as Assyria, and then Persia, are rising. In the eastern Mediterranean, we've been keeping several barrels in the air all at once, as we've been juggling these various peoples, countries, and civilizations.

Now we turn to the West and say, "What was going on over there?" The great threats to the Romans, in a certain sense. Did the Romans face threats? They had more powerful neighbors, more important, more interesting neighbors, in certain ways, than they. Latium is a region of small villages; it was not yet united in any meaningful sense. To the north, there were the Etruscans. To the south, there were the Greeks. In between the Romans and the Greeks were the Samnites, a region of small villages that very slowly but surely began to coalesce, began in a sense to pull together, to make something like the Roman people.

Tradition tells us that the Romans expelled their last Etruscan king, Tarquin the Proud, *Tarquinius Superbus*, in the year we call 509 B.C., and created a republic. That tradition bears a little scrutiny. We need to think about that just a little bit. During a couple of centuries then—two-and-a-half centuries, from 753 B.C., when tradition says Rome was founded, down to 509 B.C., when tradition says Rome created a republic—Rome progressed from being a few small, scattered settlements into being a city of some consequence.

There is always a parallel with the Greek *polis*, do you remember *asty* + *cora* = *polis*? Eventually, Rome is the *asty*. There did remain villages, and there was farmland out in the *cora*—that is to say, the plain of Latium. But inside the city, there began to emerge something that would remind us in some ways of one of the Greek *poleis*, of the *asty*, of the center of the city.

The Romans, for example, built their first forum—their first great open public square where they conducted their public business. They built their first stone buildings: temples in the first instance, other buildings thereafter.

They began to lay out streets. They erected the very first set of walls around their city.

It's interesting to think, did the Romans do all of this because this is just what people naturally do, or were the Romans, in a way, looking over their boundaries to the Greeks in the south, where, as we've seen, Greeks imported into Italy (exported from Greece) the *polis*? The chances are pretty good that influence of the Greeks in the south was decisive. That, in a way, the Romans looked at them and said, "That's what you do." It's not impossible that there was Roman originality playing a role here as well. Also, it's important to say that the Romans laid their cities out a little bit differently. The Romans accorded, for example, greater prominence to the forum than would have been the case in a Greek city, where the *agora* was perhaps the great central square.

This renders pretty controversial the relationship between the Romans and the Etruscans to their north. There's a lot of mystery surrounding the Etruscans, and we don't have time here to pursue the quite interesting story of these people, probably originally from the eastern Mediterranean, though that isn't absolutely crystal clear. Exactly when they came to Italy is not crystal clear; it is a contentious point among specialists. Suffice it to say, that they began to build a series of small towns in the area immediately north of Latium, perhaps as many as 12 small cities. Over a period of time, those cities got quite rich—as the archaeological record indicates—partly from mining, partly from farming, and partly from trade.

Roman legend tells us—and in later lectures we'll talk about some of the authors, some of the writers who leave us these legends, but also communicated them to the Romans, so we'll in a sense eavesdrop on some of this Roman storytelling. For the moment, we'll just move along and say that Roman legend tells us that the Etruscans conquered the Romans, and then, in 509 B.C., the Romans liberated themselves. That story's a bit too tidy. There almost certainly was a long period of mutual interaction, mutual rivalry, mutual influence—one party being dominant at one moment, the other party being dominant at a different moment.

Roman tradition says that Rome was ruled by seven kings, and that it was the last of these Etruscan kings, Tarquin the Proud, who the Romans expelled in creating their republic. Rome almost certainly had kings; that seems pretty clear to us. That Rome had seven kings is not so clear to us. We have no number to substitute—I'm not prepared to say that I think there were 10, I think there were 26. But the point is, we can't be sure that the seven of whom the tradition records some information are the only kings that Rome had.

Roman kings had fairly broad powers in war, in religion and in daily life. They led Roman armies, they regulated the public religion of the state and they regulated a great many civic activities in the city. They left a very deep imprint on Rome's later institutions, as we'll see in more detail in our next lecture. But the point is that the kings—although the Romans expelled the last king and did not recreate a monarchy—monarchy left a deep imprint on the Roman constitution. That's the point I wish to make and one of the reasons to talk about these first couple of hundred years of Roman history. However murky and legendary it may be, it had influence later on.

The kings were assisted in ruling Rome in these early times by a group of men called "fathers," *patres*. Hence, patricians. At Rome, the governing class, the ruling class, the ruling elite, are always called the patricians. If you know someone named Patricia, that means she is "well-fathered." If you know someone named Patrick, that means he is "well-fathered." You say, "Noble's lost it. Patrick's Irish." Well, he wasn't Irish, he was British, but never mind. His name is Roman and means "well-fathered." Patrick's not an Irish name.

These well-fathered ones, like the *eupatrids* in Greece, the well-fathered Greeks, are again an older group of distinguished and responsible citizens. They had a council, a sort of an assembly, through which they exercised their authority. It is called the Senate. The Roman Senate comes from the Latin word *senex*, which means an old man. Think of senectitude and senescence, some words that we use in English. *Senex*, a group of old men. This might prompt you to think of Sparta and the council of equals above the age of 60, though there were no age requirements, specifically, for sitting in the Roman Senate.

The ordinary people at Rome were the plebeians, the ordinary people. There's a good bit of controversy about exactly who were the plebs. Were they preexisting people in the region Latium when the people we know as the Romans came in? Were they people who lost out in political struggles at the time when the Romans were sort of settling their affairs with the Etruscans, and so on? We don't know with real confidence who exactly these plebs were. It's actually a little bit difficult to say who the well-fathered patricians were. The point is that there was a group of people, the plebs, over whom another group of people, the patricians, ruled.

There was an assembly of all citizens that could take legislative initiative. There was an assembly of all citizens. That is rather like the situation that we've seen in the Greek world. But early on, at any rate, any measure taken by the citizen assembly had to be approved by the Roman Senate. Here, again, we see something a little bit like the Greek world, a little more like Sparta than like Athens. Remember at Sparta, the assembly could propose an agenda to the council, and the council could say "yea" or "nay." At Rome, the assembly has a little more initiative in proposing things, but finally the Senate says "yea" or "nay." So there are similarities. Did the Romans, again, learn this from the Greek cities to the south? Are these simply fairly obvious ways of organizing yourself politically? Perhaps a little of both.

Early Rome was very much open to foreigners, unlike most Greek cities. Do you remember? In Sparta, you had to be a Spartan citizen to be an equal. At Athens, by the time of Pericles, for example, your mother and your father had to have been Athenian citizens or you were not an Athenian citizen, and therefore could not participate fully. In very early Rome, the Romans were quite open to foreigners. We're going to see, as time goes by, that that openness closed somewhat. It never closed wholly, but it closed somewhat at Rome.

Almost all of the evidence we have for the creation of the Roman Republic is late. By "late" I mean it follows by some centuries, and it tends to collapse into a very short period of time. It tends to compress developments that probably played out over much longer periods of time and that were very, very complex. This is inevitably the way historical writing remembers remote pasts. You simplify the story, you get it down to its basics, and then that's the story you tell yourselves. When we talk about the very early history of Rome, and when we talk about the creation of the Roman Republic—and the Roman Republic will be the object of our investigations here over the next several lectures—we have to recognize that we know most about how the Romans wanted to tell that story, and not so much about what actually happened.

What does the story look like? Two basic changes seem to have been crucial, and this seems to have been important both in terms of what happened and in terms of the way the Romans told the story. The first was the emergence of liberty, *libertas* in Latin, freedom. What freedom meant, particularly in the Roman context, was freedom of the people to participate rather than to be ruled. Again, we have seen that process unfold in Greek cities, so this is not unique to the Romans, not by any stretch of the imagination. But the Romans laid great stress on this as an early stage, as an early moment, in the development of their republic.

Closely connected to this is the notion of republic. The Latin for that is *res publica*, which quite literally means "a public thing," a public affair, something that belongs to the public as a whole. Not, in other words, something that is *res privata*. That means "private things," a private affair; for example, the affairs of a ruler, the affairs of a king. So, that people will be free, and what they do is, in a certain sense, public. The participation of people in open institutions was not a kind of an afterthought, but belonged right at the heart of the Roman system. Liberty, then, and publicness at the heart of the Roman system—not privateness, not rule by a single individual.

It's also very important to notice that the Romans did not embrace the idea of equality. There was a distinction built into the system between patricians and plebeians. The Romans understood rank, distinction, hierarchy, deference. Eventually, the Romans built a system—and we'll pursue this in later lectures—that left virtually all citizens with virtually identical rights. Some modest differences, but fundamentally, virtually everyone had the same rights. Elements of hierarchy, of discipline, and of deference and differentiation remained crucial.

The early years of the Roman Republic then beg interesting questions: Who are the people who get to participate? What does this mean? If you're going to have this freedom in the Roman system, who are the people who will be free, who get to play in the Roman game?

Two basic mechanisms drove change in the early years of the Roman Republic. Again, I invite you to reflect a little bit on what we've seen in the Greek world, for instance, where we know a good deal about the processes of political change there. Poor plebeians wanted land, they wanted debt relief and they wanted published laws. These are exactly the issues that we've seen in the Greek world. Poor farmers want some stability in their lives, and they want public law as opposed to the arbitrary rule of individuals. Rich plebeians, on the other hand, want access to public office. They want access to public opportunities, and to forms of participation initially and fundamentally reserved to the patricians.

Something else began happening very early in Rome's history, and this is a theme, again, which we'll pursue in a little bit more detail in some of our later lectures on Rome. Rome began to contend with its neighbors. The legends, the early stories of Rome, make this very, very clear. Scholars have fashioned the doctrine of "expanding defense" as a way of explaining Rome's military activities. In later lectures, we're going to see the Romans virtually conquer the world on the basis of this theory of expanding defense.

Put in simplest terms, expanding defense means this. The next village over might one day attack me. Therefore, I will attack it—not because they have attacked me, but because they might. That's a bit too cynical, because the Romans would have said that the gods will not bring us victory in any offensive war, but only in a defensive war. So what the Romans would do— and it is very interesting to watch how meticulous they were in contriving this, in their way of telling stories—is they would pick a fight in such a way that the other party would indeed offend them, and then they would destroy the other party. The point is that, slowly but surely, Rome began to conquer the other villages on the plain of Latium, and then, slowly, the people lying beyond. You either capture, you neutralize, you destroy—in one way or another, you sort of beat down your neighbors. Again, this is what we saw in the Greek world.

As the Romans were more regularly at war—as the Romans were more regularly in contention with those who lived around them—a larger and larger portion of their population had to be drafted into this military service. By "draft," I just mean drawn in; there was no Roman draft. In principle, every Roman farmer was a soldier.

If the people are going to be asked to go out and fight and die, and the people have certain political aspirations or certain political grievances, then the people are going to demand opportunities and they're going to exchange those opportunities for their military service. This is precisely like what we see with the transition from the aristocratic man on horseback, the warrior of the *Iliad*, to the hoplite phalanx in the Greek *poleis*. The story was told there in very much the same way.

The Roman plebs did something rather clever. Several times, they "seceded" from the Roman state, and that was the formal description of what they did. In effect, they went on strike, and they said, "We will not serve, unless certain concessions are made to us." Slowly, what began to happen as a result of these concessions—what are we talking about—well, across the fifth century B.C., in other words, the early decades of the existence of this Roman Republic—theoretically, in legend, founded in 509. The plebs organized themselves into a plebeian council, for example, which was permitted initially to pass laws binding on them, but not on the Roman people as a whole, which means not on the patricians. That created solidarity among the plebs, without yet necessarily anchoring the plebs into the Roman system.

In the second place, the plebs were permitted to choose, every year, 10 tribunes, who were sort of to be officers, who looked out for the interests of the plebeians. They couldn't actually lead the Roman state; they couldn't lead its armies, and that sort of thing. What they could do was veto acts of the magistrates, and veto acts or even deliberations going on in the patrician assemblies. In 449 B.C., the Twelve Tables of Roman Law were erected, published if you like, in the Roman forum.

By 367 B.C., the plebeians were regularly able to be elected consul. We shall in our next couple of lectures deal with the constitution of the Roman state.

Consul is the highest executive officer; the plebeians could be elected consul. They had gained one important and powerful concession.

By 287 B.C., the Licinian-Sextian law granted the legislation of the plebeian assembly full binding power on all the Roman people. What had emerged, in the first place, as a concession to and a way of building solidarity among the plebs turned into a capacity of the plebs to pass laws binding on all the Roman people. We'll just say here, Roman laws were always named after the officers who were responsible for passing them; so, Licinian-Sextian law was two fellows, Licinius and Sextius.

By the early third century B.C., Rome was formally, at least, a democracy. Virtually everyone could participate, vote, hold office, and so on. Rome was dominant in central Italy. What remains for us to turn to is: How did these Roman people actually govern themselves? What was their system actually like? How did these Roman people build an empire, a vast empire that would one day reach from southern Scotland to Mesopotamia? But those are subjects to which we shall turn in later lectures.

The Roman Republic—Government and Politics
Lecture 17

> The Roman government, like others, was partly institutions; it was partly ideologies—fundamental governing underlying ideas. It was, fundamentally, social practices that evolved, that changed over time.

The Roman republican constitution was a combination of institutions, ideologies, social values, and historical experience. We are fortunate to know a great deal about it. The Roman magistrates operated on the basis of *collegiality* and *annuality*: The officers cooperated formally and informally, and they changed every year.

The highest magistrate was the consul. Two, elected annually, convened the voting assemblies and led the army; ex-consuls entered the Senate automatically. *Praetors* were the judicial officers. Originally, there were two but, finally, as many as eight. They presided in courts and issued "praetor's edicts" on taking office—these added to the body of Roman law. Ex-praetors entered the Senate automatically.

Quaestors were the financial officers of the state. They received taxes, fines, and tributes and let out state contracts for such things as waterworks. They were elected annually but could also be appointed by consuls. Originally, there were two, but this rose to an undetermined number. Ex-quaestors entered the Senate automatically. *Aediles* had responsibility for the food supply, public buildings and streets, games and entertainments.

Ten tribunes were elected from the plebs and continued to have responsibility for the best interests of the ordinary people and the power to veto acts of the magistrates and assemblies. Two censors were elected every five years and served for 18 months. Their primary task was to set the census status of every citizen (see below) and to legislate on public morality.

Rome's assemblies present a slightly confusing image. The Curiate Assembly from the royal period withered under the Republic, and the Plebeian Council declined after 287. The Senate was originally restricted to patricians, then opened to former holders of high offices. It passed treaties but could not legislate. The Tribal Assembly constituted the Roman people organized according to districts, of which there were 33, four in the city and 29 in the surrounding countryside—always a boon to wealthy landowners.

The Centuriate Assembly constituted the Roman people organized according to wealth into 192 *centuries*. The wealthiest Romans made up the majority of the centuries. Legislation could be introduced by magistrates or ordinary Romans. Bills were read three times in the Roman forum, vigorously debated, and then voted on. Assemblies used the system of "block voting": There were 33 votes in the Tribal Assembly and 192 in the Centuriate (think of the U.S. Electoral College).

Stoicism taught that all visible differences in the world are illusory and accidental.

The big question is, how did this system work? The first critical point to remember is that deference was paid to age, experience, and tradition. The oldest member of the Senate—the "prince of the Senate"— spoke first. The Senate did not pass laws but issued influential opinions (*Senatusconsulta*). The Senate was made up of former holders of high offices. Tribes and Centuries caucused before voting, and the *seniores* spoke and voted before the *iuniores*.

Patron-client bonds were critical to the operation of Roman society as a whole. The rich and powerful had large numbers of people in various bonds of obligation. A remarkably small number of families—fewer than 100—provided almost all of the officers of the Roman Republic for the first 400 years of its existence. Historians speak of a "senatorial aristocracy." This is perhaps understandable before the attainment of essential equality between patricians and plebeians but harder to understand thereafter.

The central Roman political and social values contributed to the preservation of the system. *Auctoritas*: Romans placed great stress on the eminence, the inner dignity, of their greatest citizens, past and present. This was not, in principle, a matter of wealth or birth. *Mos maiorum*: The "custom of our ancestors" was to the Romans the guiding light in all things. This is how most speeches began.

Perhaps the greatest critique and assessment of this system came from the Greek historian Polybius (c. 200–c.118 B.C.). Polybius was a learned Greek captured by the Romans in Greece and brought back to live for decades in honorable captivity among the most influential Romans. He wrote a history of his times, the sixth book of which is a penetrating evaluation of Rome's system. He wanted to understand how a people so recently barbarian had come to conquer the known world in such a short time.

He attributed their success to their "mixed" constitution. Consuls were like kings: monarchy. Senators were like aristocrats: oligarchy. Assemblies were like demos: democracy.

Polybius had a characteristic Greek view of the cyclical evolution of politics: Monarchy → oligarchy → democracy → mob rule → monarchy. He believed that the Romans had escaped the cycle.

Was Polybius right? Yes and no. The Roman system was remarkably stable for a long time, and the "mixed" dimension of the constitution was there for all to see. Polybius said nothing about the culture of deference or the senatorial aristocracy. Polybius's views could not address the strains on a small, tradition-bound city-state of the acquisition of world empire.

The Roman system has been, in concrete institutional structures and in fundamental ideological notions, formative in later Western political development. ∎

Suggested Reading

Brunt, *Social Conflicts in the Roman Republic*.

Polybius, *Histories* (esp. Book 6).

Scullard, *Roman Politics*.

Questions to Consider

1. Can you see how the Roman system was theoretically open and, in practice, closed?

2. Can you detect the influences of the Roman constitution on the Founding Fathers of the United States?

The Roman Republic—Government and Politics
Lecture 17—Transcript

We're going to talk about the government and institutions of the Roman Republic. You may recall that last time, we put the Romans on the map, quite literally. We talked a little about the geography of Italy; we talked about who the Romans were, the early Romans. We talked about their neighbors, the Etruscans, the Greeks to the south, and so on. We talked about the rather intense political and social turmoil that marked the first couple of centuries of the history of the Roman people, and how one result of that turmoil was a situation where social and economic distinctions were, to some degree, effaced so that all Romans could participate pretty much fully and equally in Roman political life.

What we want to turn to today is the kind of government they created—talk a little bit about how that government actually worked, what the institutions were, what the officers were. I want to talk a little bit about the social values that underlay that government. Finally, we'll reflect a little on that government, through the eyes of the Greek historian, Polybius. Much that we say towards the end of this lecture will seem very familiar because Thomas Jefferson knew Polybius, and some of Polybius' ideas were writ right into the American Constitution.

The Roman government, like others, was partly institutions; it was partly ideologies—fundamental governing underlying ideas. It was, fundamentally, social practices that evolved, that changed over time. And it was, fundamentally, the product of historical experience. The Romans liked to think of themselves as being sort of sturdy, stable and unchanging. In fact, as we'll see in this and in subsequent lectures, things changed a good deal.

One of the things that's particularly interesting to us about the Roman government is, because of the nature of the information that survives the sources, we know a great deal about it. We know far more about the Romans than we do, for example, about the Greeks, or indeed about any of the peoples whom we discussed in the ancient Near East, or the Egyptians, for example.

The Roman constitution, in the first place, and then something about Roman society, then something about ideologies. The Roman constitution was, in the first place, led by a series of magistrates. When we talk about the magistrates of the Roman Republic, there are two principles that we need to keep in mind. The first of these is *collegiality*. They worked as a college of officers, as a group of men (they were all men) bound together, and in some ways required to cooperate with each other to facilitate one another's work. We'll see some concrete examples of that in just a second.

In the second place, *annuality*. They were elected every year. All of the Roman magistrates with one exception—one peculiar exception that we'll describe in a few minutes—all of the Roman magistrates were elected annually. Now, we have elections every four years, or maybe local elections every two years. Imagine the Romans, an election every year.

The highest magistrate of the Roman Republic was the consul. Of these, there were two. They were elected annually. They convened the Roman voting assemblies; that was one of their primary responsibilities. We'll talk about those voting assemblies in a few minutes. They led the Roman army, and ex-consuls automatically entered the Roman Senate. We'll talk about the Roman Senate in a few moments. But for a moment, let's just say that consuls are the chief executive officers of the Roman state.

Next, there were the *praetors*. The praetors were the judicial officers of the Roman state. Originally, there were two of these; the role got larger as its business grew more complicated. The number of praetors eventually expanded to as many as eight. They presided in the courts. This was their fundamental day-in and day-out responsibility; they presided in the Roman courts. They weren't exactly judges, in our sense of the term, but we might think of them by analogy to judges.

Perhaps historically, in the long term, the most important thing about the praetors is that on taking office each year, they issued a "praetor's edict." This would be a basic statement of what their priorities would be, what their goals would be, what the essential things that they would work on during their year in office would be. But those praetor's edicts gradually added together and built up the body of Roman law. This is really a fundamental source for Roman law. Like the consuls, the praetors entered the Senate on conclusion of their year in office.

Next, there were officials called *quaestors*. The quaestors were essentially the financial officers of the Roman state. They received taxes. They received fines when persons were fined, for example, in courts of law. They received tributes, tributes paid to the Romans by peoples whom they had conquered. They let out state contracts for such things as waterworks, for such things as road building. This was an opportunity for considerable peculation; letting out public contracts has sometimes been a bit seedy in modern times, and it was much the same in Roman times.

Quaestors often were able to use their year in office as a way both to enrich themselves and also to earn the favor of large numbers of people in Roman society, for whom they did sometimes very large favors. They, again, were elected annually, but they could also be appointed by the consuls. When there was a need for extraordinary quaestors, the consuls could actually appoint quaestors. As with the other officers, initially there were two, and then over time, the number grew. After the very early days of the Republic, there was no longer a fixed number of quaestors; there might be two or four or six or eight, it just depended a little bit on circumstances. And ex-quaestors, like the other ex-officers, entered the Roman Senate.

There were, next, *aediles*. Aediles had responsibility for the food supply. That was one of their key responsibilities. They also had responsibilities for public buildings in Rome, as the city of Rome grew—as it became a larger city, a more complex city, a more sophisticated city—that was a very large responsibility. They also had responsibility for the streets of Rome, which also meant for the sewers of Rome. They also were responsible for putting on games and public entertainments. This, as Rome grew larger, as the city grew more complex, was, again, a very important responsibility. Aediles did not enter the Senate automatically on the conclusion of their term of office. Generally, if one held the aedileship, for example, at a little bit later time, one would move on to hold one of the other offices, and then, perhaps, move on into the Senate.

You may remember that, in our last lecture, we had talked about the tribunes. During the times when the plebeians had seceded from the Roman state—had, in effect, gone on strike to secure their interests—on one of those occasions, they were accorded the privilege of choosing 10 of their number as tribunes, who would then be sort of persons charged with responsibility for the best interests of the ordinary people. Remember, they had the power to veto acts of the magistrates and the assemblies. They could, for example, sit outside the assembly halls if they were not elected members, and if they didn't like the direction that the debate inside was taking, they could shout, "Veto!"—I forbid—and the discussion came to an end.

The tribunes lacked, in a sense, under the republican constitution, some of the reason for being that had brought them into place in the first instance. After 287 B.C., when patricians and plebeians were essentially equal and could hold all offices, it was a little less important for the tribunes to be there, to look out for the interest of the plebs. Nevertheless, right through the Roman Republic, the 10 tribunes continued to be elected. On some occasions, late in the history of the Republic, they played a very decisive role in Roman politics. We'll come to that a couple of lectures down the road.

There were, finally, two *censors*. Remember I said everybody's elected annually, with one exception? Here's the exception, there's two of them, so we might say it's two exceptions, but it's only one office. Every five years, two censors were chosen. They served for 18 months, and then they went out of office. Then, for three-and-a-half years, there were no censors. Then they were elected again.

There were two responsibilities, and if you think about it, the word "censor" to us can imply two different things. In the first place, the Roman censors fixed the census status of citizens. What that means, I'll explain in just a second. They fixed the census status of citizens, and they issued rules on public morality. Even today, we think of a censor as: the person who, every 10 years, knocks on your door and counts everybody in your house; or the censor who tells you what books you can read or not read, or what movies you should see. The censors at Rome had both those responsibilities, but their fundamental responsibility was to fix the census status of Roman citizens.

Thus far, then, the magistrates of the Roman state. There were occasionally some minor officials, but that is basically the group of magistrates who, from the earliest days of the Republic until its end, led, organized, managed, governed, functioned as sort of the chief executive of this Roman state.

The voting assemblies, then. How did the Romans legislate? How did the Romans come together, discuss their public business and take action? They had a series of different assemblies, which are related to one another in rather complicated ways. It's sometimes a little hard to grasp exactly how the Roman system worked. I'll see if I can't at least shed some light on the situation.

In very early times, there was a body called the "Curiate Assembly." This goes all the way back to the time when Rome had kings. It withered under the Republic, and is really not particularly important, though if you were to read some early Roman history you might see mention of this. In the high period of the Republic, it's not really important, and needn't engage our attention here.

There was also a "Plebeian Council." This council also—after the Licinian-Sextian laws, in 287 B.C., granted essential equality to the decisions of the plebs and the decisions of the Centuriate Assembly—the old Plebeian Council also withered. It really didn't have the kind of significance it once did.

That leaves us with the fundamental institutions—the fundamental legislative institutions, or deliberative bodies of the Roman people. First, the Senate. The Latin word *senatus* is derived from the Latin word *senex*, which means "old man." You'll remember at Sparta that it was the group of old men who governed the state.

So, too, in Rome, a body which was in some sense imagined as that of the older or the wiser men had prime responsibility in the Roman state. But there is an irony. It was made up, originally, of patricians, and eventually open to all. It was made up of ex-office holders. It had the fundamental responsibility of passing treaties, but it could not legislate. The Roman Senate did not pass laws, and Rome did not function with a bicameral, or even with a multicameral, legislature. That is to say, issues discussed in one of the other assemblies, to which we'll turn in just a second, did not come up to the Senate for resolution. The Senate had no role—well, it did have a certain kind of role, I'll come to that in a minute—it had no formal role in legislation. It could not pass laws.

There was then the "Tribal Assembly." The Tribal Assembly constituted the Roman people, organized according to districts. Here was one of the great acts of gerrymandering in human history. There were four districts, so tribe means district; tribe does not mean a group of people related to one another. Maybe way, way back in Roman history there was some hint, some suggestion, some notion that people living together in a certain area would then act together publicly. Whatever might have been the case, once we enter this historical period, tribe means district.

There were four districts in the city and 29 in the countryside surrounding it. By the time, let's say, of the birth of Christ, the city of Rome had about a million people. All of those people had basically four districts. The people on the outside of the city had about 29. That was always a boon to the wealthy landowners, who had managed this system. Its institutional consequences, we'll see in just a second.

There was, in the second place, the "Centuriate Assembly," the assembly by "centuries." What exactly is a "century?" It's 100; that's easy enough. Was this originally a group of 100 citizens, organized for some purpose? Was it a military band of 100 men, organized perhaps for domestic defense in the event that Rome were attacked? We don't really know. We don't really know what the point of the word "century" is. By the time we enter the historic period, centuries were groups of people, grouped by wealth.

Now, we come back to our censors. Every five years, the censors tried to assess the wealth of all of the Roman citizens. According to their wealth, it placed them in census classes; it placed them in one of 192 centuries. You'll be asking yourself, "Why 192?" I can't tell you. We don't know. But there were 192 centuries. Like the Tribal Assembly, the Centuriate Assembly was also gerrymandered. That is to say, about 10 percent of the Roman population constituted about the first 100 centuries. The remaining 90 or so centuries involved about 90 percent of the population. We're going to see how the Romans voted, in just a moment, and you'll see with particular clarity why that fact is significant. The Tribal Assembly and the Centuriate Assembly—the fundamental voting assemblies of the Roman people, the fundamental assemblies that passed Roman laws.

How do we start the process? Legislation could be introduced by the magistrates. A consul, a praetor, could introduce into one of the assemblies a piece of proposed legislation. Bills were then read three times in the Roman forum. They were read from the rostrum in the Roman forum, to whatever people gathered. If it were a great controversial issue, there would perhaps be lots of people there. If it was a relatively minor point, there might be very few people around. The bills were read out three times publicly. Does any of this begin to sound a bit familiar? I think so. These issues were vigorously debated by the Roman people and then voted upon.

Now we come to the significance of that gerrymandering, to which I was referring just a moment ago. The Roman assemblies used the system of block voting. In other words, it made no difference how large the Roman population was. The Tribal Assembly had 33 votes to cast. The Centuriate Assembly had 192 votes to cast. How did they work?

The centuries would come together when the Centuriate Assembly was called, and this was direct democracy. It was not a republican system in the sense that these were elected representatives of people. Every Roman citizen was automatically a member of a tribe, because he lived somewhere, and a member of a century, because he had some wealth that fixed him in a certain status, in a certain category.

The Centuriate Assembly would come together, and each assembly, one after the other, would debate the issue that was before the Roman people, would vote among themselves and cast a vote. Century 1 casts a vote for or against a measure; Century 2 casts a vote for or against the measure; Century 3 casts a vote for or against the measure; and so on. Remember a moment ago, I had said that about 10 percent of the Roman people made up about 100 of the centuries? What that meant is that about 10 percent of the Roman people could cast about 100 votes, and normally—not always, sometimes issues were controversial—produce a little splitting. Normally, the issue would be decided before the vast majority of people ever voted. Yet, everyone participated, everyone voted. It looked as though all were equals.

In the Tribal Assembly, people came together in a voting hall, which archaeologists have discovered and elucidated very clearly in Rome. It was arranged in a series of long stalls. At the front of the room was a rostrum, a podium, with an urn. The tribes would gather together again—the tribe gathers together and they would discuss the issue. Then each member of the tribe would walk to the front, and walk past an urn and drop in either a white pebble—that's a vote for the measure, or a black pebble—that's a vote against the measure. There's the origin of being "blackballed." When all of Tribe 1 had voted, the urn was emptied out and the pebbles were counted. There is now a vote for or against the measure. And Tribe 2 votes.

It occurred to you, perhaps, that here is the origin of our electoral college: "block voting." In other words, it didn't make any difference if Tribe 1 had 10 people and Tribe 2 had 100,000 people. Each had a vote. It didn't make any difference. One vote per tribe. One vote per century.

If we think about that system for a moment, we can see that it's rife with ironies. On the one hand, everyone participates, everyone votes, everyone seems to function equally. On the other hand, the system is managed in such a way as to leave the most wealthy, most powerful, most influential citizens with the opportunity to decide issues before they actually get to the great mass of people. If we wonder why, on the one hand, Roman society was so stable for so long, and on the other hand, why there was always a certain volatility just below the surface, we can see it in these very voting assemblies.

Thus far, the system, in its formal exterior aspects, that's just what it looked like. Let's ask ourselves, how did it actually work? In other words, for instance, imagine a space visitor from Mars who landed in Washington this morning and said, "This is an interesting place I've arrived at. How does it work?" And we say, "Here's the Constitution, read this over and you'll see how it works." I daresay the person could read our Constitution and wouldn't probably know how our system worked. I mean, think of all the attitudes, the values, the historical experience, that simply isn't expressed in that document. In a way, what we've talked about till now is the Roman constitution. Now what we want to say is, how did it work? What were some of its underlying principles?

First, the Romans paid enormous deference to age, experience and tradition. Rome was a hierarchical society, and Rome was a deferential society. There was a culture of deference, a very powerful culture of deference at Rome. Certain citizens, certain traditions, certain ways of doing things were accorded great weight by the Romans. In the second place, and we can see this in a way as a manifestation of the point that I just made, the oldest member of the Senate, the *princep senatus*—the prince of the Senate—always spoke first.

I said a moment ago that the Senate could not pass laws. That's right. But the Senate could issue opinions, *Senatus consulta*—opinions of the Senate. In this culture of deference, when the Roman Senate knew that a certain issue was before the Roman people, a certain issue was being debated, and they said, "It is our opinion that this course of action, or that course of action, should be followed," this carried enormous weight. It had no binding legal force; *senatus consulta* did not have binding legal force, but it carried a tremendous amount of weight.

Let's imagine the Senate. The oldest member rises and speaks first. Then, one after another, the Senators speak on an issue. Imagine one of the younger members of the Senate, one of the newer members of the Senate. Is he going to stand up and say, "Well, old man, that's all very well and good, but I have a new idea; let's do something different?" No. The younger man, to make his way, is going to stand up and say, "That's brilliant! Yes, I agree completely with that." There would be a tendency for the old men, *senatus senex*—body of old men—to govern. "Old" would mean old by age, but also old by experience.

The tribes and the centuries caucused before voting. Before they actually began casting their ballots, they caucused. That's another good Roman word: *caucus*. And in the caucus, the *seniores* always spoke and voted before the *iuniores*. *Seniores*, the older men. *Iuniores*, the younger men. Once again, when the younger men watched what their older, more experienced fellows were doing, were saying, and how they were voting, it was in their interest to go along. They want to make their way in this society; they want someday to be important and influential people. They're not going to be rebellious, at least for a long, long time, in Roman society. They were not going to be rebellious.

Patron-client bonds were critical to the operation of Roman society as a whole. Rich and powerful people had large numbers of people in various degrees of obligation to them. These might be people whom they had helped financially. These might be people whom they had helped in a court of law. These might be people for whom, a generation or two earlier, their families had done a favor, had done a good turn. The patron-client bond could be formed for lots and lots of reasons. Influential people at Rome—remember those tribes, districts and centuries—wealth groups. Many influential people at Rome could count on the votes of a large number of people who owed them something. That is not written into the Roman constitution, but it's there, and it's a crucial part of how it worked. If you think about it for just a moment, that's not unrelated to this culture of deference to which I referred a moment ago.

One of the interesting results of this set of social and political values that attached to the constitution we described, a remarkably small number of families, about 100, provided almost all the officers of the Roman Republic during the first 400 years of its existence. That's a very small number of families. Historians, therefore, speak about a "senatorial aristocracy," because the point is, of course, that the higher magistrates then entered the Senate.

We can say, in a way, that this is perhaps understandable before the attainment of something like political equality and democracy, with the Licinean-Sextian laws in 287. It's a little harder to understand thereafter, as a political fact, just as a fact of logic. But it's easier to understand when we reflect on this culture of deference. The Romans simply paid deference to certain people.

There were two Roman political values that, it seems to me, help us a little bit more to understand this process. The first of this is *auctoritas*. That's a Latin word from which we get the English word "authority." In the Roman context, this laid great stress on the eminence, the inner dignity, of the greatest citizens. The idea was that certain people were intrinsically more eminent than others, and, therefore, ought to be observed, to be followed, to be listened to. It wasn't a matter of wealth; it wasn't a matter of birth; it wasn't a matter of power. It was a matter of inner qualities. Even to this day, we draw a distinction between authority and power. That's a Roman distinction. Authority is legitimacy; power is mere brute force. To the Romans, that legitimacy flowed from certain inner qualities of people, not simply because they had a lot of power.

The second principle to which I want to draw your attention is the *mos maiorum*, the custom of our ancestors. This was, to the Romans, their guiding light in all things. Did they ever change? Of course they did, but they never admitted to changing. This is how Roman speeches began: Here is what our ancestors did. What would our ancestors have done? There was always this tendency, this sense, this powerful feeling that one must go back to the good old days. The authority of eminent citizens, and then, more particularly, the authority of eminent citizens from the past, explained to the Romans how their system was supposed to work.

Perhaps the greatest critique and assessment of this system came from the Greek historian Polybius. He was born about 200 B.C., died in about 118. He was captured by the Romans during their wars in the Balkans. We'll turn to those wars in our next lecture. He was a very learned Greek, and he set out to write a history of his times. He lived among influential Romans. He lived a very, very elegant and graceful life, even though he was sort of a prisoner of war. He wrote a massive history of the Hellenistic world, that world that we talked about a couple of lectures back. Book 6 of this is a penetrating analysis of Rome's system.

Polybius wanted to understand—he was sort of a haughty Greek—he wanted to understand how a people so recently barbarian had come to conquer virtually the whole known world. He attributed their success to what he called their "mixed" constitution. He said the Romans had consuls, who were very much like kings. There's a monarchical dimension. The Roman Senate was like aristocrats; there was an oligarchical dimension, rule by a few. And the assemblies were like the *demos* in a Greek city: democracy, the rule by the many.

Polybius had a characteristically Greek view of the cyclical evolution of politics. Remember, in antiquity people generally—the Hebrews were different, and we'll see later on that the Christians were different—but among ancient peoples, generally, it was thought that life revolved in great cycles. The wheel of fortune was not a television program in antiquity; it was a philosophical way of talking about how everything works.

There was a notion that there was a natural evolution of societies, starting with monarchy, the rule of a strong person. Eventually, the monarch would have to share power with some number of people, and we would move to oligarchy. Oligarchs would then gradually have to share power with a larger number of people, and we would have democracy, rule by the people. A certain number of the people, of the *demos*, would then begin to rule selfishly in their own interest. We would have mob rule. Mob rule would then be ended by the man on the horse, by the strong man, by the monarch who comes in and brings order, and in a sense brings us back around to the top (or, if you will, the bottom) of the circle, and the cycle begins again.

What intrigued Polybius so much about the Romans was he believed somehow that they had escaped the cycle, that their mixed constitution, their balanced constitution, had enabled them to break out of this vicious cycle of political change. Was Polybius right? Yes and no. The Roman system was remarkably stable for a long time, and the mixed dimension of this constitution was there for all to see. And, as I said, it was admired very much by the founding fathers of the United States. There are a lot of things Polybius didn't tell us. He lived among great people; he ought to have known, but he didn't tell us, for example, anything about the culture of deference. He didn't tell us anything about the senatorial aristocracy. He didn't tell us anything about the relatively small number of families who had monopolized political power over a very long period of time. It's curious, in a way, that Polybius notes certain aspects very penetratingly of the Roman system and seems to ignore others.

Finally, and perhaps most ironic, Polybius lived at Rome at the very moment when the Romans were building a vast empire. One of the things he didn't notice was the kind of strains and tensions that the creation of this empire produced for a small, face-to-face, deferential political system. That said, the Roman system has been, in terms of strict institutional structures and in terms of ideological ideas, formative in the Western tradition. In our next lecture, we'll turn to the strains produced by the creation of the Roman Empire.

Roman Imperialism
Lecture 18

When, finally, the Roman Republic collapsed into a military dictatorship, Rome had emperors. Then the word "Roman Empire" refers to a particular kind of political regime. That regime still had an empire as a geographical entity.

In this lecture, we will explore the emergence and early history of the Roman Empire and discuss some of the ways in which that empire affected Rome. But first, let's clear up the language that we will use. Hearing the term *Roman Empire* may conjure up an image of the far-flung territories over which Rome ruled, or it may suggest the imperial regime, the government of the caesars.

In fact, both terms are appropriate, but in different ways at different times. Under the republic—and this is the subject of the current lecture—Rome acquired provinces all over the Mediterranean world, acquired, that is, an empire. Amidst civil wars, Rome's republic collapsed into a military dictatorship: The Roman Empire was born in the sense of a Roman regime in which power was in the hands of emperors. But the empire, in a physical, geographical sense, kept right on expanding.

Before Rome got entangled with other peoples in the Mediterranean world—in the *Hellenistic world*—the Romans waged war for two and a half centuries in Italy. (In the last lecture, we alluded to some of the political and institutional consequences of that warfare.)

Rome gradually forged the Latin League in Latium. The Latins revolted in the period 340–338 B.C., but the Romans successfully put down the revolt. In 354 B.C., Rome made a treaty with the Samnites. A border provocation led to a series of three Samnite Wars (343–290 B.C.), which brought Rome to a frontier with Magna Graecia. Some Greeks had aided the Samnites, which Rome considered a provocation. To protect themselves, the Greeks called in King Pyrrhus of Epirus, who was defeated by Rome (Pyrrhus lost because of

"Pyrrhic victories"!) during the period 280–276 B.C. Rome then dominated Magna Graecia and all of Italy.

Certain fundamental and longstanding aspects of Roman military tactics and diplomatic practice emerged already in this Italian phase of Roman expansion. Early Romans seem to have borrowed the *hoplite phalanx* from the Greeks. This demonstrates a constant theme of Roman history: a pragmatic willingness to borrow what works.

But in mountainous Samnite country, the phalanx was not useful. (Ask a World War II veteran who fought through that country what it is like!) Gradually, the Romans changed their tactics. By the end of the Samnite Wars, Romans had developed and deployed the legion, bodies of troops arrayed in a checkerboard pattern with great mobility and flexibility.

Roman diplomacy was the stuff of legend in antiquity and has been admired and emulated ever since. Roman diplomacy's first key principle was that of the "just war": The gods would not give Rome a victory in a war of aggression; therefore, the Romans always had to assure themselves that they were avenging an attack or, as the theory evolved, forestalling an attack. The second key principle was generosity toward the conquered. Beginning with the Latins in 338 B.C., Rome's conquered enemies (at least in Italy) were offered very favorable peace terms and accorded a second-class Roman citizenship.

The third key principle was "divide and rule." The Romans rarely made the exact same deal with any two people. Thus, potential foes did not have the same grievances. A corollary of this was the Roman principle that "Your friend is your neighbor but one." A fourth element was Rome's sheer tenacity. Once embarked on a policy, Rome simply did not abandon it. Rome's enemies came to know this.

In conquering the Greeks of southern Italy, Rome came face to face with the Carthaginians, who had important trading bases in Sicily and who may have lent some aid to Rome's enemies in the Pyrrhic Wars. Rome fought three Punic Wars with the Carthaginians (264–241 B.C., 218–201, 149–146). Carthage, the old Phoenician colony, was a naval and commercial power.

Some conflict of interest between Rome and Carthage was inevitable once Rome became dominant in Italy.

Wars are full of great stories and famous characters. In the first war, Rome had, initially, no navy. Sources tell us of Romans building ships while would-be sailors practiced in mock-ups. In the second war, the brilliant general Hannibal crossed the Alps (from secure bases in Spain: Rome now had a navy!) with elephants. Faced with a large army and a superb general, Rome first adopted delaying tactics, that is, fought a guerrilla war. Astonishingly, Rome rallied from a terrible defeat at Cannae in 216.

The Romans believed, absolutely, that the gods would not give Rome a victory in a war of aggression.

In 204, Rome took the war to Carthage when Scipio invaded North Africa. The third war was largely caused by Cato the Elder who ended every speech in the Senate with *Carthago delenda est* ("Carthage must be destroyed"). He would bring in fresh figs to show just how close Rome's foe was. (One is reminded of certain American senators and their nightmares about Cuba.) Why did Rome win? Tenacity and determination played a role. Flexibility in military tactics was important. Critical was that Rome's Italian allies did not fall away. Roman diplomacy proved its value.

During the Second Punic War, the Antigonids had provided some slight assistance to Hannibal. Rome remembered this affront. Rome fought three wars in the Balkans (199–197 B.C., 171–167, 150–146), the first against Macedon and the other two because various Greek cities and leagues had supported the Antigonids.

In the Second Macedonian War, the Seleucids rendered some aid to King Philip V. In 188–187, Rome reckoned accounts with Antiochus III and swept his forces from the eastern Mediterranean. The Seleucid heartlands and Ptolemaic Egypt were still independent, but Rome was already meddling in their internal affairs. After the First Punic War, Rome annexed Sicily, Sardinia, and Corsica. These were the first provinces. By 146, Rome had annexed Greece and Carthage. In 133 B.C., King Attalus III of Pergamum, having no heirs, bequeathed his kingdom to Rome. This act symbolized Roman domination of the Mediterranean world.

The consequences of empire were great for Rome. The institutions of a city-state had to be adapted to govern foreign territories. War provided opportunities for wealth and prestige outside the traditional Roman social and political order. Being constantly at war gradually had a corrosive effect on Rome's society. Veteran soldiers became a disruptive force in politics. ∎

Suggested Reading

Badian, *Foreign Clientelae.*

Gruen, *The Hellenistic World and the Coming of Rome.*

Harris, *War and Imperialism in Republican Rome.*

Livy, *The War with Hannibal.*

Questions to Consider

1. Scholars debate whether Rome was drawn into its conflicts (sometimes called "defensive imperialism") or whether the Romans were aggressive all the time. What do you think?

2. What connections do you perceive between Roman social values and military activity?

Roman Imperialism
Lecture 18—Transcript

This lecture will take up the subject of the rise of the Roman Empire. You may recall that, at the end of the last lecture, when we talked about Roman government and institutions, I was suggesting that the emergence of the Roman Empire produced serious and, finally, fatal strains for the Roman Republic. Let's build that empire, and see, then, what kinds of strains it might have created.

First, let's clear up a little bit of terminology. "Empire," in the Roman context, can have two distinct meanings. On the one hand, it can mean the large conqueries of territories that the Romans conquered and over which they exerted rule. Physically, geographically, an empire. When, finally, the Roman Republic collapsed into a military dictatorship, Rome had emperors. Then the word "Roman Empire" refers to a particular kind of political regime. That regime still had an empire as a geographical entity.

In this lecture, what we're going to talk about is the building of a geographical empire by the Roman Republic. In later lectures, we'll collapse that republic into a military dictatorship, we'll create emperors, and then we'll study the empire that the emperors ruled. Today, "empire" doesn't have anything to do with emperors; it has to do with an empire.

What, then, did the Romans do? How did the Romans come to build an empire all over the Mediterranean world? You'll perhaps recall that when we talked about the rise of Rome a couple of lectures back, it was the case that the early Romans, around the city of Rome, on the plain of Latium, began to struggle with other parties in Italy. They struggled with Greeks to the south. They struggled with the Etruscans to the north. They struggled with various peoples who lived in their own immediate neighborhood in central Italy. We saw that those struggles, which they had with their neighbors in Italy, had some fairly decisive, some fairly important consequences for the early shaping of the Roman political system and the Roman social system.

Gradually, the Romans achieved a degree of independence from the Etruscans to the north. The Greeks continued to live to the south. And in central Italy, the Romans built what we call the "Latin League." It was Rome's relation with the Latin League that set the Romans on a course of conquest in Italy, which would eventually bring them to a course of conquest throughout the Hellenistic world, throughout the Mediterranean world. Rome built this vast empire over a long time by small steps. That's the first thing we want to keep in mind. It was something that happened very gradually, over a very long period of time.

The Latins, the people who lived in Latium, rebelled against the Romans between 340 and 338 B.C. The Romans successfully put down the revolt. Shortly before this war, the Romans made a treaty with the Samnites. These were people who lived to the south of Rome; they lived in the hills to the south of Rome, and a border provocation then led to a series of three Samnite Wars between 343 and 290 B.C. As the Romans fought their neighbors to the south, the Samnites, they bumped up against the frontiers of *Magna Graecia*, Greater Greece—that area in the south of Italy, centered on the Bay of Naples, which had been all of those Greek colonies that we talked about in a much earlier lecture.

Some of the Greeks had aided the Samnites. During Rome's struggle with the Samnites, some of the Greeks in the south thought that these Romans were a little meddlesome. They aided the Samnites in hopes of keeping the Romans to the north. The Romans, therefore, decided that that was a provocation and began to make war upon the Greeks to the south.

The Greeks to the south then invited in one of the minor Hellenistic monarchs. His name was Pyrrhus; he was the king of Epirus—more or less what used to be Yugoslavia in the western Balkans—more or less to come in and help them. Pyrrhus was sort of an up-to-date Hellenistic monarch, and he had a very substantial military establishment. He came in, and he actually defeated the Romans twice; but both of his victories over the Romans were so costly to him—in human and material terms—that we give to those victories still the name of "Pyrrhic victories," a victory you know that if you win any more like that, you're going to lose. Eventually Pyrrhus was defeated because the Romans just wore him down. Once Pyrrhus was unable to protect the Greeks of the south against the Romans, the Romans dominated the Greeks to the south.

We can say that by about 290 B.C., Rome was dominant in the Italian peninsula. It is no coincidence that the Licinian-Sextian laws granting virtual political equality in the Roman system passed in 287 B.C., very shortly after the end of these wars. The Roman military establishment had really depended on large numbers of people, and, therefore, it could no longer exclude them from participation in the political system.

These wars against the Samnites, against the Greeks of the south and against Pyrrhus of Epirus are interesting and revealing to us for a couple of other important reasons. We see already, then, certain fundamental aspects of Roman military practice and tactics and of Roman diplomatic practice. In this very earliest phase, we see some elements that are utterly characteristic of the Romans for a very long time into the future.

The early Romans, for example, appear to have borrowed the *hoplite phalanx* from the Greeks. That was the high-tech military establishment of the times, and so the Romans borrowed it. That, we might just say parenthetically, demonstrates a constant theme of Roman history, a very pragmatic willingness to borrow whatever works. The Romans were quite willing to adapt, to adopt, to borrow, to steal ideas, notions, artistic motifs, poetic motifs, military practice. It didn't matter what it was; the Romans would borrow it. If it worked, they'd use it.

When the Romans fought the Samnites, they faced a situation where the hoplite phalanx was just useless. The Samnite hills, as any World War II veteran who fought his way up the Italian peninsula could tell you, are a series of very tough, hard, 2000-meter high ridges, one after another. In those hills, the phalanx just wasn't useful. The phalanx is useful on a great open field. The Romans began to evolve the legion, a series of military groups arrayed in something like checkerboard fashion on the battlefield. It's extremely flexible, it's extremely fast, it can move in one direction, move in another direction, apply pressure in one place, receive pressure in another place. The Romans basically learned how to build, to deploy, and to use the legion in the wars against the Samnites. It was then, with those legions, that the Romans went off to conquer most of the then-known world.

Roman diplomacy was the stuff of legend in antiquity. It's been much studied and, in certain respects, much emulated ever since. Roman diplomacy rested on a few very basic principles. Some of these, it will occur to you as we go along, we've been hearing a lot about in very recent times. The first was the principle of "just war." The Romans believed, absolutely, that the gods would not give Rome a victory in a war of aggression. The Romans always had to assure themselves that they were fighting to defend themselves, that they were avenging an attack against themselves. Or, as the theory evolved, that they were forestalling an attack which they viewed as inevitable. So, the notion of a "just war," *iustum bellum*, the war must be just or the gods will not give victory.

A second very important principle of Roman diplomacy was generosity toward the conquered, beginning with the Latins in 338 B.C., for example. Rome's conquered enemies, at least in Italy, were offered favorable peace terms and a form of Roman citizenship. The Romans did not put the boot heel on the necks of those whom they defeated. They defeated someone and treated them generously.

A third key principle was the notion of "divide and rule." In other words, if you divide your enemies, you can rule them more easily. The Romans never made the exact same deal with any two people. The very interesting element there, of course, is that no two potential foes had the same grievance. Rome's idea was that people couldn't gang up together against Rome because they would never have quite the same problems, quite the same grievances, quite the same difficulties. Roman diplomacy, as a further element of the divide and rule principle, operated on the principle that "your friend is your neighbor but one." Imagine a sequence A, B, C. I'm A. If I want to control B, I make an alliance with C. My friend is my neighbor but one. The Romans were masters at spotting someone who was difficult and making an alliance with that person's neighbor.

A fourth element was sheer tenacity. Once embarked on a policy, Rome would not abandon it. For these sturdy, staid people who believed in the customs of their ancestors and so on, that's not surprising. Rome's enemies came to know that the Romans were not going to give up; they were not going to get tired; they were not going to quit. They would persist.

Certain very basic military notions—borrow and use what works, be flexible, and certain fundamental diplomatic principles—already there in the fourth and third centuries B.C.

In conquering the Greeks of southern Italy, Rome came face to face with the Carthaginians. Remember, an old Phoenician colony on the coast of North Africa—very important commercial people, had a kind of a commercial empire, really, in the western Mediterranean basin. They were also a fairly formidable military force. The Carthaginians had lent some aid to Rome's enemies during the Pyrrhic Wars. Rome, then, regarded that as a provocation. Rome regarded that as an unwarranted interference in Rome's own internal business and, therefore, fought a series of wars against the Carthaginians. We call these the "Punic Wars." Remember, the Phoenicians are the *peony*, the "purple people," or the *puni*. Of course, the winners always name the war after the losers, so the Romans called these the Punic Wars. Their wars, not our wars. Their wars, we fought wars against them. They fought wars against the Carthaginians over more than a century: the first, from 264 to 241 B.C.; the second, from 218 to 201 B.C.; and the third, from 149 to 146 B.C.

Carthage was a very significant power. This was a big deal for the Romans to take on a power like Carthage. One by one, little by little, marching up and down the Italian peninsula, that was no small thing. The Romans were now really taking on one of the important powers in the Mediterranean world. We may very well say that some conflict of interest was almost inevitable once Rome became dominant in Italy. The Carthaginians were the other great power in the western Mediterranean; these guys were going to knock heads at some point. What was the exact trigger mechanism? The idea that the Carthaginians had helped the Greeks during the Pyrrhic Wars in the 270s.

The Punic Wars, of course, full of wonderful stories—some of the most familiar stories from Roman history are wrapped up in these wars. This is the one where, in the beginning, Rome had no navy— very small commercial navy, but really no navy. The sources tell us of Romans sitting on logs down on the beach, practicing rowing, while boats were being built. The Romans were learning to how to row ships before they even had any ships built.

This is the war where we meet Hannibal, the great Carthaginian general, who mounts an invasion of Italy in the Second Punic War by coming over the Alps. Rome had a navy by then; he couldn't sail freely across the sea, so he marches up through Spain, across southern France, down over the Alps and into Italy and brings elephants with him. One must imagine how elephants struck the population of Italy in the third century B.C.

Faced with a large enemy, with a large army and with a superb general against them, the Romans developed a new kind of military tactics. *Phabius Cunctator,* Phabius the Delayer, the Staller, fought and harassed the Carthaginians for several years. The Romans, basically, fought a guerrilla war. Instead of this time sending out their legions, which would almost certainly have been defeated by the superior Carthaginian forces, the Romans fought a guerrilla war.

Finally, however, the Romans did sustain a tremendous defeat at Cannae in 216 B.C. Probably the single worst military defeat the Romans ever suffered in a thousand years of Roman history. Yet the Romans rallied, rebuilt their military, and by the year 204, took the war to Africa, when Scipio Africanus invaded the Carthaginian territories. Finally, by 201 B.C., the Carthaginians had surrendered.

The third of the Punic Wars was produced very largely by Cato the Elder. Cato the Elder had a habit of coming into the Roman Senate and holding a fresh fig and saying that this fig had just been plucked off a tree in North Africa. Reminds one of certain figures in North American public institutions talking about Cuba. Anyway, he's talking about Carthage, just across the sea, and ended all of his speeches in the Senate—no matter what he was talking about—he ended his speeches, "*Carthago delenda est*" ("Carthage must be destroyed"). And finally, Cato's perseverance paid off; the Romans did, indeed, invade North Africa, defeat the Carthaginians, and this time they destroyed their city and plowed their fields with salt—the idea being that no one would live there any longer. The Carthage that rose again later—that's there now—is actually slightly displaced from where original Carthage had been.

Why did the Romans win? Several reasons I think we can identify. Tenacity and determination. These are hard to quantify, they're hard to measure, but they're certainly an important factor. You may have noticed, as I've been going along here, three wars against the Samnites, a series of wars against the Latins, a long war against Pyrrhus, three long wars against the Carthaginians—the Romans were nothing, if not tenacious.

In the second place, I think, flexibility in military tactics. The Romans were not so hardheaded. They may have been conservative, they may have been traditional, but they weren't so hardheaded that they couldn't adapt, try new things, work with new practices, new military strategies, new tactics that would work in particular circumstances—whether it's guerrilla warfare against Hannibal's troops in Italy, or the elaboration of the legion in the Samnite Wars.

It was very, very, very important, particularly during the Second Punic War when Hannibal had his army in Italy, that Rome's Italian allies did not fall away. Roman diplomacy had proved its value. Roman diplomacy had worked. Rome's generous treatment of those in Italy, whom it had come to dominate, led those people to see their long-term interests as better under Roman rule, under Roman influence, than perhaps under the influence of anyone else.

During the Second Punic War, the Antigonids—remember when we talked about the Hellenistic world, and we said that after the death of Alexander the Great, three of his great generals: Antigonos took the Balkans; Seleucus took Palestine, Syria and Mesopotamia; and Ptolemy took Egypt. Three of Alexander's great generals carved up his empire. We're going to bump into those three families, not Alexander's immediate successors but those who came after them, here in the next few minutes, beginning with the Antigonids in the Balkans.

The Antigonids may have lent some aid to Pyrrhus, that's not clear. It is clear, however, that they lent some aid to Hannibal. Once again, the Romans regarded that as a direct affront. This was an attack upon them, as far as the Romans were concerned. Consequently, once they had finished with the Second Punic War—after 201 B.C. when Scipio Africanus had defeated the

Carthaginians at the end of the Second Punic War—the Romans initiated a series of three wars in the Balkans. These wars, 199-197 B.C.—remember, they defeated the Carthaginians in 201—199 they're in the Balkans, right away. They don't let the issue rest. 171-167, a second war. 150-146, a third war. You may remember that 149-146, the Romans are defeating the Carthaginians for the third and final time. 150-146 they're fighting in the Balkans. Do you notice the Romans are now able to fight in two places at once?

The point is that they originally went into the Balkans to, from their point of view, even the score against the Macedonians for having had the temerity to help the Carthaginians. The Antigonids were defeated fairly promptly, but the Antigonids had received a good deal of assistance from a number of cities and leagues in Greece. The Romans, therefore, regarded that as an affront, that Greek cities had helped their enemy, King Philip V of Macedon. Consequently, a series of wars were fought, the second and third of these Macedonian Wars, to defeat these various Greek cities and their allies. By 146, Rome had come to dominate the Balkan Peninsula.

During the course of the war with Philip V of Macedon, the Antigonid ruler of the Balkans, the Seleucids from the eastern Mediterranean had lent some assistance. The Romans then regarded that as an affront. The Romans began as early as 188-187 B.C. to reckon accounts with Antiochus III, the Seleucid ruler at that time. They swept his forces, basically, off the eastern Mediterranean. They put an end to his naval power; they seized a certain number of naval bases from him. They did not yet, at that moment, penetrate inland and conquer the Seleucid realms, but they basically defanged and neutralized the Seleucid rulers.

Much the same is true of the Ptolemies in Egypt, who had lent some assistance to the Seleucids when the Romans attacked them. Once again, the Romans regarded that as an affront. The Romans largely neutralized the Ptolemies, but did not yet actually take over the land of Egypt, though it's pretty clear that Rome was meddling in the internal affairs of both the Seleucid realm and of Ptolemaic Egypt. A substantial part of the Balkans had actually been annexed and taken over by the Romans. The Romans had not yet taken Palestine and Syria in the east, and they had not yet taken Egypt. But they had largely neutralized the rulers of those areas.

After the First Punic War, 264-241 B.C., Rome annexed Sicily, Sardinia, and Corsica—the first three provinces of the Roman Empire, the first territory outside Italy governed by the Romans. By 146 B.C., Rome had annexed Greece, Carthage, a strip of territory across the North African coast, and a substantial part of the Balkan Peninsula. Rome is now moving far outside the realm of Italy. In other words, at the end of the First Punic War, we can say the annexation of Sicily, Sardinia, and Corsica made a certain kind of sense. They're very close to Italy; the Romans could view them as representing security interests, security needs—there's a certain logic to that.

They defeated the Carthaginians, but now you'll see a difference in Roman policy. In Italy, remember the policy of generosity. Treat your defeated foe well, and your defeated foe just might turn into your friend. In North Africa, they fought three great wars against the Carthaginians, and then destroyed them utterly. They basically sort of put the Carthaginians into the dustbin of history—this time, no fooling around.

The Romans went into the Balkans and fought again three times, feeling themselves drawn forward on each occasion to fight one party after another who had lent aid to Rome's foes. Again, not the old policy of generosity, not the old policy of make your enemy into your friend, but now take over. Carve up the Balkan Peninsula; make it provinces of an empire and place those provinces under the administration of Roman officials.

The Romans were canny. The Romans were wise; they were prescient. The Seleucids had lent aid to the Antigonids; the Ptolemies lent aid to the Seleucids. The Romans knew that. The Romans were affronted by it. The Romans could accommodate that to their notion of defensive war, of just war. The Romans also knew that, at that time, they lacked the means fully to conquer the Seleucid realms or the Ptolemaic realms. They didn't get themselves mixed up in a battle they simply couldn't win. They waited. Within a century or two, as we'll see in a later lecture, the Romans were able to take over those territories. But for now, they held. There's a kind of a wisdom in the Romans. We may think them a bit brash, we may think them a bit proud, we make think them a bit ambitious—and they were all those things—but they weren't crazy. They had a very measured sense of how to move forward.

In 133 B.C., King Attalus III of Pergamum—Pergamum is a state in the northern area of what we would now call Turkey, Anatolia in antiquity. It was one of the smaller Hellenistic states that emerged. Remember, we talked about this, and we talked about the Hellenistic world: that you had the great states of the Antigonids, the Seleucids, and the Ptolemies, and then a number of other small states emerged around the periphery of those large ones. We've met another of these today in Pyrrhus' Epirus. Perhaps we could actually say that the Carthaginians figure as another of these Hellenistic powers, although certainly the Carthaginians were there long before the Hellenistic world.

King Attalus of Pergamum—a man who is influential in his own neck of the woods, a man who is fantastically wealthy. His spectacular architectural achievements were, in part, dismantled and carried off to Berlin, where one can go and see them today. If anyone is ever visiting there, this is quite a wonderful thing to see, and one gets a sense of the scale of a man like Attalus, and of how powerful and important he actually was.

He had no heirs. As he's coming towards the end of his life, it's an interesting and open question: what would he do? He willed his kingdom to Rome. We'll have occasion to see, a couple of lectures down the road, that the Romans actually had a very considerable debate about whether to accept this legacy or not. There were some very interesting, complicating factors in whether or not the legacy was a good one. For the moment, what I want to draw your attention to is the very fact that an important, wealthy, powerful Hellenistic ruler, by 133 B.C., could see into the future, and he knew that that future was all Roman, and he wills his kingdom to Rome.

In a very real sense, the year 133 marks a symbolic moment in Roman history. Rome has achieved dominance, utter and complete dominance. They haven't yet taken over every square inch of territory, but they have achieved utter dominance in the Mediterranean world, in the ancient world, in the world of all those peoples about whom we've been speaking over the last 17 lectures.

For present purposes, I want to draw your attention back from that world that Rome conquered, to the city that did the conquering, because, in spite of itself, building this vast empire cost the Romans a very great deal. We're going to turn in a couple of future lectures, in the very next one for example, to Roman culture, and then we'll actually destroy the Roman Republic. We built it; we'll destroy it. Right now, I just want to conclude this lecture by putting a little focus on the ways in which the creation of this empire generated unforeseen tensions for the Romans.

First of all, for example, the institutions of a city-state had to be adapted to govern foreign territories. Remember when we were talking about the Roman constitution, I mentioned a certain number of officers, generally two at the beginning, and then there would be more and then more and then more and then more. The Romans would begin to do things like have praetors and then pro-praetors, consuls and then pro-consuls. In other words, if you're going to take over a substantial chunk of the world and govern it, you've got to put officers out there. You've got to put administrators out there. You have to have people out there to run that world for you. You multiply, therefore, the number of offices; you multiply the number of magistrates.

You'll remember, I hope, that I mentioned that over the first 400 years of its history, in Rome's Republic, about 100 families monopolized political offices. One of the things we're going to see is that, in about the last century, that changed dramatically. There were simply too many officers for a few families to control them all, and too many new men who weren't beholden to the old system.

In other ways, we can say that the empire interfered with the Roman system because war provided opportunities for wealth, for prestige, well outside the traditional Roman social and political order. Great generals, great conquerors, great battles could be fought, and these could be translated into political capital back home, which didn't quite fit with the custom of our ancestors. It didn't quite fit with what our fathers would have done because, in many cases, these were new men doing new things.

The Romans had, of themselves, a very long-standing ideology of the citizen-soldier, the farmer-soldier. The farmer would lay down his tools, would go off and defend Rome, having defended Rome would lay down his weapons and go back and take up his tools again. During the Samnite Wars to a degree, during the Pyrrhic Wars to a degree, but during the Punic Wars to a very large degree, Rome put large numbers of her men in the field, year after year after year after year. This produced large numbers of veteran soldiers, who had been away from their homes, away from their farms, away from their families for long periods of time. When finally they left the ranks, they needed settlement. They needed land. They needed money. They needed support. They became a large, new and complicating force in Roman politics.

You'll perhaps remember that last time we talked about patron-client bonds. In the old days, those were sort of local big shots who loaned the local people a little money, who took care of the local people's legal business, and so on, and who could count on the local people to vote their way in the assemblies. Now the patron-client bonds, in the last generations of the Roman Republic, shift to the veteran soldiers of great generals. Great generals not only have wealth, power and prestige, and so on gained from victories on far battlefields, they've got guys back home who will vote the way they want them to. That was something very new and different—and not at all the way our ancestors would do it.

We've talked a little bit about the constitution of the Roman Republic, and we've talked a little bit about the building of the Roman Empire. Let's leave this sort of unrelieved picture of politics of war and diplomacy, and in our next lecture turn to Roman culture. For these Romans were, indeed, cultured people.

The Culture of the Roman Republic
Lecture 19

As in their political life, as in their diplomatic life, as in their military life, Roman cultural life also looks staid, stable, conservative, structured and measured.

Like its politics and diplomacy, Roman republican culture was staid, stable, and serious. To understand it, one must start in the Roman household. An aristocratic Roman household comprised a *familia*—the totality of persons living together in one or more associated dwellings. The head of the household was the *paterfamilias*—the oldest male member of the *familia*, who had life-and-death power over all members. This society was relentlessly male and hierarchical. Romans had a positive cult of their ancestors. Statues, or burial masks, of dead ancestors were kept in every house. Family history was taught to children, especially to boys.

Shakespeare to the contrary, Cato the Elder was the noblest Roman of them all; at any rate, he was the most exemplary. Cicero wrote a book on *The Old Age of Cato the Elder* to stress, in his own troubled times, how magnificent the Romans of old had been. Cato (234–149) lived through momentous times. He fought in the Second Punic War and the First Macedonian War. He held the quaestorship, consulship, and censorship.

Cato affected a rustic demeanor to avoid all pretense of sophistication. He stood for the sturdy, manly Roman values of olden times. He helped to pass sumptuary laws regulating women's public appearance with respect to cosmetics and jewelry. He also helped to pass a law aimed at keeping "philosophers"—that is, Greeks—out of Rome. He disliked all alien influences.

He wrote a book, *Origines*, for his son. It was the first history of Rome written in Latin and was designed less to tell all the facts than to parade examples of Roman virtue. He also wrote *De agricultura*, a manual of farming. Cato's ideal was the citizen-farmer-soldier.

But as his attempt to ban Greeks shows, the current was already against Cato. From their conquest of the south and their introduction to the Hellenistic world, Romans learned the culture of the Greeks. Rome's earliest writings, of which little survives, were in Greek. High-born Romans began regularly to hire Greek tutors to instruct the *familia*.

> **The Romans refused to build a theater for a long time. They thought that that was too Greek, so the plays were just performed outdoors.**

In 155 B.C., Carneades (214/213–129/128 B.C.), the head of Plato's Academy, lectured in Rome and launched Greek philosophy on its course among the Roman elite. This is what Cato objected to.

When Latin literary forms began to emerge, they were deeply influenced by Greeks. The comedian Plautus (254–184 B.C.) brought the Greek "new comedy" of Menander to Rome. Plautus used stock figures: misers, spendthrifts, braggarts, parasites, courtesans, and conniving slaves. He is riotously funny but not very original or literarily polished. Terence (c. 190–159 B.C.) was likewise influenced by Greek comedy, but his plays present elegant Latin, well-developed characters, and restrained comedy. It is worth noting that the Romans refused to build a theater.

By the last decades of the Roman Republic, Greek influences and a growing Latin literary maturity and confidence had begun to produce poetry of a very high order. Catullus (84–54), from Verona in northern Italy, emulated Greek poets, mastered poetic meters, and treated themes of love with sympathy and emotion. Two poems by Catullus may stand for the others:

No. 8

> Break off / fallen Catullus / time to cut losses,
> bright days shone once, / you followed a girl / here & there
> loved as no other / perhaps / shall be loved
> then was the time / of love's *insouciance*, / your lust as her will
> matching./ Bright days shone / on both of you.

Now / a woman is unwilling. / Follow suit
weak as you are / no chasing of mirages / no fallen love,
a clean break / hard against the past. / Not again Lesbia.
No more. / Catullus is clear. / He won't miss you.
He won't crave it. / It is cold. / But you will whine.
You are ruined. / What will your life be? / Who will "visit"
    your room?
Who uncover that beauty? / Whom will you love? / Whose girl will
    you be?
Whom kiss? / Whose lips bite? / Enough. Break.
Catullus. / Against the past.

No. 70

Lesbia says she'd rather marry me
than anyone, / though Jupiter himself came asking
or so she says, / but what a woman tells her lover in desire
should be written out on air & running water.

In many ways, the greatest—the most prolific, profound, and synthetic—of the republican writers was Marcus Tullius Cicero (106–43 B.C.). Cicero was an influential public figure in his own day and widely read and admired ever since. His most well-known writings are his forensic speeches. These evince a mastery of the rhetorical arts second to none. Cicero upheld standards of absolute integrity in the conduct of public life (remember that Cato was his ideal).

His political writings, especially *On the Republic*, *On the Laws*, and *On Duties*, took the harvest of classical Greek political thought and added to it Stoic concepts of natural law and traditional Roman ethics. He attempted to make a case that "advantage can never conflict with right for … everything that is morally right is advantageous, and there can be no advantage in anything that is not morally right." He also spoke eloquently, but in the end, ineffectively, against tyranny.

We may sum up this account of Roman republican culture by thinking about Rome's greatest hero, Aeneas, the central figure in Rome's epic, *The Aeneid*.

We will come back to Virgil and his *Aeneid* in a later lecture, but Virgil lived through the late republic and, in writing his great poem, he looked back ruefully at what might have been. He created, in his Aeneas—*Pius Aeneas*—perhaps the dullest figure in epic literature.

But he endowed Aeneas with qualities that the best of the Romans always wished to believe were their natural inheritance. *Pietas:* This does not mean piety in our sense. It means loyalty, reliability, honor. *Gravitas*: This literally means "weightiness," that is, seriousness. *Constantia*: This means perseverance, commitment, dedication. *Magnitudo animi*: Literally, this means "greatness of spirit," but by extension, it implies a devotion to higher causes, not to praise, power, or material well being. It may be that few Romans lived up to these ideals, but the ideals themselves reveal much to us about what the Romans, at their best, wished to be. ■

Suggested Reading

Bradley, *Discovering the Roman Family*.

Cicero, *Selected Works*.

Grant, ed., *Latin Literature: An Anthology*.

Ogilvie, *Roman Literature and Society*.

Rawson, *Cicero*.

Questions to Consider

1. How do the Roman public values that we have discussed here compare with those of the Greek poleis?

2. Can you see actual examples of these values in practice in the political life of Rome?

The Culture of the Roman Republic
Lecture 19—Transcript

In this lecture, we're going to turn to the culture of the Roman Republic. We've talked about the Romans as builders of a government; we've talked about the Romans as builders of an empire. Now let's ask a little bit about these people themselves. What did they hold dear? What did they think? How did they talk? What were they interested in?

To answer these questions, we'll turn to some basic notions about the Roman family. We'll turn to some exemplary Roman figures, like Cato the Elder. We'll talk about certain important Roman poets; we'll quote a couple of poems, for example, from Catullus. We'll talk about a couple of Roman playwrights. We'll talk a little about a very funny play written by a man named Plautus, called *The Pot of Gold*. We'll talk about Rome's greatest political figure, Cicero. And we'll try to draw it together with some reflections on some very basic, elementary Roman values.

As in their political life, as in their diplomatic life, as in their military life, Roman cultural life also looks staid, stable, conservative, structured and measured. Was it really like that? To a degree, yes. Why was it like that, and how was it kept like that? Those are the questions to which we'll turn right now.

It all started in the family. It all started in the household. If you understand Rome, you have to understand the Roman family, or at least the way the Romans wanted us to understand their families. I mean, was every Roman family the perfect model of stability, order and harmony? No, probably not. But this is the way the Romans portrayed their families.

A Roman household, particularly an aristocratic household, though it would have been much the same through all the orders of society, was called a *familia*, family. *Familia* didn't mean mom and dad and 2.1 kids. It meant the totality of people who lived together, in one or more associated dwellings. Sort of everybody connected. This could be the servants, it could be the domestics, it could be two, three, perhaps more generations of a family living under one roof. That's the familia.

The *pater familias*, the father of the family, the head of the family, the oldest male member, was the head of this household. He had power of life and death over all members. We've seen already that this Roman society was relentlessly male, relentlessly hierarchical and relentlessly deferential. You can see how that began in the household. Before it ever got to an election, before it ever got to the Senate, it started in the Roman house.

Romans, for example, had a very positive cult of their ancestors. To enter the front door of any Roman house, certainly of any prominent Roman, was to see displayed there either statues of the ancestors of that family or the burial masks, masks actually taken from the face of a dead family member. Either statues or burial masks, or maybe both. To pass in and out the door was to be reminded of those who had crossed that threshold before you.

Family history was taught to children, but especially to sons. Very interesting. The Roman idea was that the family and the state were so identified with one another, that to teach your children, but particularly your sons, the history of your family was, in some way, to teach them the history of the Roman people. Very interesting. The role of the family, you see, and the key component— the key constituent of Roman society. Bear in mind that was the ideal. I'm not going to stand here and say that every single Roman family was always exactly like the ideal. That would be silly. But that was the ideal.

Shakespeare to the contrary, Cato the Elder was the noblest Roman of them all. At any rate, he was the most exemplary. We met him last time, when he was finishing all of his speeches, "*Carthago delenda est*"—"Carthage must be destroyed." Cato was a very, very interesting character and very revealing of the Romans. Cicero— about whom we'll have more to say in a few minutes—late in the first century B.C., Cicero wrote a book on *The Old Age of Cato the Elder*, in order, basically, to stress, in his own very troubled times, how magnificent the Romans of old had been, how grand they were, how if only we now could recapture the world of men like Cato.

Cato was held up as a model. Even in his own time, he was a man of enormous influence. Like so many Romans, he lived through momentous times. He was born in 234 B.C.; he died in 149 B.C. He fought in the Second Punic War; he fought in the First Macedonian War. He held the quaestorship.

He held the consulship. And he held a censorship. In other words, he held all the highest offices of the Roman state. He served many years in the Roman Senate.

Cato was sort of an interesting and cantankerous character in lots of ways. He affected a very rustic demeanor, in terms of his clothing and how he spoke. He wanted to avoid all pretense of sophistication. He thought one of the things, particularly as he grew a bit older, that offended him about Roman society was that people were taking on Greek customs and Greek manners and Greek ways of doing things. He didn't want any part of that. He wanted to be a good, sturdy, traditional Roman, stand for the old, manly Roman values; that was what was important to Cato.

Cato, among other things that he did, for example, he helped to pass a series of sumptuary laws. Sumptuary laws were passed at Rome to, for instance, in his case, regulate the cosmetics or jewelry that women could wear when they appeared in public. He didn't want them sort of tarting themselves up too much. He also passed a law aimed to keep "philosophers," or actually that meant Greeks, out of Rome. He disliked the alien influences. He disliked foreigners. He didn't like people messing about with his beloved Roman values.

He wrote a book for his son, the *Origines*—the Origins. Interesting book. It's the first history of Rome written in Latin. Previous to this, the Romans had written in Greek. We'll have more to say about this later on. Cato, in any case, wrote a history of Rome for his son, and we wrote it in Latin, and it's an interesting history. It survives only in small fragments today, unfortunately. It would be wonderful to have this book, but we don't. We have only, really, quotations of it embedded in the writings of some later authors.

It appears that, rather than sort of telling his son blow-by-blow, fact-by-fact, the rise of the Roman people, what Cato did is tell his son stories about great Romans of old. Again, you see the customs of our ancestors. What would our ancestors have done? How did they do things? This was how Cato taught his son Roman history. It was to put virtue on parade. That's clearly what the book was designed to do. He also wrote a book on agriculture, *De Agricultura*, on the care of fields, a sort of a manual of agriculture. Over the long course of Roman history, several such manuals were written. This also, in a way, was written for Cato's son. His ideal, Cato's ideal, was the citizen-farmer-soldier.

Cato also taught his son a bit of law, the idea being that you needed to know a certain amount of Roman law in order to take your place in Roman society, in order to function in the Roman assemblies, in order to behave as a citizen. He taught him, then, a bit of Roman history and taught him farming. How do we do things now? Law. How have we always done things? History. What do we really do? We're farmers. There is Cato, transmitting to his own son, and Cicero telling us about Cato transmitting to his own son, the way the Roman system was meant to work. Meant to work.

As I think his attempt late in his life to ban Greeks shows pretty clearly, the current was already against Cato. The times were changing. He couldn't stop these Greek influences. From their conquests of the south, and from their introduction into the Hellenistic world, the conquest of the Greeks of *Magna Graecia*, and then of course, one after another, their military campaigns in the eastern Mediterranean, the Romans came into contact with the culture of the Greeks in all imaginable ways.

Rome's earliest writings, as I mentioned a moment ago, were actually in Greek. Greek was sort of the language in which you wrote if you expected to talk to anybody, if you expected to have an audience, if you expected to reach anyone. Also, if you wanted to appear fashionable, cultivated. Highborn Romans began regularly to hire Greek tutors to instruct in their *familia*, in their household.

We talked two lectures ago about the Greek historian Polybius, who had been captured during the Macedonian Wars and brought back to Rome. He lived in the household of the Scipios, one of the great families of Rome. And he lived there—he was a hostage, he was a prisoner of war, yes, but, in point of fact, he was really living in a very elegant state of affairs. It was very common for Roman families; not all of them had prisoners of war, certainly not all of them had people as famous as Polybius living in their household. Prominent Roman families began to hire Greek tutors, and those Greek tutors, of course, would teach the children, not only the Greek language, but Greek literature,

Greek values. Much would creep in, you see, with the coming of these Greek tutors. That's what Cato didn't like. Those are the people that Cato wanted out, if he could possibly get rid of them.

In 155 B.C., a man by the name of Carneades, born in about 214 or 213 B.C., lived to 129 or 128. He was the head of Plato's Academy then, the head of Plato's school in Athens. He came to Rome, and gave a series of lectures there, which really sort of launched Greek philosophy, particularly Plato's philosophy, on its course among the Roman elite. This, again, is exactly the kind of thing that Cato objected to. He didn't want these kinds of ideas circulating among his beloved Romans.

When Latin literary forms began to emerge, they were deeply influenced by the Greeks. If, for instance, we even see Cato writing his Origins, his history, in Latin, and sort of putting virtue on parade as I suggested a moment ago, this is not so much unlike the old Greek idea that history was the public deeds of great men. This is what we record. The ordinary details of life—the details of ordinary people—that's not history to the Greeks. We can see that Cato is, in some way, influenced by this. Then, mark well, he writes in Latin. He's not having any of that Greek for his son.

We can see other Greek literary forms coming to Rome as well. For instance, comedy. We may ask, what about drama? It's a long time before Rome produces dramatists of any significant notel it's actually in the first century A.D. There may have been some early Roman drama which survives today only in fragments or survives only by the names of the authors. It probably wasn't very good, and it wasn't remembered as very good. Though you'll perhaps recall, when we talked about Greek drama, we saw that only a tiny portion of the once vast corpus of Greek dramatic writings survives to today. So, we should be careful about generalizing.

What the Romans did pick up on was comedy. For example, the comedian Plautus, born in 254 B.C. and died in 184, brought the Greek "new comedy"—the comedy of Menander, the comedy of the Hellenistic world—to Rome. Here we get all of these stock figures: misers, spendthrifts, braggarts, parasites, courtesans and conniving slaves. All the kinds of people who populate, for example, the plays of Menander. Or as we saw—remember, when we talked about Hellenistic comedy, the idea of what we might today almost call "situation comedy." It's funny. There's no great moral lesson in it. You don't go away edified; you go away having been entertained.

As an example, we might take one of Plautus's plays, *The Pot of Gold*. There's a man called Euclio, and his grandfather has buried a pot of gold in the house; so he's hidden a pot of gold in the house somewhere. He's placed it under the protection of this deity that protects this Roman household. Every Roman household had deities that were thought particularly to protect it. Euclio knew this gold was there someplace, but didn't know where it was. He was a real miser; he's depicted as a real miser, so he's very keen to find this gold.

In the meantime, a couple of interesting things are going on. First of all, Euclio's daughter has struck up a wonderful relationship with the household deity, who has revealed to her, but to none else, where this gold is. Moreover, she has fallen in love with a young man named Lyconides, and in fact, she's become pregnant. Meanwhile, there's another fellow who is a very rich man, a very powerful man in the town, who wants to marry Euclio's daughter.

Of course, you can imagine Euclio's position. He thinks that the young man Lyconides has only gotten his daughter pregnant so that he'll be able to get the pot of gold. He thinks the rich man is only interested in his daughter because he's rich and powerful already—he wants more, he wants the pot of gold. Euclio's always fending off all of these various people who are coming around to seek his daughter's hand in marriage.

Meanwhile, a slave finds the pot of gold and steals it, and runs away and hides it in some woods. Now, of course, Euclio's gone crazy. First of all, the thinks Lyconides, the young man, has stolen it. Then he thinks maybe Megadorus, the rich man, has taken the money. He's just beside himself. Now, in a very comic scene, Lyconides comes in to talk to Euclio, and he says that he has something to confess, something's weighing very heavily on his mind. Euclio, of course, thinks he's going to admit he stole the pot of gold, and he's going to tell him where it is and bring it back. Lyconides says, "No, actually, I've made your daughter pregnant, but I love her and I want to marry her." Euclio didn't want to hear that; he wanted to know where his gold is. Of course, the young man has no idea; he didn't steal the gold. He leaves the house crestfallen because he thinks Euclio will have nothing to do with him.

Then the slave comes up to him and says, "I've actually stolen to gold, and I've hidden it. And I'm worried that I'm going to get in big trouble." He reveals where the gold is to Lyconides, and Lyconides goes and gets the gold. He comes back to the house with the gold, and at first he's not sure quite what to do. There's a moment where he's probably considering taking off with the pot of gold, but he brings it back to the house. Euclio, of course, is beside himself with joy, and now he decides that it would be all right if Lyconides marries his daughter. But he goes and hides the gold again. In a sense we almost imagine starting the whole story again. Megadorus, meanwhile, has discovered that the daughter is pregnant, so he no longer wants anything to do with her. So, he's out of the picture. Then, finally, Lyconides and Euclio's daughter are married, and at the last moment of the play, old Euclio, the miser, goes and gets the pot of gold and gives it to the young people.

The point is that the story is funny. There might be a point or two in there about misers, and if you're too greedy, and so forth, things won't come out well for you. The point is, the play is merely meant to be funny. It's meant to be entertaining. You aren't uplifted by it; you're not taught any great philosophical principles by it. This is the kind of comedy that came to Rome. Good, funny stuff.

That's true, but then there's a certain irony, because the second of the great Roman comedians in the second century B.C., Terence—*Terentius*—born about 190 B.C., died in 159; he died as a very young man. He was also influenced by Greek comedy, but his plays are rather different. First of all, they're written in an extraordinarily elegant, polished Latin. You may say, "What's the point of mentioning that?" The point of mentioning that, precisely, is that Latin has not actually been used as a literary language very long. It has a long future in front if it, but Latin had not been being written for a long time.

Terence writes beautiful Latin. He writes very restrained comedy. One can usually read all the way through one of his plays and not smile. They're really not very funny. Moreover, the plots tend to be incredibly intricate. We can take any one of the stories, his play *The Eunuch*, for example, is a story of mistaken identity, and of love triangles, and of elaborate and complicated plot twists. It's very hard, even, to summarize the play. One almost has to read it because at every moment something new happens, and there's new characters, and different characters, and so on. Terence, not surprisingly, was never as popular in antiquity as Plautus was. Plautus was just a lot more fun. He was just a lot more enjoyable.

It's worth pointing out that the Romans refused to build a theater for a long time. They thought that that was too Greek, so the plays were just performed outdoors. When they finally did build one, they did it without seats, in the first instance. If you're going to go to the theater, then you're going to stand up. You're not going to sit down and enjoy yourself too much. Again, the Romans sort of compromised with these sturdy old values and then the new things that were coming in.

By the last decades of the Roman Republic, Greek influences and a growing Latin literary maturity—both things important. Greek influences, but also a growing Latin literary maturity, and also a certain sense of confidence. The Romans had now been writing for a while—they'd been writing in a number of genres for a while, and they were getting better at it. This led, for example, to poetry of a very high order, indeed.

Among the greatest of these, we might mention, for example, Catullus. Catullus was born about 84 B.C., died in 54, again a very young man, only about 30. He came from Verona, in northern Italy. He emulated Greek poets, he mastered poetic meters, he treated themes of love with sympathy and emotion. Let me just read two poems by Catullus that could stand for many others.

In his corpus the eighth poem, Catullus has had a long-standing relationship with a woman named Lesbia, and here is Catullus finally recognizing that things have gone sour.

Break off
        fallen Catullus
                time to cut losses,
bright days shone once,
        you followed a girl
                here & there
loved as no other
        perhaps
                shall be loved
then was the time
        of love's *insouciance*,
                your lust as her will
matching.
        Bright days shone
                on both of you.

Now
        a woman is unwilling.
                Follow suit
weak as you are
        no chasing of mirages
                no fallen love,
a clean break
        hard against the past.
                Not again Lesbia.
No more.
        Catullus is clear.
                He won't miss you.
He won't crave it.
        It is cold.
                But you will whine.
You are ruined.
        What will your life be?
                Who will "visit" your room?
Who uncover that beauty?
        Whom will you love?
                Whose girl will you be?
Whom kiss?

> Whose lips bite?
>> Enough. Break.
>
> Catullus.
>> Against the past.

Another occasion, this is just a fragment from one of his poems, Catullus said this about his friend Lesbia:

> Lesbia says she'd rather marry me
>> than anyone,
>>> though Jupiter himself came asking
>
> or so she says,
>> but what a woman tells her lover in desire
>>> should be written out on air & running water.

One suspects Lesbia might have had her own views about all that; but anyway, that's Catullus on Lesbia.

Let's remember that this was the kind of poetry that was popular among—that was known by—these very same Romans who built that government and built that empire. That those same Romans went and laughed at Plautus's plays. Maybe not Cato, but probably a lot of them did.

In many ways, the greatest, the most prolific, the most profound, the most synthetic of the republican writers was Marcus Tullius Cicero, Cicero as we call him. Born in 106 B.C., died in 43. He was an influential public figure in his own day; he's been widely read and admired ever since. He is another one whose writings were very well known to the Founding Fathers of the United States. His best-known writings are his forensic speeches, of which a considerable number survive. He took cases, sometimes as the prosecutor, more often as the defense counsel, in a number of very prominent, very politically charged trials at Rome. Indeed, this was how he got his first entrée into public life.

First of all, we may say about these forensic speeches, they evince a mastery of the rhetorical arts second to none. Cicero is just a master of the spoken word. Cicero upheld standards of absolute integrity in the conduct of public life. Remember, Cato was his ideal. It was Cicero who wrote the book on *The Old Age of Cato the Elder*, the purpose of which being to hold that up as a model to others.

His political writings—he wrote *On the Republic*, *On the Laws*, and *On Duties*—took the harvest of Greek political thought and added to them some very interesting and important elements of the world in which he himself lived. For example, Stoic concepts of natural law—that there are certain things that are inevitably and unchangeably written into the universe, and that our task is to learn those things, to discern those things, and to put ourselves into right order with them. This, in the end, will make happiness.

What Cicero tried to do was blend traditional Roman ethics. Remember when we talked about the Stoics and the Hellenistic world? We said that they often borrowed metaphors from the stage: play your role, know your role, accept your place. What could be more Roman than that? The Romans were Stoics before there was Stoicism. So he was able to take traditional Roman ethics, blend them with Stoic ethics and fold this into an enveloping context of natural law—that there are rules that apply always and everywhere to everyone.

This led him, for instance, in his book *On Duties*, to formulate a moral principle that has been a challenge ever since. It's one that is almost impossible for anyone to disagree with in principle, and almost impossible for anyone to live by in practice. He says, "Advantage can never conflict with right for ... everything that is morally right is advantageous, and there can be no advantage in anything that is not morally right." Think about that for a moment. Anything that is advantageous is morally right. I can't lie, I can't cheat, I can't steal, I can't fiddle my taxes, I can't pull a fast one on anybody, I can't do something when nobody's looking because I know I can get away with it because this can never be right, and it can never really be advantageous. That's the point.

Didn't they profit you? Of course, it might profit you, but it could never be, finally, advantageous. As I said, it's one of those kinds of things. You think about those words of Cicero and you say: Do you know anyone? Do you know anyone at all who would say, "Oh, no, I disagree with that, that's terrible"? Then, start with yourself, and then think about everyone you know. Do you know anybody who lives, always, by that rule? Could Cicero have lived by that rule? I don't know. But it's a very interesting notion, and very Roman, very sturdy, that Cicero.

I think we can sum up this picture of Roman political life, Roman cultural life, Roman social life, by thinking about Rome's greatest hero, Aeneas, the central figure of Rome's great epic poem, the *Aeneid*. We'll come back, a couple of lectures down the road, when we talk about the culture of the early Roman Empire, the empire under emperors, when we'll talk about Virgil, and we'll talk about his poem, and we'll consider the arts of the poem.

Today, I really want to draw attention to the fact that Vigil lived through the very difficult days at the end of the Roman Republic. There can be no doubt that, while he was certainly retelling stories that were very old and not of his own invention about Aeneas and all of his friends and family members and the heroes of early days, it also is the case that Virgil was talking to his contemporaries. Saying, in a sense, look what we have lost. He gives us, in this Aeneas, a character for all times, yes, but also for his time, and for the people who lived in his time.

That this is so, it seems to me, is revealed most clearly by the fact that, I think it is fair to say, that Aeneas, *Pius Aeneas*, as he is again and again and again in the *Aeneid*, is the dullest figure in epic literature. Let me repeat that. He is the dullest figure in epic literature. This guy is no Achilles. He's not a great warrior; well, he's an "okay" soldier. He's not a great leader. He can never quite make up his mind; he kind of muddles through. He does the right thing in the end. He's always worrying about things, and brooding over things. It's interesting. *Pius Aeneas*, loyal Aeneas, trustworthy Aeneas, Aeneas the guy you can count on. Not great Aeneas, powerful Aeneas, warrior Aeneas. That's not how Virgil chose to present the best of Romans, *Romanitas,* Roman-ness to his contemporaries.

There's a few basic ideals that we can see in Aeneas, that, it seems to me, taken together, unlock the picture the Romans created of themselves, the ideal they held up to themselves, what they wanted to see when they looked in a mirror. Were they always like this? No, of course not. That's less important, though, than saying this is what they wanted to be like.

First, *pietas*. That doesn't mean piety in our sense. The Latin *pietas* is not a word from the realm of religion. It's a word from the realm of social life. It means loyalty, reliability, honor. When you are pious, you can be counted on.

In the second place, *gravitas*. Have you noticed in the last couple of years, how the chattering classes in the United States have picked up this word? *Gravitas*. It literally means weightiness. You all know what gravity is. Weightiness, seriousness. Romans are serious; they are not frivolous.

Constantia. Perseverance, commitment, dedication. You start the job; you finish the job. We see already, in political life and in military life, how that played itself out in Roman history.

Magnitudo animi. If you look at that word closely, you'll see "magnanimity," you'll see the English word "magnanimity." Greatness of spirit. By extension, it implies a devotion to higher causes—not to praise, not to power, not to material well-being, not to wealth, not to the moment's notice—but a greatness of being, a greatness of soul or spirit that's above all of these petty entanglements of the world around us.

It may very well be that few Romans lived up to these ideals. But the ideals themselves reveal to us what the Romans thought about themselves, or at least some of the elite among them, and what they wanted their contemporaries to think about them, and the picture they have left for us. We must, of course, at many edges pull on the ragged threads hanging off from that picture, and unravel it a bit. At their very best, Pius Aeneas, or Cato the Elder, represent what the Romans wanted to be. Now we must destroy the Roman Republic. It is to that task that we shall turn in our next lecture.

Rome—From Republic to Empire
Lecture 20

> Some of the old conservatives, the more traditionals in Roman politics, had begun to think that this empire is not necessarily such a good idea. It's really costing us a lot in terms of domestic order.

Now we will watch the Roman Republic turn into the Roman Empire even as—mind the terms—the Roman Empire goes right on expanding. We'll ask why a system that was so stable for so long collapsed. Was the system itself intrinsically flawed? Did the men who operated within this system in the last century of its existence twist it all out of shape?

When Attalus of Pergamum willed his kingdom to Rome, there was a sharp public quarrel. A conservative party wanted no part of the legacy for fear it would just lead to more entanglements in the East. A progressive party led by the brothers Tiberius (d. 133 B.C.) and Gaius (d. 121) Gracchus wanted to accept the legacy.

The Gracchi wanted to use the money to fund land redistribution to put idle farmers back to work. Conservatives feared that this was a scheme to win political supporters, and some of them illegally held a good deal of the land that was to be redistributed. Tribunes were bribed, and when he himself tried to stand for the tribunate for a second consecutive year, Tiberius Gracchus was murdered. This was the first instance of political bloodshed in Rome.

When Gaius carried on with his brother's plans, he and 250 of his allies were murdered by senatorial agents. Perhaps 75,000 people got land, and after the deaths of the Gracchi, the Senate began trying to take the land back. The Roman people now were increasingly factionalized into *optimates* and *populares*.

Amidst these political crises, Roman armies under traditional senatorial leadership were faring badly in several places, especially in North Africa. In 107, Marius (157–86 B.C.), a "New Man" (a man without a family history of political office), was elected consul. He took over the Numidian campaign and quickly had success. He was a fine soldier and an honest man. He also professionalized the Roman army, which made the army proper, in addition to veterans, a force to be reckoned with in Roman politics. Senators were furious at Marius, even before he held the consulship several times in a row. This was not strictly illegal, but it was highly unusual.

After 100, Marius withdrew a bit from the public scene, but he remained an influential *popularis* leader. In 90, Rome's allies in Italy rebelled. Marius won the "Social War" (war with the *socii*) of 90–88 B.C., and in the end, the allies got Roman citizenship. Marius's recent successes alarmed the *optimates* even more.

Simultaneously, in Anatolia, Mithridates attacked Roman territory and killed Roman merchants and tax collectors. The Senate assigned to the *optimate* Sulla (138–78 B.C.) the task of punishing Mithridates. Marius was jealous and waged a battle against Sulla and his forces. When Sulla returned from the east, Marius was dead, but Sulla marched on Rome and massacred Marius's followers, then issued proscription lists. This was the first time that such violence, on such a scale, had been seen in Roman politics.

One immediate lesson of the careers of Marius and Sulla was that a man had to gain control of an army to make his way in the new Roman politics. The first to act on this lesson was Pompey (106–48 B.C.), who began with a command to clear pirates from the Mediterranean and wound up with several further campaigns. Close on his heels came Julius Caesar (100–44 B.C.), who got a consulship in 63 and began angling for a major military campaign.

Caesar, Pompey, and Crassus wound up pooling their financial and political resources in the "First Triumvirate," an ad hoc arrangement forged in 60 B.C. Caesar wanted a military command in Gaul to win wealth and glory and enhance his political support. Crassus was the richest man in Rome but a rather unsavory character. He wanted a military command in the East to gain an aura of legitimacy. Pompey wanted laws passed providing for landed pensions for his veterans. Cicero and others protested in vain against this outrageous manipulation of the Roman system.

While Caesar was spending eight years in Gaul, Roman politics changed dramatically. Crassus, a better swindler than soldier, died on campaign and vanished from the scene. Pompey became the creature of the *optimates* and helped to pass laws designed to ruin Caesar. By 49 B.C., Caesar had been backed into a corner: If he laid down his command and returned to Rome as a private citizen, he would be destroyed judicially. If he retained his command, he was, in effect, declaring war on Rome. Believing he had no choice, he "crossed the Rubicon."

Bust of Julius Caesar.

Rome now plunged into a generation of civil war. In the first phase, Caesar defeated the forces of Pompey and established himself as dictator. Many key figures of late republican politics lost their lives in this period, including Cicero. Caesar's dictatorship was reasonably enlightened and included many reforms, such as the calendar. In general, Caesar, and everyone else for that matter, was trying to find a solution to the almost complete collapse, or corruption, of the traditional Roman political system.

In 44, a group of disgruntled senators murdered Caesar. They may have honestly believed that Caesar was the obstacle to a return of republican politics and values, but this was a foolish hope. Rome now degenerated into

13 years of renewed civil war. There was, first, a "Second Triumvirate," consisting of Marcus Antonius (Shakespeare's Mark Antony), the heir to Caesar's forces; Octavian, Caesar's nephew and adopted heir; and Lepidus, who happened to have an army under his command.

The triumvirs first defeated the forces of those who killed Caesar. Then Lepidus was shunted aside. For several years, Octavian and Antony stared each other down. At Actium in 31, Octavian defeated Antony and became supreme in the Roman world. But what was Octavian's position? We'll answer this question in the next lecture.

Finally, Greek culture, for all its glories, eroded the simple, sturdy values of the Romans—turned them more cosmopolitan.

What happened to the Roman Republic? The opportunities and challenges presented by the empire devastated the old political system. Power, influence, and unimaginable wealth could be won in the empire and deployed in Rome with no checks by the traditional system. People became inured to violence and quite willing to use it against fellow citizens.

Disruptions in the countryside led to countless numbers of landless, rootless people who felt no sense of commitment to any old-fashioned values. Greek culture, for all its glories, eroded the simple, sturdy values of traditional Rome. Aristotle once said that in an ideal state, all citizens could be summoned by the cry of a herald. That may not be practical, but the Roman experience makes one think. ■

Suggested Reading

Bernstein, *Tiberius Sempronius Gracchus*.

Gelzer, *Caesar*.

Gruen, *Last Generation of the Roman Republic*.

Questions to Consider

1. Can you think of other political systems in which people manipulated the rules to gain their own advantage?

2. In looking at the last century of the Roman Republic, do you see a story of human failures or of the crush of impersonal trends and forces?

Rome—From Republic to Empire
Lecture 20—Transcript

In this lecture, we're going to talk about the fall of the Roman Republic and the rise of the Roman Empire. It's a very sorry tale we have to tell. We'll begin by discussing concretely what happened. Who were some of the personalities? What were some of the major events? What were some of the major crises that brought this old and stable and much admired Roman Republic to a state of utter ruin?

At the end, we'll ask a few questions about why this happened. Was the system itself flawed? Were there people who were willing to manipulate the system in ways that people had not been willing to do before? Did some people discover flaws, or perhaps opportunities, possibilities in this system to wrench it out of shape, and to turn it to their own purposes? We'll try at the end to explore some of those questions. Why did this happen? But first, we'll basically have to go through and say, "What happened, who are the players, and what did they do?"

When Attalus of Pergamum willed his kingdom to Rome in 133 B.C., there was a sharp public quarrel at Rome. You may remember my mentioning that, two lectures back, when we were talking about the rise of the Roman Empire. At the end of that lecture, I sort of used Attalus's bequeathal of his kingdom to Rome as a kind of a symbolic end for that lecture and for the emergence of the Roman Empire—for an awareness of what the future held for the Mediterranean world.

When Attalus willed his kingdom to Rome, it wasn't immediately accepted because there were some very complicated political situations in Rome. A conservative party wanted no part of this legacy for fear that it would lead to more entanglements in the East. Some of the old conservatives, the more traditionals in Roman politics, had begun to think that this empire is not necessarily such a good idea. It's really costing us a lot in terms of domestic order.

But a progressive party, led by the brothers Tiberius, who died in 133 B.C., and Gaius, who died in 121—Tiberius and Gaius Gracchus, the Gracchi brothers—wanted to accept the legacy. They had a whole host of social programs, land reforms, and others that they wanted to carry through. They felt that the Attalid legacy would provide them with the wealth, money and resources necessary to accomplish their tasks.

Not surprisingly, conservatives in Rome feared that this was a scheme to win political supporters. Some of them felt this was a scheme to win political supporters. Remember we've talked about patron-client bonds in Roman politics? Some people—these people all played by the same rulebook, they understood the system very well. Some people looked at the Gracchi and said those guys are trying to use the Attalid legacy to buy support in Roman politics.

There was another interesting little problem. Over a long period of time, going back more than a century before the Gracchi, as individual men—as individual small and medium sized farmers had spent careers in the Roman military—just by dint of circumstance as a result of these long wars, various members of the senatorial aristocracy had bought up large tracts of land. They had also, in some instances, acquired a great deal of public land, land around Rome that belonged to the state. But these people had kind of been settling on it and farming it and so on. One of the things the Gracchi wanted to do was redistribute land—get former soldiers back on the land. Some of the more conservative citizens at Rome were a little distressed by this because they had been holding that land for a long time. They didn't want to give it up.

What happened, in the midst of this sorry spectacle, was that tribunes were bribed, and when he himself tried to stand for the tribunate—for a second consecutive year—Tiberius Gracchus was murdered. This was the first instance of political bloodshed in Rome. Over all these centuries, amidst any number of controversies, amidst any number of difficult, potentially contentious situations, never before had a Roman shed the blood of another in political contention. Now that line had been crossed. When Gaius Gracchus carried on with his brother's plans, he and 250 of his allies were murdered by senatorial agents. The scale of violence was now becoming pretty dramatic at Rome.

During the regime of the Gracchi, when the Gracchi were trying to put their land reforms through, perhaps something like 75,000 people received land allocations from the Roman state. That gives us some idea of the scale of social problems—quite a large number of indigent people, or if not indigent then marginal people, to whom the Gracchi were trying to give land. The Gracchi idealistically said, "We're just trying to give these people the wherewithal to be good, functioning members of society." The Gracchi's opponents said, "You're buying support." Probably a little truth in both positions. In any case, after the death of the Gracchi, after the death of the two brothers, a lot of the senatorials began trying to take this land back.

This put the Roman people in a very, very difficult position. Society was increasingly becoming factionalized into two groups. Writers at the time used the words *optimates*, optimates, the best people—that's what they called themselves, of course—and *populares*, the popular element. From the standpoint of the optimates, of course, the populares were the rabble. From the standpoint of the populares, of course, the optimates were oppressive and dictatorial, and so on. Society was really becoming fractured in some very, very ugly ways.

Amidst these political crises, Roman armies, under traditional senatorial leadership, were faring badly in several places. They'd had very serious problems in Spain for a number of years. But at the moment, the crises were actually in North Africa. Remember, they had conquered the area of Carthage as a result of the Punic Wars and had not initially started expanding their conquests in North Africa. This began to wait until the last decades of the second century B.C., and Roman armies were doing very badly over here.

Armies had been a way for people to rise very high in the estimation of their fellow citizens, but the army could also be a place for a person to sink in the estimation of his fellow citizens if he conducted himself poorly. In 107 B.C., a man by the name of Marius, he was born in 157 B.C., died in 86 B.C., a "New Man," a *novus homo*. What a "New Man" was, in Roman politics, is a man without a history of family participation in political office in Rome. Romans had a category for the "New Man," somebody whose family had not held high office previously. Again, I've emphasized before the relatively small number of families who had held office in Rome over a very long period of time.

In 107, Marius was elected consul, and he decided to take over the Numidian campaign, and he quickly had great success, great military success. As it happens, Marius was a fine soldier. It also appears, contrary perhaps to all expectations, that he was an honest man. He really did seem to have a great problem with the fact that Rome had not been having success in the campaigns in North Africa, that there had been a lot of dishonesty, and he really wanted to clean up the situation.

He also, in some important respects, began the professionalization of the Roman army. Before this time, in principle, every Roman citizen—that means every adult male Roman citizen—could be called to serve in the army under any circumstances that might demand his service. With Marius, we begin to shift to a situation where men go and enlist in the army, where you choose the army as a career, or at any rate as something that you will do for a period of years.

This professionalizing of the Roman army, and then the very close connection between soldiers and their leaders, introduced a new shift in Roman politics. You'll remember we talked before about the fact that, going all the way back to the Punic Wars, veterans—military veterans—had begun to be a pressure group in Roman politics. Now the Roman army itself becomes a pressure group in Roman politics. This, again, was something new. We can see a linkage with the veterans having become a pressure group, but nevertheless there is something new here.

The senatorials were furious with Marius. They were furious with him for a whole lot of reasons. They were furious because he was successful where members of their group had not been successful. They were furious because, in taking his first steps in the direction of professionalizing the Roman military, they regarded him as simply having built himself a great patronage machine. Is that what Marius had in mind? Probably not, or at least it would be unfair to say that that's the first thing he had in mind. He cannot have been unaware of this issue; in Roman politics, you were never unaware of finding support.

Then Marius held the consulship several years in a row. This was not strictly illegal, but it was highly unusual. In the past, you're consul, and you had to wait a period of years till you were consul again. After about 100 B.C., Marius withdrew a little bit from the public scene, but he remained a very influential *populares* leader. He remained a very important sort of behind the scenes leader of the popular party at Rome.

In 90 B.C., Rome's allies in Italy, the *socii*, rebelled. Rome went to war against the *socii*, and we remember this as the "Social War." Marius won the Social War, and one of the ways that he was able to pacify the situation relatively quickly afterwards was that the Latin allies throughout Italy basically were given full Roman citizenship. Once again, Marius's conduct was an affront to the traditional Roman order. They hadn't been able to deal with the crisis he did. He deals with the crisis in a very traditional Roman way: be generous to your foe. Remember we talked about that? Here the generosity extends, basically, to giving the *socii*—the allies—full citizenship. So if you're on the opposite side of Roman politics, how to you view that? Marius is just building another patronage machine for himself.

Did anybody trust anybody any longer? Did anybody believe anybody any longer? This is the way Roman politics begins to go. You could view Marius's activities through several different points of view, quite legitimately. Either we today, looking back—or you could imagine his contemporaries looking at his conduct, and saying, "It's good, and it's honest, and it's serving the interests of the Roman people," or "No, it's serving his own interest, it's all self-serving." Which way was it? Probably a little bit of both. Marius' successes, then, alarmed the *optimates* even more.

Then, in Asia Minor, in Anatolia, a ruler, a local big shot by the name of Mithridates attacked Roman territories, and he killed several Roman merchants and some Roman tax collectors. Well, Romans weren't going to stand for that. They assigned a military campaign against Mithridates to the optimate Sulla. Sulla was born in 138 B.C., died in 78. He was given the task of going to the East and punishing Mithridates for having the temerity to attack the Roman people. Marius was jealous. Marius was jealous that this great military command had not been given to him. And after all, in view of recent experiences, whether his campaigns in Italy, or whether his victory in the Social War, and so on, Marius would have been the obvious choice to be given a great military command. But the *optimates* had control of the Senate. They had the capacity to influence, decisively, the Roman voting assemblies, and they weren't by any means going to give Marius this opportunity; they give it to Sulla.

Marius was jealous, and he waged a considerable political battle back home against Sulla and his forces. There were all sorts of subtle things he could do to harm, to damage, to thwart Sulla's interests. When Sulla returned from the East, he found, first of all, that Marius had died in the interim— no skullduggery, he just got old and died. But Sulla marched on Rome and massacred Marius's followers. Here, again, the scale of political violence is going up, up, up. And we notice something interesting here. It has been the *optimates* who murdered the Gracchi, who slaughtered the Gracchi's successors. It was the *optimates* who slaughtered Marius' successors. Those very people who, out of one side of the mouth, said we must stand for the old values, the traditional values, the old ways, the way our ancestors did it; out the other side of their mouth, they said let's kill these guys we don't like. Roman politics was becoming pretty ugly business.

Sulla also issued proscription lists. He published lists, publicly, in Rome. Anybody whose name was on that list could be killed with impunity and his property taken over. His property taken over. What was there to stop anybody from going to kill anybody who was a personal foe or even whose property you craved? This was a pretty nasty business, as well.

The careers of Marius and Sulla taught the Romans, at least the elite among them, one lesson incontrovertibly: You want power in Rome now? You've got to have an army. The old traditional political base, the base in Roman families, the base in your family having held office for a long period of time, this was no longer going to be enough. You're going to make your way in this new Roman political world, this world that emerged between about 130 and 80 B.C., over a period of, say, two generations. You want to rise in that world? Get your hands on an army.

The first to act on this lesson was a man by the name of Pompey. Pompey was born in 106 B.C., died in 48 B.C. He won, in the first place, a command to clear the pirates from the Mediterranean. Clearing pirates from the Mediterranean was a rather interesting command to get because it was one that could be extended, in principle, almost endlessly. A pirate is everything from a bandit to a merchant you don't like to rebels in somebody else's political struggles to your actual enemy. There was really no way of exactly defining exactly who were these people that Pompey was going to go and clear from the Mediterranean. He got himself, in principle, almost an open-ended command. Subsequently, Pompey also got armies and was able fight, even in some other campaigns.

Close on Pompey's heels—Pompey had taken the lesson, you've got to get a military command. In his case, he got a navy. Close on his heels was Julius Caesar. Julius Caesar was born in 100 B.C., he died in 44 B.C. Caesar's family situation, his political background, is actually kind of interesting. He comes from one of the oldest families in Rome, one of the oldest and most distinguished families in Rome, but a family which had been, for a couple of centuries, sort of on the eclipse. They had not been providing officers regularly, had not been providing consuls and so on. Caesar brings this family back into prominence.

Caesar was elected consul in the year 63, and then he began maneuvering for a major military campaign. You may remember, we said in an earlier lecture, that one of the stresses and strains that the creation of the Roman Empire produced for the Roman Republic was a multiplication of offices. Very often, the consuls, and sometimes even the praetors, after their period of service in office, would become a pro-consul or a pro-preaetor, and would then get a military command and go off to one or another of the areas of the Roman world where they might be expected to fight. Caesar's ambitions don't stop with getting himself elected consul in 63. That normally, historically, in the past would have been the pinnacle of a public career at Rome. Now, it's a springboard to get an army.

There was also, at the same time at Rome, a man by the name of Crassus. Crassus was crass. He came from a lower or middling family. He had going for him only this: he was the richest man in Rome. He had enormous money, but he had no respectability. Remember, we talked about *auctoritas*—that eminence, that dignity of great citizens. Crassus had none of that at all.

This rather unsavory character, he'd made a lot of his money. For example, Rome was a city very largely built in wood. It's only from the time of Augustus Caesar—we'll be talking about him in later lectures, we'll mention him at the end of this lecture and talk about him in more detail in later lectures—it's from Augustus' time on that much of Rome was rebuilt in stone and brick. Much of the city was wood, and as a result, buildings were frequently catching fire. Crassus had a habit of hanging around at night and going up to buildings that were on fire, and as people came running out, he'd buy the buildings. Then he'd rebuild things and sell them at enormous profits, and so on.

He wants office and a military command simply to get legitimacy, to get a certain measure of credibility. As a result, these three guys—Pompey, Caesar and Crassus—pooled their political resources, pooled their material resources in 60 B.C. and formed what was called the "First Triumvirate."

Crassus, as I said, just wanted legitimacy. He wanted a military command that would somehow give him a kind of an authenticity in Roman politics that he otherwise lacked. Pompey wanted laws passed providing pensions for his veterans, those soldiers who had worked with him during his campaigns against the pirates. Caesar, as I mentioned a moment ago, wants a military command. Actually, where he wants to go is Gaul, and we'll come back to that in just a second.

So, these three guys pool their political resources in 60 B.C. A political deal like this, was it illegal? No. Was it unusual? Yes. Was it unprecedented? Yes. Cicero and others protested in vain against this outrageous manipulation of the Roman system. They said this is not the way the system's supposed to be. What's curious here is these guys actually stayed on the right side of the law. They didn't actually do anything illegal, but they certainly were manipulating the system, and they were certainly manipulating it to serve their own purposes.

Caesar got his command; he went off and spent eight years in Gaul, writing his commentaries and sending them back. Virtually every student who's ever done Latin in high school or in college has read some portion of Caesar's commentaries on the Gallic Wars, very often the first Latin text that a Latin student encounters.

While Caesar was off in Gaul, Roman politics changed pretty dramatically. Crassus, first of all, who was a much better swindler than soldier, was killed on the battlefield and vanished from the scene. His particular influence is now gone. The *optimates* in Rome now turned to Pompey. They'd had some doubts about Pompey for a while, but now they turned to Pompey, largely because they figure they can't possibly trust Caesar. They turn to Pompey, and they use Pompey and they use the Roman institutions to pass a series of laws that were basically designed to ruin Julius Caesar. They were really going after him with a vengeance.

In 49 B.C., Caesar's command in Gaul came to an end. He had to return to Italy. He comes back into northern Italy. Remember we talked, several lectures back, about the political geography of Italy, about the fact that peninsular Italy was Roman Italy, and northern Italy was *Gallia Cisalpina*, Gaul on this side of the Alps. When Caesar came into northern Italy, he was still outside Roman territory. Then he marched down to a little river called the Rubicon.

As Caesar camped at the Rubicon River, he was faced with a very interesting dilemma. The dilemma was this: if he laid down his military command and crossed the Rubicon as a private citizen, his enemies would have destroyed him, and he knew it. If he crossed the Rubicon with his army, he's declared war on Rome. What's his choice?

Caesar's biographer tells us—Caesar, of course, one of these well educated young Romans who was well educated in Greek ways—his biographer tells us that he said, in Greek, "*Ho kubos balletai,*" in Latin, "*Alea iacta est.*" The die is cast. He crossed the Rubicon, giving us a phrase in our political vocabulary. There was no turning back now.

This inaugurated a number of years of rather brutal and nasty civil war. Not surprisingly. What were Caesar's goals? People have been trying to imagine, to understand, to think about what Caesar's goals might have been, for a very long time. First of all, of course, he had to survive. This plunged Rome into a civil war. Caesar always said, "This was forced on me, I didn't ask for this. I didn't want this. My enemies forced this on me"

Caesar defeated, first of all, the forces of Pompey, and then established himself as dictator at Rome. Actually, dictator was a formal office under the Roman constitutional scheme of things. Going all the way back, in times of extreme necessity, the Roman institutions more or less suspended themselves and appointed a dictator for six months. Then he was supposed to return his powers. Caesar now appointed himself dictator, but with a kind of an open-ended term. Again, it's a bit of a manipulation of the system, and it's something ever so slightly consistent with the system.

Many key figures of late republican politics lost their lives in the next three or four years. Cicero died in this period, Pompey died in this period, Cato the Younger died in this period. That's worth remembering because, as slowly but surely a new regime began creating itself, most of the great figures of the last days of the republic—however tortured those years were—most of the great figures were gone. Gone before their time. So one had, in a way, to reconstitute a political elite. That's not an easy thing to do in any society.

Caesar's dictatorship was reasonably enlightened. There were many reforms passed. I'll just mention, for example, the Julian calendar, one of the first great calendar reforms. In the 1580s, Pope Gregory XV revised the calendar yet again—the Gregorian calendar, which is the one we use today. But for a very long time, and in some places in the world still today, the Julian calendar is still used.

Caesar passed land laws, and legal reforms, and institutional reforms, and a wide variety of measures. Scholars who have looked very closely at what Caesar did have been very much divided in their opinion. Was he functioning as this sort of dictatorial guy, who was serving his own interests and the interests of his party? Or, was he really a kind of enlightened ruler, who had a great vision for the Roman people and was just trying to do the right thing? If we imagine those as ends of a spectrum, the truth is probably somewhere between those two ends of the spectrum. The point is that Caesar's activity in this period was then, and has been now, controversial. What's clear is this: everyone was looking for solution to the increasingly inevitable collapse of the Roman system. The Roman system that had been there for so very long seemed to be teetering on the brink of extinction. What to do?

In 44 B.C., on the Ides of March, a group of disgruntled senators murdered Caesar. This was a fairly stupid act, politically, actually. Whether these people simply seized an opportunity to get rid of their opponent because they were jealous of him, because he'd gotten more success than they had, or whether, as some have suggested, that they somehow honestly believed that Caesar was the problem. If you get rid of Caesar, the problem goes away. It's very hard to say. It's just very hard to say just what they were thinking. Maybe they weren't thinking very much. Anyway, Caesar was struck down in the Roman Senate house and fell, ironically, at the foot of the statue of Pompey.

Now the Roman world was plunged yet again into a period of civil war, this time lasting 13 years. There was now formed a "Second Triumvirate." It consisted of Marcus Antonius, that's Shakespeare's Mark Antony, who is the heir to Julius Caesar's forces. Then there was Octavian, Julius Caesar's nephew and adopted heir. And there was a man by the name of Lepidus, who just happened to have a big army under his command at this moment, and so accidentally became kind of a key figure, briefly, in Roman politics.

The triumvirs, in the first place, divided up the military responsibilities they faced, defeated the forces of those who had killed Julius Caesar and then had to begin thinking what's next. First thing, not surprisingly, Lepidus was shunted aside. End of Lepidus. He wasn't killed, but he was moved aside.

For several years, Octavian and Antony sort of stared each other down— Octavian generally in the west, Antony generally in the east. Antony is having his dalliance with Cleopatra, which gives us movies and novels and all kinds of stories. It's pretty clear that one of these guys was going to win, and one of them was going to lose. What was Octavian's position, for example? What did he think? What was he trying to do? With Antony, he simply looks like an ambitious guy, who, as much as anything, was profiting from the circumstances in which he found himself. Maybe he was, in some idealistic sense, kind of an heir to Caesar's position. That's very hard to say. As I was indicating a moment ago, it's very hard to say exactly what Caesar's position was.

Octavian? I think it's easier to see in prospect what Octavian's position was, and we'll turn to that in future lectures. We'll see what Octavian actually did as Caesar Augustus, and perhaps that will give us a little bit clearer picture of what he was thinking about during these 13 years of intense civil war.

The Roman Republic is gone. One way or another, it's gone. Why? What happened to the Roman Republic? What happened to this remarkably stable, effective, much admired regime? First of all, the opportunities and challenges presented by the empire simply devastated the old political system. The number of officers expanded; the number of opportunities expanded. Military situations produced a wholly new set of circumstances at Rome. It's unreasonable to suppose that the old Roman city-state of Rome could have survived with an empire.

Power and influence and unimaginable wealth could be won in the empire and deployed in Rome with no checks by the traditional system. The old system was checked. Remember those Roman families, remember that *pater familias*, remember teach your son law and the history of your family and how to farm your property? Again we saw—maybe that's an idea, maybe not—that's the way the Romans thought about things. But going off and conquering vast lands, and taking vast plunder from those lands and coming back and buying support in Roman politics was not how the game was supposed to be played. And yet, at the end, that's how it was played.

Disruptions in the countryside led to countless numbers of landless, rootless people, who moved into the city of Rome and who felt no commitment to any old fashioned values, to any great Roman way of doing things, to any Roman system. These were people who were massively disrupted, as a result of the political and also the military crises of Italy over more than a century.

Finally, Greek culture, for all its glories, eroded the simple, sturdy values of the Romans—turned them more cosmopolitan. Aristotle once said that in an ideal state, all citizens could be summoned by the cry of a herald. That may not be practical, but the Roman experience, at the very least, makes one think.

The Pax Romana
Lecture 21

Historians do indeed refer to this period, from Augustus to Marcus Aurelius, as the Pax Romana, the "Roman Peace."

Moving quickly and deftly, Octavian (31 B.C.–A.D. 14) inaugurated a new regime at Rome that proved stable and successful for two centuries. The brute reality was that Octavian controlled Rome's armies. Instead of flaunting his military power, of ruling like a dictator or despot, Octavian, in 27 B.C., made a show of offering to return all his powers and authority to the Senate.

Even those who opposed him realized that without Octavian, the state would descend into anarchy. Therefore, Octavian was confirmed in power and awarded a number of honorific titles. Among these titles, *Augustus* became the commonest.

Augustus decided to rule as *princeps*, "first citizen," and his new regime has been called the "Augustan Principate." Central to the principate were two basic policies. Augustus sometimes held one or more of the republican magistracies but regularly permitted elections to be held and prominent citizens to hold office.

Augustus retained control of the richest or most militarily insecure provinces but permitted elite citizens to hold important posts in other provinces. Augustus was also personally committed to traditional Roman morality and culture; even those who opposed his political control nevertheless embraced his cultural orientation. Most important, Augustus brought peace and security after a century of chaos.

Augustus was faced with a succession problem. Partly this was attributable to the central contradiction of the regime: a despotism masquerading as a magistracy. Partly this was attributable to the fact that Augustus had no heir: He had only one child, a daughter, Julia, who did not produce an heir. Finally, Augustus adopted as his heir Tiberius, a son of his second wife by her first marriage. He assumed the imperial office without incident; there was no return to civil wars.

From 14 to 68, Rome was ruled by members of the Julio-Claudian family, direct or indirect descendants of Julius and Augustus Caesar. The Julio-Claudians were an odd lot: Tiberius was old and suspicious and probably a pederast; Caligula was crazy; Claudius was physically handicapped and paranoid; Nero was an unbalanced genius. Caligula was assassinated, Claudius was poisoned, and Nero committed suicide. Nevertheless, new territories were added (for example, Britain), the empire was well governed, and Roman finances were put on a sound footing. The Julio-Claudian period is an eloquent tribute to the genius of Augustus's regime.

"The Romans made a great desert, and called it peace."—Tacitus, Roman historian

A year of civil war in 69 did not return Rome to the turbulence of the late republic. Four generals in succession competed for the imperial office, with the last of them, Vespasian (69–79), making good his claim. The Flavian dynasty of Vespasian and his sons, Titus (79–81) and Domitian (81–96), ruled effectively until Domitian's growing autocracy earned him assassination.

Rome then experienced a century of stability, prosperity, and good government under the "Five Good Emperors": Nerva (96–98), Trajan (98–117), Hadrian (117–138), Antoninus Pius (138–161), and Marcus Aurelius (161–180). Under Trajan, the empire reached its greatest extent in territory with the conquest of Dacia (roughly today's Romania). Hadrian and Marcus Aurelius were serious intellectuals. Of this world, the incomparable Edward Gibbon said:

> In the second century of the Christian era, the Empire of Rome comprehended the fairest part of the earth, and the most civilized portion of mankind. The frontiers of that extensive monarchy were guarded by ancient renown and disciplined valor. The gentle but powerful influence of laws and manners gradually cemented

the union of the provinces. The peaceful inhabitants enjoyed and abused the advantages of wealth and luxury. The image of a free constitution was preserved with decent reverence: the Roman senate appeared to possess the sovereign authority and devolved on the emperors all the executive power of government. During a happy period (A.D. 98–180) of more than fourscore years, the public administration was conducted by the virtue and abilities of Nerva, Trajan, Hadrian, and the two antonines.

Historians refer to the period from Augustus to Marcus Aurelius as the Pax Romana: the "Roman Peace." The wry historian Tacitus (whom we will meet in more detail in the next lecture) made two critical points about this period. First, he said, the "Romans have made a great desert and called it peace." Second, he observed that the unspoken secret of the principate was that the army could make, and unmake, the emperor.

Nevertheless, at the heart of the regime, a partnership between the emperors and the senatorial elite worked well. It was important here that Augustus had remade and expanded the old republican elite, incorporating more Italians and even some provincials. Senators did not try to seize the imperial office or to restore the republic.

Even if Rome's peace was imposed by force on people who had not asked for it, it provided many benefits. Peace within a vast zone promoted trade, and a lack of local disturbances permitted agriculture to flourish. Provincials did not have to fear cross-border depredations. Roman law, roads, public amenities (baths, theaters, temples, markets) served the interests of all people. Cities flourished.

How did the Pax Romana work? First, Rome asked for relatively little, primarily, taxes and loyalty. The Roman regime was too small to demand much, and Rome had no desire to interfere in people's daily lives. The process of Romanization was a slow, steady, largely voluntary project. Local elites wanted to get on good terms with the Romans and eagerly adopted Roman ways.

Despite all the positives, and Gibbon's glowing assessment, the storm clouds were gathering, as we will see in a later lecture. Still, the fact that Rome's empire eventually vanished should not blind us to the remarkable successes of its first two centuries. A betting person would have put a substantial wager on Rome in 180. ∎

Suggested Reading

Garnsey and Saller, *The Roman Empire*.

Millar, *The Emperor in the Roman World*.

Raaflaub and Toher, eds., *Between Republic and Empire*.

Shotter, *Augustus Caesar*.

Syme, *The Roman Revolution*.

Questions to Consider

1. Put yourself in Octavian's position in 31 B.C. What would *you* have done?

2. Do you agree with Tacitus's assessment of the Pax Romana?

The Pax Romana
Lecture 21—Transcript

In this lecture, we're going to talk about the "Augustan Principate," a regime introduced by Augustus Caesar. More explanation about that in just a few minutes. In the next lecture, we're going to look at the Augustan Principate again. This time, we'll talk about government, institutions, war, the empire. The next time, we'll talk about Roman culture in what are called the Golden and the Silver Ages.

You may recall that in our last lecture, we brought the curtain down on the Roman Republic. The Roman Republic, that long and stable regime that had existed for some five centuries. We saw that it collapsed amidst civil war, two long periods of civil war, between 49 and 46 B.C., another between 44 and 31 B.C. These had been preceded by civil insurrections in the 90s B.C., and the late 80s and early 70s B.C. So, a long and difficult period for Rome, when, you may again remember my mentioning, a considerable number of the leading members of the old ruling class had been killed off. We also talked about political manipulation. We also talked about military ambition.

When, in 31 B.C., Octavian defeated Antony at the Battle of Action and achieved a supreme position in the Roman world, the question we have to ask ourselves is: Of what was he now in charge? What had happened? What was the state of the Roman world in 31 B.C.?

Moving very quickly, moving very deftly, Octavian, who reigned from 31 B.C to 14 A.D., inaugurated a new regime at Rome that proved stable and that proved successful for some two centuries. These two centuries, more or less, from 31 B.C. to 180 A.D., we call the *Pax Romana*, the "Roman Peace."

The brute reality of this period was that Octavian controlled Rome's armies. That is the one underlying fact, without which nothing else really makes sense. Then we come to the genius of Octavian. Instead of flaunting his military power, instead of ruling like a military dictator, instead of putting his jackboots on the necks of his subjects throughout the empire, Octavian, in 27 B.C., made a great show of giving all his power and authority back to the Roman Senate. One can easily imagine the Roman senators having been somewhat flummoxed at this particular political show. What they realized, very quickly, was that without Octavian, all would be chaos. Everything would descend into complete and utter anarchy.

What they did was make a grand show of systematically giving him back all of these powers which he had, as it were, returned to them. They accorded him a number of honorific titles. Chief among these was *Augustus*. In Latin, that means eminent, distinguished, particularly important. We henceforth refer to Gaius Julius Caesar Octavius, Octavian Caesar, as Augustus Caesar.

Augustus, generally speaking, referred to himself as *princeps*. We can hear the English word "prince" hiding in there, first citizen, as the first citizen. So, historians refer to his regime as the "Augustan Principate," the time when Augustus ruled as *princeps*, and when those who came after him ruled also as *princeps*. This was not entirely a novelty. You may remember just a few lectures back that we had talked about the *princeps senatus*, the oldest member of the Senate, the prince of the Senate, the person who always, in the Roman Senate, spoke first. Surely that's the sort of thing that Augustus had in mind when he took for himself the title *princeps*.

Central to this Augustan Principate were a couple of very simple, very basic policies. First of all, Augustus generally held one or more of the old republican magistratacies. He was sometimes consul and sometimes one or another of the other officers of the state. But he permitted regular elections to be held so that other prominent citizens could be elected to one or another of the old republican magistrates, could be seen to have the kind of power, the kind of authority, the kind of eminence, the kind of legitimacy that had always attached to the holding of office in the Roman state. There can be no question about the fact that power was in Augustus' hands, but he appeared to share that power with others.

In the second place, Augustus retained control of the richest and the most militarily insecure provinces. The rich ones because they poured enormous tribute into Rome, and/or, for example with Egypt, food, grain. Managing the food supply of Rome, managing the food supply of the population of Rome, was very important to Augustus in terms of maintaining peace and maintaining order. Maintaining the wealthy provinces, of course, gave him a kind of a stranglehold on the material resources of the Roman world.

And maintaining, in his hands, control of the most militarily threatened provinces meant that rivals to him—generals at the head of armies—could not rise up as had been the experience of the Roman world going back at least to the time of Marius at the very end of the second century B.C., and coming right through that very difficult first century. Fundamentally, Augustus controlled the money and the army. Those are the two basic things that he controlled. And then in the first place, as I mentioned, he controlled offices in the state, but he appeared to share them.

Augustus was also personally committed to all the traditional Roman values, to the traditional Roman morality, to traditional Roman culture. We could say that he made great show of adhering to old Roman values, of promoting the old Roman ways of doing things, of promoting traditional Roman ethics. And it is absolutely true. He made great show of this. All of the evidence seems to suggest that he was, himself, genuinely and personally committed to these old Roman values. It will occur to you, perhaps, that he was, as a military dictator, a living contradiction of all those old values, but people have often been able to live with these kinds of contradictory opinions in their mind, all at once.

Fundamentally, and if we really try to pass a judgment on Augustus, we would say this: he brought peace, security and order after a century of chaos. If we were time travelers, and we went back to 31 B.C., when Octavian defeated Antony and was about to be launched on his career as sole ruler, and we said, "Predict what's going to happen next," most of us would predict more chaos. That would be the sensible prediction. We'd be wrong, but that would be the sensible prediction. Augustus' achievement in bringing order, in bringing stability to the Roman world, was a very considerable one, indeed.

As he drew near the end of his life, Augustus faced a very interesting and a very acute problem. He was, as I've emphasized, a military dictator. He was also, as I've emphasized, a magistrate, or he appeared to be a magistrate. He appeared to hold his power at the pleasure of the Roman public authorities, indeed at the pleasure of the Roman Senate. The reality was different, but this is how he portrayed himself. How does one transmit a regime like that? How does one hand it on? In the Republic, year after year after year, there were elections; there was peaceful transition of power from one year to the next, from one year to the next over five centuries—or at least over the first four centuries of the Roman Republic. That, of course, all came unstuck in the first century B.C. How is Augustus to hand this regime on, and what kind of a regime is it?

That's really two separate questions, isn't it? How is he going to hand it on, and what kind of a regime is it? What kind of a regime it is, we'll trace out in the next few minutes. The question immediately before us: how is he going to hand it on? Augustus had no heir. He had one daughter, who herself produced no children. He, himself, produced no sons. Finally, near the end of his life, he adopted a man by the name of Tiberius, who was the son of his second wife by her first marriage. In other words, he was looking around for someone with whom he had a plausible connection, and he named Tiberius as his heir.

The remarkable thing is that when Augustus died, Tiberius succeeded him, and there was no return to civil war. There was no return to chaos. There was an orderly succession of power. That, perhaps, in retrospect is the crowning achievement of Augustus' reign. Not only that he was able to produce, for more than 40 years, peace and order in this Roman world, but he was able to transmit it in wholly new circumstances. There had never been a transition of power in the Roman world like the one that took place in 14 A.D.

From 14 to 68 A.D., Rome was ruled by members of what we call the Julio-Claudian family. The family remembrance now is that Julius Caesar was the first ruler, Augustus Caesar the second, and then 10 more followed as members of this Julio-Claudian family, or Julio-Claudian dynasty. They are all people who have direct or indirect succession to Julius and Augustus Caesar.

The Julio-Claudians are, in a variety of ways, an odd lot. Tiberius, for example, was an old, rather suspicious man who was probably a pederast. Caligula was crazy, there's just no question about that. Claudius was physically handicapped and paranoid. Nero was an unbalanced genius;

he's the one who fiddled while Rome burned. This was also a time, in some ways, of intense political strife and political controversy, too. Caligula, for example, was assassinated; Claudius was poisoned; Nero committed suicide. We might say, if we're going to think about these Julio-Claudian rulers, "Is it the case that the Augustan Principate held, that the Augustan settlement persisted, or had Rome, in fact, descended once again into the anarchy of the first century B.C.?"

The paradox is deep, indeed. One way, I suppose, of getting a feel for it would be to say, let's imagine two space travelers to the United States. They could come now, if you please. One of them lands in Washington, and one of them lands anywhere else you like in the country, really, maybe somewhere out in the Midwest. They stay for a few months, and then they go back to wherever it was they came from and they have a conversation. Would they not suppose that they had landed in two different worlds? The world of Washington: the world of government, of gossip, of busybodies, of all of the activities, all the self-serving activity, all the self-important activity that goes on. And in most of the rest of the country, people peacefully going about their lives and business without much reference to what goes on in the middle.

Now let's imagine two comparable visitors, two comparable travelers in the first century A.D. One landed in Rome, where there was all this strife and controversy and oddball rulers and political assassinations. Another landed almost anywhere in the provinces of the Roman Empire. Then we'll send them back where they came, and we'll have a conversation between them. They, too, would imagine themselves to have visited two completely different places. Here, again, is a tribute to the remarkable success of the Augustan achievement. The Augustan Principate, the Roman Empire, the regime Augustus created went chugging along its way, working remarkably well, even though there was a certain amount of difficulty, stress, chaos, crisis, and odd goings on at the very heart of that regime. Something sufficiently stable had been produced that it didn't absolutely depend on the character or the ability of the ruler himself.

This is also a time when new territories are added to the realm, for example the British Isles. Excuse me, Britain—Romans didn't conquer Ireland. When Britain was conquered by the Romans, this was a time when the Roman world was extremely well governed. It was a time when Roman finances were put on very sound footings. In other words, in a whole variety of areas of public life and public administration, this was, in fact, a very successful period, indeed. Let me just repeat: it was a tribute to the genius of Augustus' settlement that the Julio-Claudian period was so stable, effective and well governed, when, if we only looked at the capital, we only looked at the emperors, we would conclude that things are in big trouble once again.

A year of civil war, in 68-69 A.D., did not return Rome to the turbulence of the late republic, a test of the system. Four generals in succession competed for the imperial office; three of them fell away, and finally one of them—Vespasian was his name—succeeded in making good his claim, and he ruled for a decade, from 69-79. Vespasian inaugurates what we call the Flavian dynasty of rulers. A little bit later in Roman history, Flavius actually becomes one of the honorific titles for an emperor. But now, this is the Flavian dynasty; they're members of the Flavian family. Vespasian is succeeded by his son Titus, and then by his son Domitian. Titus ruled from 79-81, Domitian from 81-96. He ruled really quite effectively until Domitian's sort of growing autocracy eventually earned him assassination. Then, as we'll see in just a moment, there was another peaceful transition of power. So, we had moved from the Julio-Claudian family to the Flavian family, and we had moved across a year of civil war in 69 A.D. Still, the Augustan settlement held.

With the assassination of Domitian, we might suppose that now, surely, trouble will come. Basically, it did not. In fact, Rome now got perhaps the best set of five emperors in a row that the entire imperial period produced. History remembers them as the "Five Good Emperors:" Nerva, who reigned from 96 to 98, a very short reign; Trajan, from 98 to 117; Hadrian, from 117 to 138; Antonius Pius, from 138 to 161; and Marcus Aurelius, from 161 to 180. I don't actually expect that anyone will remember those dates. I mention them only because, apart from the very short reign of Nerva, who died a peaceful death, you'll notice, perhaps, that the rest of these reigns are rather long. Lengthy reigns can produce—by themselves they may not—but they can produce stability and order. That is certainly what happened in the Roman world of the second century A.D. One long reign after another, of one extremely competent, gifted ruler after another.

In a dynastic system, there is, of course, no guarantee that son will succeed to father, or adopted heir will succeed to the person who adopted him, and be successful. But in this particular instance, the Roman world was blessed with a succession of very successful rulers. This was also the final period of Roman expansion.

Under Trajan, the empire reached its greatest extent in territory. Trajan conquered beyond the Danube in the northern Balkans, and conquered the area which then was called Dacia. Today this is, roughly, Romania. This was the last expansion of the Roman world.

You'll remember, perhaps, I said just a moment ago that during the first century A.D. the Roman legions had gone into Britain. That's worth pausing and reflecting on for just a second. Remember that the Romans went to war with the Carthaginians in 264 B.C., and at the end of that war in 241, they annexed Sicily, Sardinia, and Corsica—the first territories outside Italy taken by the Romans. Formally, we can date that acquisition of territory to 241. The Roman Empire continued expanding until the very first years of the second century A.D. In other words, this was an imperial system that continued to expand for some 350 years. Roman conquest did not come all at one moment, and, as we'll see in later lectures, it did not disappear all at one moment.

This was a regime that grew for a very long time. Anyone who has visited Rome and has been near the old Roman forum may have seen Trajan's column—this beautiful, very tall column, around which is carved in bas relief a history of Trajan's Dacian campaigns, the last of these great campaigns waged by the Romans to expand the size of their empire.

Of this world, of this late Augustan Principate, the incomparable historian Edward Gibbon wrote in the 18th century—we'll be occupied with Gibbon again in a later lecture—Gibbon wrote these words. He said:

"In the second century of the Christian Era, the Empire of Rome comprehended the fairest part of the earth, and the most civilized portion of mankind. The frontiers of that extensive monarchy were guarded by ancient renown and disciplined valor. The gentle but powerful influence of laws and manners gradually cemented the union of the provinces. The peaceful inhabitants enjoyed and abused the advantages of wealth and luxury. The image of a free constitution was preserved with decent reverence: the Roman senate appeared to possess the sovereign authority and devolved on the emperors all the executive power of government. During a happy period (A.D. 98-180) of more than fourscore years, the public administration was conducted by the virtue and abilities of Nerva, Trajan, Hadrian, and the two Antonines."

Historians do indeed refer to this period, from Augustus to Marcus Aurelius, as the *Pax Romana*, the "Roman Peace." Let's reflect a little bit on this *Pax Romana*. We may take our prompt from the late first century A.D. Roman historian, Tacitus—we'll meet him in a little bit more detail in our next lecture when we talk about the culture of the Augustan Principate. For now, let's just notice that he was the greatest historian of this period. He made a couple of very critical points in his historical writings about this period that we have come to call the *Pax Romana*, though he himself had experienced, seen, and wrote about only the first half of it, really.

First of all, he said, with wry humor, "The Romans made a great desert, and called it peace." Second, he observed that the unspoken secret of the principate was that the army could make or unmake an emperor. He saw that there was this dangerous element there with the military. And he saw that Rome's vast empire was not something, after all, that all of those peoples, from the north of Britain to Mesopotamia, from the North Sea to North Africa, had asked for. Old Attalus of Pergamum might have willed his kingdom to Rome, but nobody wrote to the Romans and said, "If you have some time next week, could you please come and conquer us?" The Romans marched forward always.

Remember, we talked about their notion of defensive imperialism: they had the idea that they could only fight just wars, that they could only fight if they had been attacked or affronted in some way. The Romans always contrived to describe every one of their wars as a war in defense of themselves. Somebody had threatened them, and then they went forward and conquered them. Tacitus understood the reality of the situation.

At the very heart of this regime, there was a partnership between the emperors and the senatorial elite which worked very well. Let's emphasize there that it was, slowly but surely, in the last years of the first century B.C., and across the first century A.D., a new senatorial elite that had to be constituted. It was made up, not so much of the old traditional Roman families as, indeed, of men who came from other parts of the Roman Empire as well.

Senators did not try to seize the imperial office or to restore the republic. When, for example, one or another of the Julio-Claudian—or even the one Flavian emperor who was killed, Domitian—when these men met their end, senators didn't try to replace them. They didn't try to put themselves in their place; they didn't try to recreate, to resurrect the Roman Republic. Remember, when the senators killed Julius Caesar in 44 B.C., we asked when we were discussing that: "What did they have in mind? What did they think was going to happen?" It seems that some of them, perhaps, were just blindly jealous of Julius Caesar. Others, however, seemed somewhat naively to have supposed that Caesar was the problem. Absent Caesar, the Republic would come back and all would be well.

By the time we move into the first century, people understood perfectly well that the Roman Republic, though much to be admired and written about, was gone. The senators had enough sense to share power with the emperors in this regime that we call the Augustan *principe*.

If Rome's peace had been imposed by force on people who had not asked for it, and surely that's the situation—we must always bear that in mind—and a little bit later, in later lectures, when we start to talk about the unraveling of the Roman Empire, we have to remember that we're not so much dealing with usurpation or rebellion or people being disloyal to the Romans. These people have, after all, been conquered by the Romans. In a certain sense, local autonomy, local interests and so on rose to the surface once again. But that's a story for a later day.

For now, I want simply to say that even if Rome had imposed its will on these peoples around the Mediterranean world, the fact is, Rome brought considerable benefits. First, an enormous free trade zone, which promoted trade, which promoted a lack of local disturbances; this peace imposed by the Romans made trade possible. It made agriculture flourish. You may recall that, quite a few lectures back, we noticed that the Persians had done the same thing in their very large empire. Remember, the Persians built roads, and the Persians created a post office, and the Persians created a unified system of weights and measures, and unified systems of coinage, and thus promoted trade through a world which, previous to the Persians, had been a sort of a crazy quilt of peoples. In a very real way, the *Pax Romana* repeated that kind of situation. It created a world where economic opportunity existed in ways that had not been true before.

Provincials were accorded a measure of protection, particularly those who lived along the frontiers of the Roman world. People who lived along the frontiers of the Roman world had always been subject to, victims of, cross-border depredations by various peoples who lived outside the Roman world. Rome now protected those people, protected their lands, protected their territories. Rome assumed the burden of defending this vast empire. Again, in a later lecture, we'll have to ask questions about whether Rome assumed a burden simply too large to have been carried with grace and success over the long haul. Rome provided other things, too: Roman law, a system of law; a system of public courts; a system of public justice; a system of order throughout this world.

Rome provided a vast system of roads. To understand the importance of the Roman system of roads, one has only today to drive in Britain, in France, in Italy. When you drive on the *Autoroute*, on the *Autostrata*, you're driving on the Roman roads. The Romans knew exactly where to put roads, and they built quite remarkable roads, roads that were preserved down into modern times, and then, of course, paved over and turned into modern toll-ways in various countries of Europe.

The Romans ruled through cities. Every province of the Roman world was equipped with urban government, and when Romans went into a city, they gave those cities a set of urban amenities. They would create amphitheaters, theaters, bathhouses, fora; they would create a whole panoply of great public buildings. Traveling the Roman world—in what was the Roman world, today the Mediterranean world—is to still see many of these buildings in lots and lots of places. Cities flourished. Under the Romans, urban life flourished. Largely, that was a result of Roman peace, that was a result of Roman fostering of economic opportunity, and it was also due to the fact that the Romans ruled through cities and that cities played a decisive role in the Roman system.

How did the *Pax Romana* work? How did the *Pax Romana* work, not at Rome, whereas we've seen what we have is this elegant and tenuous partnership between military dictators and senatorial elites, but how did it work out there in the empire, in this vast area ruled by Rome? First, let's bear in mind that Rome asked for relatively little. They collected taxes, but that wasn't new. People had been paying taxes or tributes to various rulers for a long time. They asked for loyalty. Now that really was a negative thing. People were not to act against Rome's interests. It wasn't a positive thing. Rome didn't actually ask people to do very much; they asked them not to harm Rome's interests. For the vast majority of people around the Mediterranean world, Roman rule was no more onerous than any of the rules they had experienced previously, and in some cases, it was actually more benevolent.

It's important, also, to bear in mind that the Roman regime was simply too small to demand very much. The entire Roman administration consisted of a few hundred administrators. A few hundred administrators, this vast world. The Roman army was not used as a police force; it certainly wasn't used as a secret police force. It wasn't used to maintain control over people; it was used to defend the frontiers of the empire. So, the Roman presence was absent. The vast majority of people in the Roman world would never have laid eyes on a Roman official or a Roman soldier, much less a Roman emperor. The Romans were not a constant presence.

The question, then, is: What made people buy in? The process of what we call "Romanization"—people going over to the Romans, adopting Latin, adopting some of the trappings of Roman culture, but in particularly showing their loyalty to Rome—was a very long, a very slow, a very steady, and, largely, a voluntary project. The Romans did not demand Romanization. People throughout the Roman Empire, slowly but surely, Romanized themselves, embraced various trappings of Roman culture.

One of the things that we will see in a later lecture is that, slowly but surely, people learned how to retain their Romanization and decouple that from loyalty to Rome. I'll just signal that now as a theme we'll come back to. Now, people Romanize and couple themselves to Rome. There was much in Rome for them.

Despite all of the positives and Gibbon's glowing assessment, the storm clouds were gathering. As we'll see in later lectures, eventually the Augustan Principate also failed, as indeed the Roman Republic had failed before it. But none of this should blind us to the remarkable achievements of these two centuries when, as I suggested at the outset, no one at their inception would have wagered that this Roman world had the tiniest chance at peace, order and security. Augustus' achievement was a quite remarkable one.

Rome's Golden and Silver Ages
Lecture 22

The reign of Augustus has often been called the "Golden Age." This was the age of many of Rome's greatest cultural achievements. It was also one of the great ages of poetry in all of Western history, and a remarkable array of gifted poets at this time.

The inception of the principate established several crucial conditions that were conducive to a high level of cultural achievement: Peace and security after a century of disturbances. Wealth and a willingness to use it to promote culture—patronage. A climate in which reflection on Rome's past and character was natural.

The reign of Augustus, often called the "Golden Age," was one of the greatest ages of poetic achievement in all of Western history. Virgil (70–19 B.C.), called by Tennyson "wielder of the stateliest measure ever formed by the mouth of man," was incomparably the greatest of them. His is a "composed" epic: Although there are stories and legends behind the *Aeneid*, Virgil composed this poem from beginning to end.

Although remembered mainly for the *Aeneid*, Virgil also composed the *Georgics* and *Eclogues*, moving and technically accomplished poems in praise of the countryside and the charms of traditional rural life. But the *Aeneid* is one of the true masterpieces of world literature. Its theme is the somber dignity of Rome's past. In the almost dirge-like quality of the poem's dactylic hexameters (six-footed lines, the fifth foot of which is always a dactyl), we meet, at line 33 of Book I: *Tantae molis erat Romanam condere gentem*. No pompous cheerleader, Virgil!

This means: "Oh what a tremendous job it was to found the Roman people." From the time when Aeneas carries his aged father, Anchises, on his back out of a burning Troy, we know that he has embarked on a mission from which he will not be deterred. Along the way, we see family devotion, honesty and integrity, determination, courage, and humanity: all the "typical" Roman virtues. Yet Aeneas was harried by Juno, the goddess who had favored the Trojans.

Venus, Aeneas's patroness, went to her father, Jupiter, to ask if he were going to remain true to his promises. Virgil put these words into the mouth of the chief of the gods and, in doing so, told us something about the optimism of the early years of Augustus's reign and of the ways the Romans saw themselves:

> … fate remains unmoved
> For the Roman generations. You will witness
> Lavinium's rise, her walls fulfill the promise;
> You will bring to heaven lofty-souled Aeneas.
> There has been no change in me whatever. Listen!
> To ease this care, I will prophesy a little,
> I will open the book of fate. Your son Aeneas
> Will wage a mighty war in Italy,
> Beat down proud nations, give his people laws,
> Found for them a city …
> To these I set no bounds in space or time;
> They shall rule forever. Even bitter Juno
> Whose fear now harries earth and sea and heaven
> Will change to better counsels and will cherish
> The race that wears the toga, Roman masters
> Of all the world. It is decreed.

Ovid (43 B.C.–A.D. 18) was learned, accomplished, and prolific. He wrote love elegies (the *Amores*), a didactic spoof (*The Art of Love*), an epic-scale encyclopedia of mythological tales (*The Metamorphoses*), and other works. There is, in Ovid, a spirit of play and a sense of deep feeling. Consider one of his elegies:

> Maidens, give ear, and you shall hear
> What is your chiefest duty,
> Pray listen well and I will tell
> You how to keep your beauty.
> 'Tis care that makes the barren earth

Produce the ripened grain.
'Tis care that brings tree-fruit to birth
With grafting and much pain.
Things that are cared for always please,
And now each man's a dandy,
A girl must be as spruce as he
And have her powder handy.

The elegant Horace (65–8 B.C.), sage, urbane, Epicurean, was prized in his own time and ever since. Patronized by Macaenas (who gives his name to patrons and patronage), Horace was one of those who flourished under Augustus. He wrote odes, epodes, satires, letters, and a treatise on poetry. Here is a 17th-century translation of one of the odes:

Strive not, Leuconoë, to know what end
The gods above to me or thee will send;
Nor with astrologers consult at all,
That thou mayest know what better can befall:
Whether thou livest more winters, or thy last
Be this, which Tyrrhene waves 'gainst rocks do cast.
Be wise! Drink free, and in so short a space
Do not protracted hopes of life embrace:
Whilst we are talking, envious time doth slide;
This day's thine own; the next may be denied.

Epic in scale, uncommonly beautiful in language, but all in prose was the great *History* of Livy (59 B.C.–A.D. 17). He did in prose what Virgil had done in verse: told the Romans the tale they wanted to hear about themselves. In the process, he tells us a great deal of what we actually know about early Rome and how the Romans in the time of Augustus "constructed" their own past.

The period after Augustus until well into the 2nd century produced another literary outpouring, usually called the "Silver Age." History, philosophy, rhetoric, and satire were its chief achievements.

In history, three authors command attention.

Tacitus (c. 55–c. 117) was the greatest of Rome's imperial historians. He wrote monographs, such as *On Britain* and *On Germany*, but is chiefly remembered for his *Histories* and *Annals* that treated the imperial period. He created fine pen portraits of individuals but mainly wished to put virtue and vice on display. He had made his peace with the imperial regime but not with the excesses it produced.

Suetonius (c. 70–c. 140) was not a great stylist, but his *Lives of the Twelve Caesars* (that is, of the emperors beginning with Julius Caesar) created unforgettable portraits.

Lucan (39–65) was a Spanish poet and historian who was put to death by Nero. He wrote the *Pharsalia*, a verse account of the civil wars of the late republic between Caesar and his foes. His work is full of trenchant political commentary, often providing a ringing defense of political freedom.

Among philosophical writers, pride of place goes to the Stoic Seneca (4 B.C.–A.D. 65), another writer who fell afoul of Nero. He wrote tragedies, dialogues, treatises, and letters. The emperor Marcus Aurelius was also a significant Stoic writer. His brooding *Meditations* was read for centuries as the deep reflections of a man faced with the awesome responsibilities of power who was all too aware of his human shortcomings.

In rhetoric, one name stands out, that of Quintilian (c. 35–c. 100), whose *Institutions of Oratory* constituted for the West the standard manual of the rhetorical art until modern times. These works remind us that in classical antiquity, education was based on training in public speaking. Rome produced several satirists.

Lucian (c. 125–c. 200) came from Syria and wrote prose satires in Greek in which he poked fun at both mythical and historical characters and, by implication, at almost anyone.

Juvenal (c. 60–c. 136) wrote 16 verse satires dealing with hypocrites, the travails of the poor (especially of poor writers like himself), women's faults (as he saw them!), ambition, pretentiousness, and people's despicable treatment of one another. He language is rhetorically sophisticated, but his message is earthy and unsparing.

Martial (c. 40–104), a Spaniard, composed some 1,500 mostly satirical epigrams. He could be rough and crude for effect, but he was a polished stylist and, at his best, hilarious.

Consider this from Martial:

You disappoint no creditor, you say?
True, no one ever thought that you would pay …
You blame my verse; to publish you decline;
Show us your own, or cease to carp at mine …
The verse is mine; but friend when you declaim it, It seems like yours, so grievously you maim it …
Why don't I send my book to you
Although you often ask me to?
The reason's good, for if I did,
You'd send me yours—which God forbid!

The principate was also a time of stunning architectural achievements. Some of these were at once remarkable pieces of engineering and powerful ideological statements. The Pont du Gard was a bridge built in the time of Augustus as part of the aqueduct that brought water to the city of Nîmes from the hills near Uzès some 50 miles away. Hadrian's Wall stretched right across Britain, partly to control the movement of people and partly to make a statement in the landscape about the might of Rome. Other buildings

The Romans were among the first to use architectural details as a way to decorate a building and not to serve functional purposes.

were urban amenities that also made ideological statements and have been recognized as masterpieces of architecture. The Pantheon in Rome (27–25

B.C.) was round, with an arched roof and architectural details as decorative elements. The use of the arch, in the roofing and as supporting elements in relieving arches, permitted the Romans to span greater spaces than Greek post-and-lintel construction could. The Flavian Amphitheater (that is, the Colosseum) is a felicitous mixture of architectural styles both structural and decorative. Seating some 80,000, it permitted games and displays on a vast scale in Rome.

Today's traveler in the Mediterranean world can see the ghosts of Rome all around. Until recently, schools taught the authors of the principate. Architects still study the buildings of this era. All roads still lead to Rome, in a way. ■

Suggested Reading

Galinsky, *Augustan Culture*.

McNeill, *Horace*.

Ogilvie, *Roman Literature and Society*.

Ramage, *Roman Art*.

Virgil, *The Aeneid*.

Questions to Consider

1. Are you familiar with Roman authors of this period? If so, what can you discern about the period from the authors you know?

2. Roman architecture was to a degree ideological. Can you think of ideological messages connected with modern buildings?

Rome's Golden and Silver Ages
Lecture 22—Transcript

Welcome again to our series of lectures on *The Foundations of Western Civilization*. Lecture Twenty-Two, on Rome's Golden and Silver Ages—that is, on the cultural life of the Augustan Principate to which we addressed ourselves in our last lecture.

Let's say, by way of beginning, that the inception of the principate provided for several crucial conditions that were conducive to a high level of cultural achievement: peace and security, after a century of disturbances. We don't want to push that point too far; we certainly know of moments in human history when tremendous cultural achievements have been associated with times of great instability—war, violence, famine, and other things. This was, nevertheless, not the case in the first two centuries A.D. This was a time of peace, stability, order, good government, and, in that climate, culture flourished.

It was a time of great wealth. It was a time when the Roman state was wealthy, when the Mediterranean basin was wealthy, and when particular families— yes, the imperial family at Rome, but individual families throughout the empire—were wealthy, and, more importantly, were willing to spend their money on great cultural achievements: financing great buildings, supporting great writers and so on.

It was, finally, a time when reflection on Rome's past, reflection on Rome's character, reflection on what Rome had once been was really quite natural because that world of older Rome, as we saw in our last lecture, was gone. Although there were people who were nostalgic about it, there were no longer people who were actually willing to lay down their lives to try to recreate it. So, in a very real way, the effort and energy that was spent recreating that world was spent by authors, was spent by people who wrote about that older time.

The reign of Augustus has often been called the "Golden Age." This was the age of many of Rome's greatest cultural achievements. It was also one of the great ages of poetry in all of Western history, and a remarkable array of gifted poets at this time. Let's begin, then, with these poets. Let's take them as our entrée to the Golden Age. We'll come to the "Silver Age," the rest of the first and the early second century, a little bit later. Let's use these poets as our entrée to the Golden Age, and let's begin with the greatest of them, Publius Virgilius Maro—Virgil—born in 70 B.C., died in 19 B.C. Called, by no less of an authority than Tennyson, "wielder of the stateliest measure ever formed by the mouth of man." Virgil is one of the true immortals, one of those poets who was read in antiquity and who has been read ever since, who has always been known by educated persons.

He is best known, of course, for his great epic, his "composed" epic. I'll explain what I mean by that in just a second. This is the *Aeneid*, the story of Aeneas, the founder of Rome. Remember a couple lectures back I talked a little bit about Aeneas, whom I called the dullest character in epic literature, by way of simply eliciting some of the values that the Romans wished to hold up to themselves, what the Romans wanted to see when they looked in the mirror. There's a great stock of stories, and of traditions, and of legends, and of word of mouth, and of probably urban legends as well that hide behind the *Aeneid*. Where this great poem was concerned, the first thing we need to say about it is that Virgil wrote it, from the first word to the last. When Virgil died, about two-dozen lines of this poem were incomplete, and he wanted it destroyed. The emperor Augustus, we are very grateful, violated Virgil's will and he saved the *Aeneid* for us. And we don't mind those few lines that are incomplete out of his 12 books and many thousands of lines.

Virgil is mainly remembered for the *Aeneid*, but it's worth mentioning that he wrote other poems, too. He wrote two books of poems, the *Georgics* and the *Eclogues*, which are technically accomplished poems, much admired in later times as models of Latin poetic meter. These are poems that were in praise of the countryside, poems in praise of traditional rural life. Let's don't forget that Virgil wrote more than just the *Aeneid*.

The *Aeneid* is one of the great masterpieces of world literature. Its theme is the somber dignity of Rome's past. There's no "boosterism" in this poem. Virgil was not the sort of fellow who would've run around yelling, "We're number one." In almost dirge-like quality, the poem's dactylic hexameters—now you may recall we talked about dactylic hexameters many lectures back, when we talked about Homer's *Iliad*. A hexameter is a six-foot line; a dactyl is a poetic foot which consists of one long and two short beats: boom, boom-boom. The fifth foot of a dactylic hexameter line is always the dactyl. The fourth might be, but the fifth must be. Virgil composed his poem, line after line, line after line, in their hundreds and then their thousands, in dactylic hexameter. We're very unfamiliar with dactylic hexameter in English because English almost cannot be written in dactylic hexameter. The rhythms of our language just don't lend themselves to it.

The 33rd line of the first book of the *Aeneid* is where, in a certain sense, Virgil gives away his theme. Here is, in a way, where he tells us what his great poem is going to be about. Let me quote it for you, and I want you to listen to the solemn, dirge-like quality of the Latin. Bear in mind that this goes on line after line after line in the *Aeneid*. "*Tantae molis erat Romanum condere gentem*." There's something very dignified about that, something very graceful, something very elegant. And it goes on and on and on. I could have read it a little bit faster.

What does it mean? More importantly, what's it mean? As I said a moment ago, Virgil's no booster. He's not going to go around, "We're number one, we're great!" This line says "Oh, what a job it was to found the Roman people." *Tantae molis erat*, such a great burden it was to found the Roman people. It was a hard job, but we stuck at it and we got it done. That's his great theme.

From the time when we first meet him, Aeneas is carrying his father Anchises, his aged father Anchises, on his back out of burning Troy. Remember in an earlier lecture, we talked about those Roman families, we talked about that *pater familias*, we talked about deference, we talked about ancestors. We meet Aeneas, not fleeing Troy, saying "I'm out of here," but carrying his aged father on his back out of the city. That's the first time we're told this is what you're supposed to pay attention to. Want to know how to be a Roman? Mind Aeneas here.

We also are somehow told—we just know that Aeneas has set forth on a mission from which he will not be deterred. Along the way, we meet family devotion. We meet honesty. We meet integrity. We meet determination.

We meet courage. We meet humanity. We meet, in other words, all those "typical" Roman values. It will occur to you in a moment that my argument here is a bit circular because a couple of lectures back I used the values in the *Aeneid* to tell you what the Romans were like. Now I'm telling you that the *Aeneid* was the book that told the Romans what to be like. It is a bit of a circular argument. Here is the mirror in which the Romans wished to see themselves.

Aeneas was harried by Juno, the goddess who had favored the Trojans. This enters an interesting note in the music because it shows that everything was not to be smooth and easy for the Romans—that there were other people out there. They had their interests, too, they had their qualities, they had their problems, and that Rome was going to struggle. Remember, it was a big job to found Rome. It wasn't easy.

At one point, Venus, Aeneas' patroness, went to her father, Jupiter, to ask if he, Jupiter, were going to remain true to his promises. He'd made her great promises for Aeneas. Virgil had put these words into the mouth of the chief of the gods. In doing so, he told us something about the early years of Augustus' reign. He tells us something about the way the Romans see themselves. He tells us something about their sense of destiny. Venus has gone to her father and said that "Juno is stirring things up and making awful problems down there; aren't you going to fulfill your promises?" Jupiter says to her:

> ... fate remains unmoved
> For the Roman generations. You will witness
> Lavinium's rise, her walls fulfill the promise;
> You will bring to heaven lofty-souled Aeneas.
> There has been no change in me whatever. Listen!
> To ease this care, I will prophesy a little,
> I will open the book of fate. Your son Aeneas
> Will wage a mighty war in Italy,
> Beat down proud nations, give his people laws,
> Found for them a city ...
> To these I set no bounds in space or time;
> They shall rule forever. Even bitter Juno
> Whose fear now harries earth and sea and heaven

Will change to better counsels and will cherish
The race that wears the toga, Roman masters
Of all the world. It is decreed.

Thus, Virgil on the Romans. And thus, that Roman sense—and we'll come back to this in a later lecture—that the world would last exactly as long as Rome. It is decreed.

Not everything in Augustus' time was quite so serious and somber. For example, the poet Ovid, born in 43 B.C., died in 18 A.D., was learned, was accomplished, was prolific. I emphasize again the technical mastery of these Augustan poets. Before they ever said anything, they were extremely gifted, skillful writers or composers of poems. Ovid wrote love elegies, the *Amores*, the Loves, for which he's well known. A didactic spoof, *The Art of Love*, it's a sort of a seduction manual; it's kind of a manual on how a man might have his way with a lady. And he wrote an epic scale encyclopedia of mythological tales, *The Metamorphoses*, The Great Changes. There is, in Ovid, a spirit of play. There's also a very powerful sense of deep feeling. He betrays something else, too. He's immensely learned; Ovid knows a lot. But it is perhaps his feelings, which are clearest.

You may recall that when we were talking about the Roman Republic, and after I'd been stressing the sturdy, manly values of the Roman Republic, I then quoted Catullus for you. Here is one of Ovid's poems:

> Maidens, give ear, and you shall hear
>   What is your chiefest duty,
> Pray listen well and I will tell
>   You how to keep your beauty.
> 'Tis care that makes the barren earth
>   Produce the ripened grain.
> 'Tis care that brings tree-fruit to birth
>   With grafting and much pain.
> Things that are cared for always please,
>   And now each man's a dandy,
> A girl must be as spruce as he
>   And have her powder handy.

Ovid could be technically accomplished, and a bit playful as well. He got a little bit too playful, actually, and for a period of time Augustus, ever stern Augustus, exiled him from Rome. Eventually he came back, and his poetry has survived as a delight and entertainment of the Western tradition ever since.

A bit different is the elegant Horace, 65–8 B.C., sage, urbane, Epicurean. He was prized in his own time; he's been prized ever since. He has been seen as, perhaps, the most technically accomplished of all the Roman poets. He was patronized by a man named Macaenas, who gives his name to patrons and to patronage throughout the Western tradition. Horace was one of those who flourished under Augustus, one of those kind of people who's provided an opportunity, in this particular regime, to do all that he was able to do. He wrote odes. He wrote epodes. He wrote satires. He wrote letters. He wrote a treatise on poetry. Again, a man of considerable learning, of considerable breadth, of considerable ability.

Here's a 17th century translation of one of the odes. All translations, of course, are in some ways interpretations. It would be entirely helpful for me to read you these poems in Latin. The last time, modern translations of Ovid and Virgil, here is a 17th century translation of one of Horace's odes:

> Strive not, Leuconoë, to know what end
> The gods above to me or thee will send;
> Nor with astrologers consult at all,
> That thou mayest know what better can befall:
> Whether thou livest more winters, or thy last
> Be this, which Tyrrhene waves 'gainst rocks to cast.
> Be wise! Drink free, and in so short a space
> Do not protracted hopes of life embrace:
> Whilst we are talking, envious time doth slide;
> This day's thine own; the next may be denied.

You note the Epicurean tone there: eat, drink, and be merry, for tomorrow you die. Of the future, who can say? Thus far, the poets of the Golden Age.

No less epic in scale, no less uncommonly beautiful in language, but all in prose was the great Roman *History* of Livy. Titus Livius was born in 59 B.C.; he died in 17 A.D. We may say in a very real way that Livy did in prose what Virgil had done in verse. He told the Romans the tale they wanted to hear about themselves. Livy's *History* is, again, virtue on display. It's a long parade of remarkable characters. The chances are very good that if anyone listening to my words is familiar with any stories from early Roman history, one has probably got them from Livy—possibly, also, from Virgil. It's not unlike the situation now, where if you hear a familiar quotation, if you wager that it came either from the Bible or Shakespeare, you'll win your wager more often than not. If we were playing that game with Roman texts, you'd wager Livy or Virgil, and you'd usually win your wager.

It's also important to say, with respect to Livy, that he was a very earnest historian. He did an enormous amount of research, he consulted a great many records. In the process, he tells us a very great deal of what we actually know about early Rome and about how the Romans, in the time of Augustus, "constructed" their own past. I draw out the word "constructed" there because this implies an issue that is very, very important to certain critics of literature and of history in our own times. That is the idea: that there may be an objective reality out there, but that if I write about that reality, I'm going to project myself on it. I'm going to construct a reality—I'm going to make a history that I need, a history that talks to me, a history that is useful to me. I may, along the way, say a lot of things that are quite true. But I may also put, as we would say, a certain spin on them. In many respects, Livy spun early Roman history. It is he who then gives us all of these remarkable tales about those noble Romans of old.

The period after the death of Augustus, down really to the very first years of the second century A.D., produced another literary outpouring, which scholars have generally referred to as the "Silver Age." This was a time when history was written, but also philosophy, rhetoric, satire—in other words, literature in a variety of genres. The variety is interesting and also revealing of the creative tensions and the creative capacities of this age.

It's also true that silver is imagined to be a bit less precious than gold. So the ideas of the world of Virgil, Ovid, Horace and Livy is somehow superior to the world of the people about whom we shall speak now. Making such cultural judgments is tricky business, at the very best. In any case, we refer, then, to the writers who come after Augustus as having lived in the Silver Age.

We ended with Livy when we talked about the Golden Age; let's begin the Silver Age and talk about some historians—Tacitus, first of all. Cornelius Tacitus, c. 55–c. 117 A.D., is when he lived. You may best recall that we talked about Tacitus as having been the person who understood the Roman principate very well, who said, "The Romans made a great desert and called it peace," and who had said, "It is the army that can make and unmake the emperor; real power is in the hands of the army."

Tacitus was incomparably the greatest of Rome's imperial historians. He wrote a couple of short books; he wrote a book, *On Britain,* for example, which, remember, had been conquered in the 1st century A.D. He wrote a book, *On Germany*, really it's the Rhineland—it's the frontier between the Roman province of Gaul and what we would think of as Germany today, which the Romans never conquered. He wrote a monograph on the peoples who lived along the frontier there. He wrote two larger works, the *Histories* and the *Annals*, which went back early into Roman history and brought the story down to his own times.

He created very fine pen portraits of individuals. He had a very cunning and discerning judgment of individuals. Like so many Roman writers before him, he took as part of his task—he took perhaps as one of his greatest responsibilities—to put virtue and vice on display, and to make very, very clear what he thought about each.

Fundamentally, Tacitus was faced with an interesting problem. He was faced with a problem of describing an imperial regime, some of whose benefits and advantages and good qualities he saw. Yet at the same time, he was a man, I suppose we might say, Republican to his core. He hated tyranny, and he hated tyrants, and he had to write about a world ruled by tyrants. Some of whom, however, he found, at least in some circumstances, sometimes to be admirable. Whether or not Tacitus successfully carried off his treatment of that tension is something that individual readers of his *Histories* will have to decide for themselves. But we would be far the poorer without his trenchant comments, particularly on the first century A.D.

Less trenchant is Tacitus' contemporary Suetonius. Suetonius was born about 70 A.D. and died in 140. He wasn't a great stylist like Tacitus, and he didn't have the kind of cunning insight that Tacitus did. But he left us a book, the *Lives of the Twelve Caesars*, beginning with Julius Caesar, going right on through Augustus and on through the first century A.D., which created a series of unforgettable portraits of the emperor. Scholars have fussed and fidgeted ever since, trying to decide if he was a bit of a satirist. Was he criticizing these emperors? Did he genuinely admire them and create loving, admiring portraits of them? Almost any of these readings of Suetonius is possible, and that's, perhaps, why he has engaged our interest so effectively and over such a long period of time.

Lucan was a Spanish poet and historian who was put to death by Nero. He wrote a book called the *Pharsalia*, which was a verse account of the civil wars of the late republican period and, particularly, an account of the great battle of Pharsalus. I mentioned that Lucan was Spanish. Here another note enters the music. We begin to see that some of the great writers of the Roman world come not from Rome and not from Italy. Virgil himself came from northern Italy; Mantua is where he came from. People come first from Rome, then from wider ranges in Italy, and then gradually from the empire as a whole. You'll recall in our last lecture we talked a little about the process of Romanization. In a writer like Lucan, we can feel some sense of that Romanization.

Lucan is an author whose work is full of trenchant political commentary, and he is another writer who wrote in defense of political freedom, in defense of liberty, against tyrants. This is something interesting: there is a constant chorus of defenses of liberty in a regime of tyrants. We see that in Tacitus, we see that in Suetonius, we see that in Lucan. One can find it again and again and again. People realized, in other words, the tensions of the world they were living in.

Among philosophical writers, pride of place in this period goes to the Stoic Seneca, 4 B.C. to 65 A.D. is when Seneca lived, another writer who fell afoul of Nero and was executed by him. He wrote tragedies, which were popular for centuries. He wrote dialogues, he wrote treatises, he wrote letters. He was, in many ways, the great popularizer of Stoicism for later times. Much of Stoicism filtered through Seneca. Or it filtered through the writings of the emperor Marcus Aurelius, who, in addition to being one of the "Good Emperors"—indeed, the last of them—was also a significant Stoic philosopher. His brooding meditations for centuries were read as the deep reflections of a man faced, I suppose we might say, with the awesome responsibilities of power, and a deeply sensitive awareness of his own human shortcomings. It is, really, his great dialogue with himself.

In rhetoric in this period, one name stands out above all others: Quintilian. Perhaps about 35 to about 100 A.D. His *Institutions of Oratory* constituted for Western civilization the standard manual of the rhetorical art until modern times. Mentioning Quintilian, and reminding ourselves that we've talked about Cicero, a great public orator—we've talked about the place of oratory, for example, in the Athenian assemblies in Greece—reminds us that the ability to speak well in public was crucial to the ancient world: crucial to their culture, crucial to their government, crucial to their politics.

Rome also produced a number of satirists. These Romans could laugh; they weren't always all so terribly serious. Lucian, not to be confused with Lucan, of whom we spoke a moment ago, lived from about 125 to 200 A.D. He came from Syria, and he wrote in Greek, but very much in a tradition that is now Hellenistic and Roman at once. Lucian poked fun at both real living characters and at mythological ones. In the end, he poked fun at almost everyone. Lucian is actually very, very funny to read.

So, too, is Juvenal. Juvenal was born in about 60 A.D., lived to 136 A.D. He wrote 16 verse satires, and what he does here—it's a little bit like the cast of characters that we talked about as having been characteristic of Plautus' plays, a variety of kind of social misfits of one kind or another. In particular, Juvenal wrote about the travails of the poor, especially poor writers like himself. He was always concerned of "why don't people give me more money, and help me out more." In the process, he exposed ambition, pretentiousness, and, with great feeling and with great bitterness, I think it's fair to say, he excoriated people's despicable treatment of each other. His language is rhetorically sophisticated; his message is unsparing. Juvenal is tough. You read Juvenal, you know exactly what—like the best editorial writers today—you know exactly what's on his mind.

Martial is different. Let's conclude this discussion of these writers with Martial. Martial was born in about 40 A.D. and died in 104, another Spaniard. He composed about 1500, mostly satirical, epigrams. He could be crude; he could be rough for effect. He could be vulgar. He was, however, also a very polished stylist. At his very best, he was really quite funny. Let me quote you just a few of his very brief epigrams.

> You disappoint no creditor, you say?
> True, no one ever thought that you would pay ...

Or:

> You blame my verse; to publish you decline;
> Show us your own, or cease to carp at mine ...

Another:

> The verse is mine; but friend when you declaim it, It seems
> like yours, so grievously you maim it ...

And finally:

> Why don't I send my book to you
> Although you often ask me to?
> The reason's good, for if I did,
> You'd send me yours—which God forbid!

The principate was also a time of stunning architectural achievements. Let's conclude our reflections on the Golden and Silver Ages with just a few words about some of the most remarkable of these buildings.

We may regard Roman architectural achievements as sort of triumphs of civil engineering. The Romans were masters at using, adapting, adopting, extending architectural forms. Remember we stressed the practical genius of the Romans? Buy all things and make them your own, and find uses for them that others had never dreamed of before. Often it's the case, whether we're talking about literature or philosophy or architecture, the Romans are not innovators; Roman creativity rests in finding uses and applications for things designed by others.

We might think, for example, of something like the great aqueduct, the *Pont du Gard*. The city of Rome, of course, was fed by a series of aqueducts that had to be tended very carefully. The *Pont du Gard*, in the south of France, one of the most remarkable of all of Rome's civil achievements, is part of a long aqueduct complex that brought water from the hills near Uzès, in the south of France, to Nîmes, some 50 miles away. Very characteristic of the Romans. We need water there; it's 50 miles. Fine, we'll build an aqueduct. Romans don't say, "Oh, gee. We can't do that."

Hadrian's Wall, built right across the north of Britain. Could Hadrian's Wall, impressive in its ruins even today, actually have served as a secure frontier between the Scottish hills to the north and England to the south? No, of course not. It was a triumph of Roman engineering. The Romans came in and said, "You mess with us, look what we can do. Can you do this?" It was an ideological statement, in brick and mortar, not really a barrier.

In the city of Rome itself, we see examples of the urban amenities that I referred to when I talked about the Romans building cities around the empire—building great buildings there to project their power, to portray their power, but also to make the cities more pleasant places to be.

One might think, for example, in the city of Rome itself, of a building like the Pantheon: a round building built between 27 and 25 B.C. initially, with an arched roof and architectural details on the outside. Very interesting. The Romans were among the first to use architectural details as a way to decorate a building and not to serve functional purposes. With its arches, with its relieving arches, with its supporting elements, the Pantheon was, in many respects, a very bold and creative building. Every element in it was older.

Similarly, for example, the Flavian Amphitheater, or the so-called Colosseum in Rome, built late in the first century A.D.: once again, a building with architectural elements as decorations; a building that would seat 80,000 people for spectacles; a building that put arches on display in a way that is quite pleasing to the eye; yet, for all of that, a building, all of whose elements were older.

Today's traveler to the Mediterranean world will bump again and again and again into the buildings of the Roman principate. Today's students will still read the literature of the Roman principate. This was a period that marked Western civilization as, before it, only Periclean Athens had done, and as after it, perhaps only Voltaire's Paris would do, although possibly Medicean Florence would be a competitor.

Jesus and the New Testament
Lecture 23

> One of the things that began to happen in the 2nd century, in what we call the post-apostolic age, and what we may also think of as the post-biblical age, is that a group of Christian writers, whom we call the apologists, began explaining their new faith to the ancient world.

In the long run, the most momentous development of the Pax Romana was the emergence of a new religious faith that would eventually sweep the Roman world before it. This is not a phenomenon that contemporaries expected or that seems so obvious in prospect as it does in retrospect.

Christians were a tiny sect in a small, backward, unimportant province. The Mediterranean world was rich in mythical, religious, and philosophical experience. It would not have been easy for any newcomer to make its way. The cults of the Roman world were not casual, not parts of people's private sphere. Religion constituted *ta patria*, one's paternal inheritance. The calendar, basic events of life, public buildings, literary culture, and so on were all deeply marked by religion.

In the second place, *from a strictly historical point of view*, our sources are late and limited in what they tell us. The oldest written materials are the Pauline and Catholic Epistles that date from 49 to 62. These represent a first attempt to begin to systematize teaching and to create an official version of the past. They give evidence of controversy.

The Gospels were written between the 60s and the 80s, perhaps even the early 90s. Mark is the first Gospel, circa 65, but Papias said in the 2nd century, "Matthew wrote the oracles in Hebrew." No such text survives, but it is possible that Matthew prepared an Aramaic book of some kind, then revised it, in Greek, in line with Mark's narration.

The Gospels differ a good deal: Only Matthew and Luke have the "infancy narrative" (the Christmas story), and they differ. The version most people have in their minds is a composite. Matthew's is the most Jewish of the

Gospels and begins with the long narration of the genealogy of Jesus (all the "begats"). Luke frankly admits that some others have told the story, but he is going to try again. John offers less narration and more focus on doctrines.

Scholars have long discussed the "synoptic problem": the literary relationship among the Gospels of Matthew, Mark, and Luke. Of the 661 verses in Mark, more than 600 appear in Matthew and some 350 in Luke. But there are about 200 in Matthew and Luke that do not appear in Mark.

The commonest explanation is the "two document hypothesis": Mark plus "Q" (*quelle*, German for "source") yields Matthew and Luke with the differences between them attributable to authorial style and intent. No one has ever seen Q. It is, by the hypothesis, a collection of the *logoi*, the sayings of Jesus. (In older Bibles, these were the words printed in red.) In antiquity, history was "the public deeds of great men" and biography was the revelation of character. Thus, we cannot expect biographical accounts of the life of Jesus to tell us all that we would like to know.

What, then, do we know with reasonable certainty? Jesus was born in Bethlehem, in Judaea, but grew up in Nazareth, in Galilee. He was presented in the temple for his circumcision a few days, presumably, after his birth, and he appeared in the temple at about the age of 12. These are the only surviving details of his youth. When already a man, Jesus went down to the Jordan River and was baptized by John ("the Baptist"). Jesus then began to preach publicly throughout Galilee. After a period that is traditionally said to be three years, but the length of which cannot be fixed precisely, Jesus went down to Jerusalem.

In Jerusalem, the teaching of Jesus aroused the ire of various factions, who denounced him to the Romans. To maintain peace, the Romans acquiesced in Jesus's public execution on a Friday. In the firm belief of his followers, Jesus rose from the dead on the following Sunday. For a few weeks more, he appeared from time to time to various groups of people before he ascended into heaven.

This narrative has to be patched together from the four Gospels because no single one of them gives the whole story straight through. The account is riddled with historical puzzles. We can mention only a few by way of example.

Luke says that when Jesus was born, Quirinius was governor of Syria and that Jesus was born in Bethlehem, where his parents had gone to register for a census. Inscriptions prove that there was a census when Quirinius was in Syria, but this was in what we call A.D. 6 or 7. There was another census in what we call 8 B.C., but no Quirinius in Syria as yet. Matthew and Luke both mention King Herod. He died in what we call 4 B.C. Most scholars, therefore, believe that Jesus was born between 8 and 4 B.C.

> **The Gospels offer us a series of very interesting, but sometimes also conflicting, pictures.**

Luke says (3.1–3) that John the Baptist began preaching in the 15th year of the reign of the Emperor Tiberius. This would be A.D. 26–27 AD in the Syrian reckoning and 28–29 in the Roman. Did Jesus meet John immediately after he began preaching or some time later?

Tradition—and only tradition—says that Jesus was 30 when he began his ministry and that he preached for three years. Much later, Christian chronographers decided that he began his ministry in what we call A.D. 30 and that he died in 33. In fact, he would have been somewhere between 30 and 36 when he began his ministry, and we have no sure information on when he died. We need to remember that these are historian's puzzles left for us by writers who did not share our interests or curiosity.

What can we say about the teaching of Jesus? As to technique, we have a number of indications. Jesus used parables, an old Jewish custom. He regularly quoted the Hebrew Scriptures, then explained their meanings; this is just what a rabbi would do. He spoke in all sorts of places, before all kinds of different groups. What seems most striking is his relative familiarity with women. On occasion, he appeared as a charismatic healer; he let his actions speak for him.

Jesus himself and those who wrote about him anchored him in the Jewish tradition. He, and they, spoke constantly of fulfilling prophecies. He said he had come to fulfill, not abolish, the law. When a Pharisee tried to trick him, he quoted the law (these are the two great laws, love God and love your neighbor). The central elements in his own teaching were few and simple.

He had come to call people to repentance. The Kingdom of God was at hand (although what this meant was, and is, subject to interpretation). He subverted the world's ways: Love the poor, the meek, the hungry, the suffering; take up for the Samaritan; hurl accusations only if you are totally pure. The disposition of the heart is more important than the letter of the law, as we see in many different parables.

Still, however attractive he and his teachings may have been, Jesus had been executed as a common criminal and he did not appear to have many followers. As things stood in the mid-30s, Jesus was no more than a minor footnote in ancient history. But we *know* that things turned out rather differently. We'll turn to that story in the next lecture. ■

Suggested Reading

Johnson, *The Real Jesus*.

New Testament (esp. Matthew, Romans, I Corinthians, Acts).

Questions to Consider

1. Compared with other figures from antiquity, do you have the impression that we know more or less about Jesus than we do about them?

2. How does Jesus compare, in both methods and ideas, with other great teachers from antiquity?

Jesus and the New Testament
Lecture 23—Transcript

In this lecture, we'll turn to Jesus and the New Testament. We'll turn to a set of phenomena that were—we can see so very clearly in hindsight—actually among the most momentous developments of the *Pax Romana*: the emergence of a new religious faith that eventually would sweep the Roman world before it. Mark well, I said we can see in retrospect. One of the great advantages, of course, of the historian's craft is that we predict the past. Our hindsight is always 20/20, our foresight somewhat less able.

Today we're going to pose a series of paradoxes as we talk about this first century world. We know how it turned out, but it is certainly not the case that contemporaries would have noted these events with the same kind of significance, would have invested these events with the same kind of significance that we have, would have seen what their consequences would be. That means, in a very real way, we sort of have two jobs here. We're going to talk a little bit about what actually happened, and then we're going to try to begin, at least—we'll follow this up in some later lectures—but we're going to begin forming some impression of why was this so very important. We have to avoid the temptation to say that it seems so obviously important to us in retrospect that it must have been important from the very beginning. Let's assume that that's not the case, and let's see if we can explain the importance.

Why is it that this all seems paradoxical? The people who followed Jesus—we can call them Christians—were a tiny sect in a small, backward, unimportant province of the Roman Empire. I would say if we were time travelers, and we went back and we stopped the clock at a certain point, and we said, "Predict what's going to happen." If you went back to Palestine in the very early years of the first century A.D., you wouldn't say, "Great things are going to come from here."

The Mediterranean world was very rich in mythical experience, in religious experience, in philosophical experience. There had been many innovations, to be sure, but it wasn't particularly clear that another innovation was called for. It wasn't particularly clear why any newcomer—religious, philosophical, whatever—would have an easy way of making its way in this Roman world.

The cults of the Roman world, we may regard as silly, superstitious, odd, peculiar, sort of amusing artifacts of literature. But in point of fact, for the Roman people, these were not simply part of people's private sphere, and not simply amusements. Religion constituted what one great historian called *ta patria*, paternal things, part of your paternal inheritance, part of your way of living. Think: the calendar was fixed by religious ceremonies; the basic events of life revolved around religious ceremonies; the public buildings of most towns included temples, buildings dedicated to the gods; literary culture was full of the gods. One could not pick up a great poem, a great work of literature from antiquity and not pretty soon encounter the gods and the goddesses marking that text.

So religion was something that people in the ancient world experienced every day, and it was part of their community, it was part of their family, it was part of their culture. For something to come along, and eventually just sweep all of that away is not something we would predict. But it is something that we will have to try to explain. That's one interesting set of problems. There's really no way to go back before the fact and predict that the Christian phenomenon is going to happen.

In the second place, if we're thinking as historians—just as historians for a moment—we would have to say that our texts, our sources, our documents are late, limited, and partisan. As we'll see in just a moment—I'll put some flesh and sinew on this skeleton—the basic texts that we have come 30, 40, 50, 60 years after the events about which they're written. For ancient history, that's not so bad; that's close. For modern history, we would say that's pretty remote evidence. It's also important to say we don't really have a lot of evidence. And it's also important to say we don't really have any evidence from the other side; it isn't as if we have kind of a balanced view, several different people taking widely divergent views and enabling us to triangulate among all these views.

What do we have, then, actually, as sources? What materials can we turn to? The oldest materials are the Pauline and Catholic Epistles. This material dates from between 49, when Paul left the Jerusalem conference in 49 (that is reported to us in a work called the Acts of the Apostles) and began his ministry, his sort of missionary work, if you like, in the eastern Mediterranean, down to 62, when Paul was executed at Rome. So we have a body of epistolary material that dates from, we can date it pretty securely, between 49 and 62.

In this material, we can begin to see, for the first time, an attempt to systematize teaching, and an attempt to create an official version of the past, to say, "Here's how we will remember the past, and here are the things that we teach." There's also, however, evidence of controversy. Paul, if we think of his First Letter to the Corinthians, he starts off as: I'm delighted to hear from you, I'm so glad you're praying for me, and I'm going to pray for you as well. Now, I have one or two things to talk to you about. And he let them have it because there were controversies about teachings and about authority in the church of Corinth. Whatever we may say about the materials that survive from this epistolary period, there were contests; there were controversies.

The Gospels—that is to say, the more or less biographical accounts of the life of Christ—we'll have more to say about those books in a few minutes. These are written between the 60s and the late 80s, possibly even the early 90s. Again, we're moving out another half generation to a generation past the epistolary material. Even where these Gospels are concerned, there are puzzles.

Mark is universally agreed by biblical scholars to be the oldest surviving Gospel—probably dates from around 65. Don't take that date to the bank, but that's a pretty good rough date. A second century writer, utterly forgettable in other respects, a person by the name of Papias, once said, "Matthew wrote the oracles in Hebrew." What on Earth does that mean? No such text survives. It is possible however, of course, that Matthew prepared some kind of a book in Aramaic, the language that he would have spoken, that Jesus would have spoken, indeed, the language spoken in the Palestine of the first century A.D. Then it is possible, because we only have Matthew's Gospel in its Greek version, that he, having written something in Aramaic, which Papias took to be Hebrew—Aramaic is a patois of Hebrew, or actually a related Semitic language to Hebrew—maybe then that Matthew revised his original text in Greek in light of Mark's account. That's an entirely possible reconstruction. I mention that, really, just to point to the puzzles that exist surrounding these books.

The Gospels offer us a series of very interesting, but sometimes also conflicting, pictures. For example, only Matthew and Luke have the "infancy narrative," the account of Jesus' birth in Bethlehem. Yet, there, go take the text off the shelf and have a look, see which one has the star in it, for example; it doesn't appear in both, the accounts are really quite different. The version, for example, of the Christmas story that most people have in mind is a composite of the two accounts.

Matthew's is the most Jewish of the Gospels; it's the one that begins with the long narration of Jesus's genealogy. All the "begats." Begat, begat, begat, begat, begat. That's not so unlike, for example, the kind of thing one meets in Genesis, where when a new figure is introduced, we get all the begats. We have to know who this person is. We have to know who is people are. John, for example, offers a great deal less narration. His focus is more on doctrine; his focus is on basic teachings.

These Gospels differ a great deal from one another. They're not only late, but they're complicated also as texts, as literary productions. Viewed in that guise, scholars have for a very long time discussed the "synoptic problem." "Synoptic," what you can see with one eye, what you can see together. The synoptic problem is a name for the way we understand the literary relationship among the Gospels of Matthew, Mark and Luke. The Gospel of John has always been understood to be a different kind of document. As I mentioned a moment ago, it takes a much more doctrinal, we might almost say later theological, point of view than a biographical one.

Concretely, the synoptic problem looks like this: of the 661 verses in Mark's Gospel, more than 600 appear in Matthew, and about 350 of them appear in Luke; there's about 200 in Matthew and Luke, however, that don't appear in Mark. It seems quite reasonable to conclude that Matthew and Luke both knew Mark's Gospel and both built their own stories on Mark's Gospel. It's also perfectly clear that Matthew and Luke had some material, the same material—or bodies of different material? That's not so easy to answer. Matthew and Luke had additional material either that Mark did not use or that he did not know. The synoptic problem, quite simply, is how do we explain the relationship among these three books—Matthew, Mark and Luke—as texts, as literary productions?

The commonest explanation, going back more than 150 years now—actually, it emerged in Germany in the 19th century—is the so-called "two document hypothesis." This holds, basically, that Matthew's Gospel and Luke's Gospel were built by two independent authors from Mark's Gospel, that's one document, and "Q." "Q" is shorthand for the German word *quelle*, which means "source." What is this source? It's imagined to be a booklet, possibly a pamphlet. One can't say. No one has ever laid eyes on it. It's a hypothetical document, but it is imagined to be a collection of the sayings of Jesus.

One of the interesting things, one of the very interesting ways, easy ways, vivid ways of grasping the synoptic problem, if you have access to an old red-letter Bible—the kind of Bibles that were printed where all the words of Jesus are in red—take a look. There's virtually no red in Mark. Luke and Matthew are full of red. That's what we're talking about here. The idea is that a lot of the red is Q, is the *quelle*. It came from this hypothetical book, pamphlet, treatise, whatever it might have been, that recorded a lot of the sayings of Jesus.

First, you have Mark, and afterwards, Matthew and Luke come along, use Mark, and add material from Q, the second document. The two documents—let's back up a stage and do it as very simple arithmetic. Mark + Q = Matthew. Mark + Q = Luke, the difference between Matthew and Luke being two different authors who have slightly different interests, slightly different intentions. Authorial intent, style and so on may have some explanations to offer us.

That, in a way, is the synoptic problem. What that really points to is, if we're going back, then, to these biblical materials and we want to elicit historical information from them, we have obviously a very complicated set of texts to use as witnesses to historical realities from earlier times.

Are there other puzzles hiding in these texts for us? Are there other things that we need to know about these Gospel narratives? In antiquity, the public deeds of great men is what history was normally understood to be. Biography was normally understood to be the revelation of personal character. We have here a couple of works—these texts, these Gospels, these synoptic Gospels—that are, in some measure, history, and yes, indeed, they do lay a good deal of focus on the public deeds of Jesus. They are, in some ways, biography, although they leave great gaps. But they do lay some stress upon the character of Jesus.

The fact, for example, that two of them give us an infancy narrative, and then Jesus disappears until he's about 12, when he appears teaching in the temple, and then he disappears until he begins his public ministry, is not unusual for ancient biography. We didn't need to know all that because biography and history, in a sense, complement. It's public, and we cannot see the character of a person until that person becomes public, as it were. For us as historians, however, it leaves enormous puzzles. Boy, would we like to know things that those texts simply did not set out to tell us, simply had no intention of telling us.

What do we know with reasonable certainty? What kinds of things can we take from these texts and say, "These seem to be established facts?" Perhaps, to put it ever so slightly differently, we're saying, "What had—between the 50s and the 90s of the first century A.D. —what had come to be the story, as it was told? What did they assume to be the facts?" There was a person called Jesus, and he was born in Bethlehem in Judea. But he grew up in Nazareth, in Galilee, quite far to the north. He was presented in the temple for his circumcision a few days, presumably, after his birth. He then vanished from us. He then appears in the temple, teaching, at about the age of 12. That's it. That's what we know about Jesus's youth.

When already a man, Jesus went down to the Jordan River, and was baptized by a man named John. History comes to call John "the Baptist." Jesus then began to preach publicly throughout Galilee, and eventually, after a time period whose length is traditionally three years but which cannot be fixed precisely—there is actually not in the synoptic Gospels a clear chronology— Jesus went down to Jerusalem. In Jerusalem, Jesus' teachings aroused the ire of various factions, who denounced him to the Romans. To maintain peace, the Romans acquiesced in Jesus' public execution on a Friday. In the firm belief of his followers, Jesus rose from the dead on the following Sunday. For a few weeks more, he appeared from time to time to various groups of people before he ascended into heaven.

The narrative that I have just given is sort of the essential minimum. That's basically what we can say the story had come to believe as the basic, definitive facts. Even in giving you that brief narrative, I have patched it together from the four Gospels because no one of them gives us that whole story, absolutely straight through, in all those details.

The account, moreover, is riddled with historical puzzles. Let me just mention a few of these by way of example—not by way of calling into question the validity or importance of these texts, but I do want to say that in viewing these texts, they have somewhat different standing if one views them as a Christian believer or if one views them as an historian. So for the moment, I'm looking at them as historical documents, as if they were like any other kinds of historical documents.

Luke says that when Jesus was born, Quirinius was governor of Syria, and he says that Jesus was born in Bethlehem, where his parents had gone to register for census. Inscriptions prove that there was a man by the name of Quirinius who was governor of Syria, and indeed there was a census taken under Quirinius's authority. But that census happened in the year we call 6 or 7 A.D. There was another census in the Roman world, fixing the tax records, actually, is what these censuses were, not counting people, but anyway, in the year we call 8 B.C. As yet, there was no Quirinius in Syria. Matthew and Luke both mention King Herod. He died in what we call 4 B.C. We can either have a census and Herod and no Quirinius, or we can have Quirinius and a census and no Herod, but we can't have them all. Most historians have said that Jesus was probably born between about 8 and 4 B.C., perhaps a bit closer to the second of those years.

Luke says (Chapter 3, Verse 1) that John the Baptist began preaching in the 15th year of the reign of the Emperor Tiberius. If they were using Syrian reckoning, that would be the year 26-27 A.D.; if they were using Roman reckoning, 28-29 A.D. Did Jesus meet John immediately after he began preaching? Sometime later on? A year, two year, three years, four years? We don't know; we're not actually told that. Our way of patching these stories together tends to link them all very closely.

Tradition—and only tradition—says that Jesus was 30 when he began his ministry, and that he preached for three years. Much later, much, much later, in the fifth century, early sixth century, Christian chronographers decided that he began his public ministry in what we call 30 A.D. Then they reckoned back and got their zero point because they assumed, traditionally, that he began preaching when he was 30 and that he preached for three years. Therefore, he died in the year 33.

It's a question: When did he actually meet John the Baptist and then begin his public ministry? How long did he actually preach in public? We don't really know. When was he actually born? Well, at least four, five, six, seven years earlier than the traditional chronology (fixed in the fifth and sixth centuries A.D.) actually had it. Jesus must have been somewhere between 30 and 36 when he began his ministry, and somewhere between his mid-30s and about 40 when he died.

I stop there with puzzles. One could go on and on. These are the kinds of intriguing little problems that the texts threw out for us as historians. Let's remember that these are historians' puzzles; they are not issues that ought to disturb or bother very much persons who turn to these texts for spiritual inspiration and not for historical detail. Our curiosities, as historians, may be different from those of other people.

What can we say about Jesus' teachings? What did he teach? We could talk a little bit about, for example, his technique. We had a lot of indications; one of the very interesting things that we find in the Gospels are presentations of Jesus as a teacher. He used parables, an old Jewish custom. When a Jew wanted to teach, he told stories, and this is something that Jesus did. Jesus regularly quotes the Hebrew Scriptures, and then he explains their meanings. He quotes a passage, he quotes an incident, he quotes a scene, and then he explains it. This is precisely what a rabbi would do. A rabbi was someone who taught what the Scriptures taught. He spoke at all kinds of places, before all kinds of people, all kinds of different groups.

What seems striking here is not all of that; that's common enough, that's ordinary enough, but his particular familiarity with women. Again and again, and again and again, the Gospels show Jesus in very close connections with women. All kinds of women, from his mother Mary, to the harlot Mary Magdalene. On occasion, he appeared as a charismatic healer. Interesting case here, he let his actions speak for him.

Jesus himself, and those who wrote about him, in other words, anchored him very much in the Jewish tradition. This has become increasingly important to scholars trying to understand Jesus himself and his teachings. If we try to uncouple Yeshua ben Yosef from the Jewish tradition, we miss all hope of understanding him. He is anchored in, he is rooted in that tradition. He is, finally, after all, Jewish.

Jesus spoke constantly, and the Gospel writers spoke constantly, of fulfilling prophecies, of fulfilling an older tradition, which again shows us Jesus attaching himself to this older tradition. He said he had come to fulfill, not to abolish, the Law. We're going to make it complete, not make it go away. When a Pharisee tried to trick him, very interesting, when a Pharisee tried to trick Jesus, he turned right around and quoted the Law to him: Love God, you love your neighbor. We talked about that in a much earlier lecture when we talked about the Hebrews. The great teachings. Remember when we talked about the *Decalogue*, the first part is about loving God, the next part about loving your neighbor. We talked about the *Shema*: "Hear, O Israel, the Lord your God is One, and Him alone shall you serve. And you shall love thy neighbor as thyself." We talked about Micah: "This God asks of you, walk humble with your God, and love justice." Jesus anchored himself very much in that old tradition.

The central elements of his teaching seemed quite few and quite simple, actually. He had come to call people to repentance, to change their way of life, to acknowledge their failings, to acknowledge their shortcomings, to acknowledge all that had gone wrong in their own lives, in their own hearts. The Kingdom of God was at hand, he said. A judgment would come. It would be a mighty judgment; it would be a final judgment. It would be a harsh, a stern, a severe judgment. One can lay great stress on the kindness, the gentleness, the warmth of Jesus, but he could be tough and uncompromising when the situation called for it.

What exactly was this Kingdom of God? That, for some 2000 years, has been subject to some interpretation. Is it something that existed only in a transcendent world, beyond us humans? Is it something that was going to be brought into being here in this world? Very hard to say. It is much easier to say what, over a long period of time, the Kingdom of God has been understood to be by Christians, than to say absolutely clearly what the Gospel writers thought it was, or what they thought Jesus thought it was.

It's very clear that Jesus subverted the world's ways. Love the poor, love the meek, love the hungry, love the suffering. Take up for the Samaritan. Hurl accusations only if you are totally pure. This was an ancient society which, after all, had its great heroes, like Achilles and so forth, like tough guys, like winners. Here, we're told to embrace the poor, the suffering, the outcast, the sick. We're told that disposition of heart is much more important than the letter of the law. The wonderful story in the Gospels about the widow's mite: the poor woman who comes to church and offers much of her little, as opposed to the person who gives much, but out of his vast fortune. He feels very satisfied and happy with himself. Jesus took a somewhat different view.

The story of the widow's mite illustrates two themes in the points that I have just been making over the last few minutes. First of all, it's a wonderful parable. It's a story where the bare facts of the story, of course, conceal and then reveal another meaning entirely. In the second place, it's an example of the way Jesus sort of upset, overturned, contraverted the customary teachings of his day.

Jesus didn't only teach in parables. We think, for example, of his famous Sermon on the Mount, when he gives his great speech: "Blessed are the meek ... blessed are the poor ... blessed are they who hunger and thirst. ..." Or, when his disciples, for example, ask him to teach them how to pray, and he taught them: "Our Father, who art in Heaven," and so on. But parables were his customary mode of making points, and he told lots of them, strewn variously through these gospels that I've been mentioning. Again, an interesting example of the synoptic problem is that we'd have some of the same parables appear in more than one Gospel, some appear in only one Gospel.

We have other ones that upset conventional thinking—for instance, the story of the prodigal son, one of the most familiar of all the parables: A man has two sons. The younger asks him to "divide up our inheritance, give us what we are due upon your eventual decease." The father agrees; he gives his younger son his half of the inheritance. The son goes off to a far land, dissipates everything he's been given; his father knows about this. His other son stays home, is dutiful, is diligent, works hard, sort of the model upstanding citizen and all of that. Always, the father grieves for the younger son. Finally, the younger son, the prodigal son, comes home. Much to the distress of his brother, the father receives him with great joy, gives him wonderful clothes, puts a ring on his finger, and treats him with great compassion, great forgiveness, great understanding.

That's not unlike the story of the wealthy person who wants to give a great banquet, a great luncheon or a great dinner, and invites all of the elegant citizens of the nearby area to come. As the time for the meal draws near, he discovers that none of these people are showing up. He goes out and meets one, and then another, and then another. They're all making excuses. I have business to do, I have to go look after my fields, I have to look after my responsibilities. Eventually, the guy decides to go down to a crossroads, and basically round up a bunch of street people, and bring them in to his banquet, and treat them to the wonderful food and drink and hospitality that had been prepared for others. Again, the idea that those who may have great wealth, great power, great position in this society, who expect much, may not, in fact, be the ones who, in the long run, get much.

We think of other stories: for example, the man who needs workers to help him in his field. Some people show up early in the morning; he puts them to work. People show up at mid-day; he puts them to work. People show up in the middle of the afternoon; he puts them to work as well. At the end of the day, he pays them all the same. This would strike us, as indeed it struck them in the story, as not fair. Of course, the idea is that the reward is the same for all, and every worker is worth his wage.

The story of the man with the talents: the harsh master who leaves and trusts one slave with five talents, one with two, and one with one. The slave who was entrusted with five talents invested it wisely, makes more, makes five more. The slave with two invests wisely, prudently, makes two more. The other slave is scared to death; he buries it in the ground. Then the master comes home, and each slave comes in turn and reports on what he has done. To the first two, he says that's wonderful, that's very good, I'm very pleased. To the last one, he says you miserable, worthless, good for nothing person. You just wasted your time, you wasted my money, you could at least have given it to the bankers and made a little bit of interest. The idea also here is that one cannot just rest on one's laurels. One must act. One must do what is right.

Disposition of heart—as with the widow, as with the prodigal son's father, as with the man giving a banquet, disposition of heart matters. But it also matters to do what is right.

Despite his remarkable teachings, despite what we know of his long-term success, we must remember that, in this world of paradox, Jesus was executed as a common criminal. He doesn't appear to have had many followers at his death, and not many people to stand up to him. In our next lecture, we'll turn to the question of how a movement was built on Jesus and his teaching that proved successful, indeed remarkably successful, over the next 2000 years, even if, paradoxically, we would not predict that success in light of the experiences of the early decades of the first century.

The Emergence of a Christian Church
Lecture 24

The apostles, who were the original disciples of Jesus, accompanied him during his ministry on the earth. We meet them, with him, again and again and again in the Gospel stories.

What sort of a movement did Jesus think he was founding? This matter is deeply controversial, and history can provide only some clues. In Matthew's Gospel, Jesus twice used the word *church*. This does not appear to be the same as the Kingdom of God. By the 2nd century, *church* was a name for an institution that had emerged because of the teachings of Jesus. The question that each person who cares must answer for himself is whether this institution was foreseen by Jesus.

Some clues come from his earliest followers. After the resurrection, a group of about 120 met to choose a successor to Judas, who had betrayed Jesus. This implies a certain "corporate" mentality. In Acts of the Apostles (2.42), we read, "They remained faithful to the teachings of the apostles, to the brotherhood, to the breaking of bread, and to prayers." This implies communities that assumed they were to behave in common ways.

The apostles were the original disciples of Jesus who accompanied him during his ministry. After Jesus's death, they decided, consciously and as a body, to obey his last command to them: "Go forth and teach all nations." Paul, an early Jewish convert to Christianity and the new faith's greatest missionary and second

Icon of Apostle Paul.

© Hemera/Thinkstock

greatest teacher, founded new communities, corresponded with communities, and corresponded with other leaders.

There was clearly some sense of a network of leaders and, implicitly, some kinds of connections among different communities (at the very least, they received visitors and prayed for one another). Paul uses the word *church* regularly of the community in a particular place.

From some of Paul's letters, we get hints about the organization of individual Christian communities. We read in various places in Paul's letters of officials called *overseers*, *elders*, and *servants*. These words have passed most commonly into English usage as *bishop*, *priest*, and *deacon*. It is hard to see how bishops and priests differed in Paul's thinking. They both presided at worship, taught the faithful, and instructed new converts. It appears that every community had officers like this. It is not clear, but initially unlikely, that there was any hierarchical distinction between them.

From some of Paul's letters, we begin to get hints about the organization of individual Christian communities.

Deacons were clearly people (usually, but not exclusively, men) who facilitated the work of the leaders and served the community. Around 100, Bishop Ignatius of Antioch speaks of "monarchical bishops." By the end of the 2nd century and the beginning of the 3rd, we hear of "metropolitan bishops."

It appears that the expanding Christian church was adapting itself to the administrative geography of the Roman Empire. Many communities (we might say "parishes" today) existed in most cities, and gradually, the oldest priest (or elder) came to have a hierarchical and supervisory role over all the communities in the town. He was the overseer in a literal sense. Within provinces of the empire, there were "mother cities," that is, provincial capitals, and the overseers in those cities began to supervise the overseers in individual towns. A highly articulated structure was growing.

Early Christian apologists began to explain the new faith to the ancient world. Justin Martyr (c. 100–c. 165) wrote *A Dialogue with Trypho the Jew* to differentiate between Christianity and Judaism, and he wrote his *First Apology* to Emperor Antoninus Pius to argue that Christians were good and loyal subjects of the empire.

Bishop Ignatius of Antioch (c. 35–c. 107) wrote a series of letters to other Christian communities affirming basic doctrines and warning against false teachers. In the 2nd century, then, we can see a clear sense that Christianity was a distinctive faith, not a version of something else, and that it had teachings that were regarded by some, but not by all, as authentic and binding.

What factors primarily account for the success and spread of Christianity? Most converts were not articulate. Those who were stressed the compelling nature of the basic teachings. Even Christianity's bitterest foes praised the admirable quality of the lives of the Christians. The heroism of the martyrs attracted people. From the time of Domitian, Christianity was illegal, but Christians were not harassed systematically before the 3rd century.

Christianity was a universal faith: open to all ethnic groups, all social classes, both genders. Most ancient cults, by contrast, were severely restricted. Christianity was an exclusive faith. Christians could not just add one more god to all the old ones. They had to renounce all other religious allegiances. Christianity was compatible with many aspects of classical culture and particularly similar to Stoicism.

Christianity was a historical faith. Jesus had lived and taught in the present. Roman writers (such as Tacitus) mentioned him. This was not one more myth placed at the dawn of time. Christianity had a particularly strong appeal to women. Christianity developed a large-scale and highly articulated organization, something no pagan cult had. The peace, security, and ease of transportation provided by the Pax Romana aided Christianity immensely. ∎

Suggested Reading

Fox, *Pagans and Christians*.

Frend, *Rise of Christianity*.

Meeks, *First Urban Christians*.

Questions to Consider

1. Can you think of ways in which a historical view of Christianity's growth might conflict with a doctrinal view of the same topic?

2. How would you assess the various factors offered in this lecture to account for Christianity's success?

The Emergence of a Christian Church
Lecture 24—Transcript

Today we're going to talk about the emergence of a Christian church. Last time we talked about Jesus, and we talked about the New Testament documents that tell us about him, and we noted a world of paradox—a paradox of a new movement emerging from a rather small, backward, out of the way place in the Roman world; a new movement emerging in a world that had large numbers of movements: religious, philosophical, cultural, literary and otherwise.

At the end of the lecture, we noticed that Jesus, himself, the great teacher, upset many of the conventional social values of his day, upset many of the conventional social expectations of his day. We were left with sort of a paradox. If we were going to predict if this movement would be successful, I think—quite legitimately, quite honestly—most of us would say, "No, this doesn't look like a winner; this doesn't look like something that I would want to back." Yet, the paradox is, 2000 years later, we know the movement was phenomenally successful.

What I want to try to do in this lecture is talk a little bit about some of the reasons for that success. How can we account for the success? It must be acknowledged right away that a Christian believer could easily say it was the will of God, and that must be expected. Historians must work with humbler materials and humbler explanations. We have to try to assemble the evidence that we have at our disposal and see what sense we can make of it, see what kinds of explanations we can offer. This is not unlike what I was doing in the last lecture, where I said if we look at the Gospels as historical documents, and we critique them, we try to understand them as we would any other kind of historical documents.

What kinds of things do we know, primarily about the first and second centuries A.D.? We will, on many occasions in later lectures, come back to the history of Christianity between about 200 A.D. and about 1600 A.D. But for now, we want to talk about, basically, the period of the first and the second centuries: What do we know? What happened? How can we explain it? And how did it contribute to the long-term success of the Christian phenomenon?

First of all, of course, there emerged a movement. We might ask ourselves, "What sort of a movement did Jesus think he was founding?" This particular matter is deeply controversial, and history can provide only some clues. Here again, it's enough just to say there are hundreds of Christian denominations and sects in the world today, each of them claiming some legitimate connection to the earliest days of Christianity and, indeed, to the life and times of Jesus Christ himself. On logical grounds, they can't all be right. It's not my place here to choose among them, to say that this one is right and this one is not right, this view is right, that view is not right. Again, what I want to do is simply look at few sources, a few kinds of evidence and say, "What do we know?"

Once we start thinking about this movement, and we start trying to imagine it as some kind of a permanent entity, something with durability, we meet some paradoxes. Jesus uses the word "church" twice. The word appears both times in Matthew's Gospel, both times in the sixth chapter of Matthew's Gospel. It seems pretty clear that Jesus' use of the word "church" is not synonymous with his Kingdom of God. What we also know, however, is that by the second century, "church" was a name for an institution that had emerged because of the teachings of Jesus. A question that each person, I suppose, who cares about this matter has to answer for himself or herself is whether this was the church of the second century, an institution foreseen by Jesus himself in the first. There's no way, on the basis of the historical record, easily or concretely to answer that question, if one is completely honest.

We do get some clues. We get some clues from Jesus' earliest followers. For example, after the Resurrection, a group of about 120 men met to choose a successor to Judas—Judas Iscariot, who had betrayed Jesus. This is interesting, significant, revealing, perhaps, because it suggests a certain kind of corporate mentality—that there had been a body of 12, one of their number had fallen out, and then a larger group of people would have to reassemble to bring the body of 12 back up to full numbers.

The Acts of the Apostles, a kind of the history of the Christian movement, beginning after the death of Jesus and carrying on, in other words, from where the Gospels leave off with their story. In the second chapter, the 41st verse, we read, "They remained faithful to the teachings of the apostles, to the brotherhood, to the breaking of the bread, and to prayers." That formulation is rather interesting because the way it's put together, it implies that there were communities in existence who were expected, or who themselves expected, to behave in certain ways: praying, meeting, the breaking of the bread. There's a sense of a certain acceptable standard of behavior.

The apostles, who were the original disciples of Jesus, accompanied him during his ministry on the earth. We meet them, with him, again and again and again in the Gospel stories. After Jesus' death, they consciously and as a body—they are depicted as being together—decided to obey Jesus' last command to them: "Go forth and teach all nations." This, again, is a little bit like the point that I made about choosing a replacement for Judas Iscariot, a sense of a kind of a corporate group, with corporate responsibilities.

Paul, an early Jewish convert to Christianity, and the new faith's greatest missionary—perhaps, indeed, one of the greatest of all—the second greatest teacher in the history of Christianity, founded new communities. He went around the world founding communities. Not converting individuals, but converting groups of people, or converting individuals who were then formed into groups of people. He instituted leaders for those communities, and he corresponded with the leaders of those communities. The leaders of those communities corresponded with him. There was clearly some sense of a network of leaders and, thus, implicitly of some kind of connection among these communities. At the very least, they received visitors from one another; they prayed for each other. Again, there is a sense of some kind of a vaguely corporate entity, an entity larger than the individual, or even than the individual community. How exactly are we to understand what those communities were? Paul uses the word "church" regularly, of a community in a particular place. The church in Corinth, for instance.

Let's bear in mind something that I had mentioned in the last lecture. Paul's Epistles fall between 49 and 62 A.D. In other words, they're earlier than the Gospels. We're left with a paradox that Paul, in the 50s, is using the word "church" routinely, but the Gospel writers between the 60s and the 80s, possibly early 90s, are not using the word "church." What are we to make of that? In truth, not much. It's just a puzzle that we cannot really explain.

From some of Paul's letters, we begin to get hints about the organization of individual Christian communities. As I mentioned just a moment ago, from his letters we also have a sense that these communities maintained certain kinds of relationships, even if we can't specify exactly what those relationships were. They maintained relationships with one another, but his letters don't provide us much detail about the nature of that networking, as we might say.

What his documents, what his letters do show us with some clarity, *some* clarity, is what the individual communities looked like. We read in various places in Paul's letter of three kinds of officials. We'll use the word "officials" as a kind of a very neutral term. One group is called "overseers." One group is called "elders." One group is called "servants." Those words have passed most commonly into the English language—though they are retained by some Christian groups—they have passed more commonly into the English language as "bishop," "priest," and "deacon."

You might be wondering, how in the world did that happen? I won't go through too much detail here, but "bishop" in Greek is *episcopos*, which means, literally (you can hear "scope" in there, *episcopos*), "to look down upon," to look over; here is your overseer. Elder, *presbyteros*. Now that word means, quite literally, "elder" in Greek. It can also mean ambassador; it can also be a wise man, someone to whom one turns for advice. The third, *deaconos*, that gives us "deacon" in English. *Deaconos* in Greek—one who *deaconane*, one who serves—is the third of these officials. Now what happens is that *presbyteros* passes, by and by, through Latin into Norman French, into English, and becomes "priest." *Episcopos* is a word that passes into the Germanic languages, where it turns into *ebscop*, and then *bischof*, for example, in German. It passes in other directions as well: it becomes *véscovo* in Italian; it becomes *eveque* in French. It's always sort of the same word, hiding in one or another of these different linguistic forms. Thus far, names and word. "Bishop," "priest," and "deacon," in the customary form, though not every Christian community today would use exactly those words.

Those are the names; what do they do? It's very hard to see how bishops and priests differed in Paul's thinking. They both presided at worship—that seems clear. They led the worshipping community; they led the prayers of the community. They both taught—that seems clear. They had responsibility for teaching, for handing on the essential teachings of the Christian community. They also were involved in, had responsibility for, identifying and bringing on new converts. It appears, as far as we can tell, that every one of the early communities had officers like this. It's not clear whether or not there was initially a hierarchical distinction. Later, of course, a bishop would be superior to a priest, who was, in turn, superior to a deacon. Were bishops and priests, overseers and elders, in the earliest Pauline understanding, hierarchical or essentially synonymous (same name for slightly different phenomena)? We just can't say. The sources just won't really permit us to say concretely.

Deacons—happily, this is a little bit easier—these are clearly people. We hear about the institution, the creation of the deacons actually, in the sixth chapter of the Acts of the Apostles. The deacons were clearly people—usually, but not always men. Usually, but not always men. There were deaconesses in the early church. They worked to serve the leaders of the community. They acquired food. They acquired rooms for the Christian community to meet. They oftentimes took alms to the poor, for example. They carried out a variety of responsibilities on behalf of those officials who are named as bishops and as priests. Here there is a kind of a hierarchical relationship.

A question we could ask, that again—if we were talking about the third, the fourth, the fifth, the sixth, or the 20th century—we could answer, but cannot readily answer about the first century: If you were a deacon, were you on your way to becoming a priest or a bishop? Or, was deacon a separate order, in which one was going to stay, more or less, permanently? The sources, again, will not permit us confidently to resolve that question, though we can make a case for either view. That is to say, to use modern language, that the deaconate was either transitional or permanent. We can make a case for either situation, but we can't say for sure that there was one prevailing view.

Around the year 100, Bishop Ignatius from the town of Antioch, a very important city in the eastern Mediterranean world, spoke of "monarchical bishops," *poiepiscopo monarchocoi*, monarchical bishops. By the end of the second century, or the very beginning of the third, we begin to hear of "metropolitan bishops." Right away, we have to say St. Paul and the Gospels never say "monarchical bishops," nor do they say "metropolitan bishops."

We don't hear of monarchical priests, and we don't hear of metropolitan priests. Clearly, over the course of the second century, but as early as about 100—that's important, as early as about 100 when Ignatius of Antioch is writing—something has begun changing, at least a little bit, in the way the church is structured in the Roman world. Perhaps, indeed, we can start to talk about a church in the Roman world.

We don't have self-conscious Christian reflections on this process. No Christian writer took thought for poor students of the early 21st century and sat down and said, "Here's what we were doing and here's why we did it." We then, looking back, have to extrapolate. What do the extrapolations look like? It appears that the expanding Christian church was adapting itself to the administrative geography of the Roman Empire. That isn't surprising, if you think about it. Remember, we are smack in the middle of the *Pax Romana*, this age of peace, order, stability. This time of good transportation, of good communications. One of the very interesting things, when you think about, for instance, Paul's letters, how easily he's able to communicate with quite far-flung communities.

The Romans built a large and substantial administrative structure in the Mediterranean world, and as Christian missions grew, and as the Christian community grew, the Christians took advantage of it. There's nothing surprising about that. There is here a paradox. We are in a world full of paradoxes, aren't we? The paradox is this. We think of the ancient world because of its great cities; we think of Rome, we think of Athens, we think of Alexandria, and so on. Yet, 80-90 percent of the population lived in the countryside. Then, as now, rural populations are spread out all over the place. So, if you want to reach reasonable numbers of people, you go to cities. Where did Paul go? He went to cities. Where do we first, then, begin to know about the administrative organization of a Christian church? In cities. We'll have occasion in later lectures to note the fact that it took a long period of time to convert the countryside. Initially, we're talking about an urban phenomenon—not exclusively, but largely an urban phenomenon.

In many of the cities of the Roman world, there began to grow up a number of different Christian communities. We could say parishes today, but that would be a little bit anachronistic. But it may give us a vague sense of what was going on. In other words, a group of communities began growing up inside individual towns. In many of these cities—we can't say confidently in all of them—in many of these cities the oldest priest, oldest—not wisest, richest, most famous, best family. The oldest priest—and how many times in ancient history have we noticed situations where old equals wise: from wise old Nestor in the *Iliad*, to the assembly of the old men at Sparta, to the Senate, the assembly of old men in Rome. In the Christian community, the oldest priest comes to have a hierarchical and supervisory role over the other communities in his town. He becomes, in a quite literal sense, an overseer, an *episcopos*. Is that was Paul envisioned at the very beginning, or was this an evolution over time? Probably the latter, but in any case, it is over the course of the second century that we can watch this evolution actually taking place.

By the end of the second or very beginning of the third century, as I mentioned a minute ago, we hear of metropolitan bishops. What is a metropolis? Remember when we talked about Greek colonization: the mother-city, the *metro polis*, sends out colonies, sends out children, as it were. In the administrative geography of the Roman Empire, capitals and provinces were metropolitan cities. They were sort of, not literally but figuratively, the mother-city of the children-cities of the province. I've emphasized several times already that Rome ruled through cities.

As it was the case that in the Roman administrative geography of the Mediterranean world, in a world carved up into provinces where each province had a capital, therefore, had a city that was the most important. Whereas in those cities, Christian communities were growing up, and in those communities the oldest priest in a given town came to be the overseer over the communities of that town, so it follows (you can watch the administrative logic here) that the oldest priest of the metropolitan city of a province of the Roman Empire came to have ruling responsibility over the urban priests—the older priests, the overseers, the bishops, if you like—of the individual towns of the Roman Empire.

Some centuries later, these metropolitan bishops will come to be called "archbishops." Then what we have is a system, which is archbishops with bishops under them, and with priests under them. Over the course of the second century, we can watch that situation begin to evolve and elaborate. But as I say, no author at the time took thought for us, and said, "Here's what we're doing, here's why we're doing it, here are the principles upon which we're operating." We have to look back and extrapolate from what we know to what they were thinking.

Another important thing that began happening in the second century is this: a group of writers, whom we call the Christian apologists, began to explain the new faith to the ancient world. So, the first point that I've made, then, is that, over the course of the second century, and maintaining certainly some faith with the teachings of Paul himself and perhaps of the Gospel writers, an administrative organization began to arise. That's one element of the movement. A second element of the movement is a clear definition of, a clear delineation of the ideas, the doctrines, the teachings of that movement. You may say, "But don't they already have that? Don't they have that in the Gospels? Don't they have that in the Epistles?" The answer to that question is "yes," but they have it, for example, in something like 20 Gospels, of which only four became canonical, became official. In a later lecture, we'll talk about that process of canon making.

We have lots of other letters we have other treatises, we have other writings, which, I should say, did not become canonical. I mentioned already that Paul, when he was writing to various communities, I think I instanced Corinth, saw controversy. One of the things that began to happen in the second century, in what we call the post-apostolic age, and what we may also think of as the post-biblical age, is that a group of Christian writers, whom we call the apologists, began explaining their new faith to the ancient world. No longer claiming that they were writing, as it were, the word of God's revelation—that to be found in the Old Testament, the Hebrew Scriptures, and the New Testament, the Christian Scriptures—but now in a sense commentary, explanation.

A quick word on "apology." When we call these second century writers the "apologists," we must make very clear that these are not people who are going around saying, "Oops, excuse me, sorry, I'm a Christian." "Apology," in its Greek sense, is a careful, principled defense of a position. An apology is a defense of a position, it's not "oops, I'm sorry." That's apology in a very different and much later sense.

The first of the apologists to whom we might devote a moment's attention was Justin Martyr. He lived from about 100 A.D. to about 165, and he wrote a book called *A Dialogue with Trypho the Jew*. What's interesting about this book is it appears that among large numbers of people who were not particularly well disposed towards Christianity, there was a growing sense that Christians were really just a renegade sect of Jews. There was also a growing sense, among at least some people, that Christians were somehow inevitably hostile to the Roman Empire. Justin Martyr writes his *A Dialogue with Trypho the Jew* to differentiate between Christianity and Judaism, to say that these are two separate things, they are two different things. Then, also, to tell the Emperor Antoninus Pius—one of the "Five Good Emperors" about whom I spoke in an earlier lecture—to tell Antoninus Pius that Christians were good and loyal subjects of the empire, that they were no concern to him, he needn't bother himself about them.

Bishop Ignatius of Antioch—we met him with his phrase "monarchical bishops" a moment ago—born about 35, died in 107, began writing a whole series of letters to other Christian communities, affirming basic Christian doctrines and warning against false teachers. What's very interesting and revealing about Ignatius's writings is that there's a growing sense that there's an authorized way to understand what Christians believe, and that there's sort of some bad guys out there who have ideas all their own, or who have ideas that are a little bit kooky, and should not be paid attention to.

We can see, then, across the course of the second century, not only a growing administrative organization, but we can see a very clear sense that Christianity was a distinct faith. It was not a version of something else. It had teachings that were regarded by some, though not by all, perhaps, as authentic and binding.

Let's put all of this into slightly different terms and say, "What kinds of factors can we, as historians, point to in accounting for the success and the spread of Christianity?" We must acknowledge, in the first place, that most of those who converted were not articulate. That is, that they were not literate people, they didn't write books, they didn't leave documents. But those who were quite regularly stressed the compelling nature of Christianity's basic teachings. Before we turn to political, social, economic, or other kinds of arguments, we must acknowledge what a great many writers in antiquity themselves acknowledged: Christianity won people to itself because of its fundamental teachings.

Even Christianity's bitterest foes praised the admirable qualities of the lives of Christians. Roman satirists (remember we talked about Roman satirists two lectures back), but not only Roman satirists, Greek philosophers, and large numbers of other people had pointed very often to the fact that, in the ancient world, there were people who espoused grand philosophies and led lives completely out of accord with the philosophies they espoused. That had become almost expected, that kind of hypocrisy had become the norm. Christianity was different. These people claimed to value certain ideals, certain ways of living, and then they actually did it.

The heroism of the martyrs attracted people. We'll have an occasion to come back to martyrs in a couple of different ways in later lectures. From the Emperor Domitian, in the late first century A.D., Christianity was illegal. Christians weren't always and everywhere systematically harassed all the time. But there were occasional outbreaks of harassment, of legal prosecution of Christians, right down to the very early days of the fourth century. The way Christians faced their fate won for them the admiration, perhaps, indeed, the grudging admiration, but nevertheless, certainly won them the admiration of many of their contemporaries.

Christianity was a universal faith. It was open to all ethnic groups, to all social classes, to both genders. Most ancient religious and/or philosophical sects, movements, traditions, groups, call them what you will, tended to exclusive: they were based in a certain place; they were based on a certain group of people; they were based, perhaps, on a certain occupation; they were for men only; they were for women only. Christianity came along and said, "This is for absolutely everyone, and for everyone equally." It wasn't more important for one group or another. The early Christians had a battle over that. Would Christianity be essentially a Gentile phenomenon, or essentially something that remained focused on the Jews? They decided it would be a

Gentile phenomenon, without excluding the Jews. In other words, it would be for all people.

In some ways, interestingly enough, the opposite of that point is that Christianity was an exclusive faith. Christians could not simply add one more god to all the old ones. They had to renounce all their other allegiances in order to maintain a Christian allegiance. Christianity was compatible with many aspects of classical culture, but particularly with Stoicism. The brotherhood of all people, knowing your role and playing your role, accepting your position, understanding principles like natural law, universal right and wrong. Christianity didn't come in utterly from left field as something wacky. Christianity sounded—the difference is sometimes merely superficial—but sounded like other classical teachings.

Christianity was an historical faith. Jesus had lived and taught in the present. Roman writers, Tacitus, about whom we spoke, mentioned him. This was not one more myth placed at the dawn of time, placed way back at a point where all reasonable people would take it to be ludicrous, preposterous, made up, and invented.

Christianity had a particularly strong appeal to women. I mentioned, for example, that Jesus was quite regularly depicted among and around women. Christianity early on denied women formal organizational administrative positions. That's true. It's also true that Christianity accorded to women a kind of status, a kind of dignity, a kind of importance in their person. It valued their domestic roles, and it valued their marriages, for example, that pagan cults had not usually done. As we'll see in later lectures, the way into the Roman aristocracy was through women.

Christianity developed a large-scale, highly articulated organization. We've already started hinting at this, and in later lectures, we'll pick up more views on it. No pagan cult ever had the kind of organizational structure that the Christian church eventually developed for itself.

Ironically, then, the peace, the security, the ease of transportation provided by the *Pax Romana* aided Christianity immensely, and facilitated, in some way, its spread through this world. Christianity was not yet triumphant by 200

A.D.; that would come by about 400. If we were, again, wagering persons, we might make a wager in 200, whereas certainly in 33 A.D. we would not have felt much inclined to do so.

We have a Roman empire in place, and a Christian church in place. In our next lectures, we will bring these two things together, and watch their twin fates in the world we call late antiquity.

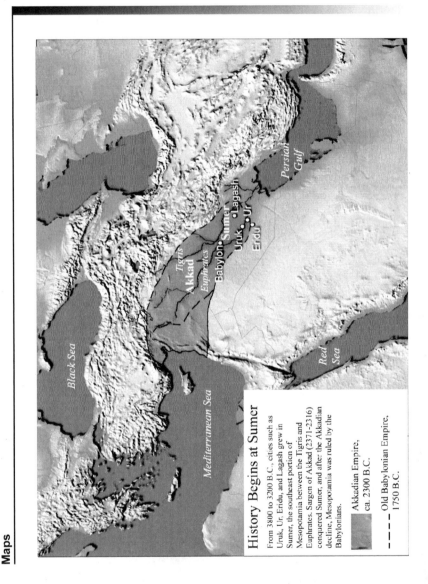

History Begins at Sumer

From 3800 to 3200 B.C., cities such as Uruk, Ur, Eridu, and Lagash grew in Sumer, the southeast portion of Mesopotamia between the Tigris and Euphrates. Sargon of Akkad (2371-2316) conquered Sumer, and after the Akkadian decline, Mesopotamia was ruled by the Babylonians.

Akkadian Empire, ca. 2300 B.C.

- - - Old Babylonian Empire, 1750 B.C.

Black Sea

Mediterranean Sea

Red Sea

Persian Gulf

Tigris
Akkad
Euphrates
Babylon · Sumer
Uruk · Lagash
· Ur
Eridu

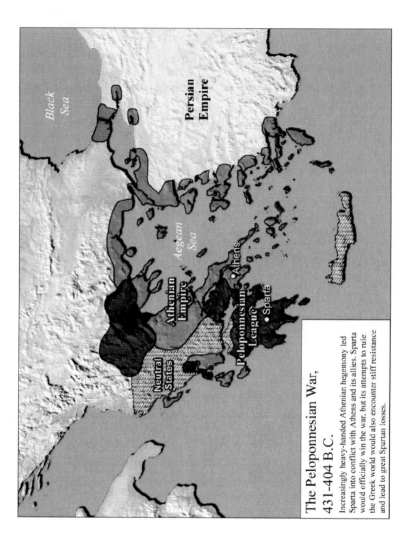

The Peloponnesian War, 431–404 B.C.

Increasingly heavy-handed Athenian hegemony led Sparta into conflict with Athens and its allies. Sparta would officially win the war, but its attempts to rule the Greek world would also encounter stiff resistance and lead to great Spartan losses.

Black Sea

Persian Empire

Aegean Sea

Athenian Empire

Neutral States

Athens

Peloponnesian League

• Sparta

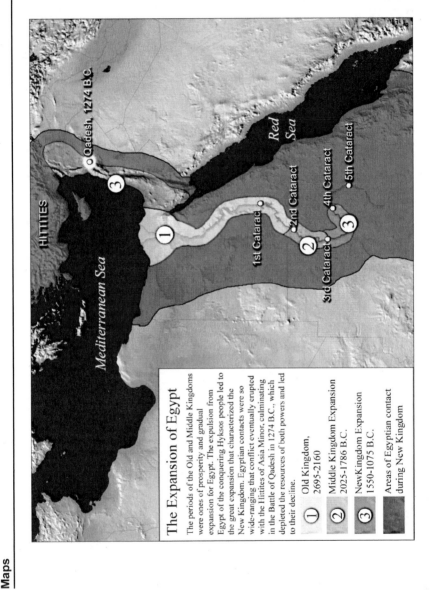

The Expansion of Egypt

The periods of the Old and Middle Kingdoms were ones of prosperity and gradual expansion for Egypt. The expulsion from Egypt of the conquering Hyksos people led to the great expansion that characterized the New Kingdom. Egyptian contacts were so wide-ranging that conflict eventually erupted with the Hittites of Asia Minor, culminating in the Battle of Qadesh in 1274 B.C., which depleted the resources of both powers and led to their decline.

1 Old Kingdom, 2695-2160

2 Middle Kingdom Expansion 2025-1786 B.C.

3 NewKingdom Expansion 1550-1075 B.C.

Areas of Egyptian contact during New Kingdom

Mediterranean Sea

HITTITES

Qadesh, 1274 B.C.

Red Sea

1st Cataract

2nd Cataract

3rd Cataract

4th Cataract

5th Cataract

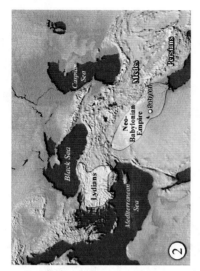

A Succession of Empires

1. The tyrannical and cruel Assyrian Empire, ruling from their capital at Nineveh, eventually evoked a challenge from a coalition of peoples: The Medes, the Persians, and the Babylonians.

2. From their own capital at Babylon, the Neo-Babylonians built their own empire in Mesopotamia. Their most famous king was Nebuchadnezzar (r. 605-562 B.C.) The Lydians of Anatolia were a minor player, most famous for their invention of coinage. They were defeated by the Persians, who had united with the Medes.

3. The Persian empire begain expanding under Cyrus (r. 559-530) and continued to expand under successors Cambyses and Darius. They built the largest empire the world had yet seen.

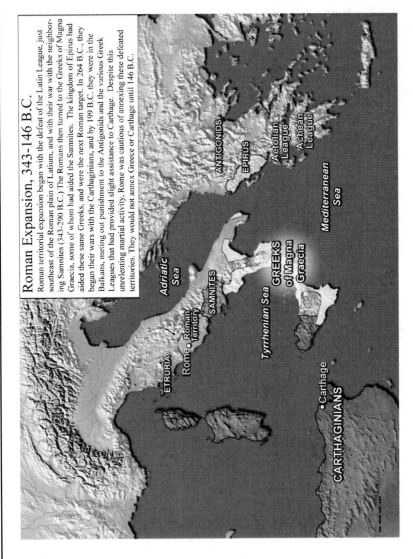

Roman Expansion, 343-146 B.C.

Roman territorial expansion began with the defeat of the Latin League, just southeast of the Roman plain of Latium, and with their war with the neighboring Samnites (343-290 B.C.) The Romans then turned to the Greeks of Magna Graecia, some of whom had aided the Samnites. The kingdom of Epirus had aided these same Greeks, and were the next Roman target. In 264 B.C., they began their wars with the Carthaginians, and by 199 B.C. they were in the Balkans, meting out punishment to the Antigonids and the various Greek Leagues that had provided slight assistance to Carthage. Despite this unrelenting martial activity, Rome was cautious of annexing these defeated territories. They would not annex Greece or Carthage until 146 B.C.

Adriatic Sea

ETRURIA

Rome○ Roman Territory

SAMNITES

Tyrrhenian Sea

GREEKS of Magna Graecia

ANTIGONIDS

EPIRUS

Aetolian League

Achean League

Mediterranean Sea

•Carthage

CARTHAGINIANS

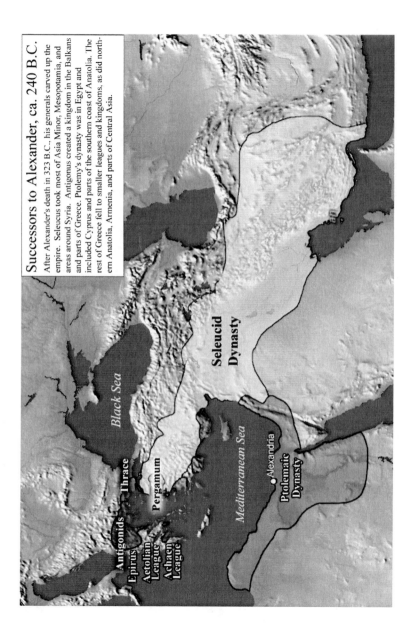

Successors to Alexander, ca. 240 B.C.

After Alexander's death in 323 B.C., his generals carved up the empire. Seleucus took most of Asia Minor, Mesopotamia, and areas around Syria. Antigonus created a kingdom in the Balkans and parts of Greece. Ptolemy's dynasty was in Egypt and included Cyprus and parts of the southern coast of Anatolia. The rest of Greece fell to smaller leagues and kingdoms, as did northern Anatolia, Armenia, and parts of Central Asia.

Black Sea

Antigonids • Thrace

Epirus
Aetolian League
Achaen League

Pergamum

Seleucid Dynasty

Mediterranean Sea

• Alexandria

Ptolemaic Dynasty

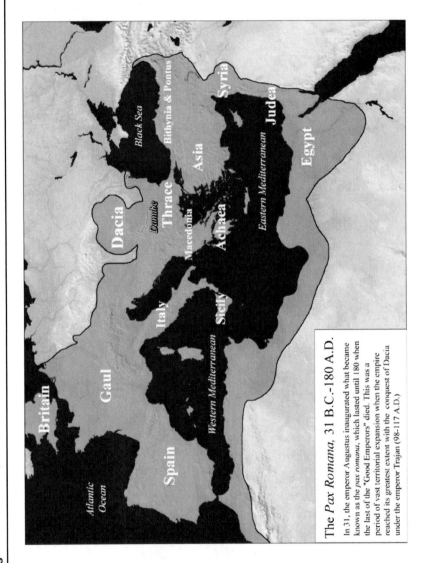

The *Pax Romana*, 31 B.C.-180 A.D.

In 31, the emperor Augustus inaugurated what became known as the *pax romana*, which lasted until 180 when the last of the "Good Emperors" died. This was a period of vast territorial expansion when the empire reached its greatest extent with the conquest of Dacia under the emperor Trajan (98-117 A.D.)

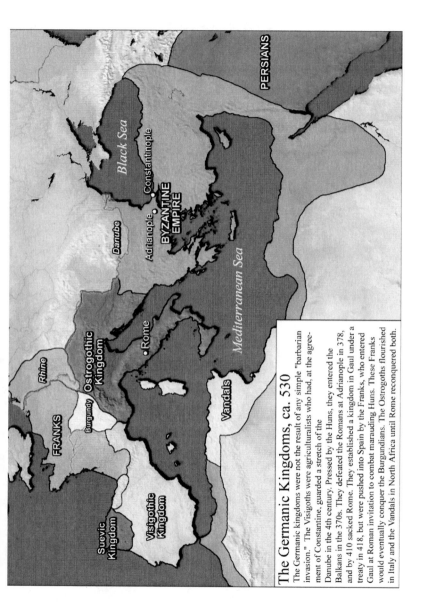

The Germanic Kingdoms, ca. 530

The Germanic kingdoms were not the result of any simple "barbarian invasion." The Visigoths were agriculturalists who had, at the agreement of Constantine, guarded a stretch of the Danube in the 4th century. Pressed by the Huns, they entered the Balkans in the 370s. They defeated the Romans at Adrianople in 378, and by 410 sacked Rome. They established a kingdom in Gaul under a treaty in 418, but were pushed into Spain by the Franks, who entered Gaul at Roman invitation to combat marauding Huns. These Franks would eventually conquer the Burgundians. The Ostrogoths flourished in Italy and the Vandals in North Africa until Rome reconquered both.

PERSIANS

Black Sea

Constantinople

Danube

Adrianople

BYZANTINE EMPIRE

Mediterranean Sea

Rome

Ostrogothic Kingdom

Rhine

FRANKS

Burgundy

Vandals

Suevic Kingdom

Visigothic Kingdom

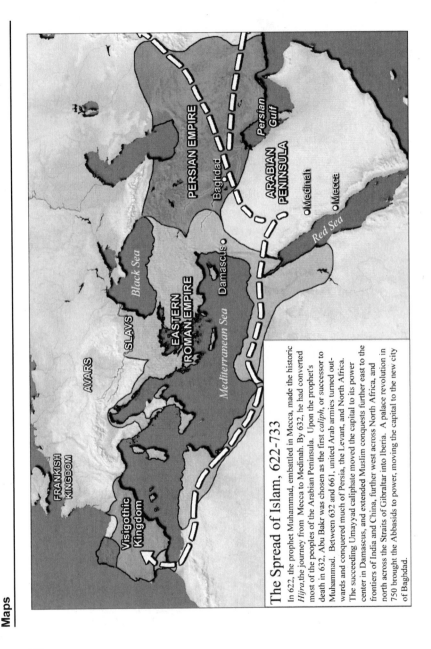

The Spread of Islam, 622-733

In 622, the prophet Muhammad, embattled in Mecca, made the historic *Hijra*, the journey from Mecca to Medinah. By 632, he had converted most of the peoples of the Arabian Peninsula. Upon the prophet's death in 632, Abu Bakr was chosen as the first *caliph*, or successor to Muhammad. Between 632 and 661, united Arab armies turned outwards and conquered much of Persia, the Levant, and North Africa. The succeeding Umayyad caliphate moved the capital to its power center in Damascus, and extended Muslim conquests further east to the frontiers of India and China, further west across North Africa, and north across the Straits of Gibraltar into Iberia. A palace revolution in 750 brought the Abbasids to power, moving the capital to the new city of Baghdad.

FRANKISH KINGDOM

Visigothic Kingdom

AVARS

SLAVS

EASTERN ROMAN EMPIRE

PERSIAN EMPIRE

ARABIAN PENINSULA

Black Sea

Mediterranean Sea

Red Sea

Persian Gulf

Damascus

Baghdad

Medinah

Mecca

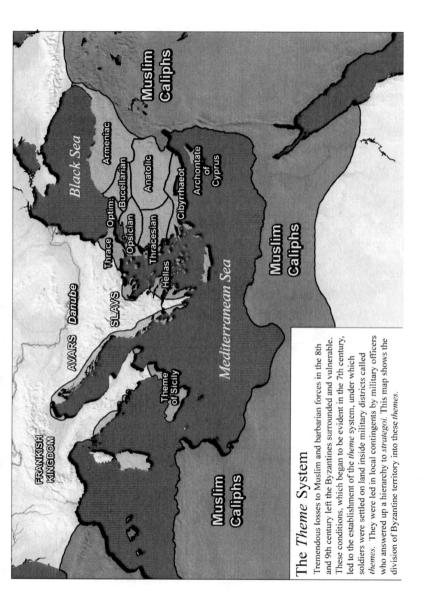

The *Theme* System

Tremendous losses to Muslim and barbarian forces in the 8th and 9th century left the Byzantines surrounded and vulnerable. These conditions, which began to be evident in the 7th century, led to the establishment of the *theme* system, under which soldiers were settled on land inside military districts called *themes*. They were led in local contingents by military officers who answered up a hierarchy to *strategoi*. This map shows the division of Byzantine territory into these *themes*.

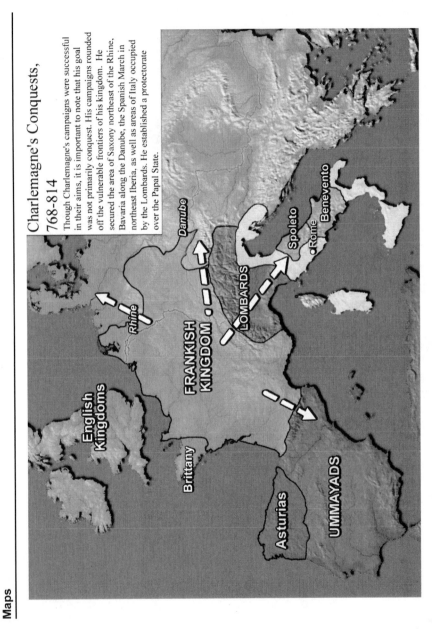

Charlemagne's Conquests, 768-814

Though Charlemagne's campaigns were successful in their aims, it is important to note that his goal was not primarily conquest. His campaigns rounded off the vulnerable frontiers of his kingdom. He secured the area of Saxony northeast of the Rhine, Bavaria along the Danube, the Spanish March in northeast Iberia, as well as areas of Italy occupied by the Lombards. He established a protectorate over the Papal State.

Danube

Rhine

English Kingdoms

Brittany

FRANKISH KINGDOM

LOMBARDS

Spoleto

• Rome

Benevento

Asturias

UMMAYADS

Western Europe, 1356

The year 1356 provides a fascinating snapshot of developments in Western Europe. The Golden Bull of 1356 promised to bring order and stability to Germany, but ultimately brought more disorder. England and the Capetian dynasts of France vied for control of French lands during the 100 Years War (1337-1453.) As German control persisted but weakened in northern Italy, the cities of Florence, Genoa, Milan, and Venice grew in power. Aragon in Iberia emerged as a power in the Mediterranean and would have influence in southern Italy later. Castile had been leading the Reconquest for centuries since the crucial victory in Toledo in 1085. In the 15th century it would unite with Aragon to complete this process. The pope had resided at Avignon in France since 1305, and the attempt to return the pope to Rome in 1378 would result in The Great Schism (1378-1417.)

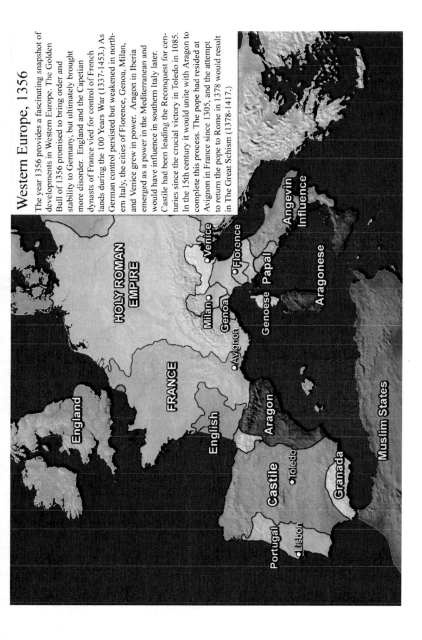

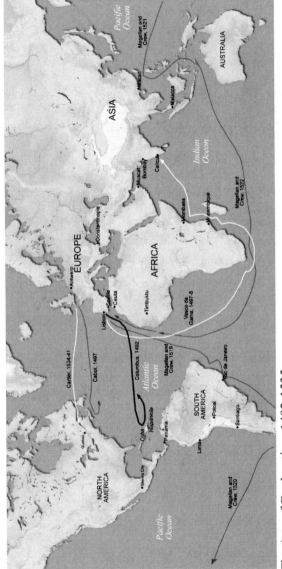

The Age of Exploration, 1492-1535

The Portuguese led the war in overseas exploration, particularly in the realm of trade. Already in the 14th century, they had been sailing up and down the west coast of Africa and had explored islands such as the Azores and the Canaries. Their trading empire was born when Vasco da Gama rounded the Cape of Good Hope and sailed to Calicut. From there, they established armed trading posts throughout the Indian Ocean basin. The Spanish were the first to establish extensive posessions int he New World stretching from Mexico and the southern part of the North American continent all the way south past Peru into present day Argentina. Christopher Columbus' famous voyage of 1492 was the seminal event that initiated this process. The English explorer John Cabot sighted Newfoundland in 1497, but this did not lead immediately to serious English exploration or colonization. Like Cabot, French explorer Jacques Cartier was looking for the Northwest passage when he discovered and sailed up the St. Lawrence River. This would lead to the establishment of Quebec and New France.

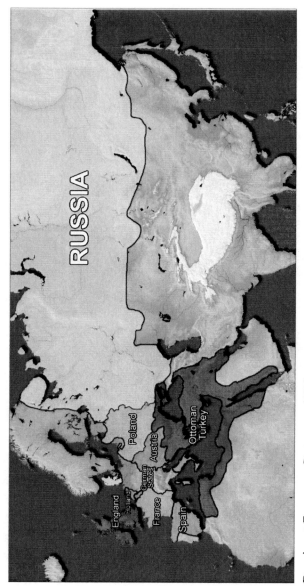

Dominant European States, ca. 1700

By 1700, the states that would dominate modern European history until the 20th century were in place. As these states consolidated and expanded their overseas holdings, Europe's struggles became globalized.

Timeline

10,000–2500 B.C.	Neolithic Era
3500–3000	Emergence of civilization in Mesopotamia and Egypt Development of cities and writing
3000–2000	Consolidation of political power in Sumer; Old Kingdom in Egypt Conquest of Sumer by Akkadians
2000–1500	Egyptian Middle Kingdom Rise of the Hittites Highpoint of Minoan civilization on Crete
1500–1000	Egyptian New Kingdom Egypt's wars with Hittites Mycenean conquest of Minoans Trojan Wars Exodus of Hebrews from Egypt Invasions of Palestine by "sea peoples"
1000–500	Highpoint, division, destruction of Hebrew kingdoms Creation of Phoenician trading networks and colonies Rise and fall of Assyria Rise and fall of Neo-Babylonian kingdom Emergence of Persia Greek Dark Ages, Archaic period Homer, *Iliad* and *Odyssey* Greek colonization Emergence of the polis Founding of Rome

Timeline

Brilliant work of assimilating Greek
philosophical and scientific heritage
Admixture of Arabic, Indic, and Persian
cultural elements

The rise of the Byzantine Empire and
Orthodox Christianity

Imperial regime focused more and more on
the east—Anatolia and Balkans
New administrative arrangements—*theme*
system marked a departure from
Roman traditions
Greek culture emphasized; Latin
slowly abandoned
Distinctive religious practices mark
Orthodoxy as a distinct Christian tradition
Efforts to assimilate ancient Greek
philosophical and literary culture

Germanic kingdoms in the West culminated in
empire of Charlemagne

Early kingdoms failed: Vandals,
Ostrogoths, Visigoths
Franks conquered Burgundians
and Lombards
Fate of Europe left to Anglo-Saxons
and Franks
Broad area of Christian culture and
common institutional characteristics led
to idea of "Christendom"

900–1300...........................Europe's medieval highpoint

Tremendous expansion

Demographic growth, expansion of
agriculture and trade
New kingdoms in Celtic world, Scandinavia,
and Slavic world
Spanish Reconquista
Aggressive expansion in Crusades

Political consolidation in England, France,
Spain, and Italian towns
    Disunity in Germany
Highpoint of power and influence of papacy and
Roman Church
Age of cathedral schools, followed
by universities
Time of scholasticism and Thomas Aquinas
Brilliant vernacular culture in *Beowulf*, *Song of
Roland*, *Romances*, *Divine Comedy*

Political crises
    The Hundred Years War between France and
    England, 1336–1453
    The Golden Bull in Germany
    Consolidation of Milan, Florence, and
    Venice in Italy
    Peasants' revolts in France and England;
    urban revolts in Flanders and Italy
Ecclesiastical crises
    The "Babylonian captivity" of the papacy
    The challenge of "conciliarism"
    The Great Schism
Demographic crises
    Bad weather and poor harvests, 1311–1322
    The Black Death, 1347–1349
    Recurring Plague

Individual figures, such as Bocaccio and Petrarch
The Florentine hegemony with Coluccio Salutati
and the Medici
The rise of humanism and courtly culture
New attitudes toward classical Greek and Roman
literature and life

The spread of printing and more rapid
dissemination of ideas
Tendency for scholars to travel more
Beginnings of European exploration
and expansion

1400–1600.........................Religious Reformations
Shifts in late medieval piety; rise of
anti-clericalism; sharp criticism of abuses in
Catholic Church
Christian humanists, such as Erasmus and
Thomas More proposed broad program
of reforms
John Wylcif and John Hus challenged theology
of Catholic Church
"Magisterial" reformers—Martin Luther and
John Calvin—created new Christian traditions
that were durable
Based on "faith alone, grace alone,
scripture alone," not on the "works" of
medieval Catholicism
There were sharp differences among
the reformers
Catholic Church also began reforming in late
15th century
New schools and universities, along with
new religious orders, deepened sense of
religious responsibilities
Council of Trent (1545–1563) a watershed
for the Catholic Church
By the 1560s, Europe was "confessionalized"
Large areas embraced different forms
of Christianity
A fragile tolerance was achieved

1600.....................................The Prospect

Europe was still Christian but badly divided

The "great power" politics and diplomacy that have dominated the modern world emerged for the first time

Growth of overseas empires was globalizing Western civilization

The dawn of modern science was challenging traditional information and ways of knowing

Glossary

Abbasids: Dynasty of caliphs (q.v.) from 750 to 1258. Moved capital to Baghdad and fostered brilliant culture. Gradually declined in power as regions broke away and Turkish mercenaries acquired real power.

acropolis: The elevated region of a polis used for civic celebrations and defense.

aediles: Roman republican officers, two elected annually, who had responsibility for food supply, public buildings, games.

Aeneid: Twelve-book epic poem on Roman origins by Virgil, characterized by praise of traditional Roman virtues.

agoge: Name for the "training," the traditional way of bringing up Spartan males.

agora: The market; a key component of any Greek polis.

Anabaptists: Literally "rebaptizers," this is a catchall name for adherents of the "radical reformation," those who felt that Lutherans and Calvinists had not gone far enough in rooting out "papism." Prominent on Europe's frontiers.

Angevin Empire: Name for the lands in France held by the kings of England of the Angevin dynasty beginning with Henry II (r. 1154–1189).

Anglo-Saxons: Catchall name for various peoples from northern Germany and southern Denmark who settled in England from 450 to 600 and built small kingdoms.

Antigonids: Dynasty of rulers who succeeded to one of Alexander's generals. They ruled the Balkans until the Romans conquered them in a series of 2nd-century wars.

Arianism: *See* **Arius** in Biographical Notes.

Armada: Great fleet sent by Catholic Spain against Protestant England in 1588 that ended in failure.

Assyrians: A Semitic-speaking people who arose in Mesopotamia in the second millennium B.C. and, after about 900 B.C., built a large and cruel empire centered on Nineveh. Defeated by a coalition led by Neo-Babylonians and Medes.

Augsburg, Peace of: A settlement made in 1555 between Lutherans and Catholics in Germany, which included the principle "*cuius regio, eius religio.*" Princes could dictate the religion of their lands and people were free to stay and practice that religion or migrate elsewhere. The settlement ignored Calvinists, yet was the first example of religious toleration in Europe.

Augsburg Confession: A statement made in 1530 of the essential doctrines of Lutheranism. Prepared by Luther's associate Philip Melanchthon (1497–1560).

Avesta: Holy books of Zoroastrianism (q.v.).

Babylonian captivity: Derisive name for the period when the popes were in Avignon (1305–1378).

barbarians: To Greeks, babblers, people who did not speak Greek; to Romans, people outside the empire. The word gradually acquired more acutely negative connotations.

Beowulf: Finest Anglo-Saxon poem. Epic account of the struggles of Beowulf, his kin, and companions with legendary monsters. Variously dated from 750 to 900 or even later.

bishops: "Overseers" in Greek, the chief religious and administrative officers of the Christian church.

Black Death: Devastating outbreak of bubonic plague in 1348; killed one-fourth to one-third of the population.

Book of Common Prayer: Issued under the aegis of Queen Elizabeth I (r. 1558–1603) in 1569 as a service book for, and theological statement of, what came to be called Anglicanism, that is, the English *via media* between Catholicism and Protestantism.

bretwalda: Contemporary name for early Anglo-Saxon kings who claimed some wide-ranging authority: "broad-wielders" or "Britain-wielders."

caliph: Successor to the prophet in Islam. Originally held only Muhammad's secular authority but, over time, acquired some responsibility for custody of the faith.

Capetians: Name for the ruling dynasty of France from 987 to 1328.

capitularies: Legislation in chapters (*capitula*) issued by Frankish kings.

Cappadocian fathers: Basil the Great (c. 330–379), his brother Gregory of Nyssa (c. 330–395), and Gregory Nazianzus (329–389) were among the greatest Greek church fathers. They wrote especially on Trinitarian and Christological issues.

cardinals: Key officers of the Catholic Church. Emerged in late antiquity and achieved real institutional prominence in the 12th century. Served as papal electors.

Carolingians: Dynasty of Frankish rulers whose most famous member was Charlemagne (*Carolus Magnus*). Became kings in 751 and ruled until 911 in Germany and 987 in France.

Cathars: Dualist heretics, in the ancient Zoroastrian-Manichaean tradition, who were prominent in southern France from the mid-12th century to the early 13th. Especially common around Albi, whence the name Albigensians.

censors: Roman republican officers, two in number, elected every five years to serve for 18 months. They determined the economic status of citizens for voting purposes and legislated on public morality.

Centuriate Assembly: Roman republican voting assembly consisting of all Roman citizens organized by "centuries," or wealth groups. Used "block" voting, that is, there were always 192 votes, one for each century.

Chaeronea, Battle of: Macedonians, led by King Philip II and his son Alexander, defeated the Greeks in 338 B.C.

chivalry: The social ethos of the medieval warrior-aristocracy that emphasized prowess, courage, loyalty, and generosity. The conduct proper for a knight, a man who rode and fought on a horse (*cheval*).

Christian humanism: Term applied to scholarship of Renaissance figures in northern Europe who tended to study the Bible and church fathers rather than the Greco-Roman classics.

christology: The branch of Christian theology that explores how Jesus Christ can be true God and true man.

church fathers: Greek and Latin Christian writers (from the time 300–750 but, especially, 350–450) who set norms for biblical interpretation and explained key Christian doctrines.

Cisalpine Gaul: Roman name for the Italian area between the Alps and the Rubicon River, literally "Gaul on this side of the Alps."

Cistercians: Monks of Citeaux, in Burgundy, or their allies; a community of reformed Benedictine monks who sought primitive purity. Spread rapidly in the 12th century.

Cluny: Great monastery founded in Burgundy in 910 to be free of all lay control. Tremendously influential well into the 12th century, not least because of its famous abbots.

Columbian exchange: Name for the process whereby Europeans and peoples in the New World exchanged crops, livestock, and germs.

comedy: A dramatic work that may be fantastic or ridiculous, whose humor may be riotous or mordant, and which may have powerful contemporary resonance.

communes: Urban institutions in Italy involving fairly wide political participation by the elites.

Complutensian Polyglot Bible: Produced around 1500 at the University of Alcala in Spain, a scholarly edition of the Bible with parallel columns in different languages and elaborate notes.

conciliarism: Doctrine spawned during the Great Schism (q.v.) maintaining that church councils and not the popes are supreme in the church.

consul: Highest officer in the Roman Republic. There were two, elected annually, who led armies, proposed legislation, and convened assemblies.

Corinthian: Name for one of the three Greek orders; pertains particularly to the columns characterized by fluting, more-or-less elaborate pedestals, and Acanthus-leaf capitals. This style was especially favored by the Romans.

Corpus Iuris Civilis: Massive codification of Roman law carried out (529–532) by a commission headed by Tribonian under the aegis of Justinian (see Biographical Notes).

Council of Trent (1545–1563): Most important Catholic Church council of the Reformation era. Affirmed traditional Catholic teachings and instituted many reforms.

Counter-Reformation: From the 1560s, an effort by the Catholic Church to win back areas lost to Protestants. Most effective in Poland and southern Germany.

covenant: Central idea in religious faith of the Hebrews. Calls for a mutual, reciprocal pact between God and his chosen people.

Crusades: Long series of "armed pilgrimages" between 1095 and 1291 designed to liberate the Holy Land from the "Infidel," that is, Muslims. The French were most prominent in the Crusades. Papal leadership was sometimes effective, but the overall results were limited.

cuneiform: Literally "wedge shaped"; customary name for the writing used in Mesopotamia.

Dominicans: Mendicant order founded by Dominic de Guzman (1170–1221) in southern France. Their ideal was to combat heresy by acquiring great learning and living exemplary lives. The order produced many great scholars.

Dorians: Greek speakers who migrated from Thessaly to Peloponnesus after about 1200 B.C. and settled around Sparta. Greek legend remembered them as invaders.

Doric: Name for one of the three Greek orders; pertains particularly to the columns characterized by convex shape, fluting, lack of pedestals, and simple capitals.

Edict of Milan: Decree in 313 whereby Constantine granted legal toleration to Christianity.

ephors: Overseers who, in the Spartan system, judged the validity of laws.

Epicureanism: Philosophy that stressed happiness or pleasure, defined as absence of pain or strife (not hedonism, as it later came to be understood).

equals: *See homoioi.*

Etruscans: Mysterious people, probably of eastern Mediterranean origin, who lived north of Latium and dominated the emerging Romans until about 500 B.C.

excommunication: Ecclesiastical punishment by which a person is denied the sacraments of the church and forbidden most kind of ordinary human interactions.

federates: People who had a *foedus*, a treaty, with Rome; usually along frontiers.

feudalism: Social and political regime in which public services and private bonds alike were arranged by vassals (q.v.), men who have sworn mutual pledges to one another, and fiefs (q.v.; from *feudum*), something of value, usually land, (a manor q.v.), which was exchanged between the lord and the vassal. There never was a uniform "feudal system" in medieval Europe in any one place or time.

fief: From Latin *feudum*, this was something of value that was assigned by a lord to a vassal in exchange for loyalty and some particular service, normally military.

Five Good Emperors: Extremely competent and successful Roman emperors from 96 to 180: Nerva, Trajan, Hadrian, Antoninus Pius, Marcus Aurelius.

Franciscans: Mendicant order founded by Francis of Assisi (1181/1182–1226) based on poverty and service to outcasts. Tremendously popular but riven by factional strife over the question of individual versus corporate property.

Franks: Germanic peoples who gradually moved south from the Rhine mouth toward Paris, and built powerful kingdoms under the Merovingian and Carolingian families of kings.

frieze: A continuous, usually narrative, sculptural program incised into or attached to the surface of a building.

Great Schism: Period between 1378 and 1417 when two or even three rivals claimed to be the legitimate pope.

hadith: The sayings of the prophet Muhammad. Collected and written down, they are studied in the Islamic world as a source of religious guidance, although not on a par with the Quran.

Hagia Sophia: The church of "Holy Wisdom" built in Constantinople on Justinian's orders. Owed much to traditional Roman architecture but also innovated. Isidore of Miletus and Anthemius of Tralles were the principal architects.

Hellenistic world: Period from the death of Alexander the Great in 322 B.C. to the Roman triumph in the Mediterranean in 31. A time of large kingdoms and empires in which Greek cultural influences were dominant.

helots: State-owned slaves in ancient Sparta, mainly Messenian people who lived to the west of Sparta and whom the Spartans conquered after 750 B.C.

henotheism: Belief by some group or people in one god without denying the existence of other gods. (Sometimes called *monolatry*.)

hieroglyphics: A pictographic form of writing in which representational symbols stand for words or ideas. Prominently used in ancient Egypt.

Hijra: The "flight," or pilgrimage, of the prophet Muhammad from Mecca to Medina in 622. Taken in the Islamic world to inaugurate a new era.

Hittites: Indo-European–speaking and institutionally precocious people who rose in Anatolia in the third millennium B.C., expanded south into Syria and Palestine, and fought debilitating wars with the Egyptians after about 1400 B.C.

homoioi: Adult male Spartans. Full citizens at Sparta.

hoplites: Heavily armed Greek infantrymen who fought in phalanx formation.

Huguenots: Name for French Protestants of the Calvinist variety; derives from a medieval romance about a King Hugo.

humanism: Term with varied meanings: love for literary culture of antiquity; concern for human beings; interest in secular rather than theological issues. Often coupled with Renaissance figures.

Hundred Years War: Conflict between France and England (1337–1453) rooted in the longstanding controversy over English royal holdings in France. The English won most battles, but the French won the war.

Huns: Fierce nomadic warriors from the frontiers of China who appeared on the Roman scene around 370 and pressured the western empire until their defeat in 451.

Hyksos: Semitic-speaking peoples from Palestine who conquered Egypt about 1700 B.C. and ruled at least the Nile delta region for approximately 150 years.

Iliad: Poem about Ilion (that is, Troy) by the mysterious poet Homer, who may have come from Asia Minor. The Greeks believed that Homer composed the poem, but he may have done no more than give familiar form to one telling of a tale that circulated orally in many versions. Probably dates from about 750 B.C.

indulgences: In Catholic theology, the remission of some portion of the temporal punishment for sin. Subject to massive abuses in the late Middle Ages.

inquisition: Ecclesiastical judicial process for the identification and reconciliation of heretics. Followed basic principles of Roman law.

Institutes of the Christian Religion: Text by John Calvin (see the Biographical Notes), originally written in 1536, that became the standard exposition of Reformed Christianity. Based on the Ten Commandments, Lord's Prayer, and Apostles Creed.

interdict: Ecclesiastical censure whereby most sacramental services are forbidden in a defined area to pressure the rulers of that region.

investiture controversy: Institutional and ideological battle between popes and German emperors in the 11th and 12th centuries; finally won by the popes at great cost to the Germans.

Ionic: Name for one of the three Greek orders; pertains particularly to the columns characterized by graceful thinness, fluting, complex pedestals, and scroll-like capitals.

Isaurians: Ruling dynasty in Byzantium (717–802). Defended frontiers, issued new laws, carried on with development of the *theme* system, and promoted iconoclasm (the removal or destruction of devotional images).

Islam: From *al-Islam*, "the surrender," the customary name for the faith taught by the prophet Muhammad and involving a complete surrender of the self to Allah.

Israel: Collective name for the Hebrew people or the name of the northernmost of the two kingdoms that emerged after the death of Solomon with a capital at Samaria. Conquered by the Assyrians in 722 B.C.

Jesuits: Common name for the religious order called the Society of Jesus, founded in 1534 by Ignatius Loyola (see Biographical Notes). The order is dedicated to poverty, chastity, and obedience to the pope. Its members are famous as teachers, scholars, and missionaries.

Judah: Southernmost of the two kingdoms that emerged after the death of Solomon with a capital at Jerusalem. Conquered by the Neo-Babylonians in 586 B.C.

Julio-Claudians: Direct or indirect heirs of Julius Caesar: Augustus, Tiberius, Caligula, Claudius, Nero.

Knossos: Site of huge palace complex built by Minoan kings of Crete.

krypteia: The Spartan secret police who watched over the *helots* and the Spartans.

Lateran councils: Church councils called by the popes to facilitate the governance of the church. The most important was the Fourth Lateran Council in 1215.

Latium: The semi-circular plain surrounding Rome. Called Lazio today, it gave its name to Latin.

Lepanto, Battle of: Great victory by Spanish naval forces over the Turkish fleet in 1571 as part of Spain's self-appointed role as protector of Christendom.

Licinian-Sextian law: In 287, this law granted the decisions of the plebeian assembly the full force of law and made the plebs equal in the Roman constitution.

Linear A: Name for writing found on Minoan Crete. Not yet deciphered.

Linear B: Name for writing found in Mycenean Greece. Deciphered by Michael Ventris in the early 1950s as a primitive form of Greek.

Lombards: Germanic people who entered Italy in 568 and gradually built a strong kingdom with rich culture, especially in law, only to fall to the more powerful Franks in 773–774.

Macedonians: Byzantine dynasty (867–1034), which presided over military successes, economic prosperity, and brilliant cultural achievements.

Magna Carta: The "Great Charter" that English barons forced King John to sign in 1215. The charter forced John to cease abusing royal and feudal prerogatives and to accept the superiority of law to royal whim.

manor: Normal English name for medieval estate consisting of a lord, the person for whom the estate was exploited, and the dependent peasants, often but not always serfs. Manors were usually bipartite in that some portion was reserved to the support of the lord and some part reserved to the peasants themselves.

Medes: People who lived in the Zagros Mountains, aided in the fall of the Assyrians, and allied with the Persians.

Mediterranean triad: Name for the three traditional and widely disseminated crops: cereal grains, olives, and grapes.

mendicants: Begging orders that arose in the 13th century. Franciscans (q.v.) and Dominicans (q.v.) were the most prominent.

metics: Resident aliens in Athens; a substantial fraction of the population and unable to participate politically, although sometimes rich and influential.

Minoan: Name (from the legendary Minos) for the brilliant culture on the island of Crete between 2200 and 1500 B.C. Its main center was at Knossos.

missi dominici: Itinerant envoys of the Carolingian kings who inspected the work of local officials and implemented royal decisions.

monk: Christian ascetic who in principle lives alone but in practice lives in some form of community.

monolatry: *See* **henotheism**.

monophysitism: Christian heresy prominent in the eastern Mediterranean holding that Jesus Christ had only one true (divine) nature. Condemned by the Council of Chalcedon in 451. Still influential among west Asian Christians.

monotheism: The belief in the existence of only one God.

Mycenae: City (flourished 1400–1200 B.C.) ruled by Agamemnon, leader of the Greek forces at Troy. Also gives its name to the earliest phase of Greek history.

Neo-Babylonians: *See* **Nebuchadnezzar** in Biographical Notes.

Neolithic Revolution: A set of processes that began about 10,000 years ago leading to the rise of agriculture and the domestication of animals.

Ostrogoths: Germanic people who built a kingdom in Italy under their king, Theodoric (r. 493–526), only to fall to the armies of Justinian (see Biographical Notes).

papal state: Lands in central Italy ruled by the papacy beginning in the 8th century.

Parliament: An English institution that grew from the royal court and the consultative function of the king's leading men. Emerged in the 13th century but took hundreds of years to reach the full potential of its powers.

Parthenon: Magnificent Doric temple built on Athenian acropolis between 447/446 and 438, with sculptures completed in 432. Chief architects were Ictinus and Callicrates; the chief sculptor was Pheidias.

paterfamilias: Eldest male in a Roman household, who possessed life-or-death powers over all members of the family.

patricians: "Well-fathered ones," the original social and political elite of Rome.

patristic era: The period of the church fathers (*patres*; q.v.).

Peloponnesian War: Contest between Athens and its empire and Sparta and the Peloponnesian League (431–404). At issue was Sparta's fear of Athenian dominance in the Greek world.

peroikoi: "Dwellers about"; resident aliens in ancient Sparta.

Persians: People from the Persian (now Iranian) plains who allied with the Medes, built a huge empire, and provided many examples in government and culture.

Persian Wars (490, 480–478 B.C.): Wars fought heroically on Greek soil and waters; took place when Persians invaded to avenge mainland Greek assistance given to Asia Minor Greeks who had rebelled against Persian rule.

Petrine theory: Idea advanced by Roman bishops that as Peter was leader of the Apostles, the successor to Peter is the leader of the church. Based on Matthew 16.16–19.

pharaoh: Customary name (from *per aa*, meaning "great house") of the rulers of ancient Egypt.

Phoencians: A Semitic-speaking Canaanite people who inhabited roughly what is now Lebanon and who began planting trading colonies in the western Mediterranean after about 900 B.C.

Pillars of Islam: Five practices that characterize the Islamic faith: profession of faith, fasting, daily prayer, generous almsgiving, pilgrimage to Mecca.

plebeians: Original lower classes—economically, socially, politically—at Rome, who struggled over some two centuries to gain full political participation.

Poetics: Title of a book by Aristotle that is the first work of literary criticism.

polis: City-state, the classic Greek political institution, consisting of an urban core and an agricultural hinterland.

polytheism: The belief in the simultaneous existence of many gods.

pope: The bishop of Rome who, on the basis of the Petrine theory (q.v.), the historical resonances of Rome, and various historical circumstances, achieved a leading position in the Catholic Church.

praetors: Chief judicial officers of the Roman Republic. Initially two, then as many as eight. Elected annually.

predestination: Doctrine particularly associated with John Calvin holding that all souls were absolutely predestined from before all time to either salvation or damnation.

primogeniture: From *primus genitus*, "first born," a social and political system whereby lands, offices, and titles were transmitted to the oldest male.

principate: Name for the Roman regime inaugurated by Augustus Caesar as *princeps*, or "First Citizen." Contrasted with "Dominate" of Diocletian (see Biographical Notes).

Protestant: Latin word meaning "they protest" that appeared in a document of 1529. Became a catchall designation for persons who left the Catholic Church and their descendants.

Ptolemies: Dynasty of rulers in Egypt descended from one of Alexander's generals. The last one, Cleopatra, was defeated by Rome in 31 B.C.

Punic Wars: Three wars (264–241 B.C., 218–201, 149–146) between the Romans and the Carthaginians (the "Puni," or "Poeni," that is, "purple people," meaning Phoenicians). Roman victory brought domination of the western Mediterranean.

Pyrrhic War: War between the Romans and King Pyrrhus of Epirus (280–276 B.C.) in which Pyrrhus won battles but so depleted his resources that he eventually lost (hence, "Pyrrhic victory"). The war was occasioned by Roman expansion into southern Italy and generated Roman involvement in the Balkans.

quaestors: Chief financial officers of the Roman Republic. Initially two in number, elected annually.

Quran: The sacred book of Islam. A series of recitations, gathered in chapters called *surahs*, given by the angel Gabriel to the prophet Muhammad.

Reconquista: The centuries-long (8th to 15th) and frequently interrupted war in which Christian powers beginning in the northwest of Iberia retook the peninsula from the Muslims who invaded in 711.

Renaissance: Generally means "rebirth," specifically of the literary culture of Greco-Roman antiquity. The term was traditionally applied to Italy during the period 1300 to 1550 but is increasingly applied to all periods of significant cultural efflorescence.

romances: Works, usually in prose but sometimes in verse, in many languages, often set in Arthurian contexts, about entanglements of love, loyalty, honor, and duty. Often reveal the courtly side of chivalry, the aspect involving relations between men and women.

Samnite Wars: A series of three wars (343–290 B.C.) in which the Romans defeated the Samnites, peoples who lived to the south of Latium. This war brought the Romans directly into contact with the Greeks of southern Italy.

scholasticism: Catchall name for the intellectual culture of high medieval Europe; more technically, the intellectual methods of the schools and universities based on logic.

Seleucids: Dynasty of rulers in Syria, Palestine, and Mesopotamia who descended from one of Alexander's generals. Conquered by the Romans in the 1st century B.C.

Senate: Originally the patrician-dominated assembly of Rome but later a body of former office holders. Made treaties and issued influential opinions but did not legislate.

Septuagint: Greek version of the Hebrew Bible, allegedly prepared by 70 translators in 70 days in Alexandria. Seven books longer than the Hebrew version. Authoritative still in Orthodox churches.

Song of Roland (c. 1100): First work of French literature. Heroic account of Charlemagne and his peers on a virtual crusade. Breathes the chivalric ethos.

Sophists: Popular but controversial wandering teachers in the second half of the 5th century who, for often exorbitant fees, would teach the arts of rhetoric, that is, the arts of persuasion.

Stoicism: Hellenistic philosophy that stressed calm, obedience to natural law, adherence to moral duty, essential equality of all. Founded by Zeno.

summa: A compendious, systematic work purporting to survey a whole field of knowledge. Best known are the *summas* of Thomas Aquinas (see Biographical Notes).

sunna: The "good practice," or the habits and customs of the prophet Muhammad, studied in the Islamic world as a guide to life but not on a par with the Quran.

syncretism: The tendency, often manifest in religion, to adopt and adapt ideas and practices from neighbors, conquerors, or even those whom one has conquered.

synoptic problem: Term that refers to the perceived literary relationships among the "synoptic" Gospels: Matthew, Mark, and Luke.

tetrarchy: "Rule by four" instituted by Diocletian. Two *augustuses* and two *caesars* would jointly rule the empire and provide for orderly succession. Only partially successful in practice.

themes: Byzantine military districts having soldiers settled on the land who were mustered by local generals. *Themes* developed gradually after 600 and partially replaced the professional standing army paid by general tax revenues.

theocratic kingship: Form of royal rule that emerged in Mesopotamia, then appeared in many Western societies. Maintained that kings ruled as specially designated agents of the gods to whom they were answerable.

three-field system: Agricultural regime with one field in spring crops, one in fall crops, and one fallow. Increased productivity over the two-field system. Introduced, probably, in Carolingian period and disseminated later.

Torah: The first five books of the Hebrew scriptures, traditionally ascribed to Moses.

tragedy: A dramatic work meant to evoke fear and/or pity whose major character, perhaps owing to a fatal flaw, suffers deeply and may be brought to ruin. The character may also earn the audience's respect through a heroic struggle against fate.

Tribal Assembly: Roman republican assembly consisting of all Roman citizens organized into 33 voting districts. Used "block" voting, that is, there were 33 votes, one per "tribe."

tribunes: Plebeian officers in Roman Republic, 10 in number elected annually, charged with looking out for the interests of the plebs.

Trinity: The Christian doctrine according to which one God exists in three distinct persons (Father, Son, and Holy Spirit).

Triumvirate, First: Informal alliance of Caesar, Crassus, and Pompey in 60 B.C. designed to secure military commands for the first two and generous settlements for the military veterans who had served under the third.

Triumvirate, Second: Formal alliance among Octavian, Lepidus, and Antonius in 43 B.C. by which they were to share rule in the Roman Empire.

Trojan War: Traditional date 1194–1184 B.C. Contest between Greeks (i.e., Myceneans) and Trojans immortalized in Homer's *Iliad*. Allegedly, the Greeks were avenging the abduction of Helen, the wife of King Menelaus of Sparta. Probably a commercial conflict or one incident in a long economic rivalry.

troubadours: Wandering poets, both men and women, of love themes, they revealed the ethos of courtly love. Most well known are the French but comparable to the German *Minnesänger*.

Twelve Tables: First codification of Roman law, posted in the forum in 449 B.C.

tyranny: A form of one-man rule, usually with popular support after social struggles, that emerged in many Greek cities between 700 and 500 B.C.

Umma Muslima: The community of all those who have made "*al Islam*," not confined to any political or ethnic boundaries.

Ummayyads: Dynasty of caliphs (q.v.) from 661 to 750 who moved the capital of the caliphate to Damascus and did much of the work of building institutions.

university: Medieval institution made up of either a guild of masters or of students. Faculties included arts, theology, law, medicine. Oldest were Bologna in Italy and Paris in France.

Vandals: Germanic people who crossed the Rhine in 406, raided in Spain for a generation, crossed to North Africa, practiced piracy in the Mediterranean, and fell to Justinian (see Biographical Notes) in 532–534.

vassal: A free man who willingly pledged *auxilium et consilium*, aid and advice, to another man in return for protection and maintenance, the latter often a fief (q.v.).

vernacular: Languages, or other cultural manifestations, that are not in Latin.

Vikings: Catchall name for those Scandinavians who raided Western Europe, the north Atlantic islands, and Slavic realms between 793 and the mid-11th century.

Visigoths: Germanic federates who crossed the Danube into Roman territory in 376, defeated a Roman army in 378, sacked Rome in 410, settled in Gaul under Roman auspices in 418, lost to the Franks in 507, and migrated into Spain and created a kingdom that finally fell to the Muslims in 711.

Vulgate: Latin translation of the Bible prepared by Saint Jerome (see Biographical Notes) on the order of Pope Damasus.

ziggurat: Temples built in Mesopotamia of mud brick and timber and having the form of a trapezoid.

Zoroastrianism: Principal religion of the ancient Persians. Revealed in songs (*gathas*) in the Avesta, the holy books of the religion. Consisted of the teachings of Zarathustra (dates controversial), who stressed dualities.

Biographical Notes

Abelard, Peter (1079–1142): Philosopher, poet, theologian, lover of Heloise.

Abraham: Hebrew patriarch who, in the early second millennium B.C., moved from Ur to Palestine.

Aeneas: Central figure in Virgil's *Aeneid.*

Aeschylus (525–456 B.C.): First author of tragedies whose works survive. His *Oresteia* is the only surviving trilogy.

Alcuin (735–804): Anglo-Saxon scholar, product of Bede's (q.v.) intellectual revival in Northumbria, who came to Charlemagne's court circa 786 and promoted intellectual reforms. Abbot of Tours from 796 to 804.

Alexander the Great (356–322 B.C.): King of Macedon (336–322) after his father, Philip II, led military campaigns that defeated the Persian Empire and extended Greek influence into central Asia.

Alfonso da Albuquerque (1453–1515): Portuguese sea captain and soldier who created naval bases in the Indian Ocean region to facilitate Portuguese trade.

Alfred the Great (r. 871–899): Anglo-Saxon king who rallied the people of southern England after Viking attacks, laid the foundations for English recovery, and fostered an intellectual revival.

Ambrose (339–397): High-born citizen of Milan who became bishop of the city and wrote extensively, bringing to Latin theology the conceptual frameworks of Greek thought. church father.

Aneirin (fl. c. 600): British poet, author of *Gododdin*, an account of the Anglo-Saxon defeat of the Picts at Catterick.

Anselm (1033–1109): Monk, philosopher, greatest logician since antiquity, theologian, archbishop of Canterbury.

Anthony (251[?]–356): Egyptian solitary who established the ideals of *eremitic* (solitary) monasticism.

Apollonius of Rhodes (b. c. 295 B.C.): Alexandrian scholar and author best known for *Argonautica*, in which Jason and his argonauts go in search of the golden fleece.

Archimedes (287–212 B.C.): Hellenistic scientist and inventor.

Aristarchus: First formulated the "heliocentric" theory (that the earth revolves around the sun, which is at the center of the "universe") circa 275 B.C.

Aristophanes (455–385 B.C.): Greatest writer of Athenian comedy; pilloried contemporary figures, including Socrates.

Aristotle (384–322 B.C.): Philosopher, pupil of Plato. Prolific writer on biology, politics. ethics, poetics.

Arius (c. 250–336): Priest of Alexandria who, in an attempt to preserve absolute monotheism, taught that Jesus Christ was slightly subordinate to God the Father. Condemned by Council of Nicaea in 325 but influential among Germanic peoples who were converted to *Arianism*.

Attalis III: King of Pergamum, a small but rich Hellenistic kingdom, who willed his kingdom to Rome in 133 B.C.

Augustine (354–430): Prolific Christian theologian and greatest of Latin church fathers. One of the most influential writers in Christian history.

Augustus Caesar (63 B.C.–A.D.14): Honorific title of Gaius Julius Caesar Octavianus, the adopted heir of Julius Caesar who inaugurated the principate.

Balboa, Vasco Nuñez de (1475–1517): Spanish explorer who crossed Central America at the Isthmus of Panama in 1513 and became the first European to see the Pacific Ocean by going west.

Bede (673–735): Anglo-Saxon monk and scholar at Wearmouth-Jarrow who wrote biblical commentaries, a book on time reckoning, and history. Greatest scholar of his day.

Benedict of Nursia (c. 480–c. 550): Italian ascetic who founded a community at Monte Cassino where he wrote his Rule, eventually the most influential of all monastic rules.

Bernard of Clairvaux (1090–1153): Greatest of Cistercians (see Glossary), prolific author, adviser to kings and popes, the most influential religious figure in the middle decades of the 12th century.

Boccaccio (1313–1375): Florentine scholar and storyteller, author of *The Decameron*, a series of 100 stories told over 10 days.

Brahe, Tycho (1546–1601): Astronomer supported by the Danish court who collected a huge amount of direct observational data on the heavens, thus supplanting ancient texts, such as those of Ptolemy (q.v.).

Brian Boru (976–1014): First Irish king to exert real authority over much of Ireland.

Cabot, John (1450–1499): English explorer who sighted Newfoundland in 1497 in an early attempt to find a "northwest passage" to Asia.

Calvin, John (1509–1564): French scholar and theologian, author of *Institutes of the Christian Religion*, founder of "reformed" tradition of Christianity, led reform of the church in French Switzerland.

Cartier, Jacques (1491–1557): French explorer who, in an early effort to find a "northwest passage" to Asia, sailed up the St. Lawrence River in 1534.

Cato the Elder (234–149 B.C.): Conservative Roman author and statesman.

Catullus (84–54 B.C.): Roman lyric poet.

Charlemagne (747–814): Greatest member of the Carolingian (see Glossary) dynasty. King from 768 to 800; emperor from 800 to 814. Secured frontiers of the Frankish kingdom, promoted cultural and institutional reform, formulated ideology of Christendom.

Cicero (106–43 B.C.): Roman lawyer and statesman who struggled for peace and concord in the crumbling Roman Republic.

Cleisthenes: Aristocratic Athenian who made major constitutional reforms around 508 B.C., thereby speeding the emergence of democracy.

Clovis (r. 486–511): Greatest Frankish king of the Merovingian dynasty who consolidated Frankish rule in Gaul, defeated the Visigoths in 507, and accepted Roman Catholicism.

Colet, John (1466–1519): London Christian humanist, trained in Oxford and Italy, studied Pauline epistles, called for church reform, founded St. Paul's school.

Colombo, Cristoforo (1451–1506): Genoese sailor and entrepreneur who secured support from the Spanish crown to find a western route to Asia. Made four voyages (1492, 1493, 1498, 1502) and explored the Caribbean region.

Coluccio Salutati (1331–1406): Chancellor of Florence, founded many schools, attracted scholars to the city, took Cicero as his ideal and republicanism as his ideology.

Constantine (r. 306–337): Roman emperor who continued reforms of Diocletian, restructured the Roman army, granted toleration to Christianity, and became Christian himself.

Copernicus, Nicolaus (1473–1543): Astronomer and, in 1543, author of *On the Revolutions of the Heavenly Bodies*, which carefully advanced the "heliocentric" theory.

Crassus (d. 53 B.C.): Wealthiest man in Rome; joined in various political alliances in a quest to earn respectability.

Cyrus (r. 559–529): King (shah) of the Persians who began building the Persian Empire. He permitted the Jews to rebuild a temple in Jerusalem.

Dante Alighieri (1265–1321): Italian poet and scholar, author of *De monarchia*, *De vulgari eloquentia*, *La vita nuova*, and the *Comedy.*

Demosthenes (384–322 B.C.): Athenian orator and statesman who warned his fellow citizens against the dangers of the Macedonians.

Dias, Bartolommeo (c. 1450–1500): Portuguese navigator who explored the west coast of Africa and finally rounded the Cape of Good Hope, demonstrating that Africa could be circumnavigated.

Diocletian (r. 284–305): Roman emperor who instituted the tetrarchy (see Glossary), reformed the Roman administration, and persecuted Christians.

Dominic de Guzman (1170–1221): *See* **Dominicans** in Glossary.

Draco: Aristocratic Athenian charged by his fellow citizens with codifying the laws of Athens and publishing them in the *agora*.

Einhard (770–840): Author of many works but best known for a biography of Charlemagne modeled on Suetonius's (q.v.) *Lives of the Twelve Caesars*.

Epicurus (341–270 B.C.): Hellenistic philosopher who taught in Athens and gave his name to Epicureanism (see Glossary).

Erasmus, Desiderius (1469–1536): Dutchman, greatest of the Christian humanists, wrote widely, edited Greek New Testament, called for church reform, eventually broke with Protestants over free will.

Eratosthenes (c. 274–194 B.C.): Hellenistic polymath who wrote on many subjects, including comedy, but best known for calculating the circumference of the earth.

Euclid: Formulated the rules of geometry about 300 B.C.

Euripides (485–406 B.C.): Third author of tragedies whose works survive. His works are typified by complex plots and moral confusion. Deeply influenced by the Sophists.

Farel, Guillaume (1489–1565): Collaborator with John Calvin (q.v.) in reform of the church in French Switzerland, especially Geneva.

Francis of Assisi (1181/1182–1226): *See* **Franciscans** in Glossary.

Galilei, Galileo (1564–1642): Scientist and astronomer, demonstrated mathematically that the earth moves and was censured by the church.

Gelasius I (r. 492–496): Pope who spelled out respective spheres of authority of kings and priests.

Gilgamesh: The main character in the Mesopotamian epic poem first composed circa 2500 B.C. and surviving on clay tablets from about 800 B.C.

Gracchi brothers: Tiberius (d. 133 B.C.) and Gaius (d. 121 B.C.) who, as tribunes, were popular leaders. Both were murdered by political foes.

Gratian: Bolognese monk who, around 1140, produced the *Decretum*, the most sophisticated and tightly organized compilation of canon law to that time.

Gregory I (r. 590–604): Pope who wrote influential books and ruled Rome as temporal overlord in the absence of effective Roman rule.

Guarino of Verona (1374–1460): Stressed an education based on Latin and Greek in an effort to form people who were like the characters in classical literature.

Hammurabi. (1792–1750): Ruler over the Old Babylonians (or Amorites). Issued a famous and influential law code.

Heraclius (r. 610–641): East Roman emperor who defeated the Persians only to lose to the Arabs. Failed to achieve religious unity. Began to promote a more Greek culture. Initiated *theme* system as a new form of administration.

Herodotus (c. 485–425): Called the "father of history," wrote a lengthy history of the Persian Wars.

Homer: *See **Iliad** in Glossary.*

Horace (65–8 B.C.): Elegant Roman poet and Epicurean philosopher.

Ignatius of Antioch (c. 35–107): Author of letters to Christian communities that show the emerging structure of the Christian church.

Isocrates (436–338 B.C.): Greek orator and statesman who argued for *Panhellenism*, a union of all Greeks.

Jerome (342–420): High-born Roman citizen who became a Christian ascetic, wrote many letters, and translated the Bible into Latin (See Vulgate in Glossary). Church father.

Julius Caesar (100–44 B.C.): Brilliant, ambitious, and enigmatic Roman politician who held high offices, won military glory in Gaul, became dictator in Rome, and was murdered.

Justin Martyr (c. 100–c. 165): Christian apologist who wrote *Dialogue with Trypho the Jew* to differentiate between Christianity and Judaism.

Justinian (r. 527–565): East Roman emperor who reconquered some western provinces, overhauled the administration, issued the Corpus Iuris Civilis (see Glossary), failed to find religious unity, and built Hagia Sophia.

Juvenal (c. 60–c. 136): Author of 16 verse satires full of social commentary.

Kepler, Johannes (1571–1630): Greatest pupil of Tycho Brahe (q.v.) who developed elaborate mathematical models to explain planetary motion.

Lefèvre d'Étaples, Jacques (1455–1536): French Christian humanist, trained in Paris and Italy, translated Bible into French, studied Greek church fathers.

Leo I (r. 440–461): Pope, gifted writer, and great theoretician of the powers of the papal office.

Leonardo da Vinci (1452–1519): Enigmatic painter, sculptor, inventor, engineer; famous for a small number of completed works, such as *Mona Lisa*.

Livy (59 B.C.–A.D. 17): Grand-scale historian of Rome's foundation and early history.

Lorenzo de' Medici (1449–1492): Financier and administrator, virtual dictator in Florence, but great promoter of cultural life and booster of his city.

Loyola, Ignatius (1491–1556): Spanish nobleman who studied in Paris, joined with fellows, and founded the Society of Jesus (*See* **Jesuits** in Glossary).

Lucan (39–65): Author of *Pharsalia*, a verse account of the civil wars between Caesar and Pompey.

Luther, Martin (1483–1536): German; educated in local universities; became Augustinian priest; became alienated from the Catholic Church over free will, good works, and indulgences (see Glossary). Initiated church reform in Germany. Prolific author.

Lycurgus: Semi-legendary figure to whom the Spartans attributed their constitution.

Magellan, Ferdinand (c. 1480–1521): Set out to circumnavigate the globe in 1519. He died in 1521 in the Philippines, but one of his ships returned in 1522.

Marcus Aurelius (121–180): Last of the Good Emperors and author of an important Stoic work, *Meditations*.

Marius (157–86 B.C.): "New Man" who gained prominence through military successes, held the consulship multiple times in succession, professionalized the Roman army.

Martial (c. 40–104): Spanish author of riotously funny Latin epigrams.

Menander (342/341–293/289 B.C.): Hellenistic author of "new comedies," which were entertaining but not philosophically or socially significant. His only complete surviving play is *Curmudgeon.*

Merici, Angela (1474–1540): A Franciscan *tertiary* who founded the Ursulines in Brescia, Italy, in 1535 as a community of women to teach girls.

Michelangelo Buonoratti (1475–1564): Florentine artist who mastered the techniques, styles, and influences of his time to produce breathtakingly original works of art, such as the statue of David and the ceiling of the Sistine Chapel.

More, Thomas (1478–1535): English lawyer, politician, and Christian humanist; author of *Utopia*; fell afoul of, and was executed by, King Henry VIII for opposing his divorce.

Muhammad (570–632): Meccan merchant who became the prophet of Islam.

Nebuchadnezzar (r. 605–562 B.C.): Reigned as the greatest king of the Neo-Babylonians, one of the peoples who overthrew the Assyrians. Ruled from Babylon, which he built into a magnificent city.

Neri, Filippo (1515–1595): Florentine who settled in Rome, studied long, embraced the ascetic life, and founded the Congregation of the Oratory to enhance the quality of worship.

Offa of Mercia (r. 757–796): Anglo-Saxon *bretwalda* who was first to call himself "King of the English."

Ovid (43 B.C.– A.D. 18): Roman poet who wrote on love and mythological themes. Exiled by Augustus.

Pachomius (290–346): Egyptian monk credited with preparing the first "Rule" and thus formulating *cenobitic* (common-life) monasticism.

Peisistratus: Instituted a mild tyranny in Athens in 560 that lasted a generation and fostered civic allegiance and economic development.

Pericles: Greatest democratic leader of Athens between 460 and 429 B.C.

Peter Lombard (1100–1160): Scholastic theologian whose *Four Books of Sentences* served as a basic theology compendium for centuries.

Petrarch (1304–1374): Florentine, greatest figure of the early Renaissance, scholar, poet, traveler.

Philip II (382–336 B.C.): King of Macedon who forged a unified monarchy and conquered Greece. Father of Alexander the Great.

Piccolomini, Enea Silvio (1405–1464): Tuscan of modest means who traveled widely, wrote scholarly and popular works in Latin and Italian, and was elected pope (Pius II).

Pippin III (r. 751–768): First Carolingian (see Glossary) to become king. He allied with the popes, defeated the Lombards in Italy, and fostered church and cultural reform.

Plato (429–347 B.C.): Pupil of Socrates, teacher of Aristotle, founder of the Academy. Philosopher best known for his theory of "forms," or "ideas." Prolific author of dialogues and treatises.

Plautus (254–184 B.C.): Brought Greek style "new comedy" to Rome. Author of, among other plays, *The Pot of Gold*.

Polybius (c. 200–c. 118 B.C.): Greek historian captured by the Romans. Lived in elegant exile at Rome and wrote a history of the Hellenistic world, emphasizing Rome's rise to greatness and the unique features of the Roman constitution.

Pompey (106–48 B.C.): Roman politician who won military glory and joined with Julius Caesar, then turned against him.

Ptolemy (127–48 B.C.): Hellenistic scientist best known for collecting enormous amounts of astronomical observations and formulating a theory of planetary motion that was dominant until Johannes Keppler (q.v.).

Pythagoras: Greek who taught in southern Italy in the late 6th century. Stressed pure contemplation as the only path to true knowledge.

Quintilian (c. 35–100): Author of *Institution of Oratory*, antiquity's most influential work on rhetoric.

Sargon (2371–2316 B.C.): Ruled over the Akkadians. Built first known imperial state.

Seneca (4 B.C.– A.D. 65): Stoic philosopher of plays and other works.

Socrates (469–399 B.C.): Athenian philosopher who developed the *elenchus*, a rigorous method of dissecting the arguments of others. Taught Plato, among others. Put to death by the Athenian authorities.

Solon: Aristocratic Athenian entrusted (c. 594) by fellow citizens with revising the laws to prevent social strife.

Sophocles (496–406 B.C.): Second author of tragedies whose works survive. Called by Aristotle the "most tragic of poets"; his *Oedipus Rex* is one of the finest plays ever written.

Suetonius (c. 70–c. A.D. 140): Wrote *Lives of the Twelve Caesars.*

Sulla (138–78 B.C.): Unscrupulous conservative politician from a distinguished family who sought to turn back the clock in Roman public life to a time before the Gracchi.

Tacitus (c. 55–c. A.D. 117): Coolly analytical historian of early imperial Rome.

Terence (c. 190–159 B.C.): Author of Latin comedies marked by brilliant, elegant style.

Teresa of Avila (1515–1582): Reformer of the Carmelite order and prolific author on the subject of Christian spirituality. Named a doctor of the church by Pope Paul VI.

Thales: Early materialist philosopher from Miletus, wrote around 600 B.C.

Themistocles: Athenian popular leader during and after the Persian Wars who got legislation passed giving the lowest classes virtually full political participation.

Theodulf of Orléans (c. 750–821): Versatile scholar under Charlemagne who was an administrator, theologian, biblical expert, poet, and architect.

Thomas Aquinas (1225–1274): Italian Dominican, trained at Paris and Cologne, taught in Paris and Rome, produced *Summa theologiae* and *Summa contra gentiles*. Greatest scholastic philosopher and theologian.

Thucydides (460/455–c. 400 B.C.): Wrote a penetrating analytical history of the Peloponnesian Wars down to 411.

Vasco da Gama (c. 1460–1524): Portuguese navigator who, between 1497 and 1499, sailed around Africa into the Indian Ocean, conducted trade, and demonstrated potential profitability of the whole region.

Virgil (70–19 B.C.): Roman epic poet, author of *Aeneid*, *Georgics*, *Bucolics*.

Waldseemüller, Martin: In 1507, published a map calling the lands discovered by Colombo (q.v.) the "New World."

William the Conqueror (c. 1028–1087): Duke of Normandy who conquered England in 1066 and ruled effectively as its king.

Xenophon (428/427–354 B.C.): Prolific writer of histories of the final years of the Peloponnesian War and the early 4th century.

Ximenes de Cisneros, Cardinal Francisco (1436–1517): Church reformer and Christian humanist in Spain. Founded University of Alcala and sponsored production of Complutensian Polyglot Bible (see Glossary).

Zeno (335–263 B.C.): Philosopher who taught at the *stoa poikile* (painted porch) in Athens. Founder of Stoicism (see Glossary).

Zwingli, Hildreich (1484–1531): Parish priest who initiated reform of the church in German Switzerland.

Bibliography

A bibliography of all relevant and instructive publications on Western civilization would be immeasurably vast. I have listed here works that are widely acknowledged to be important, even classic, treatments of their subjects and books that I myself have found helpful or influential. I adopt the following conventions: "General" books survey large subjects in readable and authoritative ways; "Essential" books are fundamental scholarly works; and "Recommended" books are primary sources and a few secondary works that are of great interest. Books that themselves contain excellent bibliographical orientations are marked with an asterisk.

General

Barzun, Jacques. *From Dawn to Decadence: 1500 to the Present, Five Hundred Years of Western Cultural Life.* New York: HarperCollins, 2001. Utterly stunning as a dissection of the fate of modernity's promise. By one of the greatest of scholars.

Boardman, John, Jasper Griffin, and Oswyn Murray, eds. *The Oxford Illustrated History of Greece and the Hellenistic World.* New York: Oxford University Press, 2001. Readable, accessible essays by a series of specialists, with beautiful pictures.

*———, eds. *The Oxford Illustrated History of the Roman World.* New York: Oxford University Press, 1991. A book just like, and as easily recommended as, the history of the Greek world.

*Bowersock, Glen, Peter Borwn, and Oleg Grabar, eds. *Late Antiquity: A Guide to the Postclassical World.* Cambridge, MA: Harvard University Press, 1999. Long and short articles by leading authorities. Comprehensive.

*Brady, Thomas A., and Heiko Oberman. *Handbook of European History, 1400–1600.* Leiden: Brill, 1994. Important articles of differing levels of readability and interest by major scholars.

Braudel, Fernand. *Memory and the Mediterranean.* Trans. Siân Reynolds. New York: Knopf, 2001. Interprets the first three millennia of life around the inland sea.

*Brunschwig, Jacques, and Geoffrey E. R. Lloyd. *Greek Thought: A Guide to Classical Knowledge.* Trans. under the direction of Catherine Porter. Cambridge, MA: Harvard University Press, 2000. Several dozen essays by world-class authorities on almost all aspects of Greek scientific and philosophical thought.

*Cartledge, Paul, ed. *The Cambridge Illustrated History of Greece.* New York: Cambridge University Press, 1998. Lively thematic essays and terrific pictures.

*Coogan, Michael D., ed. *The Oxford History of the Biblical World.* New York: Oxford University Press, 1998. An authoritative and readable companion to historical or biblical studies.

*Duffy, Eamon. *Saints and Sinners: A History of the Popes.* New Haven: Yale University Press, 1997. A beautifully written and illustrated history of the West's oldest continually functioning institution.

Fernández-Armesto, Felipe. *Millennium: A History of the Last Thousand Years.* New York: Scribners, 1995. A breathtaking panorama of the world's modern history. Serves well to put these lectures into contemporary perspective.

*Horden, Peregrine, and Nicholas Purcell. *The Corrupting Sea: A Study of Mediterranean History.* Oxford: Blackwell, 2000. A brilliant evocation of the social, political, and more important, ecological, roles of the Mediterranean.

*Linehan, Peter, and Janet L. Nelson, eds. *The Medieval World.* London: Routledge, 2001. More than 30 essays of uniformly high quality on all aspects of medieval life.

Pomeroy, Sarah B. *Goddesses, Whores, Wives and Slaves: Women in Classical Antiquity.* New York: Schocken Books, 1975. Superceded by many monographs but not yet by a single study.

Randsborg, Klaus. *The First Millennium A.D. in Europe and the Mediterranean.* Cambridge: Cambridge University Press, 1991. A distinguished archaeologist looks at what changed, and what didn't, over a millennium.

*Ward, Allen M, Cedric A. Yeo, and Fritz M. Heichelheim. *A History of the Roman People.* 3rd ed. Englewood Cliffs, NJ: Prentice Hall, 1998. The standard college textbook.

Wells, Colin M. *The Roman Empire.* 2nd ed. Stanford: Stanford University Press, 1995. A readable and authoritative survey enlivened by the perspectives of an archaeologist.

Essential

*Abels, Richard. *Alfred the Great: War, Kingship and Culture in Anglo-Saxon England.* Harlow: Longmans, 1998. An excellent introduction to Alfred and to his England.

Allmand, Christopher. *The Hundred Years War: England and France at War, c. 1300–c. 1450.* Cambridge: Cambridge University Press, 1988. The best introduction to this important subject.

Anderson, John. *Xenophon.* New York: Scribners. 1974. The basic book.

Andrewes, Antony. *The Greek Tyrants.* London: Hutchinson University Library, 1974. Remains the fundamental introduction to political change in archaic Greece.

*Annas, Julia. "Plato." In *Brunschwig and Lloyd, *Greek Thought*, pp. 672–692. A clear and succinct introduction to a vast subject.

Badian, Ernst. *Foreign Clientelae.* Oxford: Oxford University Press, 1958. Derives Roman imperialism from Roman social practices.

Bainton, Roland H. *Here I Stand: A Biography of Martin Luther.* New York: Scribners, 1950. After all these years, still the best entry point into the life of Luther.

———. *Erasmus of Christendom*. New York: Scribners, 1969. Not yet surpassed as a one-volume treatment of Erasmus's life and thought.

Baldwin, John. *The Government of Philip Augustus: Foundations of French Royal Power in the Middle Ages.* Berkeley: University of California Press, 1986. A detailed and clear exposition of institutional history.

Barnes, T. D. *The New Empire of Diocletian and Constantine.* Cambridge, MA: Harvard University Press, 1992. A major book by the leading contemporary authority on Constantine.

Barolsky, Paul. *Why Mona Lisa Smiles and Other Tales from Vasari.* State College: Penn State University Press, 1991. A book about the historian Giorgio Vasari, Leonardo, and traditions of art criticism.

Bartlett, Robert. *The Making of Europe: Conquest, Colonization, and Cultural Change, 950–1300.* Princeton: Princeton University Press, 1993. A bracing interpretation of Europe's physical and cultural expansion.

Bemrose, Stephen. *A New Life of Dante*. Exeter: Exeter University Press, 2000. A fine introduction to the life and times of the great poet and a satisfactory introduction to his major writings.

Bernstein, Alvin H. *Tiberius Sempronius Gracchus*. Ithaca: Cornell University Press, 1978. A readable and reliable bio-historical study of the great reformer.

Beye, Charles Rowan. *Ancient Greek Literature and Society*. 2nd ed. Ithaca: Cornell University Press, 1987. Smart and entertaining, this book will instruct the expert without leaving the novice behind.

*Biers, William R. *The Archaeology of Greece: An Introduction*. Ithaca: Cornell University Press, 1980. Readable and intelligent, this is an excellent book for the beginner.

Bisson, Thomas N., ed. *Cultures of Power: Lordship, Status, and Process in Twelfth-Century France.* Philadelphia: University of Pennsylvania Press,

1995. Wide-ranging essays that open perspectives on the current debate about the "feudal transformation" of Europe.

Boardman, John. *The Greeks Overseas*. 4th ed. London: Thames and Hudson, 1999. Long the standard account of the history and consequences of Greek colonization.

———. *Greek Art*. New York: Praeger, 1969. Dated in some respects but still reliable and accessible as an overall survey.

Bottéro, Jean. *Ancestor of the West: Writing, Reasoning and Religion in Mesopotamia, Elam, and Greece*. Chicago: University of Chicago Press, 2000. More current and wider ranging than Kramer but no less readable or enthused about its subject.

Bouchard, Constance Brittain. *Strong of Body, Brave & Noble: Chivalry and Society in Medieval France*. Ithaca: Cornell University Press, 1998. An outstanding introduction to the culture of the French nobility.

Bouwsma, William J. *John Calvin: A Sixteenth-Century Portrait*. New York: Oxford University Press, 1988. Stresses Calvin's relationship to the Christian tradition and to humanism.

Bradley, Keith. *Discovering the Roman Family*. Oxford: Oxford University Press, 1991. Beautifully written, engaging, and entertaining.

Braudel, Fernand. *A History of Civilizations*. Trans. Richard Mayne. New York: Penguin Books, 1993. Braudel (1902–1985) was one of the most distinguished historians of the 20th century. This book represents his mature reflections on the course of civilization on a global scale.

Bridenthal, Renate, Susan Mosher Stuard, and Merry E. Wiesner, eds. *Becoming Visible: Women in European History*. 3rd ed. Boston: Houghton Mifflin, 1998. Chapters 1 to 7 relate to the lectures in this course.

Brown, Peter. *Augustine of Hippo*. Berkeley: University of California Press, 1967. Simply brilliant.

———. *The Cult of the Saints: Its Rise and Function in Latin Christendom.* Chicago: University of Chicago Press, 1981. A sensitive, elegant interpretation of how the dead came to share a place with the living in late antiquity.

———. *The World of Late Antiquity.* London: Thames and Hudson, 1971. The book that sparked a generation of scholarship.

Browning, Robert. *Justinian and Theodora.* Rev. ed. London: Thames and Hudson, 1987. At once scholarly and readable, this book opens perspectives on remarkable times and people.

Brunt, P. A. *Social Conflicts in the Roman Republic.* New York: Norton, 1971. A penetrating analysis of the tensions in Roman society.

Burke, Peter. *The European Renaissance: Centres and Peripheries.* Oxford: Blackwell, 1998. Read Hale on Renaissance Italy and Burke on the whole of Europe.

Burkert, Walter. *Greek Religion: Archaic and Classical.* Oxford: Oxford University Press, 1985. The best one-volume survey of the subject.

Cameron, Averil. *The Later Roman Empire, 284–430.* London: Fontana, 1993. A fast-paced and highly readable interpretation of a time of decisive change for Rome.

Cameron, Euan. *The European Reformation.* Oxford: Clarendon, 1991. A superb and balanced introduction to the Reformation tradition all over Europe.

Cartledge, Paul. *Sparta and Lakonia: A Regional History, 1300–362.* London: Routledge, 1979. Not always easy going but the best single book on Sparta.

Chadwick, Henry. *The Early Church.* Harmondsworth: Penguin, 1967. Somewhat dated now but still to be commended for clarity and elegance.

Chatellier, Louis. *The Europe of the Devout: The Catholic Reformation and the Formation of a New Society.* Trans. Jean Birrell. New York: Cambridge

University Press, 1989. An erudite and non-polemical exploration of a rich and difficult subject.

Chibnall, Marjorie. *Anglo-Norman England*. Oxford: Blackwell, 1986. A wonderful introduction to the post-conquest phase of English history.

Chitty, Derwas. *The Desert a City*. Crestwood, NY: St. Vladimir's Seminary Press, 1966. A comprehensive and persuasive explanation of the rise of monasticism in Egypt.

Clark, Gillian. *Women in Late Antiquity*. Oxford: Oxford University Press, 1993. Readable, thoughtful, and instructive on a large and important topic.

Cochrane, Charles Norris. *Christianity and Classical Culture*. Oxford: Oxford University Press, 1944. The classic treatment of the question "What has Athens to do with Jerusalem?"

Colish, Marcia L. *Medieval Foundations of the Western Intellectual Tradition, 400–1400*. New Haven: Yale University Press, 1997. Encyclopedic yet readable, this is the book in which to find a few paragraphs or pages on every topic.

Connor, W. R. *Thucydides*. Princeton: Princeton University Press, 1984. The one book to start with on Thucydides.

Cook, John Manuel. *The Persian Empire*. New York: Schocken Books, 1983. An excellent survey of a vast subject.

Cornell, T. J. *The Beginnings of Rome: Italy and Rome from the Bronze Age to the Punic Wars*. London: Routledge, 1975. Richly detailed and highly readable, this is *the* book on early Rome.

*Crawford, Harriet E. W. *The Sumerians*. New York: Cambridge University Press, 1991. The best single introduction and one that opens for the reader the ways in which archaeologists change historical understanding.

Bibliography

452

Crawford, Michael. *The Roman Republic.* 2nd ed. Cambridge, MA: Harvard University Press, 1993. Easily the best survey of Rome's republic.

Crone, Patricia, and Martin Hinds. *God's Caliph: Religious Authority in the First Centuries of Islam.* New York: Cambridge University Press, 1986. A penetrating interpretation of how authority was managed after the death of the prophet Muhammad.

Crosby, Alfred. *Ecological Imperialism: The Biological Expansion of Europe, 900–1900.* New York: Cambridge University Press, 1986. Important and challenging reflections by the leading interpreter of the "Columbian Exchange."

Denny, Frederick M. *An Introduction to Islam.* 2nd ed. New York: Macmillan, 1994. An excellent introduction to all aspects of Islam from medieval to modern times.

Desborough, V. R. d'A. *The Greek Dark Ages.* New York: St. Martin's, 1972. A bit dated as a result of more recent archaeology, this book is still unsurpassed as a general survey.

*Diamond, Jared. *Guns, Germs, and Steel: The Fates of Human Societies.* New York: Norton, 1997. Brilliant and controversial, this book offers a biological, technological, and finally, cultural explanation for the distinctive characteristics of, and differences among, world civilizations.

*Dickinson, Oliver T. P. K. *The Aegean Bronze Age.* New York: Cambridge University Press, 1994. Reliable, heavily archaeological, and accessible to the nonspecialist.

Douglas, David C. *William the Conqueror.* Berkeley: University of California Press, 1967. Still unsurpassed as a study of the life and work of a remarkable figure.

Drane, John William. *Introducing the Old Testament.* San Francisco: Harper and Row, 1987. A balanced and comprehensive entrance to a huge subject that is fraught with controversy.

Duby, Georges. *The Early Growth of the Medieval Economy: Warriors and Peasants from the Seventh to the Twelfth Century*. Trans. Howard R. Clark. Ithaca: Cornell University Press, 1974. The mature reflections and interpretations of one of the 20th century's great historians.

Dunbabin, Jean. *France in the Making*. 2nd ed. Oxford: Oxford University Press, 2000. A fascinating account of the growth of France, emphasizing the regional principalities.

Edwards, Mark W. *Homer: Poet of the Iliad*. Baltimore: Johns Hopkins University Press, 1987. Amidst countless publications on Homer, this is the place to begin.

Eisenstein, Elizabeth L. *The Printing Press as an Agent of Change: Communications and Cultural Transformations in Early Modern Europe*. Cambridge: Cambridge University Press, 1979. A brilliant analysis of the changes that ensued with the advent of printing.

Fagan, Brian. *The Journey from Eden: The Peopling of Our World*. London: Thames and Hudson, 1990. A readable and engaging *introduction* (this subject changes almost annually) to human evolution and to the dissemination of our species.

Fernández-Armesto, Felipe. *Columbus*. New York: Oxford University Press, 1991. Readable and avoids both myth-making and hypercriticism.

Finley, M. I. *The World of Odysseus*. Rev. ed. New York: Viking, 1978. A brilliant treatment of how the Homeric poems can, and cannot, be used for historical information.

Flanagan, Sabina. *Hildegard of Bingen*. 2nd ed. London: Routledge, 1998. An excellent introduction to the subject, her works, and the 12th century.

Fletcher, Richard. *The Barbarian Conversion: From Paganism to Christianity*. New York: Henry Holt, 1997. A detailed and readable narration of the Christianization of Europe.

Fox, Robin Lane. *Pagans and Christians*. New York: Knopf, 1987. Long and detailed but eminently readable, this book takes the story from Jesus to the 4th century.

Frend, W. H. C. *The Rise of Christianity*. Philadelphia: Fortress Press, 1984. Easily the most balanced and readable survey of a huge and controversial subject.

Galinsky, Karl. *Augustan Culture: An Interpretive Introduction*. Princeton: Princeton University Press, 1996. A superb evocation and explanation of the most creative period in Roman history.

Garnsey, Peter, and Richard Saller. *The Roman Empire: Economy, Society, and Culture*. Berkeley: University of California Press, 1987. A readable book, full of sparkling observations.

Gelzer, Matthias. *Caesar: Politician and Statesman*. 6th ed. Cambridge, MA: Harvard University Press, 1968. A superb evocation of the complexities of the cunning Roman leader.

Glick, Leonard B. *Abraham's Heirs: Jews and Christians in Medieval Europe*. Syracuse: Syracuse University Press, 1999. A lively and thoughtful introduction to medieval Jewish history.

Goffart, Walter. *Barbarians and Romans A.D. 418–584: The Techniques of Accommodation*. Princeton: Princeton University Press, 1980. A brilliant and controversial interpretation of Rome's settlement of the barbarians in the empire.

Gould, John. *Herodotus*. New York: St. Martin's, 1989. The best place to start for a solid introduction to the historian and his work.

Green, Peter. *Alexander of Macedon, 356–323 B.C.: A Historical Biography*. Berkeley: University of California Press, 1991. The currently dominant interpretation, engaging but without myth or romance.

————. *Alexander to Actium*. Berkeley: University of California Press, 1990. An outstanding introduction to the complex Hellenistic world.

Gruen, Erich. *The Hellenistic World and the Rise of Rome*. Berkeley: University of California Press, 1984. The fullest presentation of the ("defensive imperialism") thesis that Rome was drawn into wars in the Mediterranean world.

————. *The Last Generation of the Roman Republic*. Berkeley: University of California Press, 1974. An interesting and provocative interpretation of Roman politics in the years leading up to the fall of the Republic.

Guenée, Bernard. *State and Rulers in Late Medieval Europe*. Trans. Juliet Vale. Oxford: Blackwell, 1985. A penetrating analysis of the theory and practice of government. Emphasizes France but does not slight other areas.

Gurney, O. R. *The Hittites*. 3rd ed. rev. Harmondsworth: Penguin Books, 1981. The classic study of these fascinating people.

Hale, John R. *The Civilization of Europe in the Renaissance.* New York: Athenaeum, 1994. Authoritative, elegant, and comprehensive.

*Hallo, William W., and William Kelly Simpson. *The Ancient Near East: A History.* New York: Harcourt, Brace, and Jovanovich, 1971. 2nd ed. 1998. Readable and up-to-date, this is an excellent survey of a large subject.

Harris, William V. *War and Imperialism in Republican Rome, 320–70 B.C.* Oxford: Oxford University Press, 1979. The most distinguished attack on the "defensive imperialism" thesis pertaining to the development of the Roman Empire.

Hartt, Frederick. *History of Italian Renaissance Art: Painting, Sculpture, and Architecture.* 4th ed. New York: Abrams, 1987. A charming book by a world-class scholar.

Haverkamp, Alfred. *Medieval Germany, 1056–1273.* Trans. Helga Braun and Richard Mortimer. 2nd ed. Oxford: Oxford University Press, 1992. Rich in detail and penetrating in insight, this book puts politics in cultural and material contexts.

Heather, Peter. *Goths and Romans, 332–489.* Oxford: Oxford University Press, 1991. A major interpretation of the formation of the Gothic peoples in their clashes with Rome.

Herlihy, David. *The Black Death and the Transformation of the West.* Samuel K. Cohn, ed. Cambridge, MA: Harvard University Press, 1997. The last book by a great historian, typically wide-ranging and original.

———. *Opera Muliebria: Women and Work in Medieval Europe.* New York: McGraw-Hill, 1990. An entertaining introduction to all forms of women's labor in the Middle Ages.

Holt, James C. *Magna Carta.* 2nd ed. Cambridge: Cambridge University Press, 1992. The classic study with a translation of the document.

Hussey, Joan M. *The Orthodox Church in the Byzantine Empire.* Oxford: Oxford University Press, 1986. The best single-volume introduction to Orthodoxy as a church, faith, and culture.

Hyde, J. K. *Society and Politics in Medieval Italy: The Evolution of Civil Life, 1000–1350.* New York: St. Martin's, 1973. Still the best introduction to the amazingly complicated world of medieval Italy.

Irwin, Terence. *Classical Thought.* Oxford: Oxford University Press, 1989. A superb introduction to Greek thought in all its aspects.

Jackson, W. T. H. *The Literature of the Middle Ages.* New York: Columbia University Press, 1960. Dated in many particulars but never superceded as a survey of this subject.

Jaeger, C. Stephen. *The Envy of Angels: Cathedral Schools and Social Ideals in Medieval Europe, 950–1200.* Philadelphia: University of Pennsylvania Press, 1994. A comprehensive introduction to the major schools before the universities that argues for both secular and religious learning in those centers.

Johnson, Luke Timothy. *The Real Jesus: The Misguided Quest for the Historical Jesus and the Truth of the Traditional Gospels.* San Francisco: HarperSanFrancisco, 1996. Steering a middle path between all the controversies, this book presents as balanced a view as it is possible to offer.

Kelly, J. N. D. *Jerome.* London: Duckworth, 1975. The best introduction to the life and work of the great church father.

*Kennedy, Hugh. *The Prophet and the Age of the Caliphates: The Islamic Near East from the Sixth to the Eleventh Century.* Harlow: Longmans, 1986. A comprehensive and outstanding introduction to the rise of Islam.

Keppie, L. *The Making of the Roman Army: From Republic to Empire.* Norman: University of Oklahoma Press, 1998. A readable and manageable survey of a vast subject.

King, Margaret L. *Women of the Renaissance.* Chicago: University of Chicago Press, 1991. An important book, stressing humanists, that reminds us of how much has been omitted from traditional accounts.

Kramer, Samuel Noah. *History Begins at Sumer: Thirty-Nine Firsts in Man's Recorded History.* New York: Doubleday, 1959. 3rd ed. 1981. An engaging and informative book that may, today, be a lit longer on enthusiasm than persuasion.

Kraut, P., ed. *The Cambridge Companion to Plato.* Cambridge: Cambridge University Press, 1992. Authoritative essays on most aspects of Plato's thought and influence that differ in difficulty and accessibility.

*Lambert, Malcolm. *Medieval Heresy: Popular Movements from the Gregorian Reform to the Reformation.* 2nd ed. Oxford: Blackwell, 1992. The authoritative survey of this vast topic. Stresses political and social more than theological issues.

Lindberg, Carter. *The European Reformations*. Oxford: Blackwell, 1996. Easy to recommend for its balance and brevity, yet breadth.

Lloyd, Geoffrey E. R. *Early Greek Science*. New York: Norton, 1970. A stimulating treatment of the emergence of Greek science and its relation to philosophy.

Long, A. A. *Helllenistic Philosophy: Stoics, Epicureans, and Sceptics*. 2nd ed. Berkeley: University of California Press, 1986. The title tells the story.

MacMullen, Ramsay. *Roman Government's Response to Crisis*. New Haven: Yale University Press, 1976. An impressive treatment of the 3rd century that stresses Rome's creativity in the face of challenges.

Mallett, Michael, and Nicholas Mann. *Lorenzo the Magnificent: Culture and Politics.* London: The Warburg Institute, 1996. Essays (some in Italian) on crucial aspects of the life and times of the most famous of the Medici.

Mann, Nicholas. *Petrarch*. New York: Oxford University Press, 1984. A fine and reliable entry into a long and complex life.

Marius, Richard. *Thomas More*. New York: Knopf, 1984. A lot of debunking in this book but not so much as to take the life out of the subject.

Markus, Robert. *The End of Ancient Christianity*. Cambridge: Cambridge University Press, 1991. A subtle, readable interpretation of the transformation of Christianity between 400 and 600.

―――. *Gregory the Great and His World.* Cambridge: Cambridge University Press, 1997. By far the best of many books on Gregory.

*Martin, Janet. *Medieval Russia, 980–1584.* Cambridge: Cambridge University Press, 1995. The best and most up-to-date introduction to an important and neglected subject.

Martindale, Charles, ed. *The Cambridge Companion to Virgil*. Cambridge: Cambridge University Press, 1997. Readable and accessible essays on a wide array of topics pertaining mainly to the *Aeneid* but also to Virgil's other poems.

Mathews, Thomas. *The Clash of Gods: A Reinterpretation of Early Christian Art.* Rev. ed. Princeton: Princeton University Press, 1999. A controversial explanation of early Christian art's relationship to pagan and imperial art.

McGrath, Alister. *John Calvin: A Study in the Shaping of Western Culture*. Oxford: Blackwell, 1990. An excellent introduction to Calvin's religious thought and its impact.

McKitterick, Rosamond, ed. *Carolingian Culture: Emulation and Innovation.* Cambridge: Cambridge University Press, 1994. Eleven fine essays on numerous aspects of Carolingian culture.

———. *The Early Middle Ages*. Oxford: Oxford University Press, 2001. Seven excellent essays covering all aspects of life in the period.

McLynn, Neil B. *Ambrose of Milan: Church and Court in a Christian Capital.* Berkeley: University of California Press, 1994. A fine study of Ambrose's life and thought, anchored in his social and political context.

Meeks, Wayne A. *The First Urban Christians: The Social World of the Apostle Paul*. New Haven: Yale University Press, 1983. Already a classic, this book tells why people were attracted to Christianity and who those people were.

Mellaart, James. *The Neolithic of the Near East.* London: Thames and Hudson, 1975. A readable introduction to a large and complex topic.

Millar, Fergus. *The Emperor in the Roman World, 31 B.C.–A.D. 337*. Ithaca: Cornell University Press, 1977. A detailed study of what the emperors actually did, as opposed to what law or ideology might have demanded of them.

Morris, Colin. *The Papal Monarchy: The Western Church from 1050 to*

1250. Oxford: Clarendon Press, 1989. Breathtaking in sweep and felicitous in execution.

Moscati, Sabatino. *The World of the Phoenicians*. London: Weidenfeld and Nicolson, 1968. A masterful introduction to these important people.

Mottahedeh, Roy. *Loyalty and Leadership in an Early Islamic Society*. Rev. ed. London: Tauris, 2001. A brilliant evocation of social change in Iran and Iraq in the 9th and 10th centuries that is relevant to our times.

Murnane, William J. *The Guide to Ancient Egypt*. New York: Facts on File, 1983. Packed with useful and interesting information, this book can also be used as a tourist guide.

*Murray, Oswyn. *Early Greece*. 2nd ed. Cambridge, MA: Harvard University Press, 1993. An excellent introduction to pre-classical Greece.

Nilsson, Martin Persson. *A History of Greek Religion*. London: Oxford University Press, 1963. Dated in some respects but unsurpassed as an overall treatment.

Nussbaum, Martha C. *The Fragility of Goodness: Luck and Ethics in Greek Tragedy and Philosophy*. New York: Cambridge University Press, 2001. A poetically beautiful meditation on Greek culture and the human condition generally.

Oakley, Francis. *The Western Church in the Later Middle Ages*. Ithaca: Cornell University Press, 1979. A masterful treatment of a complex and important period that sets the stage for the 16th-century reformations without sacrificing itself to their anticipation.

Ober, Josiah. *Mass and Elite in Democratic Athens: Rhetoric, Ideology, and the Power of the People*. Princeton: Princeton University Press, 1989. The first of two penetrating studies of the arguments over political culture in Athens.

*———. *Political Dissent in Democratic Athens: Intellectual Critics of*

Popular Rule. Princeton: Princeton University Press, 1998. The second of Ober's studies.

Oberman, Heiko. *Luther: Man between God and the Devil*. Trans. Eileen Walliser-Schwarzbart. New Haven: Yale University Press, 1989. Stressing Luther's connections with late medieval Christianity, this is the most influential book on the great reformer.

Obolensky, Dimitri. *Byzantium and the Slavs*. Crestwood, NY: St. Vladimir's Seminary Press, 1994. The standard introduction to the formation of Orthodox Eastern Europe.

Ogilvie, Robin Maxwell. *Roman Literature and Society*. Totowa: Barnes and Noble, 1980. Not so much a history of Roman literature as a location of that literature within the larger social and historical context.

Panofsky, Erwin. *Renaissance and Renascences in Western Art*. 2nd ed. New York: Harper & Row, 1969. One of the most influential essays in cultural interpretation.

Pelikan, Jaroslav. *The Christian Tradition: A History of the Development of Doctrine*. Vol. 1: *The Emergence of the Catholic Tradition (100–600)*. Vol. 2: *The Spirit of Eastern Christendom (600–1700)*. Vol. 3: *The Growth of Medieval Theology (600–1300)*. Vol. 4: *The Reformation of Church and Dogma (1300–1700)*. Chicago: University of Chicago Press, 1971–1980. A stupendous achievement of exposition and interpretation.

*Pellegrin, Pierre. "Aristotle." In *Brunschwig and Lloyd, *Greek Thought*, pp. 554-575. An exceptionally clear and readable introduction.

Pohl, Walter, ed. *Kingdoms of the Empire: The Integration of the Barbarians in Late Antiquity*. Leiden: Brill, 1997. Eight essays that address different aspects of the Roman incorporation of the Germanic peoples.

Raaflaub, Kurt, and Michael Toher, eds. *Between Republic and Empire: An*

Interpretation of the Augustan Principate. Berkeley: University of California Press, 1990. A collection of essays by leading scholars on various aspects of the reign of Augustus and the regime he created.

*Ramage, Nancy A. *Roman Art: Romulus to Constantine.* Englewood Cliffs, NJ: Prentice-Hall, 1996. An excellent introduction to the subject with fine illustrations.

Rawson, Elizabeth. *Cicero: A Portrait.* Ithaca: Cornell University Press, 1975. A good book, although Cicero deserves a better, fuller treatment.

Redford, Donald B. *Akhenaten: The Heretic King.* Princeton: Princeton University Press, 1984. A compelling treatment of its title subject and a good introduction to Egyptian religion.

*Reynold, Susan. *Fiefs and Vassals: The Medieval Evidence Reinterpreted.* Oxford: Oxford University Press, 1994. A stimulating reinterpretation of the medieval evidence pertaining to the cornerstones of all older arguments about feudalism.

Riché, Pierre. *The Carolingians.* Trans. Michael I. Allen. Philadelphia: University of Pennsylvania Press, 1993. Comprehensive and readable, the best introduction to the Carolingians.

——. *Daily Life in the World of Charlemagne.* Trans. Jo Ann McNamara. Philadelphia: University of Pennsylvania Press, 1978. An interesting book that delivers on the promise of its title.

*——. *Education and Culture in the Barbarian West.* Trans. John J. Contreni. Columbia: University of South Carolina Press, 1976. A learned and readable discussion of the transformation of school culture from 500 to 900.

Riley, Bernard F. *The Medieval Spains.* Cambridge: Cambridge University Press, 1993. Early and late, Christian and Muslim, Spain and Portugal—two Spains all the way through.

*Riley-Smith, Jonathan. *The Oxford Illustrated History of the Crusades.*

Oxford: Oxford University, Press, 1997. Excellent essays by leading authorities on all aspects of crusade history.

Rösener, Werner. *Peasants in the Middle Ages.* Trans. Alexander Stützer. Urbana: University of Illinois Press, 1992. A comprehensive introduction with good coverage of the often-neglected German world.

Saggs, H. W. F. *The Might That Was Assyria.* New York: St. Martin's, 1990. More positive in its assessment of the Assyrians than the lectures but unrivaled as a survey.

*Scammell, Geoffrey. *The First Imperial Age: European Overseas Expansion, 1400–1715.* London: Unwin-Hyman, 1989. Successful as an introduction to a huge subject.

Scarisbrick, J. J. *The Reformation and the English People.* Oxford: Blackwell, 1984. A major book by a leading authority; challenges a long-prevailing "bottom-up" interpretation of the English reform.

Scullard, H. H. *Roman Politics, 220–150 B.C.* 2nd ed. Oxford: Clarendon Press, 1973. A brilliant exposition of how the Roman social system and constitution interacted.

Shanks, Herschel. *Ancient Israel: From Abraham to the Roman Destruction of the Temple.* Rev. ed. Washington, DC: Biblical Archaeology Society, 1999. A set of clear and authoritative essays by leading scholars.

Shotter, D. C. A. *Augustus Caesar.* London: Routledge, 1991. Detailed yet readable, balanced yet reliable in its interpretations.

*Snell, Daniel C. *Life in the Ancient Near East.* New Haven: Yale University Press, 1997. A fine, readable, learned book that combines the evidence of texts and archaeology.

Southern, Richard W. *Scholastic Humanism and the Unification of Europe.*

Oxford: Blackwell, 1995. The first volume of a projected three-volume study by the late master of medieval intellectual history, this book argues for a common scholarly vision in courts and schools.

Strouhal, Eugen. *Life of the Ancient Egyptians.* Trans. Deryck Viney. Norman: University of Oklahoma Press, 1992. Wide-ranging, accessible, and beautifully illustrated, this book provides a panorama of daily life.

Sullivan, Richard E., ed. *"The Gentle Voices of Teachers": Aspects of Learning in the Carolingian Age.* Columbus: Ohio State University Press, 1995. Eight wide-ranging essays on Carolingian intellectual life.

Summers, David. *Michelangelo and the Language of Art.* Princeton: Princeton University Press, 1981. A difficult but rewarding exploration of the prolific artist.

Syme, Sir Ronald. *The Roman Revolution.* Rev. ed. Oxford: Clarendon Press, 1960. In one of the great history books of the 20th century, the author offers a controversial and intriguing interpretation of Rome's transformation from republic to empire.

Thompson, E. A. *The Huns.* Revised with an afterword by Peter Heather. Oxford: Blackwell, 1996. A fascinating treatment of a captivating subject.

Van Caenegem, Raoul C. *The Birth of the English Common Law.* 2nd ed. Cambridge: Cambridge University Press, 1988. A masterful introduction to a vast and critically important subject.

Von Grunebaum, Gustav E. *Medieval Islam.* 2nd ed. Chicago: University of Chicago Press, 1953. Old but still majestic as an introduction to Islamic culture.

Weisheipl, James A. *Friar Thomas d'Aquino: His Life, Thought and Works.* Oxford: Blackwell, 1974. The history book to start with on Thomas.

Whittow, Mark. *The Making of Orthodox Byzantium, 600–1025.* London:

Macmillan, 1996. The best introduction to the world of Byzantium, although stronger on politics than on culture.

Williams, Stephen. *Diocletian and the Roman Recovery.* New York: Methuen, 1985. The most recent and comprehensive interpretation of this emperor's massive reforms.

*Wolfram, Herwig. *History of the Goths.* Trans. Thomas Dunlap. Berkeley: University of California Press, 1988. A magisterial interpretation of Gothic history by a distinguished and influential scholar.

Zink, Michel. *Medieval French Literature: An Introduction.* Trans. Jeff Rider. Binghamton: State University of New York, 1995. Brief and lively, this book does just what its title promises.

Recommended

Alighieri, Dante. *The Divine Comedy.* Trans. John Ciardi. New York: Norton, 1961 (and subsequent editions). A verse translation that preserves the *terza rima* and is accessible to the nonspecialist.

Allen, Susan H. *Finding the Walls of Troy: Frank Calvert and Heinrich Schliemann at Hisarlik.* Berkeley: University of California Press, 1999. The account of the intense rivalries surrounding the excavations at Troy reads like a detective story.

Anselm of Canterbury. *The Major Works.* Brian Davies and G. R. Evans, eds. Oxford: Oxford University Press, 1998.

Apollonius of Rhodes. *The Voyage of Argo.* Trans. E. V. Rieu. Harmondsworth: Penguin, 1959.

Augustine. *The Confessions of St. Augustine.* Trans. Rex Warner. New York: Penguin/Mentor, 1963.

Bede. *The Ecclesiastical History of the English People.* Judith McClure and Roger Collins, eds. Oxford: Oxford University Press, 1994.

Bernal, Martin. *Black Athena: The Afro-Asiatic Roots of Classical Civilization.* 2 vols. New Brunswick: Rutgers University Press, 1987, 1991. A passionate and deeply controversial argument for the unacknowledged influence of Egypt on Greece.

Cellini, Benvenuto. *Autobiography.* Trans. George Bull. Harmondsworth: Penguin, 1956.

Charlemagne's Courtier: The Complete Einhard. Trans. Paul Dutton. Peterborough, Ontario: Broadview, 1998.

Connor, W. Robert, ed. *Greek Orations.* Ann Arbor: University of Michigan Press, 1966.

The Epic of Gilgamesh. Trans. N. K. Sandars. Harmondsworth: Penguin, 1975.

Erasmus. *The Praise of Folly.* Trans. A. H. T. Levi. Harmondsworth: Penguin, 1971.

Gregory of Tours. *The History of the Franks.* Trans. Lewis Thorpe. Harmondsworth: Penguin, 1974.

Herodotus. *The Histories.* Trans. Robin Waterfield. Oxford: Oxford University Press, 1998.

Homer, *The Iliad.* Trans. Robert Fagles. New York: Penguin, 1998. This translation and the following one are vigorous and readable but a bit informal for some readers' tastes.

———. *The Odyssey.* Trans. Robert Fagles. New York: Penguin, 1997.

Lerner, Gerda. *The Creation of Patriarchy.* New York: Oxford University Press, 1986. Controversial and stimulating, this book is sure to stir deep reflection.

The Letters of Abelard and Heloise. Trans. Betty Radice. Harmondsworth: Penguin, 1974.

Livy, *The Early History of Rome.* Trans. Aubrey de Sélincourt. Baltimore: Penguin, 1960.

Machiavelli, Niccoló. *The Prince.* Trans. David Wootton. Indianapolis: Hackett, 1995.

———. *The War with Hannibal.* Trans. Aubrey de Sélincourt. Baltimore: Penguin, 1965.

Menander. *Plays and Fragments.* Trans. Philip Vellacott. Harmondsworth: Penguin, 1967.

More, Thomas. *Utopia.* Trans. Paul Turner. Harmondsworth: Penguin, 1965.

Plato. *Five Dialogues.* Trans. G. M. A. Grube. Indianapolis: Hackett, 1981.

———. *The Last Days of Soctrates.* Trans. Hugh Tredennick and Harold Tennant. Introduction by Harrold Tennant. Rev. ed. London: Penguin, 1993.

The Pocket Aristotle. Trans. W. D. Ross. Justin D. Kaplan, ed. New York: Washington Square, 1958.

The Poem of the Cid. Trans. Rita Hamilton and Janet Perry. Harmondsworth: Penguin, 1984.

The Song of Roland. Trans. Robert Harrison. New York: Mentor, 1970.

Songs of Zarathushtra: The Gathas Translated from the Avesta. Trans. by Pastur Framroze Ardeshir Bode and Piloo Nanavutty. New York: Allen and Unwin, 1952.

Thucydides. *History of the Peloponnesian War.* Trans. Steven Lattimore. Indianapolis: Hackett, 1998.

Bibliography

Virgil. *The Aeneid*. New York: Vintage Books, 1984.

Xenophon, *Anabasis*. Harmondsworth: Penguin, 1972.

———. *Hellenica*. Harmondsworth: Penguin, 1966.

Notes

Notes

Notes